Forming

A Work of Grace

David Takle, M.Div.

Forming: A Work of Grace

David Takle, M.Div.

david@KingdomFormation.org

Unless otherwise noted, scripture references are taken from The New Revised Standard Edition of the Bible (NRSV), Copyright © 1946, 1952, and 1971, National Council of the Churches of Christ in the United States of America. Used by permission. All rights reserved.

NASB® quotations are from the New American Standard Bible®, Copyright 1960, 1962, 1963, 1968, 19741, 1972, 1973, 1975, 1977, 1995 by The Lockman Foundation, used by permission. (www.Lockman.org)

NIV® Scriptures taken from the Holy Bible, New International Version®, Copyright © 1973, 1978, 1984 by International Bible Society, Used by permission of Zondervan. All rights reserved.

Forming: A Work of Grace
ISBN: 978-0-9890069-0-3
Published by Kingdom Formation Ministries
www.KingdomFormation.org

Print Editions:
    Feb 2013 – Draft Version
    July 2013 – First Production Print
    Nov 2013 – Minor edits and additions

Copyright © 2012, 2013 David Takle, all rights reserved.
No portion of this book may be reproduced in any manner without the express written consent of the author, except that quotations of less than 200 words may be used, provided the following citation is included:
David Takle, *Forming: A Work of Grace* (NC: Kingdom Formation Ministries, www.kingdomformation.org) 2013, used by permission.

For Dallas.

I will be forever grateful for the path you have forged for the rest of us.

Forming: A Work of Grace

Table of Contents

Foundations
1. Changing Our Minds About Change..................17
2. God is Relational..................45
3. Focusing and Listening..................65
4. Discerning and Responding..................101
5. Grace as a Means for Transformation..................121

Practice
6. Our Manner of Engagement..................157
7. What to Expect When Engaging With God..................169
8. Common Barriers to Engaging With God..................181
Interlude: Practices for Christian Formation..................211

Movement
9. Renewing Our Mind..................255
10. Healing Our Identity and Self-Rejection..................293
11. Disarming Our Fear and Anxiety..................323
12. Two Kinds of Maturity..................341

Appendix..................381

Acknowledgments

The ideas presented here have taken shape over such a long period of time, it would be impossible at this point for me to say with any certainty who contributed what to the final result. But one person in particular has had more influence than any other in shaping my understanding of the Christian life, and to whom I am deeply indebted – Dallas Willard.

When I first read *The Divine Conspiracy* in 1998, it landed on my soul like water in a dry desert place. Every page brought relief from the spiritual fog and heaviness that had suffocated my life for so many years. I began to feel joy and hope that had eluded me all my life. As I went on to read his other works, I continued to find that same kind of beauty and clarity that reoriented my understanding of the kingdom of God into a way of life that not only made sense, but laid the groundwork for a life in God that I had always believed should be possible.

So with a heart full of gratitude, I would like to acknowledge the invaluable contribution that Dallas has made to my life and to this book.

The other person I want to thank here is my wife Jan. Her faithfulness to this work and her incredible grasp of the power of *relationship* have meant the world to me. Were it not for her love and the life we share, I would not be able to write a book about building the kind of relationship with God that is able to transform our soul.

Finally, my gratitude to God for giving me this book to write. Much of this material has felt like a gift I have been given to share with others. I hope it blesses you as much to read these words as it did for me to write them.

Preface

I never meant to write a four-hundred page book. My only goal was to share with others the things I wish someone would have told me thirty years ago. Despite the length and breadth of this work, I have tried to remain focused on a single theme of utmost importance: *How are we to participate with God in ways that actually make a difference in our life?* This one area has caused perhaps more difficulty than any other throughout the history of the New Testament church, from Galatia to the present day.

One of the greatest challenges in writing this book and the related *Forming* course material was deciding what to include and what to leave out. There were so many areas I wanted to address, but choices had to be made. To be clear, my overarching objective was simply this – to help Christians develop an authentic relationship with God that is real enough and vibrant enough to change them from the inside out. Among other things, that means spelling out as clearly as possible what it looks like to connect with our unseen God, how that connection produces change in us, why trying harder to live well does *not* work, and why Christian education alone fails to change lives.

The twelve-session course that also came out of this work, *Forming: Change by Grace*, has been met with an overwhelmingly positive response – lives are being changed as people discover a deeper relationship with God than they ever had before. The great advantage that a course has over a book is that we can incorporate the kind of experiential training necessary for transformation. On the other hand, twelve training sessions cannot possibly cover all of the nuances regarding our relationship with God, let alone the many implications of spiritual development that come out of this incredible shift toward authentic relationship. For those reasons I felt it was necessary to publish this book.

Again, I have had to limit the scope of this material, because there are so many things that could be said about how we grow spiritually. So I have followed the course itself quite closely, with the intention of providing more context and supporting theology for the things we are teaching there. I have expanded many of the basic concepts presented in the *Forming* course and provided additional examples and further clarification of the various themes covered by the workbook and video.

My intention here is to fulfill two main functions. First, I want to offer additional background and context for anyone who is facilitating the *Forming* course. The truth is that much of the understanding and many of the practices taught in the course have been neglected by much of the Western Christian world for many years. Bringing it back to the forefront necessitates an incredible paradigm shift in our thinking and practice. Anyone who wishes to lead a group through the course would be well-advised to equip themselves with as much background as possible, and by doing so enable the group to get a great deal more from the experience.

Second, there are many who will want to go deeper than the time in the course sessions will allow, and others who simply do not have the opportunity to attend a formal course. It is my hope that this book will help them to re-orient their Christian walk so that they are better able to set their feet on a path that leads to the kind of life they always believed should be possible.

All of that said, there was one additional unintended result of this work for which I am truly grateful. As I reflect on the content here and the amazing changes I have experienced in my own life that have come from this approach to our spiritual journey, I sometimes wonder how I survived the first forty-plus years of my Christian life without this relationship with God. It would, in fact, take another volume to describe how vastly different my life has become. Which means that what has emerged here is not some optional way to proceed in our Christian walk, but rather a vision that is totally faithful to the New Testament declarations of the abundant life, and absolutely foundational to how God intended for us to live.

My prayer is that this book will help others to find this same foundation, and point them to the path that leads to life.

A Note About Gender Inclusiveness

Due to the limitations of our language, every English author has to decide how to address the issue of inclusiveness regarding gender when using pronouns. Reading the phrase "he or she" all the time can be very cumbersome; using only "he" or "she" sounds very biased in modern literature; and randomly switching between the two is often disorienting.

One solution is to refer to "you" all the time, but that generally comes across as too preachy. Another approach is to use "I" and "my," but after a while that begins to sound a little too self-referenced.

By way of compromise, I have opted for the convention of using inclusive plural pronouns, despite the fact that this results in grammatically incorrect sentences. So instead of, "When a person sets aside time to be with God, he or she needs to quiet his or her mind and focus his or her heart." I will tend to use, "When we set aside time to be with God, we need to quiet our mind and focus our heart."

My assumption is that since we hear this kind of grammar all the time, most readers will have little trouble with the license I have taken with the language. I hope you will find this to be an acceptable solution.

Rowing or Sailing?

For many Christians, the spiritual life is a lot like rowing a boat. Although it may become wearisome at times, they do their best to persist and remain as consistent as possible, often in the face of considerable difficulty. Not that they try to do this all on their own. Having attended many seminars on the value of rowing and the dangers of slacking off, they keep up their energy by attending weekly meetings and praying for the Holy Spirit to give them the strength and endurance to row well.

Of course there are setbacks. Some find themselves in an opposing current and no matter how hard they row, the boat just seems to go more backward than forward. Still others could swear they were never issued both oars, and spend much of the time going in circles or switching sides to keep from getting too far off course. Most distressing of all are those who can never row for more than a few minutes at a time before becoming exhausted. No matter how much they pray they never seem to have enough energy, and may privately wonder if the Holy Spirit is holding out on them.

Sometimes those who are stronger and pulling well will call out advice on how to steer or how to hold the oars. The advice usually lands on the strugglers like an anchor, but they take a deep breath and try harder. From time to time the leaders just shake their heads and wonder why it is that so much effort is spent making so little progress.

Another Way

Imagine now a sail, full and bright, pulling each boat with all the power of the wind. The oars are gone, along with sore arms and aching backs. Instead, the boaters are learning how to catch the wind and give up the work of forward movement to something much more powerful than they could ever be. And movement it is! Waves pour off each bow and the wake they leave behind churns with foamy water. It's actually fun!

Oh, there are things to do, and lots more to learn. But this is so far removed from rowing that it's not even possible to compare the two. Even more exciting is the discovery that the wind in their sail is none other than the Holy Spirit Himself. Which means that the apprentice sailors are in truth witnessing the power of God and learning to engage with Him in tangible ways that they never experienced as rowers. Clearly they still need to learn how to sail and align with the wind. But that is light-years from asking God to give them the strength to do all the work of rowing.

Enter Christian Formation

Christian formation is every bit as different from traditional models of discipleship as sailing is from rowing. Most of us have experienced the heavy weight of knowing all the things we *should* be doing and all the things we *should not* be doing, and the exhaustion of being forever behind where we think we ought to be by now. Giving more and trying harder seem to be the only alternatives to poor performance, despite the desperate prayers for God to provide the power for our efforts. Many of us have virtually given up hope of becoming more of what God wants us to be, because we have no idea how to add any more to what we are already doing.

When we stop and ask what it is that Christians need to do in order to grow, what do we hear? Read your Bible, pray, and get involved in ministry. But Bible reading often feels more like doing homework than feeding the soul, and what many Christians seem to get out of it is an even stronger sense of how poorly they are rowing. Prayer is also hard, sometimes because we cannot seem to focus and other times because we cannot figure out how to pray for help. On the one hand we feel the need to ask for forgiveness for what we can't seem to *do* right. On the other hand, when we pray for strength we are left perplexed as to why God does not make us strong enough to *get it* right. Lastly, the prospect of getting more involved in ministry is the very thing we dread, *doing more*. We keep hearing the same thing over and over: "Row harder!"

What all of these approaches have in common is the belief that *it really is up to us* to do what Christians are supposed to do, and that God's part is to provide the energy we need to make it happen. We are more or less left with the conclusion that the only difference in "rowing" between the Old Covenant and the New Covenant is that New Testament rowers get spiritual vitamins to help them.

This paradigm is terribly mistaken!

We need to come to grips with the fact that this approach to the Christian life has very little to do with life led by the Spirit. It is essentially life under the law dressed up in New Testament terminology. No matter how much we try to give the Holy Spirit credit for whatever good happens through this approach, this whole way of proceeding is firmly rooted in our own effort, based on our own willpower and our own understanding of what we need to do in order to become better Christians.

Now as it turns out, some of those among us are really good rowers! Unfortunately, that adds to the illusion that this really is the way to go. But quite literally, this is the way of mastery as it is known in the world, not the way of transformation in the kingdom of God. All of life outside the kingdom tells us that advancement is earned, and mastery is achieved through hard work.

Not so in the kingdom of God. Purity, wholeness, healing, and restoration of the ruined soul result directly from engaging with God – not in traditional one-way prayer, but from dynamic tangible interaction in which we are involved both actively and consciously. ***Instead of trying to make ourselves do more of what we think Christians ought to do, hoping that will make us into the people we were meant to be, we need to be made into who God meant us to be so that we can do what we were meant to do.*** That's the difference between rowing and sailing!

Instead of making myself say the words that my offender is forgiven, what if God changed my heart so that I actually forgave him and my mouth then expressed the care of my heart? Instead of trying hard to *act as if* I love my enemy, what if I engaged with God in ways that changed me so that I actually loved my enemy and my actions came out of that? My task then becomes a matter of lining up my sail with the wind, rather than rowing against the current of my own heart in order to achieve an outcome I think is right.

Many people have given up the belief that such transformation is even possible. Feeling helpless in the face of their own mal-formed souls, they resort to forcing the behavior they believe Christians ought to portray out of obedience to God. But that amounts to picking up the oars because we never learned to sail.

Well, what if we could learn? What if I came to believe that God not only *can* change my heart, He very much wants to do so? What if the biggest thing by far between my heart and my transformation is my own misinformation and poor training on how to engage with God in ways that bring life? What if I *can* learn how to sail? Now *that* would be Good News!

Learning to be with God, develop a genuine relationship with God, and to engage with God for transformation is precisely what Christian formation is about – how to be formed more and more into the image of Christ, so that the life of Christ comes out of us by virtue of who we are – how to change from the inside out so that good that comes out of us *because* of who we are and not in an effort to *override* who we are.

Formation is about learning how to receive from God those things that we cannot do on our own, namely, *to change our own heart to be more like His*. We learn how to feel the wind, to tack with it, to be changed by it, until we find ourselves moved to places that would never have been possible by rowing alone.

We have a God who moved heaven and earth for our restoration and who is committed to restoring our souls as the first fruits of His new creation. What we need to do is to stop trying to get there by direct effort, and instead become apprentices of life, learning how to *be with* this God who transforms, and to engage with Him for our restoration. Then we will become free to be who He has designed us to be and to do what He wants us to do.

I say, "Let's go sailing!"

Chapter 1

Changing Our Minds About Change

You have put on a new nature which is still being renewed. (Col.3:10, paraphrased)

Have you ever looked at your own spiritual journey and thought …
"There *has* be more to the Christian life than *this*"?

If you have, you are not alone. Even though we do not say it out loud very often, most Christians who long for a deeper spiritual life at some point experience a profound sense of having missed something along the way – something very important, perhaps vital. Whatever it is, they have been unable to find it or even give it a name that might point them in the right direction.

From time to time they may wonder if they are just hoping for more from life than will ever be possible in a broken world. But then they read Paul's letters, written from a Roman prison, where he is encouraging his listeners to discover more of what God wants for them. Or they read the words of Jesus as He promises rest to the weary and an abiding presence of His Spirit, not to mention the stream of water that would well up inside those who drink of the water He offers. "What on earth is He talking about?" they ask themselves.

They may question whether they are too loaded down, too defective, too *something* to ever receive what God has promised. Maybe they have not tried hard enough or cared enough or prayed enough. Maybe they need to repent. Or perhaps they are too selfish and would see God move in their life if they just gave more or did more to prime the pump.

Or maybe God overstated His promises. The first disciples probably got more grace and more power than we could ever expect, so we need to take what they said about the Christian life with a little dose of realism and understand that we could never do what they did or live that close to God. After all, they got to walk with Jesus for three years.

Whatever it is, we find ourselves feeling cheated, that for some reason this life we were promised never quite lives up to what we thought it would be like. And we don't know why.

It seemed to work for a while. The joy we felt and the changes we went through right after our conversion were amazing. We had so much hope, and could not get enough of it. Then one day it just started slowing down. We began to notice places where we seemed to be permanently stuck, along with a few issues that never seemed to diminish in strength or intensity. Our energy started sagging and our devotional times dried up. The more we tried, the more remote those things became.

This cannot be what God had in mind. There must be something more. But what is it? How do we find it?

If you have ever felt any of these things, you have also probably made enough attempts to resolve them to know that there are a lot of people out there trying to tell you what the answer is. So if you are at all skeptical that this book will help, I understand. For over thirty years I combed the Christian world looking for the "magic bullet" that would make everything clear. I found plenty of promising leads that turned out to be mostly short-term distractions. What I wanted was a way to change who I was. All I found were more things to do and behaviors to change and ways to avoid changing the real me.

While I no longer believe in a magic wand that will suddenly make everything all right or give me instant transformation from who I am to who I want to be, I have found something far more compelling and far more life-giving than I ever thought possible.

More than anything else, I would call it *a path that leads to life,* a trajectory that brings me closer each day to becoming the person I know God has called me to be, a way of proceeding that frees my heart more and more from the stuff I carried around for so many decades, a way that helps me know my Father's heart and brings me into relationship with Him – closer than anything I have ever known before. My heart is changing, my fears are diminishing, my hope is growing. With each passing year it gets better and better.

And I am not alone. All across the planet there are thousands of Christians who are finding this path. We are learning more and more about how God intends for us to be involved in deliberately fostering our spiritual growth. We even have a name for this process – *Christian Formation*. And although that may be a strange term for some, it means only that we are learning how to be actively involved in what God is doing to form us into the image of Christ.

So I invite you to join me for a while, and see the ways that God has made it possible for us to truly become one with Him, to be formed more and more into the people He designed us to be, and to live as He meant for us to live.

I can assure you that there is nothing in here that falls outside of the true faith that was given to us in the New Testament. For that matter, there is nothing "new" in here at all. Christian formation is actually a rediscovery of what dear Christian saints have always known, but which has been lost by much of the modern world. So please come along with us as we consider how we might recapture the abundant life described in the New Testament.

What If There Really Is a Way to Live as Christ Promised?

Now if I was reading a book like this, the last thing I would want to find is another list of things that I should be doing, or worse yet, some new fad that will blow though the church and be gone in ten years. Personally, I have no desire to spend time or energy on a warmed over version of the same old stuff, or some strange variation of Christianity that somebody dreamed up when they got too emotional one day.

So what exactly is Christian formation and why should I listen long enough to find out if it makes any difference for me to know this?

The short answer is that ***Christian formation is about developing an authentic relationship with God that is vibrant enough to change us from the inside out to become more the person God created us to be***. But those are very loaded terms, and the meaning behind them is not at all self-evident.

That is why it takes an entire book and a course about formation to recapture what it means to be a Christian. What we want to emphasize here is that this approach to spiritual growth is quite different from what most of us have been taught. And as you will discover, it is also far more in tune with the spirit of the New Testament than what most of us have tried. This difference is significant enough to lead us to an incredibly refreshing, life-giving way of engaging with the Holy Spirit that causes real change in our life from day to day.

What Christian formation *is not*, is a repackaged discipleship model or a five-step program for getting more involved in your church. Rather, this is learning how to engage with God in tangible ways that go beyond saying 'grace' at mealtime; learning how to develop a conversational prayer life from which we can discover His heart for us and be taught by the Spirit of God; learning how to balance our part and God's part in the process of transformation; and making a space *for God to do in us what we cannot do* – to change our heart and mind to be more like Him.

If you have been a Christian for any length of time, you may have discovered the great unspoken secret of Western Christianity: *We have lots of good ideas about what a Christian should do, but we have almost no idea at all about how to help you actually change your heart to become more like Jesus.* If you do ask how to become more Christ-like, you will be told:

- Read your Bible.
- Pray.
- Go to church.
- Get involved.

But what you will *not* be told is that while these things may give you new information and new skills, beyond a certain point they will not change your basic character very much at all. The longer you try to make this work, the more tired you will become and the more disillusioned you will be with your own lack of transformation. Eventually, your devotional life will dry up and you will feel farther and farther from God.

What makes this even more confusing is that it seems to work for some people some of the time. If it is not working for you, then you are told there must be something wrong like:

- You are not committed enough.
- You have sin or bitterness or unforgiveness in your life.
- You have lost your first love.

Or perhaps you need a shot in the arm from some itinerant preacher or a particular ministry. Usually these explanations just pile more condemnation on us and offer very little real hope for change.

The truth is that the whole process of trying really hard to be a good Christian is a terribly misguided venture, even though this approach is what dominates much of the Christian world. Theologians and laypersons alike routinely miss the very heart of the gospel and thus fail to find the life that is promised to those who know Jesus. In fact the majority of Christians today have radically distorted views of what it means to grow up and become mature both as human beings and as Christians.

Most people have some sense that *human development* happens more or less automatically as you get older, moving from childhood to adolescence and then adulthood, and that the goal of maturity is an ever-increasing ability to stand on our own two feet. At the same time, they believe that *spiritual development* is something that we have to work at quite a bit, doing things over and over in obedience until we get them right.

Incredibly, despite the widespread acceptance of these ideas, this paradigm is wrong on both counts! Human maturity is the result of hard work that is done in the context of a well-functioning community, developing skills that enable us to deal with increasing complexity in interdependent relationships.[1] Everything from acquiring language and learning how to walk, to learning how to repair ruptures in a relationship and care for the needs of two people at the same time are skills that must be developed over many years and with many attempts, guided by those who have gone before us and learned them well.

Spiritual development, far from being acquired through hard work (or happening automatically over time) is mostly *received*, and that is a concept and a process which is very foreign to many Christians today. We are not talking about some abstract mystical work of the Holy Spirit that goes on virtually undetected in the background of our mind. God intended for us to grow spiritually by means of a concrete, tangible connection with Him that creates life and truth inside our soul and changes who we are from the inside out. You do not learn how to "love your enemy" by baking him a cake while grinding your teeth in anger. You engage with God about your heart condition, and when He shows you how He sees your enemy and changes

---

[1] This will be a recurring theme throughout the book and the main subject of Chapter 12, taken from Friesen, et. al., *The Life Model*

your heart, you actually care about his well-being and can love him without having to drag yourself down the road to "obedience."

Spiritual growth is the fruit of engaging with God, not something achieved by trying hard to do the right things. So what is *engaging with God*?

Well, that is what Christian formation is all about. Engaging with God is a multifaceted process that is learned experientially and involves a number of perspectives and practices that many Christians today are unfamiliar with. So there is no short answer to that question. But if you stay with us, the phrase "engaging with God" will soon take on a whole new meaning. To begin, we will recast a vision of what spiritual growth looks like, because there are so many mistaken ideas floating around regarding the basic nature of the Christian life.

How is Christian Formation Different from Traditional Discipleship Programs?

Although that question will be addressed repeatedly throughout the rest of this book, it is important to present a little preview to prepare the reader for the kind of paradigm shift that is necessary in order to deliberately pursue Christian growth and transformation.

At the outset, we should emphasize that a *disciple* in the New Testament is not a person who practices a certain lifestyle or learns a few ministry skills or studies theology. *A disciple is a person who participates in a meaningful mentoring relationship with a teacher.* This distinction is crucial. Being a disciple means that a person engages regularly with a mentor who trains and instructs his followers in whatever it is that he is a master of. So when we talk about being a disciple of Jesus, we are not using a catchy phrase that means we are having devotions or working in a church ministry. We are envisioning a very dynamic *relationship* in which we are actively involved with God to learn how to become more Christ-like and how to live in this new kingdom as we continue our physical existence in a broken world.

That is *why* Christian spiritual formation is different from most other discipleship programs that focus on making behavioral changes and learning doctrines, however valuable those may be. Now we will look at *how* it is different.

Our Expectations are Different

Let's begin by looking at some of the things the New Testament says about the Christian life. As you slowly read these passages, think about how they compare to your own experience as a Christian.

> Whoever believes in me, as the Scripture has said, **streams of living water will flow** from within him. (Jn.7:38 NIV)

> So that the body of Christ may be built up until we all reach unity in the faith and in the knowledge of the Son of God and **become mature, attaining to the whole measure of the fullness of Christ.** (Eph.4:12-13 NIV)

> You were taught, with regard to your former way of life, **to put off your old self**, which is being corrupted by its deceitful desires; to be made new in the attitude of your minds; **and to put on the new self, created to be like God in true righteousness and holiness.** (Eph.4:22-24 NIV)

> So that you may be filled with all the fullness of God.(Eph.3:19)

Those are amazing promises! They seem almost too good to be true!

Honestly, some of us wonder if they *are* too good to be true. When we read passages like that we have to ask, How does that square with my own life? How many Christians do I know who truly reflect this way of life?

Just look at some of these statements: "Created to be like God." What does that mean? How do we make sense of that in light of the unhealed wounds and repetitive sins that plague most Christians?

Did you ever look at verses like this and just shake your head? Have you ever compared your life to the stories in the New Testament and think, "They seemed to have something that I don't have"? Have you ever thought, "There has to more to the Christian life than this"?

For most of my life I could say that Christianity was a way of life for me, and yet in spite of that I was aware of a huge gap between what I saw in my life and what I saw in the New Testament. When I read about an artesian well of water springing up and flowing out of us, (Jn.4:14) I had to wonder what in the world He could be talking about.

But let's assume for a minute, just for the sake of argument, that this kind of life is really possible. What if we could...

- Break the patterns of the past.
- Pursue transformation by some deliberate means.
- See evidence of Biblical maturity on an on-going basis.
- Experience the reality of the kingdom.
- Have a genuine relationship with God, not just know about God.

What would that mean?

Even entertaining the idea can be difficult or painful for some people. After all, how many of us have wondered whether this is at all possible? How many have found it totally elusive? How many of us feel like this is a far-away dream or too much to hope for? Perhaps all of this talk of being Christ-like is just a target, an ideal that we can never really expect to experience. Maybe Paul and others were exaggerating a bit or talking about life after death or something else.

For most of us, if any of that stuff is truly possible, it means that we have missed something along the way. And the prospect of having to try and make up the deficit is daunting, if not shaming. We naturally equate "I'm missing something" with "There's something I'm not doing that I should be doing" and feel defeated before we begin. Others have simply ruled out such a possibility and instead adopted a theology that explains why falling short of the New Testament vision is perfectly normal.

If we are honest within ourselves, most of us will find that we have come to harbor a kind of disbelief in ongoing transformation and have settled instead for the status quo, whatever that may be. We have tried all that we know to do without seeing much change. So while we are willing to keep trying, we have lowered our expectations to be more "realistic" about what might be possible in our journey toward wholeness.

But what if there is another way to get there from here? What if becoming more Christ-like is something that we cannot do because it's God's job not ours? And the reason we have been having so much trouble with this process is that we are trying to make this happen by sheer willpower and our own effort, because we have not been trained how to engage with God in ways that will change who we are?

What if, instead of trying to do *more* to make life come out better, there were some things we could do *differently* that would allow the Holy Spirit to change us from the inside out? Then we could become the kind of people who are naturally inclined to think about and desire the things of God much like the way Jesus did. Rather than expending so much energy fighting our inner nature in order to live the way we think we should, we would do by nature the things that align with the kingdom and produce life.[2]

When we embark on a journey of Christian formation, we have good reasons to raise our expectations of what God will do in our life. Because when we give up on the failed methods of the past and seek to learn how to be closer to God, we open the doors to receiving life in ways we have not known before. As we learn how to receive life from God, we begin to change in ways that we could never accomplish in our own strength. Discovering how God can change our life in such identifiable, concrete ways gives us hope that life can be different.

So let's continue to look at some of the other ways in which Christian formation may be different from what most of us have tried in the past.

Our Goals are Different

For much of the Christian world, following after Christ means trying to do all the things He said to do and trying not to do any of the things we are not supposed to do. Of course we assume that the Holy Spirit is helping us, but only so far as we are already being "obedient." Our immediate goal in this process is to be able to do the right things, say the right things, have the right attitude about things, and to respond in godly ways to the various events of life.

Shocking as it may be, this approach to Christianity is a terrible mistake. *Aiming for obedience this way actually makes the Christian life impossible.* Now if that makes your head spin a bit, please take a few deep breaths before going on so that you do not miss this important point.

Obedience to the written code in the Old Testament was paramount to their way of life. But no matter how hard they tried to keep it, the law could not produce transformation of character. That was why God granted a New Covenant founded on different principles. "For if a law had been given

---

[2] This is precisely the heart of Paul's argument in Romans 7 and 8.

which was able to impart life, then righteousness would indeed have come through the law" (Gal.3:21; Heb.8). But that was not possible, so God gave us something else entirely.

Tragically, the Christian world has by and large failed to grasp the enormity of this paradigm shift, and has instead opted to replace the Old Testament law with New Testament Principles, all the while continuing in the belief that trying to do the right things will make you a good person. But Jesus did not just give us better principles to replace the law. He did away with the whole process of achieving righteousness through human effort! Claiming that the Holy Spirit gives us the power to keep the new principles only obscures the seriousness of this error on multiple levels:

- That is not the primary role of the Spirit.

- Whatever power we do receive from the Spirit does not change us automatically. If it did, we would be a lot farther along than we are. If change comes from our hard work aided by the Spirit, we would have to conclude that how much effort *we* supply is what makes the difference,[3] which runs contrary to Scripture.

- God never intended to empower us to keep an external set of principles. He chose instead to write His laws on our heart (Heb.8:10). That is a metaphor that means He wants to change our heart to act naturally in accordance with His laws and to not have to keep trying to do what our heart resists doing.

Instead of trying to do things right until we "get it," our goal is to be changed at the core of our being to be more Christ-like. If we take both God and our condition seriously here, we are forced to admit that this job was not finished when we were converted. Writing God's laws on our heart is a promised benefit of the New Covenant, but it does not happen all at once. The reason we try to finish the task by committing ourselves to a works-oriented process of growth, is because we have not learned how to receive what we need from God. So we make the same mistake that the Jewish nation made. "Not knowing about God's righteousness, and seeking to

---

[3] Or worse yet, that God only gives assistance to those who try really hard.

establish their own, they did not subject themselves to the righteousness of God" (Rom.10:3 NASB).

If we intend to become Christ-like, we must acknowledge from the start that we cannot get there by direct effort. We are aiming at the wrong goal. Instead, we should aim at learning how to engage with God in ways that change our heart. As our heart becomes molded by God, we will then be able to live in the way God designed us to live, the way we are called to live. If that seems hard to grasp, it is only because we have not been taught how to live this way. Our hope is that by the time you finish this book, you will not only know how to engage with God for change, but you will have actually done so!

The Role of Holy Spirit is Different

As stated above, the Holy Spirit was not given to us to enable us to keep a new set of rules. That is one of the most persistent myths regarding His role in our lives, and it comes from not understanding His real ministry and from misunderstanding the process of spiritual formation. Even leading theologians teach that "participating with God" means if you do all the right things the best way you can, the Spirit will encourage you and empower you to do those things. There is so much wrong with that perspective that it is hard to know where to begin.

First, the ministry of the Holy Spirit becomes almost indiscernible. Often a person will exclaim, "I don't know how I could have done that without God's help." Now to be clear, I do believe there are times that the Holy Spirit sustains us in ways beyond our normal capacity. But we must also stop a minute and notice that people who are not Christian, or even hostile to Christianity, do hard things all the time, even heroic things. And they often look back and say, "I don't know how I did that!" So how *do* they do that? And when I do something hard, how much is me and how much is God? To be honest, I have no real way of knowing what part is God and what part is me. So if the Spirit's main job is to give us the power to do what we are trying our best to do, we actually have relatively little real awareness of what He is doing in our life.

Second, this does not sound anything like the ministry of the Spirit as described by Jesus. According to John 14-17, the Holy Spirit's primary ministry is to mentor us about life in the kingdom. Now there are a number of reasons why this idea may be hard for Christians to grasp, so what often happens to this passage is that it gets turned into something we are familiar with, like learning from Bible studies or listening to sermons. But that's not what Jesus is talking about here. To make this into something commonplace is to miss the fact that this is a radically different approach to life.

The Holy Spirit is not someone who follows us around and gives us a booster shot when we try to do good things. He is the one that *we* are supposed to follow! *He* is the active leader, and we are to learn how to live by His direction. Most of us have never been taught what that means or how to do that, and many have only the vaguest notion of who the Spirit is and what He does. But His role in our lives was never meant to be that abstract. He was given to us as a life-giving companion and mentor with whom we would have direct contact.

While Jesus was on the earth, His disciples were completely dependent upon Him for every bit of direction and insight they had into what God was doing in the world. He opened up to them the character of God, He revealed the distrust that underwrote their anxieties, He corrected their faulty thinking, cleared up their distorted values, and gave them understanding of things that they had been clueless about before. Much of that training was in relation to whatever else they were involved with at the time – whether being confronted by religious leaders or discussing eternal life with a rich man or settling a disagreement about who would be the greatest in the kingdom. His teaching was always relevant and tailored to the people He was speaking to, because He knew what it was that they needed to hear so they could see its significance in the moment.

When Jesus left the earth, the disciples' dependence did not decrease, it became greater than ever. They were not suddenly left to their own wisdom to figure out which principles applied in a given instance. Jesus gave them the Spirit to pick up where He left off, to continue the training that they would need throughout their lives. And the Spirit continues to teach in much the same way that Jesus did, turning the spiritual world right side up, event by event, opening our eyes to the way God sees things instead of the ways that we see them.

The problem is, we have lost the art of being mentored. We no longer know how to listen or how to engage Him in conversation so that our spirit can be retrained in the light of the kingdom. That leaves us in the precarious position of being more or less self-taught, doing our best to extract what principles we can see in the text and apply them to our life. Truth is, we are not that good at it. By taking this approach we cut ourselves off from the most important resource we have been given, the Spirit Himself.

If we could clearly see the choice we have before us, between being taught by the Spirit of Truth or by the best practical theologians, it would be a no-brainer. The only reason we have trouble with this paradigm shift is that most of us have had little to no experience in being taught by the Holy Spirit, and so we cannot make sense of the choice. But if we suppose for a minute that it is possible to have conversations with God about our life, and take the time to learn how to do this, then we open the door to a way of life that we never thought possible.

Aside from the vast difference in wisdom between our thoughts and God's, a tremendous difference exists between the *voice* of God and our own. Although at times we can say true things to ourselves and each other that we need to hear, God's voice has a power that we cannot possibly imitate, a power that can birth new life and transform minds that have been malformed by life experience in a broken world. When He speaks to us, the words get in deeper and have more impact then when we say them. That is why we need His wisdom, spoken by His Spirit.

That brings us to the next main difference between spiritual formation and other ways of pursuing growth.

The Means We Depend On for Change are Different

Nearly all discipleship programs have a plan for people to follow that involves Bible study, learning about prayer and some of the more important doctrines, developing good habits, attending church and joining a small group, and for those who show potential, training on how to lead such studies and groups. This is all good as far as Christian education goes. But this approach has a hole in it that is big enough to swallow your soul.

First, what is left *unsaid* in most programs is actually the most important part – how to engage with God. We are taught how to *pray to* God, but we are almost never shown how to *listen to* Him or *receive from* Him. In terms of what we miss by way of necessary training, this is like trying to learn how to fly a jet liner by studying books and never sitting in a real jet. This deafening silence about listening in prayer has a very powerful impact on our assumptions about what is possible. We learn from its absence in our teaching that it is either unimportant or unreliable or impossible.

Second, the underlying presupposition of the average discipleship program is that with enough information and enough motivation, you can grow spiritually and make this Christian life work. For people who are converted from a spiritually impoverished lifestyle, this may actually feel like water in the desert and help them in many ways – for a while. Giving God's truth to a person who was spiritually confused can be like handing a compass to a person lost in the woods. That's a good thing.

But most people find that after about three to five years they no longer know where to go, spiritually speaking. Whatever issues they live with that have not been impacted by their church involvement become a continual source of frustration and defeat, a feeling that something important is missing in their relationship to God, something that they cannot seem to "get." Their training tells them to try harder and be more dedicated. But the harder they try the more impossible the task seems to become. They may doubt themselves, they may doubt God, or they may just give up. Many turn to books and conferences looking for answers. Some begin seeking to have power encounters with God.

Sadly, those who struggle with some stubborn sin, nagging self-doubt or painful memory are usually told they need to be more committed, more repentant, or more obedient to the things they already know. After all, Christians are not supposed to have emotional problems or sin that cannot be overcome. Anyone who is unable to "succeed" in their spiritual walk is moved to the back of the class in the hope that they will not be too noticeable or disruptive.

Christian formation takes an entirely different approach to spiritual growth and recovery. By discovering how to depend on the Holy Spirit as our Mentor, we learn to have conversations with Him about our life, our wounds, and our failings, and how to receive His healing ministry in the deepest parts of our soul. We acknowledge from the beginning that we cannot change our nature by an act of the will or by beating it into submission. Transformation is something only God can do in us. Our part in that process is *not* to do everything we can in our own strength, hoping that God will mysteriously alter our heart as a reward for our effort. Rather we give up on trying to force the right outcome by our own power, and engage with Him directly and ask Him what He wants to do in our heart and mind, and how He wants us to participate in the process. Dependence upon God is then no longer a euphemism that means relying on our grasp of doctrine, it is an everyday experience that is fleshed out in tangible interactions with Him. That is how we change and grow.

In short, we do not produce the fruit of the Spirit by trying to produce fruit. We become fruitful when we connect well to the Vine. Discipling programs often try to teach people how to *act as if* they have the life of the Spirit, without actually helping them have that life. In Christian formation, we draw our life from God rather than try to change our heart and mind by sheer resolve. That brings us to entirely different places.

Our Relationship With God is Qualitatively Different

One day when I asked a friend of mine how his relationship with God was going, he hesitated for a few moments and then began, "Well, the Bible study I'm leading on Sunday mornings seems to be going OK. As for the rest, I'm not so sure. I know it could be better. I'm still dealing with my anger issues, my wife and I fight about a lot of stupid things, and I have yet to get involved in one of the small groups at church." After acknowledging his struggles and empathizing with his efforts, I repeated my question. "How is your relationship with God going?" He responded with a quizzical look and asked, "You mean my quiet time?"

It is interesting that when you ask people about the quality of their relationship with God, they will talk about the things that they do, whether they do them well or poorly, and how they measure up against some ideal standard of what a Christian ought to be like. For the vast majority of Christians, the phrase "relationship with God" is almost synonymous with the phrase "how well I am doing in my Christian obligations."

But relationship with God is not about how we are performing or how many vices we have conquered. Imagine for a moment that when you ask someone about their relationship with a favorite professor they respond with, "Well, I get to most of the classes on time, I'm getting a 3.5 in his classes, and I'm fairly certain I'll pass the final without too much trouble." Those things might have some connection, but they tell you almost nothing about that person's relationship with the professor.

A genuine relationship has some substance to it, an emotional closeness, a trust that is tangible and meaningful, and an expression of time together, with conversations and gifts of life from one to another. Yet for most Christians, their relationship to God is about on par with their relationship to their banker. They know how to ask for help when they need it, but they have no idea what the guy even looks like.

My friend's question about his quiet time is getting closer to the point, but may or may not have anything to do with a real connection to God. A time set aside to be with God is an essential part of building a relationship with Him. Unfortunately, most of us have been taught to have a quiet time that bears a striking resemblance to cramming for a test. It looks and feels more like doing homework than connecting with a person.

The very fact that we confuse *having a relationship with God* with doing Bible study or going to church or conquering sin ought to be evidence enough that something is terribly wrong in the way many Christians have been trained.

A major part of Christian formation is understanding the nature of our relationship with God and learning how to *be with* Him, not just think *about* Him or have correct theology about Him. An authentic relationship with God is a lot more than just being legally adopted into heaven's family tree. It is something we need to give time and attention to because relationships involve shared experience and a knowing of each other's heart. Even a strong bond with another person will change us in ways we do not expect and in ways we could not accomplish in isolation. Much more, a functioning relationship with God will change us from the inside out.

Many Christians today have more of an *arrangement* with God than a relationship. The arrangement goes something like this: "God, I will believe Your explanation of reality and confess my need for Your redemption, and in return You will take me to heaven when I die. And then in gratitude for what You have done for me, I will try my best to do Christian-like things and live an ethical lifestyle." In many places this sort of thing actually passes for the gospel message.

As delicately as I can put it, that kind of transaction is a travesty, a mere caricature of the Good News. Jesus did not come to earth to make a deal with us. He came to offer us LIFE itself, an invitation to live in the presence of God. These words are not some fancy way of talking about a legal contract. They are the very heart of the matter. God came to participate in a tangible, substantive relationship with us that is as real as any we have with another human being, only far more life-giving.

Rather than view our relationship with God as primarily an arrangement whereby we get to have *life after death*, Christian formation views our relationship with God as the very definition of *life itself*, a relationship that leads to living forever with the King. Only a perspective of this nature can make any sense of the passion of the early followers and the kind of language they employed in their writings.

Growth as a *Process* Has a Different Meaning

One often hears that spiritual growth is a process. If by that we mean growth is continuous and never ending in this life, then it is a true statement. But if by *process* we mean that spiritual growth has more to do with time than it does with our actual participation, or that it happens so slowly we are hardly aware of it, then the phrase may actually have more to do with trying to explain our own *lack* of growth than it has to do with describing the realities of spiritual development. Leaving change to some abstract notion of the Holy Spirit working in mysterious ways behind the scenes will eventually foster disillusionment and cause us to resign ourselves to some "process" that we seem to have little influence over.

Spiritual growth *is* a process, one that we need to engage in actively and consciously, just as building a successful marriage is a conscious, active process. The reason it needs to be identified as an ongoing process is because we need to separate growth from any notion of *arrival* or completion. But that is not the same thing as saying we should not expect too much.

Behind a lot of training programs there is an unspoken idea that intentional growth is some kind of phase you go through before joining the ranks of those who minister to others, after which your growth will slow down and become less focused and less discernible. And while this may be an observable phenomenon in many Christian organizations, it is only because we have seriously misunderstood growth and transformation. Any spiritual plateau we experience for years at a time is not a symptom of arrival, it is stagnation from a misdirected approach to spiritual growth. Viewing the work of the Holy Spirit as a hidden process is a tremendous barrier to genuine change.

Undoing the malformation from this world and being reformed in Christ-likeness is a life-long process. There is far more work to do than can be accomplished in a single lifetime. That does not mean we are passive in this process or that it is so gradual that we are more or less unaware of what the Spirit is up to at any given moment. Extensive time is needed not because of the pace at which change can happen, but rather because of the extent of malformation that actually exists within us. There is truly far more damage in our soul than we can imagine. But the process of change is so liberating that every step is well worth our time and attention. In this way, life can be a continual experience of healing and growth that brings great joy and satisfaction every day. And this process will never end in this lifetime.

We Address Spiritual Struggles Differently

Judgmentalism in relation to our struggles is not just a symptom of an unkind spirit, it is a predictable result of the way in which much of the Christian world views spiritual development and its related struggles. In our performance-oriented approach to Christianity, those who have difficulty with old wounding or obvious persistent sin are often viewed as having a weak will or character. If we believe that it is possible to achieve the Christian life through obedience to the principles we see in Scripture, then it would only be natural to assume that most spiritual problems can be blamed on one of the following:

- Not committed enough.
- Not obedient enough.
- Too preoccupied with self.
- Failure to forgive.
- Unconfessed sin.

Of course, rebellious people do exist. So in some cases one or more of these reasons these might be partially true statements. For most people though, these explanations land on the soul like a ton of rock, condemning them for having trouble in their spiritual walk. Not only that, but those who offer such pat answers generally offer little else – nothing that will help the struggling person who asked for a life saver and got handed an anchor.

Again, all of this is entirely predictable. When Christians do not understand the true nature of spiritual recovery and growth, they cannot offer meaningful help to those who have trouble living up to the faulty paradigm they were given. For the majority who find the performance-driven life impossible, there is a double failure. First, because they were told to follow a law-based system that could not possibly give life, and then because they were condemned for not making it work!

The way out of this mess is to see the fallacy of trying to grow up by following *principles*, and return to the original message of following a *person*, developing a functional relationship that gives life and getting to know our Mentor who can actually help us with our struggles, not just cite laws from a distance.

Rather than try to coerce obedience from an already beleaguered traveler, the Holy Spirit reveals to us the underlying causes for our malfunctions, heals those wounds that keep us bound in fear, anger, and hopelessness, and then gives us what we need in order to move forward. Our part in the process is to run to Him when we are in trouble, open ourselves to His teaching and training, and receive from Him what we need in order to grow and change.

Again let me emphasize that this is not a jazzed up way of talking about figuring things out on our own "with God's help," but a direct engagement with God in order to receive His goodness, life, and love. Learning to engage with God in this way is startlingly effective in breaking the destructive patterns in our life so that we are free to live as God intended. Instead of the "try harder" approach to spiritual struggles, we come to grips with the limitations of our resolve and our energy, and ask God to do in us what we are unable to do – change who we are from the inside out.

A Closer Look at Common Approaches

I do not mean to belabor this issue, but because this is so entrenched in our current Christian culture it may be quite helpful to take another look at the dominant paradigm of Christian growth, how it came about, why we buy into it, and why it fails to deliver what it promises.

How We Got Derailed

At the risk of offending some, allow me to make some historical observations. First of all, in many ways we are still suffering from the institutionalization of the Church that took place in the fourth century after Christianity became legalized in the Roman empire. Once in place, *the institution* quickly became the means for people to get to God, and consequently came to be seen as the dispenser of grace. People were no longer taught how to engage with the Holy Spirit, but were instead instructed to go through the clergy for their spiritual needs. This made God very inaccessible and left the average layperson in perpetual need of an "expert" who would approach God for them.

With the coming of the Reformation, we reclaimed much of our access to God – we could pray to Him and receive His forgiveness directly. But in the process a new problem was created, that of hashing out doctrine. As history shows, sorting out doctrine has consumed much of the life of the Protestant movement and resulted in literally thousands of fractures between Christians. Important as it was, the fervor and dedication to pure doctrine tended to foster the belief that spiritual growth was mostly about learning the correct theological propositions. Even today many people mistake correct doctrine for spiritual development. Good theology is absolutely necessary to point you in the right direction, but it will not feed your soul.

Add to this the reverence for learning that developed during the Renaissance, and understandably you have the makings for an intellectual form of Christianity that has little room for God's direct guidance. Bible knowledge can easily replace authentic experience of God, with little notice of what has been lost. Indeed, it would seem that so much has been gained (as opposed to an ignorant kind of faith) that it could be mistaken for having a relationship with God.

With a few notable exceptions, the old problem that never got resolved was the lack of direct connection to God which is the birthright of every believer. Instead of relearning how to engage with God as our source of life, we depended on our new doctrines. We extracted the Biblical principles necessary for discerning between right and wrong, and then used those principles to try and fill the deficit left by our relative distance from God. Over the years there have been changes in the indicators that we rely on to tell who is following well and who is not. But the basic premise has remained intact, that given the right information you should be able to be a good Christian.

What Most Christian Training Looks Like Today

As noted earlier, if you were to ask the average person how you can grow as a Christian, you will probably get an answer that contains the following elements: pray, read your Bible, repent of any sins you become aware of, and get involved in church ministry. These all sound rather self-evident and make good sense. But when we begin to take these apart and look at what they really mean, there is a great deal wrong with this approach to growth, and some very important things missing.

First, we are usually taught that prayer is *talking to* God. Few places around the globe teach Christians how to *listen* to God. In many places they are even discouraged from trying. In some circles people are taught with total certainty that God stopped talking at the end of the first century, and anything we think we hear from God today must be considered suspect at best. Yet the Bible itself is *full* of stories of people who heard from God and stories about those who *failed* to hear. Those to whom Paul wrote were evidently quite accustomed to hearing from God. We might even ask how we are supposed to apply the Bible at all, if indeed is was written to people with completely different resources than we have.

If the suggestion that we can hear from God runs against your theological convictions in any way, I would ask you to suspend judgment on this aspect of spiritual formation until Chapter 3 where we take this up in detail.[4] In the mean time, for the sake of argument, consider how great a tragedy it would be if God actually did intend for us to rely on His voice for our spiritual

---

[4] I would also heartily recommend *Hearing God* by Dallas Willard

food but we gave that up because it seemed too risky. Such a vacuum might actually explain the current state of affairs in the Western Church.

Second, the admonition to read your Bible is another mixed message. We know Bible study is crucial to understanding the Christian life, because it is the only revelation God gave to His people as a whole, and because it is the only reliable pointer back to God. But Jesus Himself warned against substituting the Scriptures for the Person of God.[5] The Bible stories about people who listened to God are there precisely to show us what a Spirit-directed life looks like. Reducing those stories to ethical issues and doctrines recreates the same mistake made by those to whom Jesus was talking.

Furthermore, attempting to read the Bible without the guidance of the Holy Spirit is like trying to perform brain surgery from a medical textbook without ever having been mentored in the process. We will get it wrong, and the results are not good.

Third, we are told to repent of sin in our life. Again, a good thing to do. However, this directive is accompanied by a great many unspoken premises that may actually keep us from living as God intended. Repentance today has come to mean, "Be sorry and try harder in the future to get it right." But this assumes we can do it better if we just care enough about the problem. While that may be true for a few limited issues some of the time, this approach does little to nothing for deeply embedded problems, the kind where we get caught in a cycle of fail-repent-try-fail-repent, over and over.

As we will see in Chapter 9, repentance of this type intervenes at the wrong place in the cycle of defeat and uses the wrong tools. If we step back and consider a broader concept of repentance as "wanting whatever it takes to be free of this problem" we open the door to some highly accessible, life-giving options that come from God Himself rather than relying on our own efforts to change.

Fourth, we are told to get involved in ministry. Once again, an idea that has some merit. Yet this time the unspoken assumption is that spiritual activity will foster growth. And in some very small ways, it can. But doing good things does not make you a better person. The idea that if you pedal

---

[5] "You search the scriptures, because you think that in *them* you will find life. But the purpose of the scriptures is to *point to* the source of life, which is *me*." (Jn.5:39, paraphrased)

fast enough you will grow your character is terribly misguided and leads to all sorts of difficulties.

But the problem gets worse. An underlying presupposition often accompanies this push to "do" ministry that can obscure the very nature of growth. In some Christian circles, the group is more or less divided into those who minister and those who are ministered to, as if the need for ministry was a temporary condition. Other places have an explicit road map whereby people (1) join, (2) get trained, and (3) get involved, almost like a multilevel marketing program. When this is the dominant paradigm of church involvement, complete with charts and graphs on the wall, the whole matter of how the Holy Spirit changes lives tends to get buried somewhere in all the activity.

Motivating Christians to To Do the Right Things

Another interesting problem that is present in traditional discipleship models is that of trying to motivate people to do more in regard to their spiritual journey. The obvious question is, "Why bother? I'm going to heaven when I die. What difference does it make how much effort I make in the mean time?"

From the perspective of Christian formation, that is not even a legitimate question because it is rooted in an impoverished view of the gospel. But in much of the Christian world this issue of motivation has been a major problem. Given all that we have said so far, it is not too surprising to hear that the number one reason given for why Christians should try to grow spiritually is out of gratitude for God's gift of eternal life. "After all that God has done for you, you ought to at least make an effort to live in a way that is honoring to Him."

In practice this often translates to shaming people into trying to look like they are doing something. Yet that is only a symptom of a much bigger problem, which is turning the gospel into a transaction. There are far more compelling reasons to pursue our growth than being thankful for heaven. But those reasons are rooted in an active, functioning relationship with God, something that is noticeably missing from discipleship models that fail to emphasize the mission of the Holy Spirit to train God's people.

What is Missing?

That brings us back to the giant gaping hole that exists in the middle of most traditional approaches to discipleship. *Where is the Holy Spirit?* Virtually every branch of the Christian Church declares that the Holy Spirit is the source of all transformation that occurs in a Christian's life, a process we usually call sanctification or spiritual development toward Christlikeness. Yet most Christians are unable to articulate what that means in any practical sense. Even in a highly technical discussion among theologians of different backgrounds,[6] the question of how the Spirit works in us is left highly ambiguous. They quote lots of verses telling us that the Spirit does *something*, and then include a few vague comments along the lines of, "the Spirit helps us live the Christian life."

When they do try to describe the actual details about participating with God, they often will say that the Spirit adds His power to what we do when we are doing the right things, which is really not what the Bible teaches at all. When you think about it, if that were true, it puts the Holy Spirit in an incredibly passive position. He has to wait until we do something that He can put His stamp of approval on and then He adds His energy to whatever we are doing.

This understanding of God's action in our lives also introduces a huge problem in regard to explaining why efforts to do ministry or to get free of spiritual bondage go unrewarded. Anyone who has put their hand to any form of ministry has experienced empty results at times and even outright resistance from other people. In what way is the Spirit aiding them? For that matter, how does one explain ministry burnout? If the Spirit's job is to empower our efforts, one would think that the harder we worked the more power we would receive. But the evidence appears to say that the more you do the more likely you are to crash and burn.

There is more. Christians everywhere have experienced times when they prayed to be released from some pain or persistent sin without seeing anything change. Where is God then? Why would He not add His power to their efforts to be free? Are they doing something wrong? Do we need more faith? Is there a better way to ask? Are they being punished? Are they being tested?

---

[6] Dieter, et al. *Five Views on Sanctification*

During the summer of 2008 a leading Christian magazine published a short article from a pastor who supposedly had an insightful explanation for this dilemma. He proposed that God often withheld His hand from our efforts as a way of stripping us of pride. Of course, he had no Scriptural basis for this conjecture. The truth is he was just grasping at straws, hoping to find an explanation for this very difficult question that comes to everyone's mind when all the right prayers and actions come to nothing. Where is God's power? And how long will we need to keep trying this thing before God decides to lend a hand and do something? But these are the kinds of mistaken explanations people come up with when they begin with faulty ideas about how we grow.

Most notable in this paradigm of "God helps those who try real hard" is the complete lack of deliberate, direct engagement with the Spirit of God. Praying to God for His help is good as far as it goes. But the second we get done praying we either sit back and wait for Him to do something (which is way too passive) or put our best efforts to the task at hand and hope that God comes along and "helps" us (far too much self-effort). Either way, we fail to engage with Him directly and receive what we need for the changes we so desire. Does this not sound like a problem? Should this not get our attention and tell us that something is terribly wrong with our whole approach?

What do we do with all those verses in the New Testament that talk about God being with us, working in us, becoming an artesian well of water gushing out of us, and *leading* us? *We either have to read our experience into those verses to make them sound like something we know about, or else we have to confess that most of us have no idea what what sort of experience the Biblical authors are talking about.* I know that's a very disconcerting thought. But it *would* explain the apparent lack of God's involvement in our efforts to grow. If we have somehow found ourselves in the place of not knowing what it means to engage with the Holy Spirit in our lives, then it would make perfect sense that we cannot figure out why He does not show up the way we think He should! It would also begin to explain why trying harder does very little to solve the real problem.

Back to a Relationship With God

What if God intends for the Christian life to be an experience of God that is far more real and intense than what most of us have known? What if He means for us to know His presence within us? What if He means for us to know not just what He wants us to do *out there*, but to know *what He wants to do in us*?

This is Christian formation: *developing an authentic relationship with God that is vibrant enough to change us from the inside out, and learning how to participate with God in ways that allow Him to bring about that change, so we can become more and more the person God created us to be.*

To help put this in perspective, the following comparison shows the sharp contrast between Christian formation and traditional discipleship programs in terms of how they approach spiritual growth.

Traditional Discipleship	**Christian Formation**
Follow ethical rules	Develop ethical character
Do merciful acts	Become a merciful person
Know about God	Know God
Do different things	Become a different person
Change behavior	Change identity
Control our emotions	Transform our heart
Achieve through hard work	Receive through engaging

One approach to righteousness is to lay out all the ethically right choices and principles and then attempt to follow them. Another approach is to engage with God in ways that change our basic nature to think and desire what is good, and then live out of that new character. The difference between these two approaches is as great as the difference between the Old Covenant and the New.

Most of us have been trained to rely on our knowledge of right and wrong in order to try to live the way we think a Christian ought to live. But God gave us a new identity that could grow in the context of a relationship with Him to become the person He intended us to be. *Becoming one with Christ* is not a poetic way of describing some legal transaction that takes place in heaven, but a description of the life we are called to that can change us in ways we cannot possibly accomplish by our own effort. This is as big as the difference between rowing and sailing.

God is relational. When He declared that the greatest commandments were to love God and one another, He was not giving us an ethic to live up to, but rather He was telling us that life-giving relationship is the most important thing in the universe.

Our hope is that in the pages of this book you will find some keys to the kingdom that you may have been missing, and through them you may find a way to open the door to a new way of relating to God and living in His presence.

SHIFTING THE PARADIGM

If the ideas about the Christian life presented in this chapter are at all valid, then much of the Christian world is in need of a deep paradigm shift – away from performance-driven Christianity, toward a relationship-oriented life with God.

If we are going to actually grow and become more Christ-like, we have to stop trying to *act* like Jesus, and instead focus more on getting to *know* Jesus. Because only when the life of God is truly **in** us will we have any hope of that life coming **out** of us.

But let us not underestimate the size of this paradigm shift. As we have seen above, nearly every aspect of spiritual development has been distorted by our dominant performance-driven mindset. That is why this book has grown to the size that it is. We have many things to unlearn and relearn in order to see what God wants to do in us, and to build the kind of relationship we are talking about.

Changing how we understand change is just the beginning. By the end of this book, our hope is that you will be engaging with God in ways that are literally changing who you are on the inside. Because once you begin to experience this kind of life first hand, you will have no doubt that this is how God intended for us to live.

With that in mind, we turn to our most basic issue – what it means to have a relationship with God.

RESOURCES FOR FURTHER STUDY

V. Raymond Edman, *They Found the Secret: 20 Transformed Lives That Reveal a Touch of Eternity* (Grand Rapids: Zondervan) 1984

John Eldredge, *The Journey of Desire: Searching for the Life We Always Dreamed of* (Nelson Books) 2001

Chapter 2
God is Relational

> I pray that you ... may have power, together with all the saints, to grasp how wide and long and high and deep is the love of Christ, and to know this love that surpasses knowledge. (Eph.3:17-19 NIV)

In the first chapter we laid the groundwork for a major paradigm shift away from the traditional performance-driven approach to Christian growth, and instead moving toward building a relationship with God that is real and vibrant enough to change us from the inside out. For that to be possible, we need to lay a foundation for what that relationship will look like and why it is so central and crucial to our spiritual development.[7]

After all, who is this God we are going to learn how to engage with and receive life from? How does He view me? How is He involved in my life? What does He expect from me? Is this even safe? Most of all, how does this relationship differ from whatever it is that I already have with God?

Our Deepest Need

Deep within the heart of every child of God is an all-encompassing desire to be connected with our Heavenly Father. To know His love, to hear His voice, to feel the warmth of His arms around us – this is the reason we were saved, this is what we *know* we were made for. Even more amazing, *this is what the Father wants, too!* He wants to share life with us, more than we could ever imagine. And He wants us to know how much He loves us and how much He desires to heal and restore us. Paul's prayer at the top of this page could very well be summarized like this:

> "I pray that you will really get how much you are loved by God. Because if you could truly grasp this one thing, it would completely change your life."

---

[7] This chapter was inspired by James Bryan Smith, *The Good and Beautiful God*

Yet we sometimes talk about the love of God as if it were yesterday's news. Often God's love is equated with His historical work on the cross, but with little reference to the present. But that does not fit very well with what we read in the New Testament. Our Father's love is not just an idea. It is as real as the chair you are sitting on. And God means for you to know and experience that love as much as the original disciples did.

After following Jesus through His earthly ministry and then walking with God for several more decades, the apostle John writes these words about what he has learned: "We have come to know and have believed the love which God has for us" (1Jn.4:16 NASB). With all he had been through, he has come to the place where *he knows that he knows* he is loved by God. And when John talks about "knowing" he is not referring to some abstract head knowledge. He knows from his *experience* of God that God loves him. He *knows* he is loved, as surely as he knows that there is air in the room.

This is the kind of relationship that the Father wants with all of us. Although many Christians today have very little awareness of God's presence in their life, let alone a working relationship with Him, God truly desires to be close to every one of His children.

God Wants a Deeper Relationship With Us

On the last night before His death, Jesus went to great lengths to reassure His disciples that *His relationship with them was not over*. Having spent the better part of three years together, developing a bond of love and trust along with the hope that they would be part of what God was doing to change human history, Jesus' earthly ministry was drawing to a close. He was going to leave them physically, but He wanted to make sure that His people knew *they would **not** be on their own*. He said,

> I will ask the Father, and He will give you another Helper, that He may be **with you** forever ... **you know Him** because He abides **with you** and will be **in you** ... I will not leave you as orphans; **I will come to you** ... In that day you will know that I am in My Father, and you in me, and I in you ... He who loves me will be loved by my Father, and **I will love him and disclose myself to him** ... We *will come to him and make our home with him* (Jn.14:16-23 NASB, emphasis added)

During this "upper room discourse" Jesus told His disciples several times that He would come back to them with His Father and the Holy Spirit to continue their training. They had much more to learn, and He had every intention of maintaining His relationship with them and continuing their apprenticeship. In fact, He made it quite clear that this change in their relationship would even be beneficial to them.[8] How could that possibly be so, unless Jesus understood that this new relationship would be real enough to make a difference in their lives?

He was not leaving the disciples to their own resources or simply turning them loose to see how well they did. We have every reason to believe that He continued to reassure them along these lines even after His resurrection. One of the very last things He said to them before He left their sight was, "Remember, I am with you always" (Mt.28:20). This was no mere figure of speech, but a reality that they would know experientially.

We need to be very careful not to gloss over this as though it were some kind of flowery language Jesus employed to talk about what it means to be a believer. He is reassuring His disciples that their relationship would continue. When He says that He would make His home with them, He is talking about a life together that is real; He is not just describing a theoretical model.

Sometimes we act as if we have to beg God to be with us or give us the time of day. We even have worship songs that invite the Holy Spirit to "come" be with us, as though He were somewhere else. Maybe it is because we have so little sense of His presence with us that we have so much trouble believing He is actually here. But we need to come to terms with the truth that God is not only here, He is eager to engage with us in ways that are recognizable to us as real and substantive.

In addition to this very explicit declaration of God's intent to be *with* us, there are countless examples of God's intention to be *for* us. His love is not mere sentimentality or simply an acknowledgment of our limitations, but a robust, deliberate plan of action on our behalf to free us from the things that destroy life in this broken world.

---

[8] "It is for your good that I am going away ... if I go, I will send the Counselor to you" (Jn.16:7)

God's desire to have a relationship with us is in fact *the very heart of the gospel*. Jesus did not come and die just so we could get into heaven. He came as part of God's grand plan to remove every barrier between Himself and us, so that we could be *reconciled* to Him.[9] His very name, Immanuel, means "God with us." Everywhere we look in the Bible we see God seeking a genuine connection with a people He can call His own.[10]

Understanding "Relationship" with God

As mentioned in the last chapter, sometimes when we talk about our relationship with God we are referring primarily to our *status* as an adopted child of God. Since we have accepted Christ as our 'personal' savior, we now have a permanent relationship with Him. That may be true enough, but if we are not careful we will stop there and think of our relationship only in this cognitive sense. The term then becomes a mere euphemism we use to mean roughly the same thing as being a Christian.

On occasion we may refer to our relationship in more dynamic ways, such as "How is your relationship with God these days?" This may be closer in principle to the way we want to use the term in this chapter. Unfortunately, many of us seem to believe that the quality of our relationship is measured by our behavior or by how well we perform, spiritually speaking. That is why we answer that question by listing all the things we are doing or not doing well.

Suppose we ask a guy how his marriage is going and he responds by saying the food is great and he's learned a lot about taking care of their new house. We may well feel sorry for his wife. But we use similar language in regard to our relationship with God and think it's normal! "I try to read a chapter from the Bible every day, and I started volunteering at a food shelf last month." When we use the term 'relationship' in this way, we turn it into a kind of yardstick for measuring our performance.

This has a very unfortunate side effect. Our relationship then becomes highly conditional, based on how successful we are in various spiritual tasks.

---

[9] "All this is from God, who reconciled us to Himself … reconciling the world to Himself in Christ … we implore you on Christ's behalf: Be reconciled to God." (2Cor.5:17-20)
[10] "I will be their God, and they will be my people" (Heb.8:10)

And while this may be a common perception, it really makes much of the New Testament unintelligible. It would be like saying that our connection to the Vine is dependent upon how much fruit we are producing, when in fact it is the other way around – our fruit is dependent upon how well we are connected to the Vine. So we end up with a great deal of confusion in regard to how this all works. *If we find ourselves at some distance from God, how is it possible to perform well enough to get the relationship back, when we cannot truly do well unless we **are** already connected?*

So you see that if we misunderstand the nature of our relationship with God, we end up with a practical theology that makes little sense and turns the Christian life into a program of self-effort.

Why This Relationship is so Illusive

At least three major barriers stand between us and a vibrant relationship with God. First, here in the West we live in a culture that has a very poor sense of what relationship looks like between people. Having lost much of our sense of community and having elevated individualism to a virtue, we find ourselves devoid of the very context in which adult relationships are best formed.[11] If we have trouble building a relationship with someone we can see, how much more trouble will we have trying to have a relationship with someone we cannot see (1Jn.4:20)?

Second, building a working relationship with an invisible God presents some interesting challenges all its own. For example, many Christians wonder how sensing the presence of God differs from the experience of a four-year-old who is talking to an imaginary friend. Unless we resolve these issues, we will have tremendous difficulty believing there is anything of substance to our relationship with God.

Third, as we have already begun to discuss, much of the Christian world has abandoned authentic relationship with God and replaced it with a lot of religious activity in the name of relationship. So we are now in the place of needing to unlearn a great deal of baggage in order to relearn what it means to engage with God directly. For example, the general lack of teaching about

---

[11] See Wilder, *The Complete Guide to Living With Men* for an explanation of how relational maturity is formed in community.

authentic relationship or how to hear God's voice is itself quite educational – it says very loudly that none of this is important.

So it is with these barriers in mind that we take the time to revisit some of the most fundamental elements of the Christian walk.

God's Intentions Toward Us

In order to emphasize how substantive God wants this relationship to be, let's take a look at some of the ways He works in us and His plans for our future. First and foremost, God does not condemn us for being unfinished works.[12] Sadly, there are many Christians today who live as if God actually does condemn them for every mistake they make. The phrase "God hates sin" dominates their every thought, and they live in constant fear of God's disapproval. But this makes sin out to be bigger than God's desire to set us free. We need to get used to the idea that being a clay pot is really alright with God. He does not demand perfection any more than He would demand that we sprout wings and fly.

What He *does* want is for us to become great *receivers* of His grace and goodness toward us.[13] Instead of trying to act righteous by sheer effort, God wants us to learn how to receive from Him what we need in order to transform our heart, so that we can then live more like Christ by our very nature. Our life here is not a test of our resolve to see if we will do the right things, but an invitation to become part of what God wants to restore. His intent is to free us from the very things we long to be free from and to recreate in us a heart that is so filled with love that it spills out of us like water from a spring. That certainly requires our participation. But approaching this as if it were a job assignment misses entirely the relational aspect of our new life. Our main task is to learn how to work with Him so that He can work on our heart and make it more like His. After that, the way we live becomes a natural outgrowth of who we are instead of a test of our will, trying to compensate for who we have not yet become.

So what about sin? Does God not care if I sin?[14]

---

[12] "There is therefore now no condemnation to those who are in Christ" (Rom.8:1).
[13] "The riches of God's grace that He lavished on us with all wisdom and understanding" (Eph.1:8).
[14] See also the article in the Appendix, "What About Sin?"

Of course He cares! Sin destroys His creation and His children. The question is not whether or not God hates sin, but rather, *what does He do about it?* Far too many people think that God simply punishes sin after it is committed, and that our job is to try to be as good as possible in order to avoid God's judgments. Pardon the analogy, but that is a bit like training a dog by shocking it when it leaves the yard. Such a view of the Christian life turns the whole process of spiritual growth into a kind of behavior modification program with rewards and punishments to coerce us into good behavior.

To put it bluntly, God is not that foolish. In the first place, His vision for a new creation is not one in which His followers are merely compliant, and especially not when their primary motivation is fear of judgment. God's desire is for a renewed people who thoroughly enjoy giving away the goodness that God has woven into their heart and mind, people who rejoice by nature, who live in purity simply because they are being made pure, who pour out to others what is being poured into them. Those are things we cannot do by trying to make all the right choices. Character like that is something we can only receive from engaging with God.

Secondly, training through reward and punishment will never transform our heart. In many ways, this is what God demonstrated in the Old Covenant of law. As the New Testament authors argued so well, the law never made anyone perfect (Gal.2:21; Heb.7:19). It only served to expose our limitations and drive us to Christ, from whom we can receive that which we could never get by trying to follow rules and doing the "right" things. And coming to Christ is not just about going to heaven. Reconciliation to God includes all of our restoration to wholeness. We are no more capable of living as God intended by our own effort than we are capable of redeeming ourselves. The same principles apply to both salvation and spiritual growth – we need God to do in us what we cannot do.

So there is no reason why God would reject us or condemn us when we sin. Again Paul makes a great case. If He loved us when we were His enemies and brought us to Himself, how much more – having already been reconciled to Him – will He restore us to wholeness in all those areas where we repeatedly fail (Rom.5:10). This is how God deals with sin in His children! Not by beating them over the head, but by rooting out the underlying causes for sin and removing those things that keep us in bondage. By transforming our heart to be more Christ-like, He frees us from the power of sin so that it no longer has reign in our life. That not only makes more sense, it fits better with what we read in Scripture.

Everywhere we look in the Bible, we see God at work in His people, wanting the best for them, revealing truth to them, guiding them, so that they can become one with Him in love and in purpose. He *has* to be actively involved in that process, so that He can do in us what we would never be able to do by our own effort.

Listening to Others Who Walked With God Before Us

If we pay attention to the way the biblical authors talk about God, we will see in their writings a great deal of evidence that the connection God had in mind was much more than some kind of arrangement with humanity. Clearly what God intended all along was a relationship with His people, a working relationship that has real substance to it.

Many of those who have had this kind of relationship with God left a record for us to see. Among the most obvious writings are those we find in the Psalms. Here the song writers give full expression to their experience of God, describing their relationship in numerous ways.

> Taste and see that the Lord is good. (Ps.34:8)

> The Lord is my shepherd ... He restores my soul. He leads me ... you are with me ... you prepare a table before me ... you anoint my head with oil. (Ps.23)

> One thing I ask of the Lord, this is what I seek: that I may dwell in the house of the Lord ... to gaze on the beauty of the Lord ... My heart says of you, "Seek His face!" Your face, Lord, I will seek. (Ps.27:4,8 NIV)

> You show me the path of life. In your presence is fullness of joy. (Ps.16:11)

> Hide me in the shadow of your wings ... I shall behold your face in righteousness; when I awake I shall be satisfied, beholding your likeness. (Ps.17:8,15)
>
> He rescued me, because He delighted in me. (Ps.18:19 NASB)
>
> How precious is your steadfast love, O God! All people may take refuge in the shadow of your wings. They feast on the abundance of your house, and you give them drink from the river of your delights. (Ps.36:7-8)
>
> Your steadfast love is better than life ... my soul clings to you; your right hand upholds me. (Ps.63:3,8)
>
> May your unfailing love come to me, O Lord ... may your unfailing love be my comfort ... turn to me and have mercy on me, as you always do to those who love your name. (Ps.119:41,76,132 NIV)

Notice how these verses all speak of a first-hand *experience* of God's love and His involvement in their life. Part of what makes these verses so amazing is that they reflect the experience of a person *prior* to the New Covenant, before Jesus opened the door to kingdom life in all its abundance. How much more we should expect to have a fulfilling relationship with God now that He lives within us! Not surprising, that is exactly what we find in the New Testament writers.

> And because you are children, God has sent the Spirit of his Son into our hearts, crying, "Abba! Father!" (Gal.4:6)
>
> If we live by the Spirit, let us also be guided by the Spirit (Gal.5:25)
>
> He chose us ... in love ... for adoption as His children ... according to the riches of His grace that He lavished on us (Eph.1:4-8)
>
> Our fellowship (koinonia) is with the Father and with His Son, Jesus Christ (1Jn.1:3)
>
> Abide in me (Jn.15:4,5,6,7)

When you add to that all of the things Jesus taught about the Father and His promise to send the Holy Spirit to continue His teaching, and all He said about abiding in Him, it becomes quite plain that God intends for us to know Him experientially, and not just theologically. If the stories in the Bible tell us anything at all, they tell us that God is intensely interested in being involved in our lives.

Distorted Views of God

Now, in spite of all of the evidence that God's intentions toward us are good, we know from well-documented surveys[15] that over half of all professing Christians in America believe God is highly critical and judgmental, and the majority of those also believe He is looking for an opportunity to punish them for what they are doing wrong. Another large segment of the Christian population believes that God is very distant and uninvolved in people's lives, perhaps just sitting up in heaven watching all of us to see how well we do with His demands.

David Benner poses an interesting question that is very revealing:[16] "Imagine that God is thinking about you. What do you suppose He feels as you come to mind?" By far, the number one answer for most Christians is "disappointment."

But these perceptions of God simply do not correspond at all to the Jesus we see in the four Gospels. Jesus is present, He is involved, He touches the most diseased among them, and He gladly accepts dinner invitations from the most despicable people in town. Everywhere He goes people flock to see Him, taking time away from their farming and labors to hear the wonderful words that flow from His lips, and to see Him set people free from every sickness there is. They cannot get enough of this man!

What's more, the great distinction between Jesus and the Father that many people today hold in their mind is simply not supported by the text, the evidence, or the words of Jesus Himself.

> He [Jesus] is the image of the invisible God. (Col.1:15)

---

[15] Barna Research Group has numerous publications supporting this data.
[16] David Benner, *Surrender to Love*

> Jesus is the reflection of God's glory and the exact imprint of God's very being. (Heb.1:3)
>
> Jesus: "Anyone who has seen me has seen the Father." (Jn.14:9)

When Jesus talked about His Father, He spoke of a God who loves His creation, who seeks out those who are lost, who opens the doors of His house and invites anyone who will come. This is a God who is scandalously generous and forgiving, a God who clearly wants to be with His people, to meet their deepest needs, and to help them become active participants in the New Creation He has begun.

Shortly, we will talk about how we manage to arrive at such distorted images of God when the New Testament clearly reveals Him to be far more grace-filled than we can imagine. But before we do that, let's line up these two main views of God side-by-side and look at how vastly different they really are. On the left side in the chart below are the commonly-held views of God as highly judgmental and punitive. On the right are the characteristics of God as He is revealed to us by Jesus and the apostles. The contrast is rather startling.

Love Does Not Imply Permissiveness

Surely some readers are still wondering, "What about God's justice? What about His problem with sin? Aren't you forgetting about the other side of His nature?"

Let me assure you there is plenty of room in formational theology for the holiness of God, how He views sin, and what this means in terms of God's justice.[17] That is not the problem. Quite often this question about God's justice is born out of a fear that if we only emphasize God's grace and love that people will take it as a license to sin. If we do not also make a point of the severity of God's judgment, we may end up with people who have no fear of God at all.

But this is a false dichotomy, and a dangerous one at that, because it can put closeness and intimacy with God out of reach due to fear that it will compromise His tough stand on sin. The rationale goes something like this:

---

[17] For a very balanced presentation on this issue, see the chapter "God is Holy" by James Bryan Smith, *The Good and Beautiful God*, p.113-127

It might be alright to pardon sinners so they can go to heaven. But after that they have to be held accountable, otherwise there is nothing to stop them from continuing to live in sin.

There are several major problems with this perspective. First, the notion that love and grace are inherently permissive is born out of an incredibly deficient understanding of both. God's love is not just soft pity for the plight of His creatures that brings Him to the point of wiping the slate clean and giving us a shot at immortality. Rather, *His love is the will and the effort to rescue us from the power of sin*, to reconnect with us, and to change us from the inside out so sin no longer has dominion over us at all (Rom.6:14).

Judicial God	**Relational God**
Watches from a distance	Present, abides within us (Jn.14-15)
God is up in heaven	Christ is in me (Col.1:27)
Hands out work assignments	Asks us to join Him (2Cor.5:18-19)
Expects performance	Works with us and in us (Phil.2:13)
Judges our behavior	Loving, giving to us (Rom.8:32)
Angry, demanding from us	Understands our weakness (Heb.4:15)
Gives standards to live up to	Changes us to live well (Phil.1:6)
We earn His approval as servants	Delights in us as children (Mt.19:13)
Mostly disappointed in us	Wants to be with us (Jn.14:23)
Spiritual growth from trying hard	Spiritual growth from engaging with God (Phil.1:11; 3:9)
He waits for us to repent	He works to change us from the inside out (Heb.8:10)
Values doing the right thing	Values receiving and giving (Jn.13:34)
Commanding	Mentoring (Jn.16:12-15)
Life is one big divine test	Life is an ever-growing experience of God (Eph.3:14-19)
Salvation story is about sin, punishment, and pardon	Salvation story is about a relationship that is broken and restored (Lk.15:11-32)

Second, this misunderstanding of love also reflects a deficient view of the gospel. The good news is not about getting a pardon from the *results* of sin, but about God destroying the *source* of sin so that we can be free and He can live with/in us. That is why there is nothing passive or permissive about His love. What He wants is to restore us and have a relationship with us. And an important aspect of that intention is His dedication to root out whatever darkness still resides in us. License to sin is nowhere to be found here.

The third problem with the view that a relational God would be soft on sin has to do with another mistaken notion about the nature of love. One reason why people fall for the judicial image of God is due to an underlying belief that fear of judgment motivates people to change, while emphasizing God's love lacks any inherent motivation. People will simply take advantage of God's grace and love, and not bother to change their behavior.

What we are dealing with here is a half-truth, which is one of the reasons that this faulty view is so hard to dislodge. What *is* true, is that merely an *idea* of God's love *by itself* will not be enough to change a person's heart. As long as God's love is understood in the abstract, it will fail to impact us sufficiently to make any difference in our life. But *experiencing* God's love is altogether different. To be loved as much as we really need to be loved is far more compelling than fear of consequences would ever be. Witness the response of those who were healed by Jesus or delivered from demonic spirits. One after another, they could not wait to leave their old life behind and follow Him, telling everyone they saw what great things God had done for them. Such is the effect of real love. Once they experienced the transforming power of real love, license became a non-issue for them.

Instead of using shame and fear of a judicial God to motivate people to try hard, we need to be help them personally experience more of God. Because the greater their experience of real love, the greater will be their desire to be more like their Father. That is change from the inside out.

Why We Have Trouble Seeing God for Who He Really Is

That we tend to dismiss His love for us or have difficulty believing that real intimacy is possible, is only evidence of how great the distance is by which we have missed the mark. But we need to ask why this problem is so common, and why this has been the case for so much of church history despite the amazing revelation of God in the person of Jesus and the repeated references to God's love in the Biblical text.

Ever since Adam hid from God in the garden, people have been distancing themselves from His presence and dismissing the possibility of connecting with God as a normal part of life. And this is by no means limited to those outside of Christ. Christians for the most part today have very little first-hand experience of God's abiding presence, and many have even incorporated that deficiency into their practical theology to explain why they have no awareness of God being with them. Yet, clearly this was not what Jesus intended when He announced the good news that people now have direct access to God. Nor can it be what He had in mind when He gave His famous final discourse in the upper room and told them repeatedly that He would be with His disciples and abide in them.

Tempting as it might be to blame human nature for the persistence of this tendency, that point of view is not very helpful. It is simply too broad a stroke to shed any light on the process of restoration. If at all possible, we need to identify this issue with as much clarity as we can, as precisely as we can. Getting closer to the core problem may very well help us see how to recapture what we have lost. And given that the early disciples eventually did "get it" and passed this on to many of the new believers in the first century, we know that some level of experiential knowledge of God can be a reality for more than just a few.

Our Broken "Truster"[18]

More than anything else, I am convinced that the difficulty we have with maintaining an authentic relationship with God is really symptomatic of a much greater problem we have of maintaining relationships at all. After all, how many of us have ever received the kind of love we truly needed? How many of us ever felt entirely safe within the care of another human being? These deficits are not at all trivial.

Due to the nature of life in a fallen world, at some point nearly all of us experience enough relational wounding and deprivation to break our "truster" and give us reason to suspect that self-reliance might be a better way to live. We learn how to hold most people at some distance from us emotionally, become quite conditional in our willingness to give to others or receive from others, and often settle for connections with others that would

---

[18] The term "broken truster" comes from Dallas Willard

be better characterized as *arrangements* rather than *relationships*. In short, our truster gets broken and we become highly guarded, highly protected individuals.

Unfortunately, our lack of trust in people gets carried over into our relationship with God. We remain guarded and untrusting, despite His promises to be faithful and ever-present. Our truster is simply unable to respond to anyone, including God. What's more, our broken truster has a way of distorting our perceptions. Instead of seeing ourselves as broken and in need of healing, we tend to see others as *untrustworthy*. And while there are plenty of untrustworthy people, that is not our real problem. Our difficulty lies in the kind of lens we see through that makes it almost impossible for us to trust at all.

Why Our Understanding of God Matters

About fifty years ago, a great little book was published with the title *Your God is Too Small*.[19] Within this brief volume, Philips identifies a number of perceptions of God that, although common, are seriously distorted caricatures of who God is. Some see God as a "Policeman" who enforces the rules. Others see Him as an "Old Man in the Sky," or as a "Santa Claus" figure.

Most important was Philips' observation that it is almost impossible to have a relationship with God if we see Him in some distorted way. We cannot trust or get close to a God who is small, petty, or judgmental. Unless we rediscover God as He truly is, there is little chance of developing a close, trusting relationship with Him.

The real issue here is that there is so little experience of God's love by His own children that many have come to believe He is either too distant or too angry most of the time for us to even think about being close to Him. And that is a terrible distortion of the spiritual realities we see in the New Testament where Jesus shows us God's true heart.

One of the most important reasons Jesus came to earth was to reveal to us the true nature of God and His heart for His creation. But far too many Christians think of God primarily in judicial terms. Which is a serious problem, because having a life-giving relationship with a judicial God is

---

[19] J. B. Philips, *Your God is Too Small*

almost impossible. Only when we discover how much God truly delights in being with us can we have any hope of trusting Him enough to join Him in the process of restoring our soul.

God Wants to Be With Us!

Even in the Old Testament, the one thing that distinguished the people of God from other nations more than anything else was that God was with them (Ex.33:16). In telling the story of Jesus' birth, Matthew quotes the prophet Isaiah saying that Jesus would be called "Emmanuel" which means "God with us" (Mt.1:23). And Jesus promised His disciples that He would "dwell" with them (Jn.14-17).

God is not far away. He did not give us the Bible as a way to fill in for Him until He returns in glory. Nor were His references to being with us ever meant to be taken as mere figures of speech. God wants to be a *known* presence in our life, and to have a relationship with us that is real and substantive and meaningful for us.

Most Christians would agree in principle that God is with us all the time whether or not we can sense His presence. There are certainly enough verses letting us know that this is a reality we can count on. But for many, this idea is filed away under the category of "things I *believe about* the spiritual world" and has almost no connection with their actual *experience* of God. Many Christians even have memories of times when they sensed God's presence, but have little awareness of Him in their everyday life.

Wanting to experience God's closeness may be a nearly universal desire. Perhaps every Christian has entertained the fantasy of speaking with Jesus or God the Father face-to-face. But the "invisibility" factor for many seems to be insurmountable, as if God purposely distanced Himself from us and is only accessible to the super-spiritual. So when we pray, we may feel a lot like we are sending messages out into the void in the hope that He is actually getting them and giving them some consideration.

When we have almost no memory of God's presence, it is inevitable that we would begin to think of God as being a great distance from us, if not geographically, at least in terms of His involvement in our life. Even if we are deeply committed to doing our utmost for Him, the reality is that our relationship to Him feels more like following in the footsteps of an historic figure than walking beside our dearest friend and mentor.

This implicit distance and its accompanying silence have a way of blanketing our aspirations about engaging with God on a day-to-day basis. We no longer expect to hear from Him or experience His presence. If someone suggests this might be possible, we feel our disappointment with God yet once again and think if He really wanted a working relationship with us, He could do more to make Himself available.

Please do not misunderstand. Even though I often refer to this relationship with God in human terms, I am fully aware that relating to an unseen Spirit is different from relating to another human being. But at the same time it is important to note that many Christians have *too little* direct experience of God and what He has for us.

So how do we break through this barrier? What do we need to know or do that will help us perceive God's presence and get to know His heart, beyond what we know *about* Him?

Believing

I was a very young child when I was first told that Jesus could live in my heart. For many years I held an image in my mind of this tiny two-inch Jesus standing inside my beating heart, riding around in my body wherever I went. From my conversations with others, perhaps I was not alone in this perception.

As fun as it was to think of Jesus being inside my heart, the truth is that image was far too weak to be of much value to my life. Watching was about all He ever did. As much as I wanted to believe He was all-powerful, there was something about His tiny stature that made Him seem puny. After all, I was bigger than Him!

What we really need is some way of understanding His presence with us that is true to scripture, does justice to His "otherness," and gives us a sense of being connected with Him all at the same time. He is in us in all His fullness, yet He is bigger than us, so that if we could see the unseen, we would be more "in" Him than He is "in" us. Furthermore, His presence is not merely some ethereal extension of Himself, but a real conscious presence. He is aware that He is with me and He knows who I am. Even more amazing, He *cares* that He is with me. All of this I embrace when I take into my soul the belief that He is with me.

Believing is, among other things, seeing with our spirit what is not well perceived with our five physical senses. So my first step in being connected to God is to believe with all my heart that He really is as close as my next breath, that He permeates the membranes of my body and exists in and between every cell of every part of me.

Belief is also more than a rational choice I make to accept the above ideas as true. I *want* Him to be with me, I am glad to know *He wants to be with me*, and I am already appreciating the wonder of His presence with me, even before I can sense His presence.

Paradoxically, one of the biggest barriers to experiencing God is our desire for a signal that He is with us. We want to have a chill run up and down our spine, or hear Him speak into our head, or see a glow when we look in the mirror, waiting for indisputable evidence that He has decided to come to us and reveal Himself. But this kind of waiting misses the point – that He is already here. To believe He is with us is to be mindful and reflective of what is already true.

Rejoicing

That brings us to thanksgiving. Rather than beginning with an almost skeptical waiting to see if we can detect His presence, we begin by giving ourselves over to rejoicing in His presence with us. Most of us can, with little effort, allow ourselves to feel appreciation for almost anything good that we have in our life. By turning our focus and attention to what we know is good, we can quite naturally feel gratitude well up within us and know that we know we are blessed to have what we have. Bringing this kind of focus into our relationship with God is an act of faith that gives us a wonderful bridge to seeing Him in our life.

Believing that God is *in* us and purposefully *with* us is expressed and experienced, in part, by allowing our heart to feel grateful for His love. This gratitude is something we can practice intentionally, not just experience spontaneously at serendipitous moments. So again, instead of waiting for an experience of God for which we can be grateful, we can open our heart to

Him in a spirit of gratitude for His abiding presence. As we do so, we can begin to take notice with our spirit that He is closer than our own breath.

Receiving

God is life. His presence within us is life, for both our body and our soul. As we open ourselves up to Him, we do not just wait in anticipation of a sign that says He is with us, we actively take in life itself. It is a bit like stopping to notice you are living in a mist-filled oasis, with green leaves and ripe fruit abounding all around. Each breath feels like a renewal of life within you. Each minute that you are aware of your surroundings brings peace.

Often Christians are consumed with trying to do the right thing in order to get God to respond, or with attempting to give God something worth responding to. But we have a wonderfully lop-sided relationship in which God is doing most of the work and loves to give away what we need most, love and life. Our side of this relationship is largely that of learning how to receive all the good stuff that He lavishes upon us, to bask in His amazing love, and to let it fill us up to overflowing.

Being with God is like going to a feast (Isa.55:1-3), not as the cook or the janitor, but as a guest. Let us learn to receive His love.

Asking

Finally, we can ask Him to open the eyes of our heart to see. "Ask and it shall be given you, search and you will find, knock and the door will be opened for you" (Mt.7:7). Our Father invites us to desire and pray for what we need. Jesus said He and His Father would come to us and reveal themselves to us (Jn.14).

Among other things, we can ask Him to give us a way of seeing Him in our mind's eye. The psalmists viewed God in many ways: as a mother hen; as a rock or fortress; and so on. According to John, God the Father, God the Son, and God the Spirit have come to dwell within us. That means we have the entire Community of God with us wherever we go. We are never alone. That is a visual image worth having embedded in our heart and mind.

God wants to be with us and has already done everything He can to move toward us, reveal Himself to us, and make a way for us. All we have to do is respond to Him with our whole heart.

God is Relational

"We have come to know and have believed the love which God has for us. God is love, and the one who abides in love abides in God, and God abides in him" (1Jn.4:16 NASB).

This is our God. He loves us more than we can imagine; getting to know Him is the most important thing we will ever do. When we step back and look at the big picture of life as God created it, we are literally "wired" or designed neurologically, emotionally, physically, and spiritually for relationship. We might go so far as to say that *authentic relationship is the organizing principle of life*. People learn to organize their life around many things. Some organize their life around consumption or accumulation of wealth, some around the assumption of power, others around avoiding pain, some even organize everything around their fears. But we were designed to function best when our lives are organized around relationship with God and others. That is why the two greatest commandments are to *Love God* and *Love One Another*. These are the organizing principles of a life well lived.

That is also why the greatest focus in Christian formation is on developing our relationship with God. More than anything else, we need to come to know Him well, to know His heart for us and how incredibly good He is.

RESOURCES FOR FURTHER STUDY

James Bryan Smith, *The Good and Beautiful God: Falling in Love with the God Jesus Knew* (Downers Grove, IL: InterVarsity Press) 2009

David Benner, *Surrender to Love: Discovering the Heart of Christian Spirituality* (Downers Grove, IL: IVP Books) 2003

Chapter 3
Developing a Conversational Prayer Life
Focusing and Listening

And they shall all be taught by God. Everyone who has heard and learned from the Father comes to me. (Jn.6:45)

The single most important thing about the Christian Life is the quality of our relationship with God. One of the strongest indicators of our relationship with God is the quality of our conversations with Him.

We need to *listen* to God every bit as much as we need to *talk* to God. Learning how to listen to the Holy Spirit is vital to daily life, for recovery from our wounds, for victory over sin, and for growing up into the person God created us to be.

Chapters 3 and 4 present some of the more significant aspects of conversational prayer that will provide a foundation for your Christian life. For many Christians, the whole matter of hearing God is a difficult one, both in terms of its potential pitfalls and in terms of how to listen at all. We hope that these two chapters will help alleviate much of the anxiety around this issue and provide enough guidance to help you to build a stronger connection with God through receiving more of what He has for you.[20]

Many Forms of Prayer

Many forms of prayer are evident in the Psalms and elsewhere in the Bible, each with its own style and purpose:

Petition: Asking God for what we need.
Praise: Expressing our wonder and adoration for who God is.
Confession/Repentance: Bringing our sin and failure to God for His forgiveness and restoration.
Intercession: Asking God for something on behalf of someone else.
Praying the Psalms: Reading a psalm and making it our prayer to God.

---

[20] Chapters 3 - 4 are based on *Whispers of my Abba* by David Takle

These are all important and necessary. But there is another form of prayer that is far more vital and life-giving than any of those noted above. If God's *recorded* Word is life-giving and food for the soul, then so also is His *spoken* word a source of life. His spoken word is the feast of Isaiah 55, life itself in John 6, our defense against stumbling and our source of peace in John 16.

When we learn how to be taught by the Spirit the written Word comes alive in ways that we could never experience by systematic study alone. In speaking with God and listening to His heart for us, we get to *know* God as someone who is glad to be with us. We discover the care He has for us, the amazingly gentle ways that He can correct us, how much He longs for our companionship and how relentlessly He pursues us. As He shows us things we would never see on our own, we learn to view life and others through the eyes of heaven, as it were. One of the most wonderful aspects of all of this is how His voice can alter our life in ways that we could never imagine.[21]

Sadly, this approach to communion with God is largely neglected in many of our Christian organizations. Consequently, the only information that many Christians have in regard to hearing God comes from stories of others who claim to hear God, some of whom are clearly unstable and *not* spiritually sound. That leaves a lot of people rather leery of the idea that we can hear directly from God, and understandably so. Because of this disturbing context, we will begin by laying a Biblical foundation for what we are about to discuss.

God Speaks!

Like many others, I grew up believing that God stopped speaking around the time the last few words of the Bible were penned by John, and that today God speaks only through His written Word. We were taught various ways of discerning God's leading in our lives: through the Word, through the wise counsel of friends, and through specific circumstances that might confirm whatever it is we think God is trying to tell us. But apart from a very few miraculous exceptions, the notion of direct communication was theologically unacceptable, even unthinkable.

---

[21] "My word shall not return to me empty, without accomplishing what I desire, and without succeeding in the matter for which I sent it." (Isa.55:10-11)

Part of the rationale for this understanding was that if God spoke to us, we would have to call it "divine revelation" which by definition meant that it would be on par with the Bible. And since the Bible has clearly been completed, one must conclude that God no longer gives out such revelation. But that kind of reasoning rests on the faulty assumption that everything God says is normative for the entire body of Christ, and that He could not or would not speak to each of us about our own life and in a way that would be particularly meaningful to us at that moment in our journey. Certainly there is no justification anywhere in the Bible for that kind of assumption.

Of course there are good reasons to not think every claim of hearing God is valid. To begin with the obvious, there have been many "prophets" who claimed to hear from God and led people on humiliating ventures to sell all their stuff and go sit on a hill and wait for the rapture. Then there is the problem of people getting contradictory "revelations" that cannot possibly all be from God. How does a person sort out who is telling the truth and who is confused or deliberately misleading? One might easily conclude that it would be better to hear nothing at all.

Why God Speaks to Us Directly

At first take, it would appear that we can solve a lot of problems by simply limiting God's word to what we find in the Bible. Unfortunately, this not only fails to solve the above problems, it introduces still more.

First, even among conservative scholars who agree on the basic principles of interpretation there can exist a wide range of understanding on very fundamental issues.[22] Limiting God's voice to the written Word in no way ends the confusion about how to live the Christian life. The very fact that we need a course in Christian formation in order to restore transformation to its rightful place may be an indication that people have just as much trouble using the Bible to live as they might have in hearing from God directly.

Second, the Bible is primarily a collection of stories about people who were led or not led by the Spirit – written down to show us what that looks

---

[22] One glaring example is Romans 7 where Paul exclaims, "O wretched man that I am!" Whether or not Paul is speaking about the Christian experience has *profound* implications for bondage and freedom for believers. Yet theologians are divided over how to make sense of Paul's literary style and meaning.

like. Paul tells us that we have those stories specifically to show us what we need to know about how to live.[23] *If then we have no direct means to be led by the Spirit, how are we to make any sense of those stories?* The one thing they do *not* tell us is how to live life without God's direct leading. In fact, they often provide examples of how our best idea of what to do apart from God's leading falls short of what God has in mind, such as when the disciples wanted to keep the children away or send the crowds home, or when King Saul decided to do Samuel's job. Consider how very different the story of Cornelius might be if God had not visited Peter previously and given him the understanding he needed in order to override his preconceived ideas about Gentiles. If anything, *these stories show us how utterly dependent we are upon the Spirit for navigating through life.*

Third, these stories make a lot of sense when we see the bigger issue, that the level of discernment needed and the kind of perspective required to see what God sees is way beyond us.[24] If God does not show us how to see and discern, then we are left to "our own understanding"[25] which is precisely what gets us into trouble in the first place! To say that your understanding is guided by Biblical principles does not solve the problem. You must still rely on your powers of reason and judgment to decide not only what principles to apply in a given situation, but when to be proactive in loving someone, what kind of love would be most appropriate for this one person at this time, and so on. We may feel very "Scriptural" in our actions and yet be way off base in terms of what is truly needed or loving at the time. How often have we looked back on something we did years earlier (even as a Christian) and wished we had known then what we know now? That should be evidence enough that we have a lot to learn besides doctrine. What if we had known better at the time how to engage with our Mentor to ask for help?

Fourth, Jesus was very explicit about the ministry of the Holy Spirit as a mentor for life (John 16). As He was preparing His disciples for the coming

---

[23] "Now these things happened to them as an example, and they were written for our instruction." (1Cor.10:11)

[24] "For as the heavens are higher than the earth, so are my ways higher than your ways, and my thoughts than your thoughts." (Isa.55:9)

[25] "Trust in the Lord with all your heart and do not lean on your own understanding." (Prov.3:5)

changes, Jesus told them directly that He was passing on His job of training to the Holy Spirit. Given the context of His statements, one would have to perform some very interesting theological gymnastics to interpret those promises as a prophetic description of the Bible. And we today are as in much need of a mentor as were the first twelve disciples.

Fifth, if the Bible is our only source of God's living word to us, then one would have to say that for much of history the majority of His Word was beyond reach for most Christians. That being the case, in what way would His promises to be with them and guide them make any sense at all? Is Christianity a way of life that requires literacy or access to another literate person in order to grow? Did Christianity require the invention of the printing press in order to flourish? These are not trivial problems. It may be easy to equate God's word to the printed text in modern times in modernized countries, but that perspective has some serious implications for millions of Christians over many centuries who would have no significant access to the truth necessary for life.

Sixth, Jesus addressed this very issue with the religious leaders of His day. Having no other direct source at the time, they were looking to the Scriptures for every detail on how to live. But Jesus changed all of that, arguing that the purpose of the Scriptures was to point to Jesus Himself, and that life was something that came from engaging with Him, not the printed Word (Jn.5:39-40). How are we to make sense of this interchange if His intention was to point us back to the Word as our source on how to live?

Seventh, while the Bible is "living and active" we can all see that it does not do its work automatically. Nearly every Christian who has attempted a devotional life has gone through periods of time where reading the Bible seemed more like doing homework than feeding the soul, despite their best efforts. We can try to find ways to fault the person involved, or we can consider the possibility that we need divine help to quicken the Word to our heart and mind, and most of us have had little to no training on how to engage the Holy Spirit in this way. If we are routinely missing God's ministry to us of bringing the Word to life, our experience with dry devotionals actually makes perfect sense.

Finally, the Christian life is not just about knowing the right things to do, and that is not the only reason God would want to speak to us. His word is life, bread for the soul (Isa.55:1-3). His presence with us is more than an idea, it is a living reality that we can experience and be aware of. God wants to have an authentic relationship with us, and relationships are almost impossible without direct communication. Our needs go way beyond correct answers to our questions about what to do. We need to be loved! We need to hear God's heart for us. And just as *the manner* in which a person says something to us is as important as *what* they say, so hearing God speak things into our hearts in exactly the way we need to hear them is part of what makes a conversational connection to Him so life-giving. God's voice carries with it the power of life. And we need that life in order to live as God intended.

As important and inherently full of life as Scripture is, we need God Himself in order to live. God created us as relational creatures, He desires a relationship with us, and His directives are ultimately about being relational. He promised to be with us and guide us in all things, not just by giving us principles to live by, but by mentoring us in life and by speaking truth into our heart that we need day by day. And He was very careful to be quite explicit about this matter of our listening to His voice.

What the Bible Says About God Speaking

Here are just a few descriptions of how God speaks to us.

Isa.55:2-3. Listen carefully to me, and eat what is good; delight yourselves in rich food. Incline your ear, and come to me; listen so that you may live.

Mt.4:4. One does not live by bread alone, but by every word that comes from the mouth of God.

Jn.5:25. I tell you, the hour is coming, and is now here, when the dead will hear the voice of the Son of God, and those who hear will live.

Jn.10:3-5,16,27. The gatekeeper opens the gate for him, and the sheep hear his voice. He calls his own sheep by name and leads them out. When he has brought out all his own, he goes ahead of them, and the sheep follow him because they know his voice ... I have other sheep that do not belong to this fold. I must bring them also, and they will listen to my voice ... My sheep hear my voice. I know them, and they follow me.

Focusing and Listening

Jn.14:26. The Advocate, the Holy Spirit, whom the Father will send in my name, will teach you everything, and remind you of all that I have said to you.

Jn.15:26. The Spirit of truth who goes out from the Father – He will testify about me. (NIV)

Jn.16:12-14. I have much more to say to you … But when he, the Spirit of truth, comes, he will guide you into all truth. He will not speak on his own; he will speak only what He hears … He will bring glory to me by taking from what is from mine and making it known to you. (NIV)

Collectively, these verses tell us that God loves to teach, that we have much to learn, and that He wants to show us life as He sees it. Most of all, God speaks to us as part of being fully present with us and relating to us. For those who need more help in believing God speaks today, I would recommend the book, *Hearing God* by Dallas Willard.

FOUR ASPECTS OF CONVERSATIONAL PRAYER

Conversational prayer, sometimes called listening prayer, is made up of four major aspects that provide a context for engaging directly with the Holy Spirit for the purpose of hearing what God has for us. The four parts are:

Focusing: Quieting our soul and focusing our attention on God.
Listening: Paying attention to the promptings of the Spirit as we engage in conversations with Him.
Discerning: Noticing the process and the content of our conversation.
Responding: Acting on what we have received from God.

These are not *steps* to hearing God, but four elements of having a reliable and life-giving conversation with Him. We will discuss Focusing and Listening in this chapter, and Discerning and Responding in Chapter 4.

Focusing

"Be still and know that I am God." (Ps.46:10)

Most of the time, God does not force Himself on our conscious awareness. We need to turn our mind toward Him as deliberately as anyone who made a pilgrimage to the Temple. Few of us are capable of quality time with God while we are driving down the highway or reading the news. Focusing on God means that we set aside time to meet with Him and make every effort to honor that time as we would any meeting with a friend or sweetheart. Within the space that we make to meet with God, we must take the necessary steps to be deliberate about bringing our thoughts into focus and engaging with God with our whole mind.

The word *focus* describes the dual process of setting the eyes of our heart on "things above" and taking them off "things on the earth" (Col:3:2). One of the greatest barriers to hearing God is the sheer magnitude of distractions that exist in our life. Aside from being overly busy, most of us have a lot of mental "static" going on in our head including anxiety, stress, expectations, not to mention the electronic gadgets that fill every spare moment we may have. In order to pay attention to what God wants to teach us, we must learn how to let go of all of these things and quiet our mind and soul so that we can give our full attention to the Spirit of God.

Learning to quiet our mind is an ability that God has given to us as human beings. With a little practice and training, most of us can put aside the things we are concerned about and relax our mind and body for a few minutes before resuming our duties. This way of oscillating between intensity and rest is a very healthy way to deal with the pressures of life generally, and the ability to put our mind at rest is an important part of connecting with God.

As Christians we have additional help quieting because God is with us and holds us in His heart. When we remind our self that we really *can* trust Him with our life, we can by faith relax in Him, the way a small child leans into a trustworthy father and receives his peace.

Now some people have a great deal of difficulty slowing down their mental processes. One person described it this way: "Every time I try to quiet I find there is a highly-caffeinated chihuahua running around in my

Focusing and Listening

head." There can be many reasons for this sort of problem, ranging from simply never having learned how to be quiet to a continuous sense of anxiety to a severe need to keep from noticing one's own life. On the lower end of the spectrum the problems can often be solved through persistence and prayer, taking each anxious thought to God (as described in the pages to follow) and asking for His healing hand in whatever may be the root causes. At the high end of the continuum, people who cannot quiet may need to seek outside help in addressing the underlying issues that keep their mind in high gear all the time.

In any case, if quieting seems difficult, do not despair. Often by pressing through to focusing on God and listening to His voice, many of the issues that keep people from quieting can be addressed and healed, paving the way to fewer distractions and better connections with God.

In addition to quieting our mind and turning off the distractions of life, the other half of focusing is to turn our mind and heart toward God. This prepares us to connect with Him and to receive from Him whatever He has for us. As part of this process we also ask God to protect our heart and mind as we open up to Him so that we do not have to be afraid of engaging with anything other than God.

In part, this aspect of focusing is an act of faith in the character and presence of God. "Those who come to God must believe that He is here, and that He willingly engages with those who seek Him" (Heb.11:6, paraphrase). If we believe that God is far off in space somewhere, chances are we will have a hard time believing it is even possible to hear from Him. If we have doubts about whether God *wants* to be anywhere near us or whether He is too disgusted to talk to us, we will have great difficulty believing that He has anything to give us. On the other hand, if we believe God is in the room and engulfs us with His presence, our mind and heart will be far more receptive to whatever He has for us.

Focusing on God means that we *expect* to meet Him, and turn to Him in anticipation of our soul finding air and water and food from His voice and His presence. We trust His heart, that He is *for* us, that He holds us in love and desires to be with us. We believe that we ourselves are included in His plan to redeem that which was lost and broken. His main reason for redeeming us is to have a substantive relationship with us. That is why we can count on Him to meet us when we seek to connect with Him in this way.

Focusing also involves a prayer for God to open our heart and mind to Him. Within each of us there resides a protective system that works below the conscious level to keep people and things at a distance that seem too big for us or beyond our control. For most of us, God falls into that category. We may have a lot of reasons to try to keep Him at arms' length, however impossible that may be, reasons that we may not even be aware of. So asking Him to calm our fears and to help us let down our guard is an important part of letting Him have full access to our heart and placing ourselves in a willing place of receiving.

Help With Focusing

From a purely practical perspective, there are some things we can do that will help with this process. To begin with, the time of day you choose can make a big difference in how successful you might be at eliminating external distractions such as the phone or children. A physically calm environment is far more conducive to hearing the whispers of God than a noisy room with lots of interruptions.

Because of how God has joined together the physical, mental, and spiritual aspects of our being, and because there are physical components to anxiety and stress, we can influence the quality of our focus with such simple things as taking a few deep breaths, stretching our back and legs, and getting adequate sleep the night before.

Music is another way to help us relax and calm our mind. In an interesting story in the Old Testament, there was a meeting of three kings who needed some wisdom about how to proceed. So they called on Elisha to ask God what they should do. By the time Elisha finally agreed, he was fairly upset, so he asked for someone who could play the harp to come and minister to him. As the musician was playing, Elisha had an encounter with God and received a word for the kings (2Kings.3:4-19). On a larger scale, the book of Psalms is in its entirety a collection of songs and poems that were used by the Jewish people for hundreds of years to help them remember who they were and what kind of God they were dealing with.

Focusing and Listening 75

Many of those Psalms are wonderfully effective in bringing us to a place of receptivity and anticipation of God's presence.

Sometimes the act of quieting can cause all sorts of things to bubble to the surface that had been temporarily forgotten, such as bills to pay and errands to run. One way to deal with this kind of distraction is to keep an extra piece of paper handy on which to write down anything that comes to mind you do not want to forget. Letting the paper hold the thought frees you to relax again without worrying about whether you will forget that bit of information.

With certain kinds of nervous energy, you may on occasion find it difficult to relax at all, especially when feeling angry or excessively anxious. And some people just seem to have an over-abundance of energy that makes them fidgety whenever they try to sit for very long. In these cases, pacing around in a fairly calm area may be more beneficial than trying to sit in one place. While this can present some challenges in terms of recording your time with God, it is preferable to have a qualitatively better connection with God than to be so uncomfortable that your focus suffers.

Using the Eyes of Our Heart

In relation to focusing our attention on God this way, a question sometimes surfaces as to whether or not it is alright to use our imagination to connect with God. Very prominent Christian leaders have spoken against holding images of God in our mind, usually citing the commandment that prohibits the creation of physical images of God. Some people fear that such practices are inherently New Age in nature and therefore bad for us.

While I want to affirm that there is such a thing as a misuse of our mind, we need to be careful lest we "throw out the baby with the bathwater." If we stop and think about it, it is actually quite difficult to turn off our imagination. Many people reading this will have already imagined a baby being poured out with the water from a small tub! Or you may even have imagined what it would be like to turn off your imagination with a switch!

The truth is that God deliberately created our minds with the capacity to "see" things that are not in our immediate field of vision, and we use that ability constantly: every time we read a story; whenever we think of better ways of doing something; or whenever we rehearse possible outcomes before attempting a difficult task. Perhaps most importantly, our ability to picture things we cannot see allows us to transmit meaning narratively in ways that are far more potent than by precept alone. That is one of the reasons why Jesus used word pictures all the time in His teaching. Bible stories stir up our imagination and give us a chance to compare our own responses to those of the characters in the text. And many times in both the Old and New Testaments we are told to remember the things that God has done for us. In that sense we are *commanded* to use our imaginations.

Our ability to misuse our imagination does not prohibit its use any more than our ability to curse should prohibit us from talking. Aside from the fact that we would probably have to be in denial in order to pretend our imagination was turned off, giving up on our ability to picture holy things makes parables incomprehensible, puts part of our mind out of reach of God's redemption, and violates the command to love God "with all your mind." How does one think about whatever is pure, true, just, honorable, or commendable (Phil.4:8) without imagining how those things might look in the real world? How do you remember the Lord's death (1Cor.11:26) without seeing Him on the cross? How do we "fix our eyes on Jesus" (Heb.12:2 NASB) when He is no longer here in the flesh?

We could go on. Story telling has been used from the beginning of time to teach important principles to children so they can learn from the experiences of others without having to make all the mistakes themselves. That is most certainly a use of our mind intended by God. When we read that the psalmist longed to "behold the beauty of the Lord" what are we supposed to think went through his mind, given that he could never really *see* God? When Jesus told the disciples that the Holy Spirit would become their new teacher, did He not mean for them to think about how those conversations would be both similar to and different from the way Jesus had taught them? When the first generation of disciples broke bread together in remembrance of Christ, did not images of Jesus necessarily come to mind? Is it now wrong for us to imagine that because we never saw Him in the flesh? In John's revelation he paints many word pictures of what things look like in the heavenly realm. Why would he do that if we were not supposed to "see" those things in our mind's eye?

This fear of using our imagination really makes very little sense. Consider the beauty of seeing a "treasure in earthen vessels" or envisioning ourselves as clay in the potter's hands. Imagination is a good thing, because it helps us know who we are, where we have come from, and who this God is who cares so much about us. It truly is a good thing to imagine ourselves having a conversation with God!

As for the possibility of crossing over to New Age practices, filling our mind with thoughts of God and seeking to connect deeply with Him separates this kind of focusing from any form of New Age mysticism or humanistic meditation where the goal is either detachment and emptying the mind of virtually every thought, or connecting with whatever happens to be flying through the cosmos. All we really need to do is ask God to guard our heart and mind, and trust Him to meet us in the process. The only caution we might add is that for those who have had extensive experience in the occult in the past, this may be a complex task. People with such direct contact with demonic forces may need special help sorting things out in their mind and prayer life, even after being set free from those elements. But we do not need to be afraid of inviting God to fill our vision.

Quieting our mind and focusing on God are an important part of hearing well. We need to quiet and focus each time we approach having a conversation with God, and most of us will need to stop and refocus from time to time while we are engaged with Him.

LISTENING

"Listen carefully to me and eat what is good" (Isa.55:2)

Hearing from God is a learned process. Many of us have had a lot of experience doing Bible studies where the main goal is a better understanding of history, theology, and Christian practice, and those are all good things. But hearing from God has a different intent and is engaged in differently. Whereas Bible study enlists primarily the logical, analytical parts of our mind, conversational prayer seeks to engage the whole mind, with emphasis on the reflective and relational parts of our brain. Listening involves multiple layers of attention, including the thoughts we already have about things, new thoughts that spring to mind, connections those ideas may have with our present reality, and our own physical and emotional responses to the what we read or think about. Most of all, listening is an act of trust in our relationship with God, an expectation that He will reveal things to us that we need for both our relationship with Him and for our life.

How Does God Speak to Us?

The biggest questions people have at this point are usually things like: What does God's voice sound like? What am I listening for? Should I expect some kind of voice inside my head? Words in big letters hanging in the air in front of my eyes? Is it like listening to see if the television is on in the next room? What are we supposed to *get*?

To be sure, it is always challenging to describe any kind of experience on paper, but we will try to come as close as we can. While our sense of God and His revelations to us may vary quite a bit, we can identify some common threads that most Christians learn to recognize in their connection with God.

First, God's word to us is usually not very dramatic, as some might think, nor do we need to have any special spiritual gift. Rather, God's Spirit speaks into our spirit in ways that we can learn to sense as we pay attention to our heart while engaging with God. Christians who hear from God, both regularly and reliably, report that most of the time His voice comes to them in the form of impressions, words, or pictures that are rather spontaneous in nature. Sometimes their awareness of His voice begins as an impression that is accompanied by a feeling of hope which then gracefully unfolds into words like a spring of water rushing up out of the ground. Other times there is a stunning clarity to the thought, as if it had been spoken out loud by another person in the room.

Quite often God speaks to us while we are actively involved in spiritual reflection. As we focus on a verse of Scripture or some question for which we need discernment, we turn it over in our mind and reflect on the issue in various ways with the knowledge that God is engaged in that experience with us. Somewhere in the process we begin to take notice of things we had not seen before, or we receive a flash of insight that feels true or that clears

Focusing and Listening 79

up a lot of confusion we may have had previously. These thoughts are often accompanied by feelings of joy or peace, and when they prove to be life-giving and fruitful, we can be fairly sure we have heard from God. Over time, we learn to identify the nature of these insights and the force that is inherent within them, which then allows us to more readily discern what thoughts are indeed from God and not from our own creative mind.

Perhaps one way to describe how He talks to us is to think of how an ideal mentor usually works with his apprentices. When you ask your mentor a question like, "What should I do about my unreasonable boss?" you do not expect him to give you some compact ready-made solution like *Three Steps to Managing Your Unreasonable Boss.* Rather, you expect him to ask questions about your interactions with your boss, why you think he is unreasonable, and what might be some areas that your boss is triggering in you. He may well challenge some of your underlying assumptions about what the workplace ought to be like, and so on. By the time you get to an "Aha!" and a clearer vision of how to view your situation, you may not be able to identify who said what or how you got to the truth you needed. All you know is that you spent time with your mentor and came away with something you did not have before that experience. Hearing from God is often very similar to that process.

When Jesus was asked whether or not we should pay taxes to Caesar, He could have responded with a "Yes" or "No." Instead, He engaged the crowd in a discussion about *what belongs to whom*, and those who were paying attention and were teachable came away with an appreciation for the claim of God on their lives and a lot less anxiety about paying taxes to Rome. Jesus' way of approaching the issue went far beyond the crowd's desire to know the "right" answer to a very legitimate question. He helped them see their dilemma though the eyes of heaven, which not only pointed them in the right direction as far as their choices were concerned, but gave them a better understanding of how to discern God's heart in a matter. He changed the entire discussion from a question of ethics (Is it wrong for a Jew to pay taxes to a pagan ruler?) to a question of relationships (Who am I as a Jew and how does my relationship to God change how I relate to this world?)

This is very much how God trains us in regard to everyday life. As we learn how to share our heart and discuss our life issues with Him, He can show us ways of viewing life that we have never seen before.

How Do I Begin?

There are several good examples in Scripture that illustrate how we can engage with God for His mentoring words. For our purposes here we will use a section of Psalm 143 where the writer models quite well the progression of moving from his own thoughts to hearing from God.

> I remember the days of old, I think about your deeds. I meditate on the works of your hands. I stretch out my hands to you; my soul thirsts for you like a parched land. Answer me quickly, O Lord…let me hear of your steadfast love in the morning…Teach me the way I should go, for to you I lift up my soul…Teach me to do your will, for you are my God. Let your good Spirit lead me on a level path. (Ps.143:5-10)

The first thing we notice here is the Psalmist's act of focusing. He has deliberately turned his thoughts toward the works of God he already knows about and for which he is grateful. These are not fleeting thoughts, but things he spends time considering and reflecting on.

What follows is a stirring of his heart: "I stretch out my hands to you; my soul thirsts for you like a parched land." He allows himself to get caught up in the feelings of desire that he has for God, and he expresses them freely. His desire very quickly becomes a prayer to connect and hear God's heart for him: "Let me hear of Your steadfast love in the morning." Finally, he expresses his desire and willingness to be mentored by God. In effect he is saying, "Show me whatever it is I need to know for this day."

The great thing about this model is the way it begins with wherever we are, what we know, and what we remember of God's goodness, and works its way into the cry of our heart and our need for God's light in our life. Focusing and reflecting on God opens a doorway to a heart-to-heart connection that creates a desire to be taught in the ways of the kingdom. We will now slow down this process a bit more and look at some of the nuances of its various components.

We have already talked about focusing our attention. But as we transition to more of a receptive, listening state we need to clarify what we mean by pondering and reflecting on the things of God. For example, I could go about recounting the ways that God changed the world, and do it in a way that is mostly a mental challenge to see how many Biblical milestones I can name. I might even think of it as getting the right answer to a Bible quiz. On the other hand, I can allow the events to come to mind one at a time and savor the meaning and impact of each one before looking for another. As I consider them, I might wonder at the heart of God who moved heaven and earth in such amazing ways to bring us to Himself. That is an altogether different process than the previous approach which is primarily academic. Pondering and reflecting for meaning and being emotionally connected to our reflection, is very different from a purely rational analysis.

In this way we are more prepared to *receive* our perceptions of whatever we are considering rather than to *work them out* by reason alone. Instead of trying to master a subject, we allow ourselves to be led through it, making observations along the way about its nature and significance, and noticing our own internal reactions as well. We may feel led to ask more questions or to make connections to other Scriptures or other events in our lives. As our thoughts progress, they tend to become more exploratory and we become more receptive to receiving thoughts and images from God.

Part of what we want to do with this is allow the Spirit of God to reveal our own heart and the areas where we need His perspective. To do that we need to be brutally honest with ourselves about what we really think, rather than try to get the "right" answers and thus avoid the realities of our brokenness. For example, if I read a verse about the Father giving us whatever we ask for and in the back of my mind I think, "Not in my life!" then I need to take notice and talk to God about my thoughts and feelings. If instead I try to pretend I really believe what the verse says when in my heart I do not, then I miss an opportunity to allow the Spirit of God to probe more deeply and to deal with Him about my trust problem.

Moving from Impressions to Concrete Words

A very important element in this process is making sure our thoughts become fully formed and do not remain as a mere abstraction or vague sense.

Impressions that we have about God's heart in a matter, about the meaning of something important, or anything else that comes to mind during our reflection needs to be verbalized in whatever words best capture our thinking.

This verbalization should be either vocal or written, but preferably not left as a silent thought. Since most of us do not have the discipline to hold a single train of thought for any extended time without wandering off or dealing with other intruding thoughts, writing out our conversations with God or speaking them out loud to God helps us to focus and even heightens our grasp of the things we are considering. Insights we receive are better anchored in the soul when they are verbalized, and any mistaken ideas we arrive at are more easily discerned when we put them into concrete terms.

My own preference is to write out my conversations with God, often in complete sentences. In addition to helping me stay focused, this way of reflecting provides a number of significant benefits. For one thing, I literally *see* what I'm thinking and that provides another feedback loop for my mind. Once it is on the page I can question it, discern whether I'm going in a helpful direction, and make choices about how to proceed. Sometimes I look at what I've written and know immediately that the words fail to capture what I think God is trying to tell me. So I make a note of that and try again. If I'm captured by another thought that seems more pressing, I can switch gears without worrying about whether I will lose what I have received up to that point on the current matter. When I come back the next day, I do not have to try to remember what I was talking to God about or whether any of that needs to be addressed further. Rereading my previous entry is usually very helpful in getting focused for my time with God and helps to provide continuity to His mentoring from one day to the next.

In contrast to that, when I try to talk to God while hiking or pacing around, it may be fruitful at the time, but I will usually need to write down the significant elements later so I do not forget them in the days ahead. And if I just let myself drift from one impression to another without verbalizing them at all, I usually come away dissatisfied with my connection or simply fall asleep from the quiet.

What Can We Expect in This Process?

Once we get started with pondering and reflecting, what sort of things can we expect to receive? What can we expect to happen as we listen? Hopefully, answering some of these questions will help to bring more clarity to the nature of conversational prayer.

Spontaneous Thoughts and Images

As we learn how to receive God's word to us and to be led through this conversation, rather than always trying to work out His will for us by logic and reason, we will begin to notice thoughts and images coming to mind that we would not have come up with on our own. This seems to be the most common way in which God speaks directly to our heart.

Of course, we are all capable of being spontaneous and having thoughts jump into our head that are not from God. We will take this up in more detail in the next chapter under the topic of discernment. But for now, be aware that when God speaks to us, we often experience it in a manner that is similar to getting a spontaneous thought. In time we can learn to tell when our thoughts are being guided by Him, primarily by the fruit we experience, especially joy and peace.

I used to wonder why He talks to us this way rather than just speak into our inner ear or something similar so we could be sure of what He said. But I'm beginning to think He really does know what He's doing! First, He wants to write His words on our heart, not simply say the words and leave it to us to internalize them. This seems to be particularly true when He is giving me an insight into something I had not known before or when He is in the process of reframing an event for me so that I can see what I have been missing. He is able to reveal truth to my heart even before I have the words for it. I feel it as an intuitive leap that my mind has not quite grasped. As I reach for it mentally, it begins to take shape in words that make sense. And when I finally speak it out, the words have the ring of truth to them.

Second, I find mysterious beauty and wonder in the idea that Evil is loud and violent in its manner, while a small whisper from Father is enough to dispel the darkness and heal the wounds. Third, God is speaking with us as Spirit to spirit, not person to person. It makes sense that our spirit would hear differently than our body would. Fourth, this way of speaking to us is consistent with His desire to draw us to Himself and not overpower us or coerce us in any way. We need to be deliberate about paying attention or we will miss what He wants us to know. Seeking Him out is part of what we need to do in this relationship.

Physical and Emotional Reactions

Often when reading Scripture in a receptive manner we will experience a physical response to something we read. We might feel a twinge of shame or a quick wave of anxiety when we see something that reveals a bit of our heart that we did not really want to see. Or conversely, we may feel a rush of God's love or a longing for more of His presence in our life.

These are very important indicators of deeper issues in our heart. When they are negative in nature, we need to be willing to stop and talk about them with God and listen to what He has to say about them. One time when I ran across the verse that says, "to whom much is given, much is required" I felt a huge stab of guilt. I began to confess to God that I had a pitiful record and had done very poorly in proportion to what I had been given.

As I was on the verge of beating myself up with this, I suddenly had the thought that *God loves to give* and that there was no way I would ever keep up with Him and respond "proportionately." He's just not that stingy. I felt a huge weight of condemnation lift off my soul as well as great gratitude for God's generosity. I was then more drawn to God and able to talk to Him about what else I needed to know in regard to working with Him to give away the life-giving things I had received from Him. But we were able to have that conversation without me trying to get out from under the crushing weight of failure, or trying to make up for what I had not done, or whatever else might come from being overwhelmed. God wanted me to notice that we had some things to talk about, but He had no intention of shaming me with my poor record. Still, if I had brushed aside the initial gut reaction, I would have missed an important point of contact with God.

When our internal reactions are very positive in nature, we would do well to savor those moments and not rush on ahead. Spending time adoring our God, feeling His love, or being filled with gratitude for His work in our life, is very important for strengthening our bond with God and our trust in His goodness toward us.

Either way, listening to our internal reactions is an important part of engaging with God.

Internal Resistance, Hesitation or Doubt

Given our unfinished state, we can expect to run into internal resistance to what God is doing in our life, to the things He wants to teach us, and even to spending time with Him. Most of us probably do not doubt the truth of the words we read in Scripture, but we may have a great deal of doubt as to whether they will ever become a reality in our life. Or when God brings up an issue that we need to deal with, we may feel a strong resistance to even thinking about it. In spite of the fact that we know it is serious enough to warrant our attention, we still resist.

Occasionally, I feel reluctant to sit down and spend time with God. I may be particularly busy or simply not feel like talking to anybody. I suppose I could force myself to open up my Bible to where I had left off the day before and go through the motions of journaling. But what usually works a lot better is to start writing about why I would rather not be doing this right now. God sometimes shows me things about my attitude that I need to see or opens my eyes to some truth I need at that particular time.

In most cases it is best to notice our resistance and take it to God without trying to sanitize it first or fix it on our own. Ignoring it or running over it will only deprive us of an opportunity to be mentored in our time of need and grow closer to God as a result.

Better Questions

Spending time with God can have a number of unexpected side effects, such as discovering that we know far less than we thought we did. As we learn to be led through our conversations with God, seeking to be taught by Him, we may find that our questions need as much help as our understanding.

Stopping to *ask the obvious* is one of the ways our eyes can be opened to valuable insights. Something as well-known as, "O Lord, you have searched me and known me" (Ps.139:1) may yield multiple treasures by asking things like:

- Is being searched a good thing or a bad thing?
- What does it mean to be *known* by God?
- What fears, if any, does this elicit in me?
- What comfort can I find in this?

Or when we read in Isaiah 55 that we can buy wine and food without money, is this simply a poetic way of saying "free food" or is there more to it? In what ways do I expend a lot of energy on "that which is not bread"?

In similar fashion, instead of assuming we know what some word means, asking God to "unpack" terms we are familiar with can be very rewarding. For example, when God invites His people to come and feast on good things in Isaiah 55, what does He mean by "food" and "water?" How do we actually "eat" His words? Or when Jesus says, "*Abide* in me" what does that mean? What would "abide" look like? Is that different from just being a Christian? Seeking to be curious about the ordinary things we encounter in the text or in life can be very revealing.

Another way that better questions can rise to the surface of our awareness is by paying attention to our reactions, as noted above. While trying to help a friend deal with his self-rejection I suggested that he ask God, "Lord, how do you see our relationship right now?" He seemed somewhat apprehensive and said he was not at all certain he wanted to know God's answer on that particular question. So I suggested he slow the process down a bit and ask, "Lord, what do I need to know about my own heart, about grace, or about You, that would calm my fears about that other question?" My friend said he thought that was something he could do. So we approached God together with that question and came away with an amazing insight. God wanted a relationship with my friend no matter how battered he saw himself! There was no need to "clean up his act" before God would have anything to do with him. Instead, we get the relationship first, and that forms the context for the work that needs to be done. For my friend that was great news, and it paved the way to meeting with God more deeply than he had known before.

As we begin to see ourselves as students of Jesus who are truly in the early stages of discovery, who do not need to have all the right answers, a whole new way of life can open up to us as we seek to relearn about life from the one who created it in the first place. There is great beauty in the simplicity of not knowing or having to think we know more than we do. Learning to ask obvious and simple questions is very much a part of that process.

What Can We Expect Him to Reveal?

Up to this point we have focused primarily on the *process* of listening to God. But as a prelude to learning how to discern His voice, it is helpful to know what sort of *content* we can expect to receive from God – what kinds of things He will actually say or not say to us.

His Heart and Character

Sometimes directly, sometimes indirectly, God will reveal Himself to us in many ways.[26] As we learn to pay attention to how He is with us, we get to know who He is through our experience of Him. We discover how much He wants our restoration and how He enjoys being with us and drawing us to Himself. By the gentle ways He confronts us we learn that He is not disgusted by who we are, but rather He is incredibly understanding and patient with us as we relearn how to live. Which in turn means that it is completely safe for us to go to Him with our failures and brokenness, to be totally transparent before Him, and to ask for His help. All of this builds incrementally over time, as we get to know who God is by our very experience of Him.

The Secrets of Our Own Heart

The closer we get to the Light, the more our flaws will show up. Thankfully, the closer we are, the less our flaws will condemn us. As our relationship with God continues to grow and we let down our defenses in His presence, more and more things will come to the surface that we may have had little awareness of before. Any lack of trust in God's provision for us or any belief in the scarcity of good things may become evident in the light of His goodness and the extent to which He calls us to depend on Him. Problems we thought we had solved will resurface in new and unexpected ways. But through it all, God holds us in His heart and takes care with each new revelation to heal and mentor us through our restoration.

---

[26] "I will love them and reveal myself to them." (Jn.14:21)

Much like a master painter gently corrects a novice's use of color, texture, and light, the Holy Spirit shows us what we need to know about our own character, and then does the work of repair, because we cannot. I have become quite accustomed to the way that God confronts, sometimes even boldly. He does it with such grace that it is never harmful. I may not like what I see in myself, but I have the full assurance that God knows what to do about it and that I will not always be like this.

Since God is committed to our restoration, it is necessary from time to time to expose our brokenness so that we can cooperate in the process. Although the work of healing is His, not ours, He usually requires our conscious participation. Our alignment with Him in the task is an essential element of releasing His life within us.

Clarification and Insight

Having the creator of life as our Mentor means that He can show us things we have never seen before, as well as the significance of things we are already familiar with. Reading through the book of Matthew, I stopped at the first Beatitude where Jesus said, "Blessed are the poor in spirit, for theirs is the kingdom of heaven" (Mt.5:3). For several reasons, I have never liked the interpretation that says those who *realize* they are poor in spirit will get to enter the kingdom. So my first step was to ask God to help me paraphrase the verse into something I could make better sense of. What came to me was, "Blessed are the spiritually impoverished, because they get to be in the kingdom, too!" I liked that, because I believe it captures better the spirit of the Good News Jesus was announcing.

But then I asked what seemed like an obvious question. "Lord, if your kingdom is wherever your will is done, then how can spiritually impoverished people be in your kingdom? How can they be *in your will?*" As I contemplated what it might look like for broken people to be in God's kingdom, it dawned on me that over time they would become more whole. At that point a flash of insight broke into my awareness: "My kingdom is not about perfection, it's about restoration! My will is for the restoration of all people. So those who seek my restoration are in my will." That was a wonderfully succinct clarification for me of some very important matters. God's kingdom *is* wherever His will is being carried out. We can be truly impoverished and be in God's will at the same time! Now when I think of this verse, my heart is more drawn to God and I am more hopeful about His involvement in my life.

Clarifications and insights like this are common in our conversations with God. He wants us to know how life works in the kingdom, how much He cares for us, who we are in His eyes, where we need to go next, and so on. All of these things become more clear as we engage with Him for His light of truth.

Reinterpretations of Life Experience

Given that God's ways are higher than our ways (Isa.55:9) we can assume that no matter what we are considering, we have to be missing something! That is why one of the best questions we can ask God in regard to any area of our life is, "What am I missing here?" And when God fills in the missing pieces and reinterprets our story, we become more whole.

Daniel's life-long conflict with his family is one example of how this can work. For nearly fifty years, Daniel had held deep resentments toward his parents and several of his siblings because of his early family life. This issue had come to a head many times and Daniel had prayed, cried, repented, and done everything he could to let go of his anger and hate. But every time he was in the same room with any of them, all the feelings of resentment would come flooding back and it was all he could do just to clench his jaw shut and stay civil.

One day God gave Daniel a picture of his family out in about twelve feet of water with everyone thrashing around trying to get some air. In order to breathe, each person would grab the next one and push them under, and they in turn would then get pushed down by someone else. As Daniel contemplated the image, it suddenly dawned on him, "They're not being mean ... they're desperate!" The revelation broke his heart, and he no longer felt bitterness and hate. Instead, he felt compassion for them and longed for their healing. Once God reframed his understanding of his family, Daniel's heart changed and his resentments died.

This way of healing our wounds is an important part of why we need to connect with God and receive His truth deep into our soul. As we learn how to bring our brokenness to God and hear His penetrating truth, we can be set free of many of the things that keep us in bondage and begin to live more the way God intended.

Not all reinterpretation needs to be this dramatic. God can take even simple misunderstandings or hurt feelings and give us a bigger picture that helps to make sense of things. One day I got rather irritated with my wife because it seemed like she was leaving an unpleasant task to me that we had agreed to do together. I no sooner began to talk to God about my anger than He virtually interrupted me with, "She is really overbooked right now and needs your help." The situation was completely obvious once I saw it, but I had been quite blind to that perspective before. I know what it is like to be overbooked – I have been there myself. My resentment dissipated, replaced by my concern for her well-being; I began to seek out ways to help lighten the weight of her schedule.

We need to learn how to see life through the eyes of heaven. Spending time with God, asking Him to reveal what we do not see, is an important part of being an apprentice of the kingdom.

What Will We Probably Not Hear?

One of the common expectations about hearing from God is that we will be able to get direct guidance for decisions we need to make. I may want to know which car to buy so I do not get a lemon, or which job to take, or whom to marry. We often think of God's will as a particular set of right and wrong choices we can make, in which case we would want to get a clear direction from Him as to what to do. Any time there is a seminar on how to know the will of God for your life, the place is usually packed out.

While seeking guidance from God is important, this particular emphasis and approach to finding God's will is somewhat misguided.[27] First, God's will involves much more than choosing "A" or "B." Thinking about God's will only in this way can severely limit the quality of our connection with Him. Second, people sometimes seek these kinds of answers as a way of avoiding the work of deciding or taking responsibility for making decisions. Third, getting the right answer without going through the process of getting there can sidestep the learning that may be available in that choice.

---

[27] See David Benner, *Desiring God's Will* for a superb understanding of this area.

Focusing and Listening

As noted above, Jesus often preferred teaching over giving short answers to questions, choosing to help people see a given situation through the eyes of heaven rather than telling them what to do. Asking God *what we need to see* in order to make better choices is something that we can have confidence He will help us with. Generally speaking, our perspective on life needs to come from God, but it is up to us to intentionally choose what is good based on what He shows us.

And yes, sometimes God does have something specific in mind that He wants us to know. If that is the case, we can be fairly certain He will not play a guessing game with us, leaving vague clues around for us to pick up on. Whenever we ask for direction and find that clarity is not on the horizon, we might want to consider asking God what else He wants us to know about the issue and seek to become learners in the process.

Of course, you will not receive anything that runs contrary to Scripture.

The Shape of the Conversation

What does a conversation with God look like? We have talked about some of the things you can expect to hear and some of the process involved in having a conversation with God. We have also described one of the most common forms of conversation, which is basically a time of spiritual reflection in the presence of God, where we anticipate that He will give us some insight into the issue at hand. Now we will look at a few other forms that these conversations can take. But before we do that, we need to be sure we understand our part in this process.

How We are Involved

An important thing to understand here is the nature of inspiration and the manner in which God speaks to us. Because He mostly communicates Spirit-to-spirit, much of what we receive from Him comes to us in the form of impressions and images that we then shape into words so we have real content to deal with. In the process, we generally end up with mental pictures and ways of speaking that we already have some familiarity with. God's word to us may connect with old memories, previously memorized Scripture passages, metaphors that are meaningful to us, hymns or worship songs we know, and many other elements of our prior learning and experience. So while we can refer to the end result as "something we received from God," in most cases it would be inaccurate to say that we are quoting Him verbatim. We are virtually always *translating and interpreting* what we have received from Him. Even with very clear messages, we must understand that we ourselves are in some way instruments of His communication and that we are not infallible in how we express what He gives to us.

That said, rather than continually qualify everything we believe God gave us, I think it is alright to relax and speak in terms of "what God told me" and the like. At the same time, we need to learn to submit what we have received to the wider body of Christ and be willing to receive feedback on whether those things sound consistent with the heart of God. More on that in the next chapter on Discernment.

The point is, these conversations to not "happen to us." We ourselves help to shape them as we follow God's leading. That does not necessarily diminish their reliability or their value to our spiritual life. We just need to understand how we are involved in the process.

Two-Way Dialogue

Sometimes our conversations turn into a sort of back and forth style of interaction in which we might ask a question or make an observation, and immediately we experience a spontaneous response that sounds a lot like a two-way dialogue with God.

For example, several places in the book of Ephesians, Paul prays for the Christians in that city. At one point he prays that they would know "his power toward us who believe, the same power he worked in Christ when he raised him from the dead" (Eph.1:19-20 paraphrase). One time after reading that, I began to wonder aloud to the Holy Spirit whether I really knew what Paul was talking about, and it turned into a give-and-take dialogue.

Me: What power? Are you kidding? All I feel today is defeated and hopeless.
HS: But you know what to do. Why are you still trying to run on your own steam when you can see you are crashing?
Me: Because I'm broken, and the world is broken... nothing is working the way it's supposed to.
HS: Maybe now we are getting someplace.
Me: But praying just doesn't seem to help.

Focusing and Listening

HS: You've hit a logjam, that's all.
Me: I don't want another logjam. I'm tired of logjams. It makes me feel shameful to run into another one.
HS: The only shame is trying to hide a mountain of logs. The mountain is not the problem.
Me: Then tell me what is.
HS: Your resistance about going to the mountain with me and pulling logs.
Me: Don't you hate me because I'm stuck again?
HS: No, that is why I am here. And why I will not let you go.
Me: Don't leave me. I can't take this by myself.
HS: You have my word. It's you I'm concerned about – *you* are the one who keeps thinking about leaving.
Me: Yes, I've considered that. But I can't stay here unless you hold on to me.
HS: You have to ask?
Me: I'm sorry. I just feel so hopeless.
HS: Then let's go to the hopelessness.
Me: Lord, I bring to you my hopeless despair. I ask for you to guide me to whatever it is that is buried here. Whatever it takes. I need you desperately.

This way of interacting feels very much like a direct conversation with a mentor regarding a life issue. After a little bantering back and forth, I arrived at the point where I was willing to take my helplessness to God rather than allow it to continue to be a barrier between us. While I do not experience this form very often, in this case it was the process I needed to move my heart and seek him for help.

The beauty of this style is the sense that we are intimately engaged with God, wrestling with something of value that we need to know in the depths of our soul. When an "Aha!" leaps from these conversations, we usually feel very triumphant, as if we have wrenched a truth free of the debris in our mind.

Teaching New Insights

Sometimes the insights we receive are much broader than a single idea or phrase. Fresh ideas often have many implications that connect to multiple themes and need some expression in order to have their full impact. When this happens we may find ourselves writing down thought after thought in a fashion that feels like we are teaching something we have never studied before. We could also characterize this form of listening as an extended spiritual reflection in which most of the material is received rather than drawn from our prior knowledge.

For example, one time I was reflecting on Hebrews 12:1-3 where the writer talks about how Jesus endured the cross by focusing on the joy that was set before Him. As I asked myself what that particular joy was that meant so much to Jesus, the ideas began to flow quite freely:

> Joy? What joy? From where? How did You find it?
> "For the joy set before Him" of redeeming the earth!
> I have tasted of this kind of joy when people say that what they have received from my writing has touched them, set them free, or captivated their heart. It feels so good to be part of giving life to others. To see them heal and recover. It warms my heart.
> Oh, the JOY of destroying the Destroyer! Of pushing back the darkness – of witnessing the Dawning Light.
> The joy Jesus must have felt, crushing death beneath His feet.
> HE WON!
> By enduring, overcoming, trusting in His Father, right up to His death, He won! He cheated death. No, He destroyed death, the power of death. Death and hell and suffering could not break Him. The joy of bringing life and love and goodness to us was worth whatever it took.

The words came out as if I was teaching about joy, but I was learning it all for the first time as I wrote it. In the process, I learned a lot about the nature of joy. Being taught in this manner can open our eyes to spiritual realities that we have never seen that clearly before.

Whatever shape the conversation takes, our part is to remain teachable and open to discovering fresh views of who God is, who we are, how God is involved in our life, and how life generally works for us.

Listening to the Word

Structured approaches to Bible study abound, many of them quite good. Probably one of the most effective methods is called "Inductive Bible

Study." For those who are looking for a sound approach to extracting the original flavor of the text and ways in which those principles might apply to today's world, this works fairly well.

But there is another approach to encountering the Bible that has been used throughout the history of the Church to engage with God and breathe new life into our soul, often referred to as "Listening to the Word." This approach to reading Scripture differs from popular Bible study methods in several ways. But the biggest difference is that the primary goal of listening to the Word is to engage with the Spirit of God even more than engage with the text. This is not a trivial distinction. Traditional Bible study relies heavily on our powers of reason and reading comprehension to analyze the text and figure out such things as the author's original intent, the context in which the passage was written, what principles might be behind the text, and how we might apply those principles to our lives.

In contrast, listening to the Word lays the text before God and asks Him to be our teacher. We ask God what He wants us to pay attention to, how He wants us to approach it, and where He wants to go with it. Sometimes He digs into the text to show us things we have not seen before, making it come alive with a richness we would have missed had we studied it on our own. Other times He uses the text to speak into our life for the purpose of providing direction or healing or correction. On occasion He will use the text as a springboard for another discussion that is not even directly related to the original meaning of the text. The goal is to spend time with God.

Listening to the Word usually means digging a lot deeper into a smaller segment of the text. Our entire time may be focused on a single word or phrase that has captured our attention. Working phrase by phrase through a single chapter in this manner might take days or weeks, depending on how many ways we feel led to pursue the thoughts that are brought to light by the Spirit. Depth is more important here than breadth.

How to Listen to the Word

1. Begin by asking God to help you join Him in seeing what He has for you. Spend a few minutes appreciating His presence with you.

2. Select a fairly short passage to read. If you are doing this regularly, you can simply pick up where you left off the previous time. If you are just

beginning or looking for a place to start, please see the suggestions below. Try to limit how much of the text you will try to process. A whole chapter is generally way too much to digest. If your Bible is divided into paragraphs, that can be a good boundary to use. Otherwise, just read a few verses until you see a transition or change of idea, or until something catches your attention.

3. Read the passage slowly, several times. If something seems to jump off the page, you may want to move on to the next step right away. Otherwise, let the words wash over you and ask God to draw you to something as you read the passage again.

4. Write down the reference and the words that you have been drawn to. Start writing what is on your heart, why you feel drawn to these words, what they mean to you, what gets stirred up in you when you see them.

5. Continue writing as you invite the Spirit of God to open the text, unpack specific words, show you how it matters, how it intersects with your life, and so on. Everything that was said above relating to conversations with God applies to this process.

6. If you start to run out of steam but feel as if there is more to receive, reread the passage again or reread what you have written, being sensitive for whatever new thoughts may come to mind, and then resume writing.

7. When it seems as if you have exhausted what you need to receive for that day, ask God how you can best hold on to what He has given you. He may lead you into a time of thanksgiving, a prayer of repentance, a healing of a memory, or any number of things. You may want to memorize a few verses or write something down on a paper and post it up where you can be reminded of what God is teaching you.[28]

8. Thank God for your time together.

For those who are just beginning to learn to engage with God in this way, I would suggest that you *not* try to read through the entire Bible. Choose something that is rich in terms of its descriptions of our identity or God's character or what He has done for His people. Some of my favorites are:

---

[28] "Recite them to your children and talk about them ... bind them as a sign on your hand ... write them on the doorposts of your house" (Deut.6:7-9)

Focusing and Listening 97

Isaiah 55, Psalms 23, 27, 84, 100, and 139, John 14-17, Ephesians 1-4, and Colossians 1-3. Then break each passage down into small bites and take time to savor them phrase by phrase. Resist the temptation to try and cover a lot of ground.

Reading your previous entry can help to create a context for your time with God and even help you open your heart to be more receptive. If you read a few verses and they do not seem to have anything to offer, try reading them again a few more times, asking God if there is anything there He wants you to see. If they still do not yield anything, feel free to move on to the next few verses and continue the process until you feel led to the words you need to interact with God about.

This single practice is the one of the most rewarding things you can do for your spiritual life. Engaging with God is life-giving in and of itself. To engage with Him over His Word can be absolutely incredible.

A Prayer Journal

Even if you are reluctant about writing down your thoughts, please consider the suggestions in this section. The benefits of a prayer journal far outweigh any discomfort or effort involved in learning how to use one. And for those who decide in the end not to keep such a journal, the thoughts presented here are still important and will be helpful as you engage with God in your own way.

First, the mechanics of a prayer journal.

1. Date each entry.
2. After asking God to open your heart and mind, read the previous entry.
3. Discern whether to continue the prior thought or move on to something else.
4. If moving on, discern whether you want to work from a Biblical text or some life issue.
5. Begin writing your thoughts, impressions, questions, reactions, feelings, discernment, and prayers.
6. Make stars or other notations near items that seem particularly significant.

7. Write down the ways you decide to respond.

Throughout your prayer time, be willing to search for the words that best capture your impressions. Be aware that some of your impressions may take a few moments to form into complete thoughts. Allow the words to come to you and do not force them. Try several approaches to the wording if necessary, writing them all down. Consider using full sentences, but do not worry about proper style. Do your discerning on paper as well, so as not to censor your thoughts (although if you know your mind is wandering, you do not need to write that down). Other than that, follow the guidelines given above for conversational prayer.

There are many good reasons to write out your time with God. Perhaps most important is the level of focus that it requires and the discipline of moving all of your impressions and feelings to the point of concrete words. Without specific words, our ideas and impressions can quickly become a kind of mental fog, with no real sense of direction or purpose. Getting our ideas into full sentences (or at least to the point of readable notes) also improves our discernment, as we have specific words to work with instead of vague notions. Putting words to our impressions also means that we are using our whole mind, processing everything from images and emotions through language, which helps us to determine the meaning of things.

Once our thoughts are down on paper, we may have reactions to them that we would not have experienced had the thoughts remained a bit more vague. In some cases, God will reveal the faulty premises we believe inside or the intentions of our heart. Other times the words will hit us with all the force of a revelation. Having them on paper allows us to return to them over and over in the days ahead, if necessary, to work them into our heart.

For those who hate to write and those who are reluctant, I would encourage you to try this for a while to see its impact on your prayer life. If you are among those who find this to be more distracting than helpful, feel free to carry on your conversational prayer without it. But be sure to have your conversations with God out loud, so that you form real words and experience your thoughts in concrete terms. Then be sure to write down the salient points so you do not forget them.

RESOURCES FOR FURTHER STUDY

David Takle, *Whispers of My Abba: From His Heart to Mine* (NC: Kingdom Formation Ministries) 2011

Dallas Willard, *Hearing God: Developing a Conversational Relationship with God* (Downers Grove, IL: IVP Books) 2012 edition

Jan Johnson, *When the Soul Listens* (Colorado Springs: NavPress) 1999

Chapter 4
Developing a Conversational Prayer Life
Discerning and Responding

"The sheep follow him because they know his voice. They will not follow a stranger ... because they do not know the voice of strangers." (Jn.10:4-5)

To review, there are four main aspects to conversational prayer:

Focusing: Quieting our soul and focusing our attention on God.
Listening: Paying attention to the promptings of the Spirit as we engage in conversations with Him.
Discerning: Noticing the process and the content of our conversation.
Responding: Acting on what we have received from God.

The last chapter discussed Focusing and Listening in some detail, with special attention on how to allow the Spirit of God to open our heart and the Word to us at the same time. Now we will look at Discerning and Responding.

DISCERNING

> We speak of these things in words not taught by human wisdom but taught by the Spirit, interpreting spiritual things to those who are spiritual. (1Cor.2:13)

For our time with God to be fruitful, we not only need to pay attention to what God may be saying to us, we need to pay attention to how we are paying attention. We need to notice when a thought runs contrary to the character of God. If we have been sitting quiet for several minutes with no thoughts of anything at all, we need to notice and ask God if there is anything we could do in order to get back on track. Discernment is almost like having another pair of eyes present, observing our interaction with God and being willing to be honest about what is seen, both in terms of what is life-giving and what is not.

The Importance of Humility

Two very interesting features of discernment are that it is partly an acquired wisdom and partly dependence on God. We will always be limited in discerning what goes on in our own mind. Not only are we biased, but our vision is fairly clouded. So there exists a kind of circular process in which we need to ask God for His discernment about what we are discerning. This may be the best argument for why we need to study the Word and involve other members of the body in our spiritual journey, seeking their help in making sense of what we are receiving. With help and practice, we can learn to tell the difference between true discernment and telling ourselves what we want to hear. As we begin to develop greater discernment, we can then participate better in the larger body to help others.

An important part of maturity is the ability to see *how we ourselves are involved* in our own life. In the case of conversational prayer, no matter how much we feel carried along by the process, we must be mindful at all times that we are intimately involved at all levels of the interaction. There is no such thing as infallible listening. Our trust level influences the quality of our connection, our presuppositions filter what we "hear," and the choices we make each step of the way determine whether we become more or less engaged in what God has for us. These are all reasons why we must remain teachable and open to revising our prior assumptions. The more receptive we are to "readjusting our sails" the more we will see our discernment grow over time.

As we will see, discerning is primarily an act of *noticing or observing*. In order to discern well, we need to take notice of both the *process* we are involved in and the *content* of those things that are coming to mind.

Discerning the Process

Discerning the process means paying attention to the way our conversation is proceeding. One way to describe the kinds of things we want to notice and consider is to list them as questions we might ask as we reflect.

Discerning and Responding

In Regard to Focusing:
- Am I focused on God and receptive toward Him?
- Am I being distracted by external noise?
- Am I being distracted by internal thoughts?
- Am I wandering in my thoughts?

In Regard to Listening:
- Do these words capture my impressions well enough?
- Is the process slowing down?
- Is it time to re-read what I have written so far?
- Am I still missing something?
- Do I need to "shift gears" and try something else?
- Are there better questions I can ask God to help me go deeper?

In Regard to Responding:
- Am I at the point where I need to close?
- How can I best hold on to what I have received here?
- Which of the various ways of responding fit well here?

The reason we need to consider these types of questions is because we can easily become distracted, drift off topic, run out of steam or hit a wall that is not fruitful, depend too much on our prior assumptions instead of receiving from God, trivialize important things, emphasize non-important things, and so on. Of course in practice, if we stopped to ask all these questions every other minute we would end up being distracted with the process of "discernment" and never get around to listening. This is not a checklist to be followed but rather a mindset that aids us in hearing well from God.

As stated earlier, humility is a great asset when trying to listen to the Spirit because we are fallible human beings. We must pay attention to how we are proceeding and be willing to learn as we go. We are apprentices not only of the material we want the Spirit to teach us, but also in how to be a student, and how to sense what it is like for God's Spirit to communicate with our spirit.

Sometimes it feels a bit like walking along in a fog, from time to time checking the walkway under your feet to see that you are still going in the right direction, and feeling your way along so you do not run into anything that will hurt. After a time, you do not have to continually ask yourself if your feet are in the right place. You know what the cobblestones feel like and so your mind is alerted when your feet feel something else. But you are in a continual state of sensing so that you notice the change in terrain.

What About Pauses?

Occasionally we will have pauses during our conversations, moments when we seem to draw a blank. Nothing else is coming to mind, but we do not feel as if we are done. What do we do with these?

In most cases, we can simply notice that the flow of thoughts has slowed down, and go back to an earlier point in the conversation to pick things up again. If we are working with a particular bit of Scripture, sometimes rereading the text will stimulate our thinking. Otherwise, rereading what we have written so far can often trigger another thought or something about which we would like to probe a little deeper.

Then we can always ask the question, "Is there anything else you want me to know about this?" which can be asked several ways such as, "Is there anything here I am mistaken about?" or "What am I missing?" No matter what we are addressing we can be sure that there is more that God could show us about it. Bear in mind that not everything God wants to reveal to us can be reduced to words. He may want us to know that He is with us, that He cares about us, that He is sufficient for our needs, and so on, truths that we may encounter more experientially than verbally.

Sometimes a pause in writing (or speaking out loud) can be very important. If we feel a rush of gratitude, love or joy, or something similar, we can do our soul a favor by taking a few minutes to let those feelings wash over us, bask in them, and let them penetrate deeply. Enjoying the presence of God and His love for us is wonderful gift in and of itself that we honor by pausing to take in what God has for us. When our time with God has been particularly intense, spending a few minutes in quiet before moving on to the rest of our day helps to anchor our experience and gives our nervous system a chance to calm. If we find that our time seems to be coming to a close, we may want to write down any thoughts that we would like to pursue further so we can pick up there again at a later date.

Discerning and Responding

Discerning Blocks in Our Connection

Sometimes the dead space we have while talking with God is not just a pause but a significant block or barrier in connecting with God or perceiving His presence with us. This issue will be addressed in some detail in Chapter 8. But for now, just be aware that there can be any number of things within us that make hearing from God difficult. For example, if we are angry at God for not preventing some painful event in our life, we may have difficulty letting down our guard and trusting Him enough to listen. Similarly, if we are afraid of what He might say to us, it will be very hard to open ourselves up to His Spirit.

When we can discern that there is a barrier between us and God, the best thing to do, paradoxically, is ask God what we need to know about that barrier. Surprisingly, very often when we cannot hear what God has to say about a passage of Scripture, we *can* hear what we need to know about what is blocking the connection. When that, too, seems to be unfruitful, it is best to seek help from others who have some experience in helping people connect with God.

Discerning the Content

In addition to discerning the *process* that we are involved in, we must also learn how to discern the *content* of what we are writing or speaking out as things come to mind. Making sense of the impressions we receive from God is something we learn experientially over time. Learning the difference between God's voice and other thoughts we might have is important.

To begin with, there is nothing unholy or undesirable about hearing your own thoughts and writing them down. That is simply a part of spiritual reflection. The Psalms are full of this kind of writing, through which we benefit greatly by hearing the struggles of those who have gone before us and have wrestled with hard questions about where God is in difficult times, as well as those who rejoice when they see the hand of God in their lives. It is important to know where we are at a given point in time, and writing our deepest thoughts can help us to become consciously aware of what is going on inside us.

Discerning the content of what we reflect on means, in part, that we are aware of when we are writing things down that are clearly our own thoughts. Most of the time, most of what goes through our mind during conversational prayer is our own reflective thinking and remembering, even when the direction of our thoughts is guided by the Holy Spirit. But that does not mean those thoughts are unimportant. Our own reflections are a valuable part of the process.

In writing down our own thoughts we also want to discern as much as possible between those things that *feel* true and those things that are *actually* true. To make more sense of that, let's step back and look at some of the different kinds of thoughts we might have about something.

Observations and Raw Data

This would include things we have seen or heard or experienced previously, but not our ideas about what those things mean. For example, regarding some disagreement I had with my brother, the raw data would include his intensity and voice tone, as well as what he said. However, I need to be aware that some of my perceptions may be inaccurate. We are all quite able to filter our observations for many reasons, and thereby distort what we perceive to be the case. So I want to be sure to check in with God to see if He will shed any additional light on how I view things.

Interpretations of the Raw Data

We continually try to make sense of what we see and hear, both consciously and subconsciously. When we verbalize those interpretations during spiritual reflection, it is important to be aware that no matter how true our interpretations *feel*, they may very well be an incomplete or inaccurate understanding of the situation and in need of God's perspective to be more complete and accurate.

Going back to the previous example, I might conclude that my brother was trying to belittle me. That is an interpretation on my part which may or may not be accurate. Or it might be partially correct but miss the larger picture that God wants me to see. It is always important to ask God how He understands our situation.

Discerning and Responding

Patterns in Our Life that Seem to Have the Force of Truth

Noticing the things we have come to believe about life is a critical step in healing our wounded soul. For example, a person may read in Romans 8 that there is no condemnation in Christ, but feel like God is condemning them all the time for what they are doing wrong. The condemnation *feels* true, despite what the text says. Getting this out in the open where they can talk about it with God is extremely important. Proper discernment would tell them that some kind of disconnect exists between their experience and what the text is saying. Even though a person may not be able to see *how* at the moment, they can still acknowledge that it might be possible to receive healing and freedom from that internal sense of condemnation. Being able to separate out what feels true and what is actually true helps to point the way to inner healing.

This list is by no means exhaustive. The point is that every thought needs to be weighed, and discerning the nature of what is going through our mind helps us to ask better questions and to participate better with our Mentor and what He might want to reveal to us.

In addition to those thoughts that we can clearly identify as our own, in conversational prayer we seek to receive from God whatever *He* wants to reveal to us. As we open up to His mentoring, we will have spontaneous thoughts that seem as if they came to us without effort and may feel like they have been given to us. This is often how God speaks to us. Of course, we are capable of spontaneous thoughts of our own. And this is where some of the most important aspects of discernment come into focus.

How Can We Tell Where Spontaneous Thoughts Come From?

The two biggest concerns that people usually have when they first consider trying to have a two-way conversation with God are:

- Insecurity about how to discern what is God and what is not.
- The fear of opening up to something evil.

Of course no one should ever create an opening for evil, and getting confused about whether or not something is from God is a serious matter. So we need to resolve these things in order to feel safe hearing from God. But the other problem these two concerns bring up is the fact that we can inhibit the flow of spontaneous thoughts altogether out of fear. Ironically, being overly fearful of hearing wrong actually makes a person *more* vulnerable to the devices of the enemy. Our relationship with God is one that is based on trust in His character more than our own vigilance. The goal then is to find a way to allow the Spirit of God to speak to us, to insure that the enemy cannot use this opportunity to injure our soul, and over time to develop a conversational prayer life that is filled with joy and not fear.

There are two good reasons why we would want to do the work of learning how to do this. First, if we decide to err on the side of not hearing anything, then the enemy has already won. In our attempt to avoid error, we have actually given up the battle and lost our best resource, the voice of God. Second, learning to navigate these waters and develop a rich conversational prayer life with God is probably the single most important thing you can do for your soul. Life is received from interacting with God. We need to learn how to do this.

God, Self, or Satan?

We really have only three possible sources for spontaneous thoughts, each with its own characteristics which necessarily influence the spirit of the thought. When God speaks, the message is consistent with Scripture and with His own character. His voice carries the power of life within it and brings truth that sheds light on whatever it is that He is addressing. Very often the words feel "clean" as though they purge darkness from our soul. They have a ring of truth to them, a clarity of meaning and a gracefulness about the way they land on our heart and mind.

When Satan plants a thought in our mind, it is far different.[29] In its extreme forms his voice breathes death, hate, violence, despair, or some other vile characteristic. His thoughts will often attack God's character or our identity in Christ very directly. Even in their more subtle forms they divide, accuse, or condemn. His words are almost always contemptuous of someone, somewhere. At the very least they will appeal to our darker instincts or lead us to our own desires.

---

[29] "There is no truth in him. Whenever he speaks a lie, he speaks from his own nature, for he is a liar and the father of lies" (Jn.8:44)

In contrast to either thoughts from God or Satan, our own spontaneous thoughts are far less definable and cover a broad range of possibilities. First, we can simply recall thoughts we have had before, bringing them into the current context. Because the previous thoughts could have originated from any of the three sources, we are back to square one in discerning their source. Second, God has given people the capacity for inductive logic (some more than others!) which means we are quite capable of making an intuitive leap and coming up with a hypothesis about why things are the way they are. While there is no guarantee that our guesses are correct, they may appear to be true unless they are later disproven.

This kind of thinking can be very helpful when analyzing new objects or when trying to make sense of an experience, but can also cause a great deal of distress if we try to act on faulty conclusions. In any case, at the point of making the intuitive leap we may experience the idea as a spontaneous thought that seems true to us. If we do not recognize it as our own thought, we could easily think that it came from God, especially if it appears to make sense of whatever we are considering at the time.

Last, spontaneous thoughts can be the result of deeply internalized beliefs rising to the surface of our awareness. For example, suppose while reading Psalm 63 I see the words, "My flesh faints for you, as in a dry and weary land where there is no water" and I have an instantaneous sense of desperate deprivation, accompanied by a strong belief that God has been very stingy about giving out the water I need. I also see an image in my mind of being perpetually thirsty and begging God for relief. While that may feel very true, it is not what the Psalmist is talking about, nor is it a revelation from God about how life works in the kingdom. If I have learned to be sensitive to the Spirit of God and to lean on Him for discernment, this should flag me as something deep inside my heart that needs to be brought out into the light, where God can deal with my sense of deprivation.

So what does all this mean? First, this task of discernment is truly a matter for the spiritual community. Having been steeped in an individualistic culture this may be a difficult step for us. But we may need the help of other Christians to learn how discern the voice of God. In many instances this can protect us from giving heed to weird thoughts like, "Go sit on your roof and wait for the rapture." As the body of Christ learns how to discern, we create a context in which it is safe to learn how to listen for God, learning from those whose lives reveal that they have been with God.

Second, God truly honors our desire to seek truth and will proactively help us in this process. That does not mean we will not encounter resistance or difficulty. If the enemy hates anything, it is when people connect with God. So we should not be surprised if we have trouble with learning to hear well. But neither should we let this difficulty have the last word. If we continue to seek God's heart, He will reveal Himself to us and help us to hear His voice.

Third, we can ask God to help us with our discernment. While this is somewhat a circular process (asking God to let us know whether He is speaking to us or not) there are good reasons to ask Him. For instance, even when we have a good sense of what God is saying to us, we can still have thoughts of our own that we might not be sure of. In those cases, God is quite able to reveal to us His perspective on what we were just thinking. Another possibility is that when we ask for discernment we get no clarity at all. That in itself is a fairly good indication that we are not hearing very well at the moment and ought to hold any previous thought rather loosely, and that we need to reconnect with God about that idea at another time.

As an aside, one of the advantages to writing out our conversations with God is that we can go back to them at a later date when we are connecting better and ask for discernment about what we wrote down. God can then use those as teachable moments.

Finally, as noted above, God's voice is very powerful. Although people often hear from Him for years without recognizing the source, once we learn what to look for we can usually tell when it is Him.

How Do I Know It's God?

While this was covered briefly above, this issue is important enough to warrant some additional description.

One of the amazing things about God's voice is that it carries the power of life. Another person can tell me something a dozen times without much impact. When God says it to me, it can change my life. When we hear God clearly, His words have the weight of authority that can declare how things really are. For example, a man I know had lived for years with condemnation over the mistakes he had made in his parenting. No matter how much he tried or what his friends told him, he felt as if the things he had done and left undone were virtually unforgivable. Only when he heard God declare him forgiven did he finally find relief from the guilt and shame he had carried around.

Another aspect of God's words is that they carry so much truth within them they can surprise us with their brilliance. The earlier story of Daniel seeing his family as desperate instead of mean is a good example of this. As Daniel explains it, God's perspective made so much more sense than his own. Sometimes God's word feels like turning on a light in a dark room so that we can see what we have not seen before. God's words to us have a quality of grace about them that can amaze us. When He confronts us, He does it in ways that communicate His care for us and His desire to walk with us through our healing. Sometimes he even uses humor. Other times we may feel a great deal of tenderness in the words themselves, or feel as if we are being held as He tells us what we need to hear.

Very often He will say things that we simply know we would not have thought of. The words represent a different way of thinking or a kind of perspective we do not have by nature. In every way they are qualitatively better than our normal thoughts.

Perhaps the most telling evidence that God has spoken into our spirit is the fruit that it bears. Often His words have an immediate impact in the form of peace or awe that covers our whole being. Or we may experience an instant burst of excitement or joy that makes us smile or want to dance around the room. In the long term we may notice our attitude changing about certain things or our expectations changing in regard to God or life.

After one particularly intense conversation in which God revealed the true source of my self-hate, I noticed a complete change of heart and my constant self-berating simply stopped. If there was any doubt about whether it was a true healing or whether I just talked myself out of a bad mood, the long-term fruit was evidence enough.

Censorship vs. Discernment

When it comes to discerning our spontaneous thoughts, the issue of censorship is an important one to consider. If we are afraid that we might receive thoughts from Satan or that we might mistake our own thoughts for God's thoughts, we may set ourselves up to dismiss our spontaneous thoughts out of fear of taking in something harmful. In doing so, we may stop the thoughts even before they take shape, which is a kind of mental censorship of our thinking process.

As stated previously, fear is sufficient by itself to prevent us from receiving anything from God. Fear can also keep us from hearing our own inner thoughts that would be better brought to the surface where they could be exposed to the light. If we are afraid that we might harbor theologically incorrect attitudes, we can actually keep ourselves from seeing what needs to be healed.

For example, if I read in the Word that God knows my heart, I might feel a brief twinge of fear or shame and move on because it is uncomfortable, when it might be better to honestly say to God, "I wish I could hide that stuff from you because I think you don't like what you see there." Trying to ignore that thought because we are not supposed to think that way is a kind of self-censorship that can keep us from having a very teachable moment. Or if we read that sin shall no longer have dominion over you and think, "I have no idea what He means by that!" then we should let that thought take shape and ask some hard questions of God and our self rather than push the thought down until we are no longer aware of it.

The antidote for fear is trust. When we set aside time to listen for God's Spirit to speak to us, we need to believe that God will protect our time with Him such that we will not be overrun by anything evil. In opening up to God, we are not opening up to whatever is in the vicinity, spiritually. God will protect our soul from invasion against our will.

This does not mean we cannot have thoughts that are misleading or even evil, which is why we need to learn to discern what is true from what is not. But we do not need to be *afraid* of those thoughts. We are learners, not masters. The kingdom of God is about *growing* in grace and discernment, not *perfection*. Grace truly does cover the deepest thoughts that come from our flesh as well as any accusation we might hear from the enemy. As we present our thoughts to God (and our fellow Christians as needed) He will reveal what we need to know about them. If we find that we are harboring thought patterns that need to be changed, He will work with us without condemnation to bring about the transformation we need. If the thoughts seem like *insights* but sound a bit odd, He will make it possible to tell the difference between what came from Him and what did not. Trust is the key issue here. Can we trust that (1) God will show us what is true, and (2) that God really is fine with our attempts to learn how to hear from Him?

Discernment is not about *preventing* faulty ideas form forming in our minds, it is about *noticing* the thoughts that do form and making a *decision* about what direction to go once we have made some evaluation. We simply need to remain teachable, open to changing any assumptions that we make along the way, and trust that God is able to show us what we need to see. Censoring our thoughts is an attempt to control our conversation out of fear of getting it wrong or believing that it is necessary to come up with the "right" answer.

Discernment must always be rooted in grace and trust. Every good gift from God is an opportunity to grow closer to Him and receive His word deep into our heart. Every doubting thought and faulty "insight" is an opportunity for transformation, which also brings us closer to God. Either way, we win! Fear has no place in our conversations with God, no matter whether it is God's voice we hear or some deeply buried thought we did not know we held or an unexpected voice from the pit. Rather, every time we discern that a thought runs contrary to God's intention for us, it becomes an *invitation* to pursue more dependence and renewal, not condemnation for being an unfinished clay pot.

Bear in mind, too, that in hearing from God the goal is to engage with Him and learn from the conversation, not to come away with infallible quotes that "God said." Receiving clear messages is wonderful when it happens. But we do not need to have a quoted statement in order to know that God spoke to us about something. Being anxious about whether we wrote something down exactly the way God might have said it is counterproductive.

Many times after writing a thought in my prayer journal it will catch my attention in a negative way. Something about the tenor of the statement does not sound right. Having noticed my reaction to the thought, I then ask God what I need to know about that, and what usually follows is some form of clarification or a rephrasing of the statement so that it better reflects what needs to be said. On occasion it will lead to better understanding of my own mistaken thinking that God wants to heal. The point is to remain teachable, depending on God for my security instead of expecting my fear of the unknown to protect me.

Experience

Nothing is as valuable as first hand experience to teach us how to discern God's voice to us. As we seek to engage Him and see the evidence in our own transformation, we learn how to tell what His connection to us feels like and sounds like. We gain familiarity with the heart of God and learn to tell by the life we sense in the words whether the ideas behind them come from Him or not. Which means the best way to learn discernment is to spend a lot of time in conversations with God.

Our experience and familiarity over time become an important aspect of our relationship with God. We *know* this God whom we can trust with our lives and our secret thoughts. Our trust is real and experiential and personal. Discernment then becomes as much a matter of our heart as it is a matter of our mind.

An Example

Let's take an example of what the process might look like as we attempt to discern our thoughts. Suppose while reading about loving one another, I begin to feel intense shame in regard to how I have treated a certain person. Some initial thoughts that cross my mind to explain this might be:

- The enemy may be trying to accuse me of something untrue.
- God is revealing something I had overlooked before, and I often feel a lot of shame when I make mistakes like this.
- God is trying to motivate me to do something about my behavior.
- I'm really a bad person.

How do I tell what is really going on?

First, I need to notice that I am reacting. At that point I can ask God to reveal any false accusations that might be involved here. I take what part is true and discern if I have a problem with shame that needs work, or what God wants to do in my heart toward this person, or what actions I might

Discerning and Responding 115

need to take. As long as we are open to whatever God wants to do in us, we will find the resolution we need from Him.

The key to discernment is to be willing to ask a lot of questions, remain teachable and curious, while allowing God to mentor us in how to see life from His point of view.

Responding

> For we are what he has made us, created in Christ Jesus for good works, which God prepared beforehand to be our way of life. (Eph.2:10)

Spending focused time with God is life-giving in and of itself and receiving life from God is reason enough to engage with Him. However, throughout our time of conversational prayer there are usually many opportunities to draw us deeper into our connection with God as well as ways that we can participate more actively in the process of internalizing truth. As our focused time draws to a close, it is important to discern ways in which we can help to hold on to what we have been given.

Sometimes the insights we receive are so powerful that they instantly replace mistaken ideas we have about life, about God, and about our self.[30] In that case our response is probably mostly one of gratitude and thanksgiving, and may arise quite naturally from the freedom we feel. Other times we may need to be more deliberate about our response and give it as much care as the process of listening itself.

As with every other aspect of listening prayer, we can ask God how to respond. Our basic questions at this time might be:

- What do I want to or need to take with me from this time?
- How can I hold on to these gifts or these insights?
- What do I want to come back to again?

Generally, our responses will fall into four major categories: Prayer, Relational Quiet, Action, and Sharing. In any given encounter with God we

---

[30] More on this in Chapter 9, *Renewing Our Mind*

may choose one or more ways of responding, according to whatever seems fitting.

Prayer

Although conversational prayer is itself a form of prayer, we can employ any of the other forms of prayer to help us hold on to what God has given us in our time together. We have already mentioned thanksgiving and praise as natural ways to respond as we notice the value of what we have received.

Often our conversations will reveal things in our life that we were either unaware of or had been pushing aside for some reason, and from which we need to be set free. Sometimes we can best respond to these kinds of issues with prayers of repentance and renunciation. Now in many Christian circles, repentance has become a term that is loaded with shame and condemnation. That is unfortunate, because repentance can be such a liberating experience when it is initiated by the Spirit of God. As described later in the Interlude under the practice of repentance, we do not need to get beat up in order to repent. All we really need is to see whatever God wants to show us and run to Him for help.

Keeping in mind that repentance is primarily a change of heart regarding something we have done or thought, we want to be careful not to fall back on our own resources for the solution. Many of us have been taught that repentance means, "I'll try harder, God, I promise!" But that is the wrong approach to transformation. Repentance is fundamentally a *relinquishing* of the self. Change comes from living in the presence of God and internalizing reality as God sees it, not from trying harder. Repentance is simply a way of identifying a specific area in which we want God involved, and for which we desire His transforming hand.

Renunciation is, in a sense, a very specific form of repentance. Sometimes we come face to face with the realization that we have been actively participating in something that is harmful or evil. Turning away from that may require a deliberate pronouncement on our part that we will no longer be a willing participant in our own destruction.

Suppose a father discovers that he has developed a kind of hatred for his teenager because of the severity of the conflicts between them. Seeing that his hate is now part of the problem, he may need to renounce it out loud as a way of declaring to himself and the powers of the air that he will no longer be an active agent of destruction in his home. In doing so he aligns himself with the principles of life, and can then submit himself more fully to the rest of the work God wants to do in his heart.

Still another form of prayer that we can be led to is intercession. Our time with God may highlight the needs of others as well as ourselves. Learning to pay attention to the needs of those around us is part of seeing life more the way God sees it.

Taking a few minutes to write out our prayer to God can be even more rewarding. Writing helps us to be more thoughtful and intentional. By involving our body and more of our mind in our prayer, it becomes more firmly embedded in our heart.

Relational Quiet

A particularly powerful but often neglected way of responding to God is to simply *be with Him*, quietly, to "be still and know" that He is God. In our busy world we are prone to say about our devotional time, "Well, that was nice" and rush on to the next thing on our agenda for the day. But when we experience the presence of God in some significant way, whether His love for us, His goodness, His faithfulness to our healing, or whatever, one of the most important things we can do in that moment is to be still and allow our self to feel the impact of that awareness.

Taking a few minutes to rest with God has another benefit. Alternating between joy and rest with those we love is a powerful way to build stronger bonds.[31] That holds true for our relationship with God as well. After meeting with God in an intense interaction, being quiet with Him has a way of strengthening the bond we have with Him.

Please understand that this is not an endorsement to seek emotional experiences. But it *is* a plea to honor the presence of God and His impact on our bodies and minds. Jesus promised us joy in His abiding presence, and we should receive it as a treasured gift to be savored and enjoyed.

When conversational prayer yields life-giving insights, it is often very good for our soul to let those thoughts "simmer" for a while, sinking deeper

---

[31] Wilder, 2004 Thrive lectures

into our heart and mind. Spending time this way in quiet can feel a bit like "marinating" in the presence of God.[32] Receive it as a gift and enjoy it.

Action

Conversational prayer can sometimes stir us to action. We may feel led to contact someone and get together with them so we can both give and receive life between us. We may feel led to offer amends to someone we have hurt, to ask forgiveness or to forgive. And because our God is such a giving God, we can feel moved to give time or resources to others, to serve in some way to lift up another person.

Acting in concrete ways like this helps us connect our conversational prayer life with the rest of our world. We become participants with what God is doing all around us, and learn what it means to be agents of the kingdom. At the same time we place ourselves in positions where our weaknesses and unfinished parts will become exposed, giving us lots more to talk to our Mentor about.

Sharing with Others

Finally, we all need to be connected to other members of the body, both those *upstream* from us and those *downstream*. By sharing some of what God reveals to us in our conversational prayer time, those upstream from us can rejoice with us, encourage us, and mentor us in our walk with God, while those downstream from us can be encouraged as they witness the ways that God works in those He loves.

In addition, sharing some of our reflections with others can help to anchor those times in our soul. By going over our encounter with God and expressing it in a way that is intelligible by another person, we internalize the reality of that experience and the accompanying insights even more.

LONG TERM IMPACT OF CONVERSATIONAL PRAYER

Being fed by God and receiving life-giving insights day after day are reasons enough to connect with our heavenly Mentor in conversations. Yet that is only the beginning of the rewards that come from engaging with God.

---

[32] See also the section on Relational Quiet in the Interlude on spiritual practices.

Discerning and Responding

First, the process itself will become more fluid over time. Our ability to quiet and focus, to listen, discern, and respond will become more fluid and interwoven with each other so that we learn to involve all four aspects at the same time without really thinking about them. We develop a kind of sensor, if you will, that helps us to know what God is leading us to, and all the elements combine to build a connection that is rich and vibrant.

Second, we get to *know* God personally in a way that is vastly different than knowing *about* God. As important as good theology is, having conversations with God is a point of direct contact where we receive food for our soul and life for our spirit. Learning experientially how He cares for us, how He speaks to us, what He wants for us, are all part of getting to know what our amazing God is really like. Our relationship becomes a reality with substance, not just a theological proposition.

Third, engaging with the Author of Life will bring about healing and transformation like nothing else. We will discuss this in more detail later in the book. But be aware that the wounds we carry around and the sins that plague our life can lose their power one after another, as we learn how to bring these to God for the truth, life, and love that only He can provide. God's voice carries with it the power of resurrection. Having conversations with God can be like standing under a waterfall of life, love, and good.

Communion with God is a Feast!

ADDENDUM TO CHAPTER 4

What About People Who "Hear" Crazy Things?

Having said quite a lot about God's protection from the enemy, we must acknowledge that there are people who "hear" some very strange things and attribute them to God. In my experience, these anomalies can be divided into several groups. Identifying these distortions will help us experience God with more confidence in what is truly Him.

First, there are those who literally fabricate conversations with God. They are usually seeking glory or power, and their immaturity will generally give them away.

Then there are those who hear what they want to hear in order to justify some personal desire of theirs. Honestly, most of us have done this at one time or another. So we need to be understanding and graceful. One way of reducing our vulnerability to this is to remember whenever we are praying about things that we have a vested interest in, we should also seek help in our discernment from others.

Then there are two groups that are in great need of our prayers and support. One has to do with people whose brains have been injured or are malfunctioning in some way. As embodied spiritual beings, our mind, spirit, and physical brain are woven together in some mysterious ways in which each impacts the other. When our neurological circuits are mis-firing in some maladaptive ways, we can experience problems in our spiritual life as well. The community of believers needs to hold these people in their hearts and if necessary be spiritual eyes and ears for them.

Please notice that up to this point, even though people may not be hearing from God very well, they are mostly hearing their own thoughts, and nothing from the enemy is involved. That brings us to the last group, which includes those who have been involved in the occult in some manner and have not yet received complete deliverance from all that entails. There is some danger here that having opened themselves up to evil in the past, they may not yet have done the work necessary to seal off those avenues of access to their soul, and may still have some measure of dividedness within themselves that makes it difficult for them to discern good from evil.

Finally, we will all have strange thoughts that go through our mind from time to time as we listen for God's voice. Trying to prevent those thoughts from ever happening is usually counterproductive. Our best hope lies in learning how to pay attention to how we ourselves are involved in these discussions and how to discern what is life-giving from what is not.

RESOURCES FOR FURTHER STUDY

David Benner, *Desiring God's Will: Aligning Our Hearts with the Heart of God.* (Downers Grove: IVP Books) 2005

Chapter 5

Grace as a Means for Transformation

> And God is able to make all **grace** abound to you, so that always having all sufficiency in everything, you may have an abundance for every good deed. (2Cor.9:8 NASB)

Next to love, *grace* is perhaps the most broadly applied term in the New Testament in regard to God's action in the lives of His people. Learning to live in grace is absolutely foundational to receiving life from God and being transformed into the people He created us to be.

Yet in the common language of Christians today, grace is so limited in its meaning that it seems to have little relevance apart from getting us into heaven. "For by grace you have been saved" (Eph.2:8). That is true enough, and completely necessary to keep us from trying to earn our way into heaven. But salvation is only an *introduction* to grace,[33] not the whole of it. As powerful and far reaching as conversion can be, it is but a taste of a way of life that God has prepared for us to walk in. Our hope for this chapter is that we might be able to recapture the tremendous wonder of grace and how crucial it is to our development as apprentices of Christ.

OVERVIEW

Familiarity can have a strange way of actually distancing us from the very thing we are familiar with. For many Christians, this is indeed the case with the term "grace." We think we know what it is, but have become so familiar with the term that we toss it around and use it synonymously with "salvation" and "forgiveness" without a second thought. So in order to grasp how comprehensive grace truly is, we need to go back to the basics and re-establish a foundation that makes sense of God's activity in our life. Our

---

[33] "We have obtained our introduction by faith into this grace in which we stand." (Rom.5:2)

goal in this chapter is to answer some very core questions about grace in ways that help us to recapture its true meaning.

- What is grace?
- What does it have to do with forming Christian character?
- How do we make use of grace for growth?

To help us with this exploration, we will make heavy use of a single overarching definition that captures quite well the extent of grace and why it is so vital to Christian development. *Grace is everything God does joyfully in us and for us that we are unable to do for ourselves.*[34]

Grace is God healing an old wound that is still causing me a lot of pain. Grace is God changing my heart so I can honestly forgive a person from the depths of my soul for something I would otherwise consider to be unforgivable. Grace is God working His love into the fiber of my being until I begin to love someone I had previously despised. Grace is the joy that grows in me over time as I spend time with God. Grace is the peace of God that calms the anxieties in me I cannot calm on my own.

The list is endless, because life is complex and God's ability to create life in me is limitless. When I learn how to align with God, He can cause my heart and mind to go places I never thought possible. He writes His laws on my heart and I become a different person. This is the difference between rowing and sailing.

God doing in us what we cannot do – God's grace – is the means by which we become more Christ-like. We do not have it within ourselves *to be* Christ-like or *to do* what it takes to become more Christ-like. Only God can do that work in us, which makes it a work of grace. This is not an abstract description of something that happens to us in theory, but a concrete reality in which we must become active participants.

Furthermore, God performs His work in such a graceful manner that we are free from the condemnation of being unfinished, and free from condemnation as a motivator for change. We are His workmanship, to the extent that we can learn to submit to the work He desires to do in us.

Learning how to *participate with grace* is precisely what this book is about (and why we created the *Forming* course). Once we learn how to make a

---

[34] This definition comes from Dallas Willard.

space for God and participate with Him for change, we discover a path that leads to life-long growth and transformation!

More than a Pardon, More than Kindness

Grace is not just being pardoned from something we deserve or getting something we don't deserve. Those are certainly great gifts that we cannot achieve on our own. But grace is far more than a legal transaction in heaven. It is God's persistent work *in* us to transform us and involve us in His kingdom. In the broadest sense, *grace is every aspect of God's mission to overturn evil in this world*. It includes who God is, how He acts, and what He does.

Among other things, this means that God is tender toward our weakness rather than condemning. Jesus assured us many times that the Father welcomes the spiritually sick and broken into the Kingdom. We do not have a God who resents having to drag His miserable creation back to wholeness, but One who loves us so much that He would die to break the yoke of bondage we live under.

That is grace! Not only because of *what* He does but *how* He does it. That is why as creatures of disgrace we can open our arms and reach up to Him in total trust that He wants us and desires to embrace us, despite our terrible condition. And of course God's mission to overturn evil in the world is an act of grace because we would be hopelessly lost without His intervention and work of redemption.

Once we realize that grace is *the* primary characteristic of God's entire mission, we begin to see how much His desire to transform us permeates the gospel. Much more than being saved from sin and going to heaven, grace is connecting with God instead of being alienated,[35] being alive instead of spiritually dead,[36] having light to live by instead of groping in darkness,[37] seeing good things formed out of bad things,[38] and being indwelt by God

---

[35] "So then you are no longer strangers and aliens, but you are fellow citizens with the saints, and are of God's household." (Eph.2:19)

[36] Described in detail in Romans 6:3-11.

[37] "For God, who said, 'Light shall shine out of darkness' is the One who has shone in our hearts to give the light of the knowledge of the glory of God." (2Cor.4:6)

[38] "God causes all things to work together for good to those who love God, to those who are called according to His purpose." (Rom.8:28)

regardless of our condition.[39] In short, the whole enterprise of reclaiming creation is God's grace at work, as these are all things *we cannot make happen*! God has decided to bond with us, to live inside us, to heal and restore in us that which was ruined beyond repair – these are all acts of grace, amazing gifts of restoration.

In the well-known movie *The Blind Side*, we are introduced to a young man who leads a very impoverished life with no future to look forward to. But one day a woman comes along who gives this boy a home with love and a chance to make something of himself. It is a wonderfully redemptive story, a beautiful drama of grace at work.

The gospel is a story of God coming to us, to rescue us and to do for us what we could never do for ourselves. And we will never outgrow our need for His grace in our life. Becoming more deeply attached to God, more cleansed by His ministry within us, and more involved in His good will for us, all brings with it a far greater dependence upon Him. We need more grace, not less, as we grow.

CHARACTERISTICS OF GRACE

This section will describe a few of the many facets of grace that reveal our need for *more* grace, not *less* as we grow closer to God. We will then compare grace and legalism to sharpen our understanding of how grace is involved in the Christian life. And finally, we will look at how grace is necessary to bring about transformation itself.

Grace as an Invitation to the Broken

Grace means that God has opened the door of the kingdom to those who have no chance whatever of getting in there on their own. Although this is fairly elementary theology, we dare not lose sight of its amazing implications. The key thought here is that God did for people what they cannot do for themselves. That is in fact why we call it an act of grace.

While we understand this fairly well in terms of conversion, we tend to overlook the need for grace in the life of those already in the kingdom. But

---

[39] "We have this treasure in earthen vessels that the surpassing greatness of the power may be of God and not from ourselves." (2Cor.4:7)

the truth is, we all begin the Christian life in a spiritually impoverished condition, unable to correct the problems of the past or see things in the present from God's point of view. Only God can heal us, cleanse us, feed our soul, and mentor us in His ways – which means we need His work in us for the rest of our life. Grace means we all get to *participate* in the kingdom, not just *enter* the kingdom.

> For if while we were enemies, we were reconciled to God through the death of his Son, much more surely, having been reconciled, will we be saved (rescued) by his life. (Rom.5:10)

> Blessed are the spiritually impoverished, because they are precisely the ones the kingdom is for. (Matt.5:3, paraphrase)

The invitation is to all, Christian or not, who are spiritually impoverished. We get to live in the kingdom even while we are still in poor shape. And kingdom life is based on grace.

Grace Makes it Safe to Come to God

To underscore the fact that we are all invited into His presence, the New Testament authors spoke repeatedly about God's relationship to us as unfinished works of grace.

> For we do not have a high priest who is unable to *sympathize with our weaknesses*, but we have one who in every respect has been tested *as we are*, yet without sin. Let us therefore approach the throne of grace with boldness, that we may receive mercy and may find grace to help *in time of need*. (Heb.4:15-16, emphasis added)

God understands our weaknesses even more than we do. He knows that we are but jars of clay, and it was *His* idea to have a relationship with us. Our problems are no surprise to Him, and practical theologies that teach God is offended and repulsed by our sin are simply not dealing with reality. We are terribly flawed people and our minds are all badly malformed by life in a broken world. In contrast to God we are all unbelievably impoverished spiritually. If God were put off by our mess, He would have nothing to do with any of us.

To even consider that we could be good enough to make God give us the time of day is downright presumptuous, and deeply rooted in self-righteous religiosity or a mindset that has never made it out of an Old Covenant paradigm of obedience to a written law.

No, the reason we can have access to God is because He has taken the issue of our spiritual poverty off the table. Instead of making us try hard to be good enough to get close to Him, God has decided to destroy the power of sin (Rom.6:14) and move close enough to us to cause change in us by His very presence and His impact on our heart and mind. That's grace – God doing what we cannot do – bringing us together and close enough to matter. That is how grace makes it safe to relate to a Holy God, especially when we are broken and failing.

Grace is Relational

Under the Old Covenant there was a strict code that limited direct access to God. Beginning with the court of the Gentiles and working inward, we eventually end up in the Holy Place where only priests could enter, and then finally the Holy of Holies that could only be entered once a year by one priest. The implication is that there are lots of criteria that must be met before engaging with a Holy God.

All that changed under the New Covenant where God turned the whole thing on its head and declared that we get access first, and *then* we will work on the purification issues within the context of that relationship. *Grace means we get the relationship first.* The good news is that our relationship with God depends on His character and His heart for us, not our performance or the level of our spiritual development. "This is love: not that we loved God, but that He loved us" (1Jn.4:10 NIV).

When we are most lost or broken in our spiritual life, we don't need to be told we are bad; we need to be told we are loved, that we are worth fighting for, that we matter to the kingdom and to others around us. And the closer we get to God, the more important this becomes, because the closer we get to the Light, the more our flaws become visible and the more grace we need. Fortunately, getting closer to God also includes learning how to *receive* more (not *do* more!) which is precisely what we need in order to stand in His Light without being condemned by our imperfections.

Grace as a Means for Transformation

As we participate with God in our restoration, He deals with each area of our life that is broken or malfunctioning, one at a time. Very often when He reveals our heart to us, it feels like a confrontation, but one that is graceful and caring. These life-giving confrontations are only possible because of the loving, grace-filled relationship we have with God. Thankfully, we can plunge into our restoration with joy, knowing that God is with us and for us in this process. Thus, grace is fundamentally a relational process, initiated by a relational God.

Grace and Truth

Paul often prayed that Christians under his care would continue to "grow in grace and truth." In many ways these two gifts from God are inseparable.

First, God's revelation of the truth we need for our healing and our daily life is an act of grace. To whatever extent we fail to receive His continual guidance, we will be unable to live as God intended. Seeing what is true with "the eyes of heaven" is something we cannot do on our own and something we can only receive from God.

Second, if it were not for God's grace, the truth that He wants to reveal to us would quickly overwhelm and condemn us. Much of the work of restoration God wants to do in us requires that He expose our heart to the light and show us what He wants to change in us. Only the knowledge that He truly loves us and does not condemn us will keep us from being destroyed by the truth of what He finds there.

God's grace makes it safe to know the truth of where we are in the process of restoration. Grace makes it *safe to be known,* because God knows us fully and loves us totally at the same time. More than that, God is delighted when we trust Him with our brokenness and ask Him to restore us and mentor us in the ways of the kingdom. Once again, the more truth we receive, the more grace we need.

Grace as a Way of Life

Restoration is a life-long process (maybe longer!). We need to accept the simple truth that our renewal will take us the rest of our life, and that was God's idea, not something that shocks Him or presents any kind of barrier between Him and us. We really are small, limited creatures with a big, holy

God who actually *likes* being God to us and working in us to bring His new creation to life. That is not something to feel shameful about.

We make a very grave error if we think that after we have been converted the rest is up to us. The truth is we cannot do much of what really needs to happen once we are *in* the kingdom, any more than we could do what it took to get us there. Paul has this clearly in mind when he spoke of the possibilities of the Christian life.

Paul argues forcefully in his letters that since God brought us into the kingdom when we were in the worst possible shape, spiritually speaking, we can be certain that He will do the remaining work that needs to be done, given that we are now in His family. The work of grace continues in us after conversion, because we still need to be changed in ways that are beyond our ability.

"We are *His* workmanship" Paul says (Eph.2:10 NASB). We do not restore ourselves by our own effort. Rather, God does in us what we have never been able to do, which is to heal the wounds and create new growth. And this is not a one-time event; it is the Christian way of life. Our biggest job in this task is to learn how to participate with what He wants to do in us. This is a very positive and hopeful processes – to be able to spend our lives purging the remnants of a malformed mind and receiving the mind of Christ, all without any condemnation for the state we are in or the work that remains to be done. Grace is meant to be our way of life with God, beginning with our spiritual birth and continuing on for the rest of our life.

LEGALISM

To better understand the nature of grace we must wade into the very difficult topic of legalism. To begin with, there are several things that make this subject a bit challenging to attempt on paper. First, people rarely see the extent of their own legalism. So to whatever level a person's practice has become legalistic, they will tend to misread this discussion. Second, a significant percentage of the Christian population is so deeply committed to the principles of legalism (although they deny being legalistic) they can actually become offended by the implications of grace. Third, legalism is insidious in its nature because it masquerades as truth and righteousness.

Grace as a Means for Transformation 129

Attempting to clarify the issues at hand is a bit like walking a tightrope: the slightest misuse of a single word can look like a huge mistake in theological judgment. That said, I pray that those who read this may allow the Spirit of God to speak to their heart and mind, and that the things I say will in fact be true to the Scriptures.

Please note that many people who are legalistic are not at all rigid or hard to get along with. Christians who tend toward legalism usually care a great deal about the things of God and live exemplary lives. Lest we think of legalism in too limited a sense as something that only applies to Pharisees or grumpy, narrow-minded people, we will try to open the definition up a bit so that its opposition to grace can be fully appreciated. Proper understanding of the nature of legalism can aid tremendously in making sense of how grace can be a practical reality and a means for growth and change.

Legalism is **not**, as is commonly thought, primarily about having a long list of rules you need to follow, although it generally includes that. The truth is, doing what is right because it is good, even when you do not feel like it, is just plain *common sense*. Non-Christians are also quite able to learn how to do important things they do not feel like doing. Legalism comes in at the point where *we believe following the rules is what makes us more acceptable to God, or how we grow spiritually*. At its core, legalism is both a belief and an action:

- *The belief that righteousness is primarily a standard of behavior.*
- *The attempt to become righteous by trying to live up to that standard.*

This is a profound thought, perhaps even shocking to some. I confess that I had reservations about using so broad a definition, but I think it is necessary in order to convey the nature of the problem we are dealing with. Truthfully, at one time or another we have all tried to grow spiritually by sheer resolve to live better. We see places in our life where we fall short of God's standard, we feel convicted, and so we promise God we will try harder. What we fail to realize is that this is a legalistic approach to spiritual development. Trying to grow spiritually by following rules or principles is legalism by definition.

This was a problem in Judaism that carried over into the early church and has been with us ever since. Grace is simply too radical for a lot of people to grasp or believe, and so they gravitate toward legalism as a way of comprehending their part in spiritual growth and supposedly taking control of their development. To better understand how and why this happens, we will take a look at various aspects of legalism and how it relates to grace, which is the only true means for transformation.

Features of Legalism

Legalism is a wide-reaching phenomenon that manifests itself in a number of ways along a broad spectrum of activity. Consequently, it can be hard to pin down exactly what legalism looks like, and any single description below may or may not apply to a person who has legalistic tendencies. What we can say is that in whatever form it takes in a person's life, it seems to have some common detrimental effects which we will cover later.

Being Right

Perhaps the most common characteristic of legalism is an attempt to improve our spiritual standing before God by abstaining from certain bad behaviors and practicing certain good behaviors. There are many ways in which this can be played out. In its worst form, people may attempt to earn their way into heaven. A meritorious view of salvation is fairly popular among non-believers who think Christianity teaches that you get into heaven by having your good stuff outweigh the bad. However, this is not the form of legalism that we want to concentrate on here. Our focus is on the belief that once you are a Christian, you then become a better Christian by being obedient to the principles laid down in the New Testament.

Curiously, a legalistically inclined person often sees no contradiction whatever between the *inability* to earn salvation and the *ability* to earn sanctification. Or to put this another way, they see no problem with the idea that on the one hand they cannot be good enough to *become* a Christian, yet on the other hand, once saved, it is up to them to become a *more virtuous* Christian through their own effort. The Christian life is seen as a lifestyle and system of rules that must be adopted and worked out in daily life.

Exactly what system of rules is used and the attitudes involved can vary greatly from one group to another or from one person to another. Some Christians become super vigilant about the dangers of being contaminated by the world. They follow a carefully detailed set of rules regarding what is good or bad because they are extremely concerned about keeping themselves pure and undefiled. Others are more focused on the rightness or wrongness of every action, attitude, and doctrine, and believe that the most important thing in the Christian life is to be right about everything. Those who get things right and have the right answers to theological questions are strong Christians; those who do the wrong things or think the wrong way are weak or spiritually lazy; and those who do not care enough about right and wrong issues or who rationalize away the good and bad aspects of things are considered liberal. Nearly everything in life is evaluated on moral grounds and given a status of either black or white.

Having the right answers does not by itself make you a better Christian.[40] Yet there are many today who truly believe their superior grasp of Bible facts and theology makes them more spiritual than those who lack that knowledge. But we are fully capable of storing theology in our brain while at the same time leaving our character virtually unchanged. We can even put on a lot of "right" behaviors without changing our heart. The Pharisees were great examples of this process.

Doing what is right is certainly a good thing in itself. But when your efforts to be good become a substitute for a relationship with God or for receiving what you need from Him to change your heart, then it is actually an attempt to clean the outside of the cup – a legalistic approach to life.

Mistaken Emphasis on Obedience

While the New Testament has much to say about obedience, when viewed through the lens of a legalistic mindset, these passages on obedience take on a form of self-effort that was never intended by the original authors.

The one thing we should have learned from the Old Testament is that righteousness does not come from trying to keep laws, no matter how good those laws may be. That is the crux of Paul's argument in the first half of Romans. What so many Christians fail to grasp is that by replacing Old Testament law with New Testament principles, the possibility of earning

---

[40] "If I understand all mysteries and all knowledge … but do not have love, I am nothing." (1Cor.13:2)

righteousness becomes *even more* remote, no matter how much we think the Holy Spirit is helping us. *We simply cannot do what Jesus says* by direct effort.

If Jesus had given us a list of things we could actually do, like feed the dog and take out the garbage, it might be a different story. But He said, forgive seventy-times seven, love your enemy, do good to those who hate you, and take up your cross. These are all beyond our ability. And even if we could force ourselves to do those things in spite of our feelings, it would only prove the point, that doing the right things is merely cleaning the outside of the cup and does not change our heart.

Believing that obedience to rules is the way to grow is like thinking you can manufacture grapes if you smash enough amino acids together. Fruit comes from connecting to the Vine, not from trying to make fruit. Obedience comes from being transformed, not the other way around.

When I was about six, my parents sent me to a piano teacher to learn how to play the piano. I was overjoyed, because I loved the piano. No matter what the teacher asked me to do, I would practice until everyone else in the house begged me to stop. There was no need to "command" me to practice, because my heart was already in it. You could say that I was obedient to the teacher, but how different that is from our common perception of obedience as something we have to do just because it is the right thing. Teaching that obedience is the basis for our life is truly a distorted understanding of what it means to be obedient, but it is a fairly predictable symptom of legalistic perspectives.

There is much more that could be said and needs to be said regarding this terribly mistaken paradigm of the Christian life. Please refer to the Appendix ("The Trouble with Obedience") for a more in-depth discussion of this pervasive problem.

Viewing the Bible as a Technical Manual

One of the more prominent characteristics of legalism is the tendency to treat the Bible as if it were primarily a legal document that lists all the rules and consequences for human behavior. As with other aspects of legalism, this idea can be very tricky to rectify, because it masquerades quite well as a reasonable way to use the Word. The differences between a graceful reading and a legalistic reading may be subtle, yet profoundly impact how we live.

In this mindset, the Bible is understood to be *primarily* a collection of principles and directives for us to follow. Our job is to distill the spiritual principles from the stories and discourses in the text and apply these principles to our lives so that we know what to do in any given situation.

Now on one level, that approach is really hard to argue with, because all scripture is "useful for teaching, for reproof, for correction, and for training in righteousness" (2Tim.3:16). We need the light of scripture to help us see the unseen realities of spiritual life and to make choices differently because of what we see.

The problem comes in identifying precisely *what we see* and what we mean by *application*. In practice, legalism becomes a lens through which we read the Bible, such that every description of a holy life becomes either an edict to be obeyed or a condemnation for disobedience. For example, let's take a short excerpt from the great Love Chapter:

> Love is patient; love is kind; love is not envious or boastful or arrogant or rude. It does not insist on its own way; it is not irritable or resentful. (1Cor.13:4-5)

Many people who read these verses immediately think something along the lines of, "I guess I should try to be more patient and less selfish." They view the text as a directive on "How to Love" and what to do differently in order to be more loving. In reality, Paul is simply painting a word picture of love. He is telling us, "When you run into love, this is what it will look like." He is **not** saying that being more patient makes you a loving person, but rather, a person who has a heart of love will be more patient because that is what love does. *Love produces patience*, not the other way around. The passage really says very little about how to *become* a loving person. That is left to other places in his writings.

Again, the reason we misread this text is because we are so prone to view everything in terms of, "What should I *do*?" How can I make this happen in my life? How do I measure up against the standard or principles in this passage, and what can I do to measure up better? But the Bible is much more than a book of rules and principles for us to figure out and follow, just as the Christian life is much more than following the right principles. For the most part, we cannot follow biblical principles in our own strength anyway. So the whole venture is misguided and in the process the Bible gets misunderstood and misused.

When carried to an extreme, the Bible ends up being used to justify all sorts of practices that are truly "rules of men" which have very little to do with spiritual life. My apologies here, because in an effort to offer some examples of this I may offend some of my readers.

Take the style of clothing that is considered appropriate in a church service. For some reason, certain traditions think that men should wear a suit coat and tie to church. But on what basis? There were no ties and suit coats in the Bible. How can a standard of formality that was *defined by our culture* sometime in the last two hundred years become the criteria for reverence to God? Yet, this standard is defended with all the fervor of protecting the integrity of the Bible.

I personally remember an instance in my youth where people were terribly upset the first time they saw a guitar used in a church service, because it was too "worldly" an instrument. Never mind that a few hundred years earlier their ancestors were upset at the introduction of the organ (which many would now refuse to part with), or that a guitar is a lot closer to a Biblical lyre than the piano sitting over on the side of the stage. But someone can always find a verse about "being in the world and not of the world" and say that it means we cannot have guitars in church. This is legalism at its worst.

Still, there are even more disturbing aspects of this phenomenon.

The Fruit of Legalism

If we believe spiritual health is something we have direct control over and we are expected to produce it by our efforts to live up to some standard, then it is inevitable that at some point we would feel self-righteous pride for our accomplishments. Those who do well are often quite judgmental about others who struggle and can even be contemptuous toward them. Spiritual maturity takes on a kind of competitive spirit in which there are winners and losers. Thus, self-righteousness can be an early warning sign of an underlying belief in achieving righteousness by self-effort.

At the other end of the spectrum, legalism bears a bitter fruit in the form of defeat and spiritual exhaustion. Many Christians who buy into the performance oriented mindset of legalism find themselves constantly falling short of the expectations they have of themselves. Over time this can lead to spiritual burnout, including a pervasive disbelief in real transformation, and even a loss of faith. Trying to live out the Christian life by willpower without the necessary transformation of our heart is a recipe for disaster.

For those who come to Christianity already burdened by self-hate, legalism can be deadly. Although self-hate can initially take root for any one of a number of reasons, it is severely aggravated by exposure to performance-oriented teaching. The worse a person's self-hate, the more difficult it is for them to achieve any kind of standard, religious or otherwise. Telling them that the Christian life is achievable if they would just try harder only increases their self-hate. Every defeat is internalized as further condemnation of their failures, and any hope for change is pushed out of reach. Self-hate is a problem that is too deeply embedded in the soul to respond to willpower or external commands. This is so important that we will take a closer look at how to deal with this in Chapter 10.

When surrounded by other Christians who are working from a legalistic framework, most people feel an intense pressure to perform well in order to be accepted. Consequently, it becomes necessary to hide as many flaws as possible and to look good, even if things are not going well. Marital conflict, parenting difficulties, addictions, and all other kinds of problems stay hidden and out of sight. Eventually, the appearance of spiritual vitality takes precedence over substantive growth. Parroting the right answers becomes more important than honesty. These attempts to hide are not just coincidental. They are predictable results of distorting the Christian life into a moralistic system of behavior.

Because a performance-driven orientation to the Christian life is unlikely to produce real change, this approach to spiritual growth is doomed to failure. Sooner or later, one of several things will happen. A person may become so entrenched in and enamored by their own performance that they become, in their own mind, part of the Christian elite. Some may simply give up and settle for doing the best they can with little hope for any realization of the kingdom life found in the Bible. Still others will manage to grow spiritually for a short time but then discover they have outgrown their church and that it has lost its relevance for them. In all cases, the results are less than desirable.

Legalism, People, and Relationships

I remember speaking with a man in his thirties who was trying to sort out the truth of Christianity to see if it made enough sense for him to believe. His greatest barrier to finding answers to his questions? The very people who claimed to have all the answers. In his efforts to learn what he wanted to know about history, the Bible, and how faith works in everyday life, he repeatedly encountered condescending attitudes and spiritual pride among the "knowledgeable" believers who looked down on his lack of religious training. Such arrogance is not only shaming toward the seeker, it casts serious doubt on the credibility of the faith of those who seem to have the most information about the Bible.

This is fairly typical of the impact that legalistic behavior can have on others, and not just on those outside the church. Legalism by its very nature divides people rather than bring them together. As noted above, Christians who see themselves as inadequate and judged by the group standards may feel compelled to project a persona that is more in line with the expectations. This form of denial and dishonesty effectively distances people from one another and prevents a lot of important healing from occurring.

Taking this one step further, a person with an emotional or spiritual problem may be reluctant to seek help at all because of the stigma attached to those who struggle. Often those who do seek help are met with pat answers and injunctions to "repent" and try harder. This insensitivity to the real needs of people is common among Christians who think all that is needed for spiritual vitality is a strong will and the desire to try hard enough. They may feel no qualms about condemning a person who struggles, on the grounds that "they need to hear the truth even if it hurts." But what it really boils down to is that rules are more important than people, contrary to the teachings of Jesus.[41] This is the source of "shooting our wounded" for which Christians have often been criticized, and justly so.

---

[41] Example: "Sabbath was made for man, not man for the Sabbath" (Mk.2:27)

Distance can also be created between a person and God this way. One very common problem among Christians is the belief that when they commit some sin, God turns His back on them. So it can be a while before they dare to approach Him again. Such attitudes belie a whole host of underlying assumptions about the need to perform well in order to be acceptable, what it means to repent, and so on. In the long term, these assumptions damage our faith and our relationship to God.

Again, I do not mean to say that a legalist cannot have a good heart. That is not the point. The problem is they have been terribly misled as to the meaning of spiritual maturity and the means for growth. Above all, they have not been shown how to develop an authentic life-giving relationship with God. For if they had, they would have abandoned their performance mindset. Once we experience what it is like to be mentored by God and receive what we need from Him, we can see more clearly why trying to make it on our own is such a hopeless cause.

Summary

Legalism is fundamentally the belief that righteousness comes from trying hard to follow the commands in the Bible. This is a life-killing approach to spirituality that has the potential to quench our joy, destroy our understanding of grace, and leave us in perpetual bondage. Either that or we will fool ourselves into thinking we actually are able to pull it off and that we can become righteous through our own effort. Either way, the fruit of legalism is offensive to non-believers and cruel to those who suffer under the impression that they are failures in the kingdom because they cannot do what is expected of them.

Motivations Behind Legalism

Despite all that can be said about legalism, many people who approach the Christian life in this way do so with pure motives. Their heart's desire is to please God and to incorporate all that He has for them into their life. Unfortunately, they have been taught that the way to proceed is to be as good as they can, try to live up to a high standard, get involved in the church, and so on. Without realizing it, they have been tutored in the art of legalistic religion. So while their motives might be pure enough, their training has led them away from the way God fosters growth and into an imitation of righteousness.

But there are other reasons why people become legalistic and even defend their legalism with vigor. Many Christians have been taught to fear their old nature, to think of it as a caged animal waiting to get out and destroy something. Unless they keep a tight reign on their passions, their old nature will betray them and they will fall into sin. With such a view, it makes sense why they would develop a broad set of guidelines and boundaries to keep them "safe." Furthermore, they see any attempt to dismantle their safeguards as foolishness or a form of disobedience that can only lead to sin. So they strongly resist a message of grace that claims to depend on a relationship with God for sanctification. Sadly, they are fighting the wrong fight, and have never been shown how to put those passions to rest so that they do not need to live in fear of their own body.

Another primary motivation for legalism is toxic shame, which can take several forms. First, there are those for whom mistakes in life are deemed to be unacceptable or evidence of some detestable character defect. These people have great difficulty accepting any critical feedback or admitting their responsibility in any problem. Their preferred method of dealing with mistakes is to minimize or cover things up. If that fails, blame someone else. Rules provide a means for knowing who is good and who is not, a way to assign blame and exonerate the innocent. Being good rule keepers, they can stay on the safe side of the law and feel blameless. Of course, the entire process is truly little more than shame management dressed up in Christian terminology. But because the fear of shame is so basic to their way of perceiving the world (even if it is completely below the conscious level) they are unable to make the connection. To them, the rules are as important as being able to breathe.

Another way that shame can drive a person to rule-based living is the fear of God's disapproval. If I think that God is really disgusted with whatever part of me that is still carnal, then I may be driven to do all I can in my power to make Him like me and not be disappointed. I figure out what He hates and what He likes and then perform for Him so that He will like me. If I think that I am mostly successful in this attempt, I may become rather proud of my accomplishments. If on the other hand I see myself as a failure,

I may be overwhelmed by self-loathing and believe that I can never show my face in the presence of God. Either way, I am using a moral yardstick to measure my performance to see if I am doing all right, and beating myself into submission out of fear of God's displeasure. We even teach this to little children by telling them "God can see you all the time, so you better be good!"

A related issue that draws people to legalism is the desire for control. Addictive family systems or other environments where life seems random and unpredictable can often cause a person to become a "control freak." Everything has to be just right or their anxiety level starts to rise and they need to do something to bring life back under control. As a Christian, a set of rules to control their moral standing with God seems like the best thing they can hope for. They know exactly where they stand and how to keep from rocking the boat, spiritually. When a person's need for certainty is extremely high, a set of moral rules looks like a God-send. Asking them to give up their control in favor of a stronger relationship with God is like asking them to jump off a cliff. To a person with control issues, relationships are inherently unstable. And a God they cannot see is even more uncontrollable. Why would they trust someone like that? Emotionally, trusting a set of fixed rules seems much safer to them.

Then there is the person who is in continual need of affirmation from peers. When they are told there are a lot of things they need to do well in order to be a good Christian, they may set their mind on doing the best they can. It even feels good to have people come up to them and say, "I've never seen anyone so dedicated and sold out for God." Performance is their way of getting what they need emotionally from the group. So to say that keeping rules is not how we mature is to challenge the basis of their reputation, their social life, and the means by which they feel valuable and important.

Closely related to the person who fears their old nature, and perhaps the most vocal advocate for legalism, is one who has a deep conviction that Christians are every bit as depraved as their unsaved neighbors, just forgiven. This comes out of a "miserable sinner" theology that says Christians may have received the Spirit of God, but they still have that terrible sin nature inside that is bent on destruction. Only severe treatment of the body will hold that monster in check. And that means there are rules to follow. This form of Christianity often produces radically religious Christians who hold onto self-hate as if it were a shield of protection against the flesh and the world. Helping them get free of this bondage is often difficult, because their perception of love has been twisted beyond all recognition, making the idea of a loving relationship with God almost incomprehensible.

Understanding Motivations for Legalism

Stepping back and looking at the big picture, legalism is largely a substitute for a strong Christian identity and life-giving relationships. For many, legalism is simply the way they have been taught to pursue the Christian life. They have never been shown how to build a strong relationship with God that is substantive enough to purify their soul and renew their mind, so they follow the rules and hope that they improve as time goes on. But for many others, *legalism is actually an unintentional way of managing their emotional problems in a religious context*. Whether fear-based control issues, or deep shame-based inner conflicts, their internal problems seem to lend themselves to a performance-oriented approach to the Christian life. Finding a substitute for relationship may actually be a real motivating factor for them.

In any case, legalism fails to deliver on its promise and instead *interferes* with our spiritual growth. Reducing *who I am* down to *what I do* is a terribly destructive assault on who we are in Christ. And running our lives by rules instead of living out of a renewed heart is a sure way to bring death to ourselves and everyone around us. Although the pride of being "right" may carry us for a long time, it can collapse in a moment when life becomes too hard to manage.

The truth is that there are a great many people in the world who, for whatever reason, are motivated enough to keep a moral code by sheer willpower, no matter how detailed or how inconvenient it is to do so. Regardless of what religion they join, they become outstanding examples of discipline and self-control. If they happen to be Christian, they bring their strong-willed character into the kingdom and appear to conquer all the deeds of the flesh overnight. On the surface, this seems to support the theory that we can achieve the Christian life through dedicated effort. But the Bible authors say otherwise.

Legalism in the Bible

The Bible has much to say about the laws given by God: why He gave them, how they were misused, and why He had to eventually offer something better than rules to obey. Understanding this big picture will go a long way toward building a foundation for transformation as a way of life.

Legalism in the Old Testament

A very interesting thing happens in the Old Testament. Under a covenant of law, legalism becomes a problem that God gets very concerned about! How is that possible? One would think that a law-based covenant necessarily leads people to live by rules. Many aspects of the covenant were conditional, dependent upon the obedience of the people. How can God accuse them of being legalistic?

Prophets throughout the Old Testament had much to say about the way the nations of Judah and Israel were living. Idolatry had become a major problem, as had oppression of the poor and various other issues. One of these problems was that certain segments of the population continued to observe the law, but in a way that was offensive to God. For example, Amos charged the people with meeting the external requirements of the law while at the same time oppressing the poor (Amos 4). Isaiah went even farther, accusing the nation of going through the motions of religion without any real desire for God at all.

> "What are your multiplied sacrifices to Me?" says the Lord. "I have had enough of burnt offerings of rams and the fat of fed cattle; And I take no pleasure in the blood of bulls, lambs or goats." (Isa.1:11 NASB)

> These people come near to me with their mouth and honor me with their lips, but their hearts are far from me. Their worship of me is made up only of rules taught by men. (Isa.29:13 NIV)

The law was never meant to be a religion unto itself. It was more like a boundary on the relationship or a description of holiness so the Israelites would know how they were designed to live. What caused God so much grief was that they gravitated toward a concept of legal requirements with its emphasis on external compliance, and they lost track of the relationship which focuses on the heart.

Imagine a gardener that dutifully tills the soil, waters the plants, and goes through all the motions of gardening but pays no attention to the fact that the plants are actually wilting, the blossoms fading, and the fruit non-existent. Although he may be meeting the legal requirements of his job description, he is not really fulfilling his purpose. This was much the case with Israel at the time of Isaiah and Jeremiah.

Legalism in the New Testament

At the time of Jesus there were several sects among the Jews who were particularly meticulous about keeping the law. The group we are most familiar with is that of the *Pharisees*. Today we sometimes use the word in a pejorative sense. But in order to fully appreciate the nature of their conflict with Jesus, it is important to understand that the Pharisees were some of the most dedicated and conscientious Jews of their time.

The main problem Jesus had with the Pharisees was their belief that practicing their laws made them pure. Or to put it another way, people who kept those rules were considered righteous while those who did not keep them were defiled in some way. Jesus did not simply disagree with the set of rules they had chosen. His concern was over the fact that righteousness has to do with the heart rather than external conformity to a prescribed system of ethics.

> You blind guides, who strain out a gnat and swallow a camel... you clean the outside of the cup and of the dish, but inside they are full of robbery and self-indulgence. You blind Pharisee, first clean the inside of the cup and of the dish, so that the outside of it may become clean also. (Mt.23:24-26 NASB)

Much of Jesus' Sermon on the Mount refers to this distinction between changing our behavior and changing our heart.[42] "You have been told not to murder, I say do not even hate or feel contempt toward others. You have been told not to commit adultery, but I say that adultery is a thing of the heart as well. Much of what passes for spirituality among you is nothing but

---

[42] "For I say to you that unless your righteousness surpasses that of the scribes and Pharisees, you will not enter the kingdom of heaven." (Mt.5:20)

religious behavior done to gain the approval of others." As a result of these types of observations, Jesus was continually at odds with the Pharisees over this misuse of the law.

Years later Paul wrote to the Galatians about a similar problem. Some outsiders had come in and convinced them that without the law of Moses they were not true followers of Christ. His entire letter to them is an extended argument about the nature of law and grace, and how conforming to rules in the hope of obtaining righteousness was a deeply flawed approach to the Christian life.

Theology of Legalism

If we condense all that the Bible has to say about legalism, three basic issues come to light.

- Legalism fails to produce the spiritual growth that it claims to.
- Legalism is actually counterproductive to spiritual development.
- Legalism obscures the meaning and function of grace.

First, the law cannot make us into the people we were meant to be, no matter how well we think we can follow it. The law has several functions, but none of them have to do with making us more righteous. Most importantly, the law drives us to Christ, because we discover through the law how terribly defective we are.[43] A secondary function of the law is to provide basic guidelines for some of the weaker souls who would otherwise be completely without a compass.

Perhaps one of the most explicit passages regarding the inability of laws to change us is found in Colossians.

> Since you died with Christ to the elemental spiritual forces of this world, why, as though you still belonged to the world, do you submit to its rules: "Do not handle! Do not taste! Do not touch!"? These rules...are based on merely human commands and teachings. Such regulations indeed have *an appearance of wisdom*...but *they lack any value* in restraining sensual indulgence. (Col.2:20-23 emphasis added)

---

[43] "Through the law comes the knowledge of sin." (Rom.3:20)
"Therefore the law has become our tutor to lead us to Christ." (Gal.3:24)

What Paul is driving at is the idea that living by a set of rules may look like a good way to live, but in the end it does nothing for my inner being. I can make myself go through the motions of forgiving. But I cannot change my heart by an act of the will to forgive someone I do not want to forgive. I may be able to stop myself from acting on my lust, but there is no law that will remove the lust from my body. I can repress it and discipline myself against it, but I cannot eradicate it.

The bottom line is that following laws does not make a person more righteous. "For if a law had been given which was able to impart life, then righteousness would indeed have been based on law" (Gal.3:21 NASB). Paul is telling us that following rules will never make us good. Although we might think that doing the right things makes us an inherently better person, Paul says no. Even if I were to somehow succeed in producing the desired behavior, I still would not have changed my heart.

As it turns out, following laws not only fails to bring purity to our soul, it can actually be harmful in several ways. Often those who are fairly successful at complying with external rules become quite convinced they are more spiritual than those who struggle or are unable to follow the rules. They may even feel contempt for those who behave more worldly or try to shame them into acting like better Christians.

At the other end of the spectrum are those who do poorly with keeping all the rules. They may be hooked on cigarettes or alcohol, or swear too much, or suffer from depression or other emotional problems that Christians are not supposed to have (according to the rules). Since they are unable to change by an act of the will, they are often made to feel like second-class Christians or labeled as backsliders who need to repent. Unfortunately, the self-hate they experience from this condemnation only makes the problem of restoration that much harder. "If I ask God to free me from my problem and nothing happens, what does that say about God's care for me? Or am I too bad in some other area for God to answer my prayer?"

All this leaves little common ground for the self-righteous and the defeated Christian to share. In this way legalism divides the body of Christ and prevents true unity that could aid both groups in their journey toward true spiritual development.

Legalism also obscures our need for grace. When we tell people that the way to grow as a Christian is by trying to conform to a certain lifestyle, we lose sight of both our need for grace and how it actually does for us what the keeping the law cannot.[44] Many Christians have so little experience of transformation that they cannot even conceive of a process by which God changes their heart through His interaction with them. They can only envision trying to do something by direct effort (which is truly nothing more than behavior modification dressed up in religious terminology).

Taken together, the above observations highlight some very important truths. First, we can try as hard as we want to apply all the spiritual principles we find in the Bible, and still barely impact our heart. Second, once we start down the road toward self-effort in our attempts to grow, we create additional barriers to spiritual development that make the Christian life into a burden rather than a joy. Third, our emphasis on obedience through willpower obscures the work of the Holy Spirit and keeps us from learning how to receive from God what we need for life.

God does not want us to try to override sin in our life by continuous effort to do good. He wants to eradicate the power of sin entirely! That is why He made a better way.

The Law has been Superseded by Grace

As commonly understood, grace is what happens when God sets aside the guilty verdict we all deserve and grants us eternal life through the redemptive work of Christ. That is true enough as far as it goes. But grace is much more than a pardon and a gift of life after death. *Grace is everything that God does for us and in us* that we cannot do for ourselves. And that includes changing our heart and mind to be more like Christ. When we set about to conform to the image of Christ by means of our best understanding of the principles of Scripture, we circumvent the means of grace for change.

Of course we try to credit the Holy Spirit with "giving us the strength" to do what we need to do. But in reality we have almost no way of knowing how much is us and how much is God. And when we get tired of the effort, we have trouble explaining why God does not give us what we need to prevent exhaustion. Furthermore, we are at a loss to explain burnout or why

---

[44] "What the law was powerless to do ... God did." (Rom.8:3)

God does not help those who struggle to do the right things, except to blame them for something they must be doing wrong. If they would just care enough and try hard enough then God would help them. But until they do, He will just wait for them to get it right. This is the spiritual equivalent of telling a person in a car wreck that you will not help them unless they first try to get out of the vehicle by themselves.

Pastor burnout is almost legendary. But how is that possible? If the Holy Spirit is supposed to energize our efforts to do good, it seems like pastors should be fairly high on God's list of people who qualify for His help. No one can say they do not try hard enough. It should be clear to us that there is a huge disconnect between what our practical theology tells us and what we actually observe in the real world. All the evidence says that this is not how we should expect God to work in our life.

We need to come to terms with the truth that trying to figure out what Jesus would do in a given situation and then attempting to do it by direct effort is a terribly mistaken goal, completely outside of our ability, and not the means by which we enlist the help of God. That approach to the spiritual life has far more in common with behavior modification than with transformation. Trying to live by rules of right and wrong may look like wisdom, but it does nothing to change the inner life of a person (Col.2:23).

Perhaps the real reason why people attempt this is because grace is simply too hard to believe. If Christians do not understand how God can directly change their heart and mind, and if they have not experienced that kind of change for themselves so they know what it feels like, then there is little else for them to count on besides their own attempts to maintain control over their inner world and try to live the best they can by their own means.

Does Grace Give Us License?

If we stop demanding accountability to a standard of behavior, then what prevents people from doing their own thing and ignoring God's Word entirely? This is a common concern among proponents of obedience-based approaches to Christian living. If we stop insisting that people live up to the standards portrayed in the Bible, then people will go the way of the world and live whatever way they want to.

There are at least two things very wrong with this point of view. First, it presents a false dichotomy by setting up obedience to a standard as the only alternative to giving people a license to sin. Second, this perspective fails to comprehend both the nature of grace and the availability of genuine transformation.

The key component to understanding such faulty thinking is this: If a person's heart is sufficiently changed and barriers are removed so that they truly desire holiness and wish to love their neighbor, then why would they need laws? There is no good reason to tell an adoring husband that it is wrong to cheat on his wife. Such a rule is completely unnecessary and might even be crass and sorely out of place. If we have the means to help a husband develop an adoring heart toward his wife, what need is there for rules about what not to do?

Laws and obedience are not the remedy for sin they claim to be. In fact they are quite powerless to change a heart that is bent toward sin. The real problem is that far too much of the Christian world has no idea how to pursue the kind of heart that has no need of coercion in order to live well. What is needed is to learn how to engage with God in ways that alter our very character.

So is it wrong to have standards?

Even when we know how to live by grace, there are three good reasons for knowing what God's laws say about right and wrong. The first reason is that transformation is a life-long process. Rules help those who have not yet experienced the changes they need in order to live well in some area of life. If my real inclination is to retaliate and escalate whenever anyone crosses me, then my knowledge of the Sermon on the Mount can be a real life-saver that may keep me from acting on my rage. I may not have the heart to love my enemy, but I may be able to stop my arm from swinging in his direction if I know that I am supposed to return good for evil. In that sense, the law has stopped a greater evil, even if it cannot stop the hatred in my heart. Notice, however, that if Jesus could teach my heart to love my enemy, then any statement about returning good for evil would only be a reminder for me.

The second good reason for law is that without it we would have no idea what holiness even looked like. We need a vision of righteousness so that we know what we are aiming for and what it will look like when we get there.

In that sense the law is largely **de**scriptive in nature, even more than it is **pre**scriptive.[45] Moral law instructs us in the ways of God and in how He designed human beings to function best. Violating those laws injures our soul even as it unleashes more problems into the world around us. We need God's law as surely as we need a compass in a foreign countryside.

The third reason, which is related to the second, is that the law illuminates what is wrong in our hearts. When we see a disparity between what holiness looks like and what our inner world is inclined to pursue, we learn of our need for God. Paul said that the law brings us to the end of our self so that we will come to Christ. That does not just apply to the pre-Christian non-believer. As Christians we need the healing work of Christ every day of our life because we have so much in us that needs to be reconciled to God's way. His law shows us where we need more help.

Grace is not the abolition of standards – it is the means by which our heart can be remade so that we live out those standards by nature instead of by edict. If the only reason we do something is because God said so, then what does that say about our basic character? And conversely, if we are able to follow God's way because our character has become inclined that way naturally, then of what use are the rules?

The law may restrain us from more evil, but it does not remove the bent in our heart that wants to go in the opposite direction. Counting on obedience to live the Christian life through willpower bypasses the most life-giving option available to us – transformation of the heart.

With all that said, this talk about grace being superior to obedience still makes a lot of people nervous. Some Christians are so committed to a works-based approach to spiritual growth that they resist messages of grace. When we say that people need grace and love in order to grow rather than accountability groups to keep them obedient, it sounds to them like wishy-washy liberal thinking. Why the disconnect? Most often this position comes from a lack of personal experience of love as a sufficient motivator, or perhaps lack of experience in life-changing relationships. In our world, such a vacuum is common. But it does not mean that we must resort to shame and fear and striving for excellence as primary motivators. It means we need

---

[45] An observation borrowed from Dallas Willard

to encounter God on a deeper level until we experience love deeply enough to change who we are on the inside.

GRACE AS A MEANS FOR CHANGE

Thinking that spiritual growth is something we are meant to achieve by trying hard to do all that God has said to do is probably one of the greatest mistakes that the Christian world has made. The truth is that spiritual growth is something we cannot do at all. Righteousness is not a *standard of behavior to be achieved* by effort but an *attribute of the heart* that is imparted by God.

> This is the covenant I will make with the house of Israel after those days, declares the Lord: I will put my laws in their minds, and write them on their hearts, and I will be their God, and they shall be my people. (Heb.8:10)

Writing God's laws on our heart means that He will change us from the inside out. This is an act of grace because we cannot do that ourselves. Paul is even more explicit:

> For what the law could not do, weak as it was through the flesh, *God did;* sending His own Son. (Rom.8:3 NASB)

Going back to Romans 6, Paul explains that grace changes who we are and changes our relationship to God along with destroying the power of sin in our lives. That is, God does for us what following the law could never accomplish. That's the whole point of the good news. God doesn't want to just rescue us from the *consequences* of sin, He wants to rescue us from the *power* of sin. Over and over we are told that righteousness is something only God can create in us:

> For not knowing about God's **righteousness** and seeking to establish their own, they did not subject themselves to the **righteousness** of God. (Rom.10:3 NASB)

> If a law had been given which was able to impart life, then **righteousness** would indeed have been based on law. (Gal.3:21 NASB)

> But by His doing you are in Christ Jesus, who became to us wisdom from God, and **righteousness** and sanctification, and redemption. (1Cor.1:30 NASB)
>
> Found in Him, not having a **righteousness** of my own derived from the law, but that which is through faith in Christ, the **righteousness** *which comes from God* on the basis of faith. (Phil.3:9 NASB)

Receiving righteousness from God is not merely a judicial act that happens at our conversion; it is a real experience of change that occurs over a lifetime of relationship with God.

Grace Alters our Life

Once we understand that grace is everything God does for us and in us that we cannot do, and begin to get a glimpse of what kinds of things He actually wants to do in us, we see why Paul said that God would do far above all we could ask or think (Eph.3:20).

Christians almost everywhere would agree readily enough that God gives us the new birth and eternal life, ushers us into the kingdom, and glorifies us after we die. But that is just the beginning. God wants to heal the wounds we have suffered from life in this broken world. He wants to transform our mind so that we no longer think according to whatever destructive patterns we may have learned from our family and culture. Our distorted images of who we are, who God is and how life works are all places that need God's redemptive work. Our very character traits, attitudes and dispositions to act in certain ways – the ways in which we get triggered by events and people around us all need to be restored.

Then there are the many causes of sin that still reside within us and the twisted parts of our soul that have grown around those remnants of sin. Add to that the scars left behind by the sins committed against us and the ways we have been malformed by life experience and our attempts to compensate for our brokenness. These are neither benign problems we carry around nor things we can resolve by willpower. We need God to do in us and for us what we cannot do, so that we can become more and more free, and more able to live as He intended us to live.

Grace as a Means for Transformation

Assuming for the sake of argument that God can and will work with us to do that kind of internal renovating, it does not take much to see why as Christians we need far more grace after we have been saved and not less. We are all in desperate need of transformation in areas that we cannot even reach, let alone repair. If God does not do the work, it will not get done. But if that is indeed the case, most of us are faced with the obvious question as to why we do not experience very much of this kind of grace. If it is up to God, then why is He not doing His job? Most of us have even asked Him to change us and wondered why nothing changed. So what is going on?

Trying to Participate with God

Almost all of our difficulties with living the Christian life involve some level of imbalance in our participation with God. In order to make sense of this, it is helpful to begin by looking at the two extremes.

If we assume too much of the responsibility for change, as in the case of legalism, we end up with a religion of self-effort. Forcing myself to go down to a local soup kitchen every Saturday to "serve" even though I hate doing it is an example of trying to be a better person through my own efforts.

On the other hand, if we assume too little responsibility we can become so passive in the process that we end up blaming God for our lack of growth. Suppose I grow tired of my anger problem and ask God to take it away. When I get done praying I do not feel any different, so I just wait a few days to see if anything changes. When nothing happens, I feel let down by God, when in truth I have not entered into the process enough to work with God for the change I need.

Either way, whether you assume too much or too little, the end result is the same – a failure to engage with God. What we need is to find an approach that *balances* our part and God's part in such a way that is both meaningful and fruitful.

Traditionally, participation with God has been defined along the lines of, "If we do as much as we can in our own strength, God will do the rest." Although we have already discussed this error, we need to look at that idea of participation a little closer. First, "doing whatever we can" is not really engaging with God at all. It is engaging in activity or doing something differently. The Holy Spirit is relegated to some behind-the-scenes role of giving us the energy and the will to do something hard. Unfortunately, that does not sound at all like the role of the Spirit as Jesus described it to His disciples in the upper room (Jn.14-17).

Not only that, there is very little evidence that this is even true! As stated previously, if God works in proportion to our effort, then how would you explain burnout? Wouldn't a pastor who works sixty hours a week be more joyful and resilient than when he worked forty hours? If this was really true, couldn't we guarantee almost one hundred percent recovery for addicts by having them go to meetings seven nights a week until God cured them? Do any of us really believe that if we just try hard enough, God will step in and end our bondage to whatever it is we are struggling with?

Anyone who really believes God helps those who try hard enough will likely sooner or later also believe they are complete failures. Given that everyone is shot through with flaws, anyone who has tried unsuccessfully to make some change and is paying attention will conclude one of two things: either they must not have tried hard enough to get God to do His job, or else God is not really interested in helping them, because they tried all they could and He failed to show up.

Does any of this sound like the fruit of the Spirit?

As we think about this, it gets even more confusing. Christians will often say that they do not know how they made it through a difficult time except for God. That may well be true in many instances. But since non-Christians do hard things all the time, even heroic things, to what do we credit *their* ability? If human beings can do some things by nature that seem beyond their ability, how can Christians tell the difference between what is their effort and what is God's?

Almost any way we look at this, we cannot with any integrity claim that God helps those who try hard to do good or try hard to change. Quite honestly, there is no real evidence in Scripture that this is even His job. The only reasonable conclusion is that this is not the kind of participation God wants from us. The bottom line is that this understanding of what it means to participate with God is actually an attempt to give the Holy Spirit credit while at the same time pursuing a legalistic approach to growth!

Grace and Participation

A great analogy for how we need to participate with grace can be seen in the relationship between good parents and a young child. The parents may have all the resources necessary for the child's well-being, but the child needs to work with his or her parents in every way. When hungry, the child has to come to Mom or Dad for food and eat what is set before them. When they scrape their knee, they need to let Dad cleanse and treat the wound. When sick they need take the medicine Mom provides. When they break a toy, they need to bring it to Dad so he can repair it.

There are also hundreds of areas for training that the child does not even know they need, such as how to make friends, how to calm down when they get upset, and how to do what they do not feel like doing. All of these places where the parents are involved are examples of grace in the child's life – things small children cannot do for themselves, but in which they need to cooperate with Mom and Dad in order to receive what they need.

Participating with God means knowing what is our part and what is God's part. If we try to do too much of the work, we fall into a religion of self-effort that will fail to transform our inner life. If we do too little and just wait for God to take over our life and fix everything, we do not learn the tasks necessary to mature spiritually, and again nothing changes. Our real job is to become His apprentices, not so much to *master* the Christian life as to *submit* to it.

But this still begs the question, what does it mean to participate well? What does an apprentice of Jesus actually *do*?

Grace is Not Opposed to Effort[46]

One of the most misunderstood aspects of grace has to do with how human beings are involved in the process. Does it cease to be grace if there is something we must do? A lot of Christians think that as soon as we contribute something to what God is doing, as soon as we are responsible for some aspect of an event, then the whole thing turns into "works" and ceases to be a matter of grace.

But this is simply not the case at all. We experience grace all the time while being heavily involved. Nearly everything we do involves far more

---

[46] Willard, *The Renovation of the Heart*

elements over which we have no control than things we can control. When a farmer plants a field and reaps a great harvest, he is the recipient of good weather and relatively few pests. When we take medicine to get well, we are actively involved in the process of healing, but our actions do not heal us. The drugs and our immune system do most of the work. In the same way, grace and effort can join together to bring about life.

If you are hopelessly lost in a forest, and a rescue team finds you and helps you get back to civilization, you have become a recipient of grace. Whatever effort you expend as you cooperate with them in the process of rescue does nothing to diminish the fact that they did something for you which you could not do for yourself.

The key is this – grace is not canceled by effort. But it can be lost when we try to do God's part or try to gain His involvement as a reward for our effort. For example, when we act as if we love someone we really cannot stand and say we are loving our neighbor, we frustrate grace. Or when we say the words, "I forgive you" without ever having had a change of heart, perhaps because we do not want to think of our self as unforgiving, we are not participating with God so He can work on our heart.

But if we would go to God and tell Him why we cannot stand our neighbor or why we still harbor a grudge against the person who hurt us, and then begin to wrestle with Him for what we need in order to change our heart, we become open to a work of grace that can make a real difference in who we are. To be clear, I am not talking about praying for a change of heart and then waiting to see if anything happens. That's *too little* participation. We need to learn from the psalmists who poured out their heart to God in their distress and walked through the issues with God until they were able to see what God saw and receive from Him what they could not do for themselves. That is participating in grace. While it is not within my ability to make myself have a forgiving heart, it *is* within my ability to approach God and begin a dialogue with Him that will give me what I need and change my attitude toward a person I need to forgive.

Grace requires that we become actively engaged with God, just as the disciples were actively engaged with Jesus. Most of the remainder of this book will discuss what that participation looks like and how we are to be involved with God for spiritual growth and recovery. Our primary goal at

Grace as a Means for Transformation

this point has been to emphasize the need for a shift from self-effort to receiving life from God, as well as a better understanding of what it means to participate with Him in that process.

Grace Creates Joy

Joy is our natural response to encounters with *good*, expressions of *life*, and experiences of *love*. We encounter *good* in many ways, sometimes being surprised by it in all its glory (like the innocence of a small child catching us off guard), sometimes as it emerges over time (like a bumper crop on a family farm), and especially when we see good overcome evil (as in when we are set free from old regrets). Expressions of *life* that create joy can be anything from the birth of a baby, to noticing the wonder of nature, to watching your child choose well when faced with difficult decisions. And experiences of *love* can be as simple as someone being glad to be with us or as incredible as witnessing a person extend themselves for the good of another.

Since grace is goodness given to us that we would not otherwise have, it quite naturally creates joy. When God touches an old wound and brings healing into our heart and mind, we rejoice with a gratefulness we did not expect. When He births new life in us we did not even know we needed, we cannot help but experience His joy. And when we feel Him envelope us and hold us in His heart, His love flows into the deepest recesses of our soul and bursts forth like an artesian well of water springing up. Grace begets joy.

Joy, in turn, feeds our soul even more! We now know (scientifically) that joy actually creates new growth in the brain, giving us greater resilience, endurance, and capacity for the challenges of life. But ancient writers knew that a long time ago: "The joy of the Lord is your strength" (Neh.8:10).

Greek philosophers knew this as well, and even the Greek language of the New Testament brings these two ideas together. Grace (*charis*) and Joy (*chara*) belong to the same root word, and not merely linguistically. The Greeks knew that any form of kindness toward another person would naturally produce joy in the one who received that grace.

That is why Jesus could say that the words He spoke to His disciples would be the cause for their joy – that same joy He lived with all time. God wants us to live in grace, because He wants His children to be filled with joy!

CONCLUSIONS

Why do Christians need to know more about grace?

- A proper understanding of grace is necessary for a working relationship with God, and any hope of outgrowing our tendencies toward sin.

- We need grace to live. It is as vital to life as forgiveness is to a relationship.

- Without grace our participation will be skewed toward either self-effort or passivity.

- A legalistic approach to the Christian life makes it hard to engage with God in life-giving ways.

- If we are too ashamed to approach God or too afraid of His disapproval, we will not be able to take our stuff to Him, we will not allow Him to walk through our life and expose our need, and we will not be able to surrender in faith and trust.

- If the only reason a person does something is out of obedience, then by definition they are *not* doing it by nature. They still need change that can only come by grace.

Christians generally have no trouble believing that engaging with God can result in the new birth. Why should it be so much of a leap to see that engaging with God causes spiritual growth as well? Attempting to achieve an ideal standard by direct effort (even with help from Holy Spirit) is rooted in law and will not result in much growth. Engaging directly with the Holy Spirit allows God to change us from the inside out. And that makes everything else possible.

RESOURCES FOR FURTHER STUDY

Steve McVey, *Grace Walk: What You've Always Wanted in the Christian Life* (Eugene, OR: Harvest House Publishers) 2005

Chapter 6
Engaging With God for Change
Our Manner of Engagement

Take my yoke upon you, and learn from me. (Mt.11:29)

We are always being formed spiritually, all the time, by everything we do, everything we think and feel, and everything we experience. There is no escaping spiritual formation – whether we want it or not.

The whole point of *Christian* spiritual formation is for us to become aware of how this happens, and to learn how to steer our course in ways that cause us to be formed into an ever-growing image of Christ. Seeing this clearly is a crucial matter, because even though we are being formed all the time and our choices in this process are of utmost importance, the means by which we participate are not necessarily obvious. To draw from our sailing analogy, we cannot make the boat move much by direct effort; but we *can* learn how to align the sail so that we get somewhere we actually want to go, instead of being left to drift or driven by the prevailing current.

Learning how to have conversations with God and to appreciate His goodness and presence with us are two of the most important elements of aligning ourselves toward spiritual growth. That is why we have spent so much time laying the foundations for this kind of life. Spending time with God in spiritual reflection, appreciation, and listening provide us with some of the most important course corrections we need in order to live in the kingdom as God intended.

We now turn our attention to an entire array of spiritual practices that we can employ to deepen our connection with God, improve our focus, and strengthen our heart and mind for this journey. Each of the next three chapters will deal with very practical issues regarding how we can become more intentional about how we are being formed. In this chapter we will look closely at what it means to balance our part and God's part as we make use of spiritual practices for growth. In particular, we are going to examine the factors that so often cause spiritual practices to dry up and become lifeless rituals instead of life-giving experiences.

Nearly everyone who has attempted to set aside a devotional time has run into a brick wall at some point and given up the practice because it turned into drudgery. Once that happens, we tend to question the value of such practices or limit ourselves to those moments when we feel inclined to open the Bible. Unless we understand what makes the difference between a practice that is life-giving and one that is empty, we will not be able to make good use of them to form our mind and heart.

In Chapter 7 we will broaden our understanding of what we can expect when we use spiritual practices to engage with God. The more we know about how God can reveal Himself to us, the more we will be able to anticipate His love and presence with us. Expecting good things from God also births more faith in us for what God will do with us, and helps us to see with the eyes of our heart what He is up to.

Of course, none of this learning happens in a straight line. Our journey toward God and our attempts to take part in His grace toward us are filled with detours and side roads. So in Chapter 8 we will talk about some of the most common barriers we can encounter when engaging with God. As in everything else about spiritual formation, the barriers we encounter are not obstacles to be overrun by sheer willpower, but issues of our heart that need God's attention. Learning how God works with us to remove our barriers is an important part of this whole process.

Before moving on to the final section of the book on healing and growing, we will take time out to discuss a number of specific spiritual practices in the **Interlude: Practices for Christian Formation**. With each practice we will offer a number of fresh perspectives to help rescue them from whatever old images we may have concerning them that cause us to avoid them or discount their value. Our hope is that they will become so inviting and functional that Christians everywhere will begin to make use of them to be more intentional about their walk with God.

Very briefly, the spiritual practices we will be discussing are outlined in the list below. To learn more about how to make use of these practices, please refer to the Interlude.

Making Space to Engage With God

- Rest and Quiet
- Private Worship
- Spiritual Reflection
- Abstaining or Extending
- Confession
- Fasting
- Listening to the Word
- Dialogue with God
- Inner Healing Prayer
- Telling Our Stories
- Service to Others
- Recovery Support
- Encouragement
- Forgiveness
- Intercession
- Repentance

For what it is worth, John Ortberg once responded to a book on spiritual practices with, "Great! Here are twenty more things I'm supposed to be doing that I'm not!" Please relax. We are not trying to add another list of things for you to do. The reason there are lots of ways listed in the above chart is that each one offers different possibilities for spiritual awareness and discovery. But they should not be viewed as a to-do list. Rather, they represent a rich array of possibilities for change and growth. With help from the Holy Spirit, we can be led to one practice or another as needed. We do not have to do them all or worry too much about which ones we have not tried. It may take a life-time to experience even a portion of them to any extent. So do not let the number of choices overwhelm you. For now, just keep them in mind as we describe how life-giving they can become for us.

CONNECTING WITH GOD

As discussed in previous chapters, spiritual growth is utterly dependent upon the quality of our connection to God. I almost hesitate to use the phrase "relationship to God" because it has become so trite and meaningless. Nearly all Christians claim to have a personal relationship with God even when they may have no real awareness of Him at all for years at a time. That said, we need to redeem the phrase so it refers to an authentic relationship that is known and experienced, rather than a euphemism about our conversion.

Recall from Chapter 2 that relationship is the organizing principle of life. By design, everything important about life is rooted in relationship with God and others. That is why the two greatest commandments are to Love

God and Love One Another. As we look at the gospel, we see over and over the primacy of relationship. "For God so loved the world" is the cornerstone of the Good News. Not surprisingly then, relationship with God is the key factor in our spiritual renewal. He is our source of life. Only by connecting significantly with Him can we hope to have a relationship that is vibrant enough to change us from the inside out.

The bottom line is that we need to engage with God in order to grow our relationship with Him, which in turn will transform our life. Other things you may have been told you need for growth as a Christian all have their place. But beyond a certain point, the only way we will continue to grow is if we learn how to connect with God. If connecting with God is the key to spiritual development, then the next obvious question is, "How can we connect with God in ways that make a difference?" That is where spiritual practices come in. But again, we need to be careful, because the life we can gain from them is entirely dependent on how we approach them.

Balancing Our Part and God's Part

In terms of making the difference between life-less and life-giving practices, the single most important factor is how we balance our part and God's part. We addressed this issue when talking about grace as a force in our life. If we take on too much of the task of spiritual formation, the focus swings to self-effort and attempting to achieve growth in our own strength. If we are too passive, then we fail to participate sufficiently with what God wants to do in us. Either way, the imbalance leaves us disappointed with the results.

The chapters on hearing God helped to flesh out this issue of balance experientially. As we learn how to listen to the Spirit of God, we are nourished spiritually and are able to grow in the things He reveals to us. If we try to figure out the Christian life on our own, we end up with a cognitive religion that resembles Christianity in many ways, but leaves us spiritually weak and undeveloped. On the other hand, if we simply wait for revelation to strike us out of the blue, we usually receive very little and end up feeling as if God has abandoned us. But when we learn to actively reflect on the things of God and engage in conversation with Him, we receive what we need for life.

Learning this balance is so crucial to fruitful engagement that we want to state it as straight-forward as possible. Simply put, *spiritual disciplines do not change us, in and of themselves. They only make a space for encountering God, and that is what changes us.*[47]

Do not underestimate this distinction. I am not a better Christian for having fasted for a week or for going on a pilgrimage or spending an hour a day in my prayer closet. My growth is a gift from God. If I make a space for Him and engage with Him and allow Him to do in me what only He can do, my soul will be satisfied, my wounds will heal one by one, and my heart will desire more and more the things of God. Spiritual practices offer us a number of time-tested ways to make a space for God to work in us. But we must bear in mind that this is only true if we keep them in perspective and do not expect them to change us merely because we do them. The truth is that we can easily go through the motions of a spiritual practice without engaging with God at all. That does not make us bad; it may simply mean we are having trouble connecting with Him that day, or we have not yet learned how to engage with Him. Nevertheless, we experience the practice as a dry and lifeless exercise.

When I participate in a spiritual practice well, I align myself fully with the truth that only God can change and grow my spiritual life. In deliberately making space for Him to work in my heart, I open myself up to His wisdom and healing, whether by what He shows me, what He says to me, or how He loves me and ministers to my spiritual needs. My aim is not to practice a discipline, but to engage with God. The discipline is only a container for the experience.

Engaging with God is life-changing in and of itself. That is why I want to be with Him, know Him, and experience His work in my heart and mind. I do not try to make spiritual exercises an end in themselves, because they do not have life and do not give life.

Misuse of Spiritual Practices Will Lead to Their Death

Approaching a discipline with the intent of earning merit or being a better Christian because of my practice is a sure way to destroy their value and create disillusionment. As already stated, most Christians have had the

---

[47] Dallas Willard, *Spirit of the Disciplines*

experience of a devotional time that feels like treading water at best or fingernails on a chalkboard at worst. The reason we feel like it is a waste of time is because we are trying to work something out in our own power, using our reason and best judgment to try to pull something out of the text and apply it. Unless you are the kind of person who simply enjoys study, or unless the lesson is particularly relevant and helpful, you are likely to feel bored or even burdened by the whole process. Any insights gained from the experience may leave you feeling shame for not doing well enough or weighed down from new demands you had not previously seen so clearly.

Furthermore, if we persist in this approach for very long, we start to develop an additional layer of resistance to what we really need. For example, if we read our Bible month after month expecting that effort to change us, we can become deeply discouraged by our lack of progress. Consequently, we may swear off Bible reading for a while because, "it was feeling too legalistic." Then we have an additional layer of disbelief to overcome before we can be open to the Spirit ministering to us from the Word.

Fasting provides another good example. Fasting in itself does not make you more spiritual. What it does do is set up ways to connect with God that are far more vibrant than when you are completely satisfied by natural means. Fasting also holds your attention differently. You are far more aware of being involved in something important as you go about your daily tasks. God's presence does not so easily slip away. If we make use of this heightened awareness, then fasting offers us a valuable context for engaging with God that we would not have otherwise. But the practice of going without food itself has relatively little spiritual value (although it may help you learn how to quiet some of your cravings).

In similar fashion, you are not more spiritual if you practice solitude. But solitude will strip you of most of the things you rely on for identity and purpose, so that issues can rise to the surface you are not normally aware of. If you use those awarenesses for conversations with God, you can be given much grace that you did not know you even needed before the experience. Yet it was not the solitude that made you more whole. Solitude provided the means for meaningful dialogue with God.

When people expect these practices to do more than they are capable of doing, the inevitable disillusionment that comes from that faulty expectation can lead them to faulty conclusions:

- There is something wrong with me and that is why I do not grow.
- Spiritual disciplines are fundamentally hard.
- Transformation is really rare after all.

Understanding that spiritual practices provide a context for growth rather than the growth itself, is a major step toward finding a balanced approach.

Indirect Means For Growth

Another way to think of the issue of balance is to view our involvement in spiritual growth as a very indirect process, much like that of a farmer. When a farmer decides that he wants to produce corn or apples or anything else, he has to commit himself to a process that is much broader than anything he can do by direct effort. There is no way to assemble a pile of amino acids and go about arranging the molecules and smashing them together to make apples. He knows instead that he must plant some trees, water them, fertilize them, and protect them from bugs. In the end, apples will "happen" without any direct effort. There are forces at work involving air, sunlight, photosynthesis, DNA and a whole host of other things that cause fruit to grow, over which he has no control. All he can do is participate with nature and provide a context that fosters that process.

Similarly, we do not "make" spiritual growth happen. A regular quiet time is not any more "spiritual" than no quiet time. Practicing solitude is not by itself a fruit of the Spirit. But these practices can foster fruit if we use them as a means to engage with God. Spiritual disciplines create a space to meet with God. His part is causing fruit to grow. There are things for us to do, but we do not change our character by direct effort. We engage with God and He heals and grows our character.

Now some people may object that planting, watering and trimming sound like a lot of work, perhaps a bit like "rowing." After all this talk about relating instead of doing, the conversation has suddenly turned to doing things. The truth is, sailing also takes work. But it is a very different kind of work than rowing. Spiritual practices require some effort, but nothing compared to the work of trying to shape your own heart through willpower, which is an impossible task. In order for an apprentice to learn what his Mentor knows, the student must become actively involved in the process of learning with their entire heart, soul, mind, and body. That is the nature of experiential learning. So yes, there is effort involved, but it is very different from the old paradigm of trying to achieve spiritual growth by direct effort.

The point here is to emphasize how little we have to do with the actual change. All we can do is learn how to participate with God in the process. Spiritual practices make a space for us to align our "sail" so we can be moved to places we could never get to on our own.

Practicing vs. Mastering

On a related note, it is important to understand that we are not trying to master spiritual practices. That would take us back to a mindset of achievement. Instead of mastering the disciplines, we submit to them and remain learners indefinitely, always apprentices of the Master. We learn by our experience to trust more and submit more readily to the process with less hesitation and less anxiety. With the healing that we gain from our life with God, we have fewer blocks between us and the Spirit. We will also learn how to vary our practices to provide the context we need on any given day. But in all these areas we remain the learner and greet each new day as a new opportunity to be refreshed in God's presence.

That said, many spiritual practices do have a learning curve associated with them. For example, if you plan to fast for a long period of time, there are certain things you must know about your body and how to begin and end a fast safely. There are also some things you can do to curb your cravings during the first few days of an extended fast. But learning these steps does not mean you have "mastered" the discipline. If you are submitting to the work of God in the fast, He will continue to meet with you and minister to you in ways that you cannot manage on your own. That is the point of fasting in the first place, and that is something you can never master.

Taught by God

The Holy Spirit loves to teach and train His apprentices. But keep in mind He does not teach in the conventional sense. His purpose is not to fill our head with information. Rather, He engages with us personally and experientially. He teaches in a manner that penetrates our heart and alters our perception of reality. As we begin to see things from His perspective, it does not merely enrich our knowledge about God, it changes how we feel and react to life.

One of the reasons spiritual practices generally include our whole body is that spiritual learning is experiential in nature, not just an accumulation of information. Reading about the violin may give you good background for becoming a musician. But the real learning happens as you take the bow and pull it across the strings. So it is as we are taught by God. He takes very common elements of life – accidents, illnesses, successes, failures, encounters with others, even memories – and uses them to teach us, revealing to us what we usually miss in our own interpretations of events. In the process He may speak words of truth, reveal the heart of God, reveal things in our own heart we did not see before, and reinterpret life events for us.

One of the values of spiritual practices is that they provide a context within which our internalized values from life experience can be brought to the surface and examined in the light. By their very nature these practices involve our entire self in the process, and thus allow us to learn at a level deeper than what we can achieve through a purely academic mindset.

Our main job in all of this is to remain teachable. As apprentices of kingdom life, we are always learning, always curious, listening, observing, asking questions – allowing the Spirit of God to open our eyes to things we have not known. This is another reason why it makes little sense to attempt mastery in any of this. God's ways are infinitely higher than our ways, and His thoughts higher than ours (Isa.55:9). That means no matter what we are dealing with, we are always missing something; there is always more of God's way to internalize than what we had before. So bringing our preconceived ideas about life to God for Him to reshape and refine is an important part of renewing our mind.

A Model for Spiritual Practices

Now that we have laid a balanced foundation for spiritual practices as a way of creating a context for engaging with God, let us consider some of the major types of practices that Christians have found helpful. While much has been written about spiritual disciplines (or practices), especially in the last few decades, the model laid out in this book provides a fresh way of approaching these practices and understanding how they impact our soul. We hope you find this helpful.

	In Solitude	In Community
Appreciating God's Presence	Relational Quiet Private Worship Spiritual Reflection Abstaining or Extending Fasting Confession	Appreciation Stories Service to Others Recovery Support
Interacting Directly	Listen to the Word Dialog with God Repentance Healing Prayer	Encouragement Healing Prayer Forgiveness Intercession

Practices of Appreciation and Interacting Directly

The two rows of practices in the above chart make a distinction between those that involve our ability to hear God (Interaction) and those we can actively participate in whether or not we can perceive God's voice (Appreciation). Among other things, this separation offers a lot of hope to those who are still having difficulty with hearing God. There are many ways to spend time with God that do not require experience in conversational prayer. Exactly how and why these practices are helpful will be left to the Interlude following Chapter 8. For now, we will simply outline a few major characteristics of each type of practice.

In short, appreciating the presence of God allows us to exercise and strengthen our soul through fairly simple, highly accessible activities that involve our entire mind and body. For example, one that has already been highlighted several times is spiritual reflection. By turning our thoughts toward the goodness of God or some other restorative understanding of the kingdom, we are able to bring our whole body into alignment with who God is and who we are in His presence and in relation to Him. This alone is worth the time it takes, because everything we do helps to shape our entire being. Over a period of days or weeks, persistently acting on these practices can have a profound impact on how we view life and God and our own sense of self.

In contrast, when we interact directly with God we open ourselves up to even more light, life, love, and truth that can transform our heart and mind in ways we never thought possible. Hearing God speak directly into our heart brings about healing, shows us more of life as God Himself sees it, and gives us glimpses of the heart of God that can liberate us like nothing else.

Personal Practices and Communal Practices

Going back to our list of spiritual practices, the columns in the grid cut across the list in a different manner, separating those practices that are primarily done in solitude from those done with others in community. Again, both are important.

From this vantage point, the use of solitude for spiritual growth takes on a very broad range of meanings. Solitude is not just a practice in itself, though it does have value as such. It is actually a context for many of the other spiritual practices. Jesus often went off by Himself to be with His Father, and He encouraged His followers to do the same. The time we spend in solitude can run anywhere from a few minutes to several days, depending on our purposes and what we need. And within that context we may fast, pray, seek God's voice, spend time basking in His presence, reflecting, and so on as we feel led.

We also need to engage in deliberate practices with our larger community of believers. Evidence to this need abounds in the New Testament. But this goes far beyond sitting in a pew listening to a speaker or singing a song next to our neighbor. It involves sharing stories of our journey with one another, listening to each other's needs, encouraging one another, and many other interactive, relational practices.

Integrating Our Practices

As we integrate these practices into our daily existence, we become more and more formed by them rather than formed by the pressures of the fallen world around us. Even more, in moving from one quadrant to another, oscillating between solitude and community, between appreciation and directly engaging, we create a multifaceted and balanced context for our relationship with God that touches nearly every aspect of our spiritual life.

Please note too that this model is not completely rigid. For example, listening to the Word is not limited to a context of solitude. In fact, a wonderfully life-giving practice is to listen to the word in a group setting. After choosing a short passage, everyone spends about twenty minutes reflecting and listening for any insights from the Holy Spirit. Then for the next hour they share their thoughts with each other regarding what they are getting from their reflections and conversations with God. The end result can build amazing bonds between members of the group, strengthen each person's walk with God, and help everyone involved see how God can speak in a variety of ways that are suited to the distinct needs of each person at that moment in time.

Conclusions

Spiritual practices have been used for centuries as a means of training our soul to seek God in all things and to make a space for engaging with God. As such, they are invaluable in helping us grow up into the character of Christ.

But they have also been terribly misused and misunderstood. The one thing we must be very clear about is that spiritual disciplines do not change us merely by "doing" them. Fasting does not make us holy. Nor are we better Christians because we read a chapter a day from the Bible. The primary value of a spiritual practice is that it provides a way in which we can deliberately make space for engaging with God, and to do so in ways that predictably alter the context of our life.

Please take a few minutes to read about the practice of spiritual reflection in the Interlude section, paying close attention to the balance between our effort and our expectations of God's involvement.

Resources for Further Study

Dallas Willard, *The Spirit of the Disciplines: Understanding How God Changes Lives* (New York: HarperOne) 1990

Chapter 7
Engaging With God for Change
What to Expect When Engaging With God

> And hope does not disappoint, because the love of God has been poured out within our hearts through the Holy Spirit who was given to us. (Rom.5:5 NASB)

What can we expect to happen when we engage with God? What sort of things will we hear and see? How will we be impacted?

We will explore a number of answers to this question, but above all, we must learn to *expect the unexpected*. Jesus constantly surprised the people around Him in ways they least expected, like touching lepers, recruiting a tax collector, forgiving an adulteress, and challenging the religious establishment. God is a God of infinite possibilities, and we should be careful not to limit our expectations. He will act in unforeseen ways, often because that is the best way to get our attention and help us see his perspectives.

That said, there are a few things we *can* expect when engaging with God. For one thing, we can be sure of uncovering whatever expectations we already have that miss the mark. When He shows up and ambushes us with love, we may realize that we never expected to feel cared for that much. When He heals us of a long-standing wound, we realize that we never expected to be free of that pain. In the process we learn to hold our preconceived notions more loosely and stay more open to God's innovative ways of restoring our soul.

Expect to Be Led in Unexpected Directions

Part of the work of discernment is deciding what our conversation will be about, and changing direction when it seems appropriate to do so. We may begin our devotional time with a verse about God's provision for us, which might stir up feelings of doubt, leading us to a conversation about trust, and finally ending with God healing us of some long-ago forgotten experience of broken trust. We need to be open to being led along the way to whatever is important in that moment, whatever our heart may be ready for whether or not we know what that is, and whatever God wants to do with us.

When it comes to inner healing prayer, unexpected direction is almost the norm. Suppose we are talking to God about our overreaction to a comment made by a co-worker or a difficult interaction with a son or daughter or parent. If we ask God what is behind the intensity of our reaction, He may bring to mind a painful experience from many years earlier that left us with the same feeling we have now, and help us resolve that issue first. Such transitions are common in our conversations with God, because only He knows what we need.

In addition, remember that we are dealing with a God whose ways are far above our own. He has within Himself the ability to bring life out of death, to create something out of nothing, and to set bushes on fire without consuming them. This is the God we are interacting with in order to learn who we are and how to live. It would be surprising if such encounters did *not* go to unexpected places. Our job as an apprentice is to learn how to notice and to pay attention to the longings of our spirit or the resistance of our flesh, along with the urgings of the Spirit of God. In doing so we will discover new things we did not know before and rediscover old things in new ways that we had not seen or experienced before.

Expect Reactions, Both Positive and Negative

Another thing we can expect is to have a variety of positive and negative reactions as we listen and reflect. One time I was following an exercise where we were to take off our shoes and approach God as Moses did on holy ground. I was surprised to discover that I had very strong reservations about coming in contact with any "holy ground"! At first I thought it might be because I was afraid of contaminating the ground. Then I was afraid that the "holiness" might creep up my body and take me over. At last I hit upon the real issue, which was the idea that it was simply unacceptable to me for holy and unholy things to touch each other. They must be kept separate. Of course that is not really true, as we can see in the life of Jesus, who touched many "unclean" people. Noticing my reaction and digging around a bit provided me with a whole host of things to talk to God about that I had not even been aware of before I began the exercise.

The key here is to pay attention to what is going on inside our mind and body as we approach God to listen and reflect on spiritual things. This is learning by experience rather than by a purely academic, cognitive process. Experiential learning is very dynamic, requiring persistence, discernment, and continual submission to God and His training. Everything we encounter needs to be brought back to God for His help in understanding and internalizing what we need.

For example, if I read something about service to others and realize that I dread the very thought of serving, I have several options. I could try to slug it out and perform some service out of duty. I could try to figure out what is bugging me about service. I could even rationalize that obedience without the heart is too legalistic and ought to be avoided, and then drop the issue. But what I really need is to bring this to God and say, "Look, Papa! Another piece of me that is broken and not working the way you meant it to. Can you help me? What can you show me or tell me that will get into my heart deep enough to change how I see this kind of service?"

We do not have to try to impress God with our resolve or our ability to do things we do not want to do. We do not have to earn His approval or overcome obstacles on our own. Instead, our task is to take everything to Him for understanding, for the insight that we lack, for discernment on how to proceed, and for a change of heart that we need.

On the other hand, suppose I decide to try not saying anything bad about anyone for an entire week, no matter what, and get surprised by the result. I might actually feel a lot lighter and discover that my normal constant flow of disparaging remarks about people is actually harming me! In this case I can rejoice in my new found freedom and perhaps even commit to making this a life-style and not just a temporary experiment.

If we are fully engaged in a spiritual practice, we can be sure we will have some emotional responses. And all of our reactions are important to our learning, because we cannot renew the things we dismiss without thinking. Noticing our reactions and taking them to God will go a long way to growing our heart and mind.

Expect Internal Resistance

Another thing we can expect to encounter as we engage with God for change is our own internal resistance. In spite of all the good that God wants for us, no matter how many times we hear that God loves us, there are parts of our soul that seem to resist the next step of grace, whatever it might be. Again, we should not be surprised by this for a number of reasons.

Most of our ingrained patterns were established for a purpose. Take, for example, the issue of generosity. An adult who is trying to learn how to loosen their grip on possessions may discover something inside them that wants to hold on, perhaps selfishly, to whatever they have, and that they are unable to give much without feeling robbed. Such feelings can come from a great many sources:

- Children raised in poverty might associate survival with possessions.
- Children raised in affluence might draw a sense of identity from ownership.
- If asking for things was often met with scorn, children can grow up believing that it is shameful to ask for anything, and that they should be offended when someone asks something of them.
- In a culture where earning one's way is highly prized, possessions may be viewed as an icon of accomplishment.

We can see there are many ways to arrive at internal values that are at odds with the kingdom, values that might even have made sense to us at the time we adopted them. And when we engage with God to renew our mind, we can expect these old values to resist what God is revealing to us.

Since this world presents us with thousands of such messages over the course of a lifetime, and since we also arrive at these kinds of faulty conclusions on our own from personal experience, we can find ourselves feeling resistance to things we know are good and true, without really understanding why we resist, or how to change our heart so that we can stop resisting.

As we will see in Chapter 9, it is a major mistake to assume this resistance is something entrenched in the old nature for which there is no remedy. Although many of us have been taught this perspective, the truth is that such a theology leads directly to bondage. It tells us our inclinations cannot be changed, and worse, that we must fight those inclinations with willpower and self-effort.

As to how they can be changed, we will leave that for later. The short answer to this question, though, is that we need to take everything back to God. So when He asks us to be more generous and we feel an inner twinge of anxiety, we need to dump that out on the table and honestly confess to God how we would rather not give up too much. Then we can ask Him what we need in order for our heart to change, and begin a conversation with Him about our inner resistance. He can help us see the roots of our inner struggle, and reach into our mind and provide the words and images we need in order to replace the faulty beliefs we hold about being generous. In that way He does what we cannot, and we will watch our resistance recede without even trying.

Then there is the resistance we have toward God Himself or what He wants to do in our heart. God may want to work with us in regard to forgiving someone who has wounded us deeply, and we may not want to go there. "No, God, I really do prefer to hold that person hostage. They deserve to be hated, I'm not letting them off the hook, and I'm not giving them another chance to hurt me."

Once again, the answer is not to "forgive in obedience" as some would say, but rather to engage with God regarding the firm resolution we have come to about not doing this work. We can begin with something as simple as, "God, I don't even want to have this conversation. What do I need from you in order to be willing to talk to you about this issue any further?" Once we have become convinced that we need to pursue forgiveness, we can then move on to questions like, "How do I stop resenting what they did to me?" and "How do you see this person, God? How do you even stand them?"

Learning to slow down the process and take smaller steps like this will lead us to much greater healing, revealing more of our heart and addressing more of the stuff in us that keeps us from growing and living more as we were designed.

There are other forms of resistance as well, such as being too afraid of God to approach Him or feeling too ashamed to be in His presence. These will be covered in the next chapter dealing with barriers to engaging with God. The key things to remember about inner resistance are:

- Resistance is to be expected, due to the extent of our malformation.
- Resistance is a God-sized problem, not something for us to work out on our own before coming to God.
- Do not suppress resistance, rather expose it and take it to God.

As we have said many times, always take everything back to God. Internal resistance is just another sign of how deeply we need Him in order to heal and grow.

Expect a Variety of Communication Styles

Reading through the Bible, one thing that becomes obvious is that God has used a variety of ways to reveal truth and reveal Himself to His children. For example, we have stories of those who have gone before us, as well as prophetic voices that call us back to dependence and trust, and poets who express the deepest pains and longings of our heart. Perhaps one reason God chose so many ways to talk to us is that the life He wants us to know is very hard to reduce to the written page. So when it comes to engaging with God within the context of various spiritual practices, there is every reason to expect Him to communicate in a variety of ways.

Sometimes He uses word pictures, as when Jesus spoke in parables. Images may come to our mind, sometimes as frozen snapshots of life that capture meaning for us, or as short video clips that demonstrate something we need to know, or as icons that encapsulate a dozen thoughts in a single mental picture. Often these images are even metaphorical, like "trees planted by streams of water" (Ps.1:3) or free wine and milk (Isa.55:1-3).

Of course, much of our reflection and conversation will take shape in words. But there can be a variety of styles here as well. Sometimes our reflections are mostly just that, our musings of spiritual things, thoughts we turn over in our mind and look at from multiple directions. Other times it can feel like we are being taught almost word for word from the Spirit. We may even get the sense that we ourselves are teaching on a matter we have never really studied. Occasionally, we may experience times of rapid question and answer, back and forth communication with God.

The point is to follow His lead. Be sensitive both to what you need and what God is leading you to. Write out prayers, thoughts, questions, and impressions as they come to mind. Listen. Respond. Reflect. And do not expect to find any "right" way for the conversation to take shape.

Expect to Encounter Truth

Jesus is the Way, Truth, and Life (Jn.14:6). Engaging with Him necessarily means encountering truth. Although this will be covered in depth in Chapter 9, it warrants some mention here as something for which we can have high expectations.

In many Christian circles, truth gets reduced to the set of propositions we hold and the right answers to some important questions. But the truth we need for life goes far beyond that. Truth is everything there is to be known about how things really are, both seen and unseen, both temporal and eternal, both as they were intended to be and how they are now distorted. One of the most important gifts we can receive is the understanding that the truth we need in order to live well is far beyond what we could ever figure out by our own study and reasoning of Scripture. We desperately need the Holy Spirit to interpret life for us, to unravel the mysteries of our own heart, and to reveal the mysteries of God's heart to us.

Among other things, this means the truth we encounter as we engage with God will be extremely personally relevant. We have all internalized hundreds of lies about God, about our self, and about life, many of which we are only partially aware of at best. Deep inside each of us is a vast reservoir of distorted perceptions and interpretations that drive our life in ways we rarely notice. In order to renew our mind, these lies need to be exposed and replaced with deep abiding truth that only God can give us.

Many examples of this process can be seen in the Gospels. Earlier we mentioned the time when the disciples were arguing about who would be the greatest in the kingdom. Jesus could have responded with a simple rule about not arguing and told them to stop. Instead, He exposed their underlying mistaken notions about the nature of greatness and power. He knew that if they really grasped what true greatness looked like, they would have no need to argue or compete over being in first place. It would be like arguing about which one of you should own the restaurant when your job is to prepare and serve the food. The argument becomes irrelevant, even counter-productive.

Truth can take a variety of forms, as God reveals to us the things we need. Sometimes it is primarily a matter of exposing our mistaken beliefs. When I was expecting our very first shipment of newly printed books, I spent much of the day stewing about whether they would come at all, whether they would get shipped to the right place, what shape they would be in when they arrived, and so on. When I talked to God about my distress, I came face to face with the startling fact that I still firmly believed in Murphy's Law, that anything which can go wrong will go wrong. God used that experience to bring this deep-seated belief to the surface where I could see it for what it was, and so we could talk about its origins and I could seek our God's view of how my life really worked.

In addition to exposing our faulty beliefs, we can expect God to reveal His point of view on things that matter in our life. Having spent over twenty years trying to convince a certain agnostic of God's existence and his need for Christ, giving him all of the best arguments I could muster and all the best books on apologetics I could find, I finally gave up and asked God what else I could possibly tell him. God said, "Tell him your story." I objected, "That won't do any good. This guy is really smart and rational and needs hard data. My story about what you have done in my life is way too subjective. He will just laugh." But God said, "Tell him your story." I finally relented and told this guy the story of how God has been working in my life for the last fifty years. When I finished, he was astonished. Within a few short years he became a professing Christian.

See, my best wisdom was no match for what was actually needed. Only God knew how to proceed. We need to learn how to seek God's point of view in all of life, because we are simply not clever enough to figure it out.

Sometimes encountering truth means that we see new significance in things we thought we already understood. This is a common theme in the biographies of famous Christian leaders. One day they are deeply discouraged, seeking God for something that will set them free to move on in their spiritual life. Then they read a verse that says something incredibly basic, like, "The just shall live by faith," and suddenly a door opens in their mind and an entirely new world becomes available to them.[48] They see the heart of God as never before and they are profoundly changed. Of course,

---

[48] This was basically what happened to Martin Luther.

this happens in far less dramatic ways as well. But even small steps in opening our eyes to the true nature of things can be transformational.

Still another way that God reveals truth is to help us get beyond the false dichotomies we cling to. Often in our attempts to make sense of the world, we are too reductionistic and view an issue in mostly black and white terms. One example was described in Chapter 5 on Grace, where people sometimes object to giving up legalistic ways of thinking on the basis that without law there would only be anarchy. This is a classic case of dualistic thinking that arises out of a faulty understanding of grace. Because once we see grace as a powerful force for change from the inside out, we are no longer limited to a choice between obedience and lawlessness. We have a third alternative, which is genuine transformation leading to a life that is in accordance with the law of God by virtue of who we are.

The whole point here is to not underestimate the level of distortion that we carry around in our mind. Truth is not just information or doctrine, but the very essence of *what* we see, and *how* we see it, and how we *interpret* what we see. Again, more about this will be covered in Chapter 9.

The Holy Spirit loves to mentor, and what He most wants to mentor us about is our own life. We are all students of Life 101, with far more learning ahead of us than we think. To whatever extent we can submit to His training, we will encounter truth we need for kingdom living.

Expect Confrontation

Of course, if we are carrying around distortions of life and living in accordance with those distortions, then we can expect quite often that God will confront us with what we believe and how we live it out. The good news is that God does not condemn us. When He needs to bring something to our attention, He knows how to do it with grace and hope, without beating us up with our shortcomings. Remember that His will is not our effort to be perfect, but His work of restoration. He is well aware that we are dust and that our restoration is a life-long process. It would make no sense for Him to get upset with every detail of our broken lives.

In fact, His confrontations are often framed as invitations. "I really want more of your heart" may be painful to hear, but it is not condemning. As God's children, we can expect Him to confront us in loving ways.

While God does not beat us up with our failings, neither does He ignore them. That would actually be thoughtless of Him, since everything within us that needs purging is inherently harmful to our soul. He heals and restores us in part because He loves us too much to see us suffer needlessly. It would be like watching your little girl suffer from a painful sliver and not helping her get it out. The challenge, of course, is getting her to cooperate with what needs to be done in order to do the necessary work. And so it is with us. But if we come to see His probing as an act of love, it becomes a lot easier to drop our resistance and even learn to welcome an opportunity to participate with Him for a deeper life.

Not only does God want to remove the stuff in us that is harmful and destructive, He also wants to build us up and give us the desire and inclination to give life to others. That, too, may require tapping us on the shoulder once in a while and calling our attention to some things in us that are too self-protective, selfish, or otherwise preventing our movement in the direction of being more life-giving.

For example, at one point in my life I shifted much of my hatred of self to hatred of my mother. I saw her as the main cause for my self-rejection and the pain that it caused. So God had to confront me about my "healing" process and deal with me about my new-found rage toward my mother. Yet, I can say that He never condemned my for either my hate or my anger. Rather it felt like an awareness that all I had achieved in regard to my deep-seated anger was to alter the object of my rage, and God wanted to do a much deeper work in me.

This is a great example that highlights both the fact that we can expect God to confront our mistakes, and that sometimes He will revisit what seemed like a previous victory and redeem it even further.

Expect Deeper Relationship

Thankfully, one of the greatest benefits we can expect from engaging with God over time is a deeper relationship with Him. That is something we can count on. As we meet with Him daily and discuss everything of importance with Him, we get to know His heart for us, His desire to see us grow and develop, and how He speaks and heals and changes us from the inside out. In short, we get to *know* God, not just know *about* Him.

It bears repeating that a closer relationship with God is not merely an abstraction or a statement about our official standing with Him, but something we actually experience. Often we hear Christian leaders tell us that we should not go on feelings because God is present whether or not we are aware of it. They are correct insofar as our feelings do not dictate reality. And yes, God is with us whether or not we feel anything. But a relationship that we are rarely aware of is not much of a relationship! That is more like an association we might have due to some contractual arrangement. Calling that a relationship lowers our expectation and diminishes our hope. When you stop and think about it, the idea that the God of the universe could take up residence in our soul without any sense on our part of something good happening inside us would be a very strange thing indeed.

If this idea of a tangible relationship with God is still a bit foggy, I would suggest re-reading the section in Chapter 1 titled, "Our Relationship With God is Qualitatively Different" and then Chapter 2 in its entirety.

Discovering how much He *wants* to be with us, how *glad* He is to be with us is all part of getting to know God. He does not just tolerate us or love us because He has to. He loves to parent! He loves to train us up in the way we should go.

Furthermore, this desire of His is not conditional. He is glad to be with me all the time, even when I'm hard to be around, even when I do not like myself, even when I am dead wrong. He is forever the loving Father, patient, long-suffering, and infinitely passionate about giving to us and renewing our heart and mind.

In spending time with God we learn how to abide with Him and know experientially that He is with us. The continual presence of Jesus, the Holy Spirit and God the Father is our birthright. The more we make time to engage with Him intentionally, the more we will be able to sense His presence with us throughout the day.

Expect to be Fed

Jesus said He would give us spiritual food and water that would truly satisfy us (Jn.4:14; 6:27). Isaiah portrayed the words of God as food for our soul (Isa.55). Since God is the essence of life and love and good, merely spending time in His presence with our mind focused on Him and His love for us is enough to fill up our emptiness and satisfy our deepest longings.

But God will never force-feed us. It is our job to make a space for Him to speak into our life, and that is exactly what we can expect when we participate in these spiritual practices for this purpose. Perhaps the single greatest barrier to being fed spiritually and experiencing this kind of life is our own reticence to set aside the time to engage with Him. Our impatience with the process and our drive to perform and make something happen all get in the way and keep us on the verge of spiritual malnutrition.

We were never meant to live without spiritual food. It is as important to our soul as the meals we eat every day are necessary for our body. One of the most amazing things about spending time with God and submitting to these spiritual practices is that we discover how much we need to be fed, and how wonderful it is to *actually be* fed! In fact, once we get used to it, our soul will hunger for it even more.

Conclusion

Being an apprentice of a Master like Jesus means that we will never be finished with our learning and growing. There will always be something more for us to discover about who we are, who God is, and how life works in His kingdom. The higher our expectations and the more we know about the kinds of experiences we can expect to have with God, the more observant we will become and the more teachable we will be as His students.

The Holy Spirit *loves* to teach and give! May we learn to love being taught and trained by God Himself!

Resources for Further Study

Dallas Willard, *The Renovation of the Heart: Putting on the Character of Christ* (Colorado Springs, NavPress) 2002

Chapter 8
Engaging With God for Change
Common Barriers to Engaging With God

> For now we see only a reflection of Jesus, as in a mirror; then we will see Him face to face. Now we know Him only in part; then we will know Him fully, just as we are fully known by Him. (1Cor.13:12, paraphrase)

Anyone who has been a Christian for any length of time knows there are many things that can interfere with our desire and ability to engage with God. If we are paying attention and know what to look for, most of these barriers are sufficiently evident to be easily identified. However, it is quite common for people to try to push through some of these barriers by sheer willpower or to assume it is up to them to resolve the problem on their own so they can reconnect with God.

Removing barriers between ourselves and God is one of the most important matters we deal with as Christians. Reconciliation is the very heart of the gospel and the reason for the Incarnation of Christ. So we are at odds with fundamental kingdom principles if we ignore these barriers or attempt to do God's part in removing them.

A "Barrier" that is Not a Barrier

Before we get too far into this topic, there is one thing needs to be made very clear, which may be very hard for some people to believe. *One thing that is **not** a barrier to engaging with God, is our own sin or poor spiritual condition.*

If it were, we would have no hope of engaging with God at all! Yet many Christians live as though God is supremely disappointed in them, that they are not fit to approach Him or that He will not hear anything they have to say, much less offer them His words of life. Many even believe that God can barely stand to look at them. And until they "get their act together" and straighten out their life, they have almost no hope of hearing His voice, much less living in the presence of God.

Ironically, the real barrier faced by someone like this is *not* their general spiritual condition, but their attempts to correct the problems and their difficulty in accepting God's grace. *Buying into the premise that they must be "good enough" or "obedient enough" in order to have a relationship with God is sufficient by itself to keep a person from connecting with Him.*

We are small creatures who are far from completion. God already knows that! He knew we would never get close to completion in the time we have left on this planet. So we need to stop making performance an issue, and get on with the matter of being with God. Remember: grace means we get the relationship first!

We will revisit this issue later. For now, we will cover some of the more common problems that create real distance between us and God, and we will offer some thoughts on how you can move toward resolution. By helping you identify and understand these barriers, you can be more focused and purposeful in your dialogues with God about the things that hinder your relationship.

Emotional Barriers

We are going to look at four very powerful emotions that often become barriers to engaging with God. Each in its own way represents a breach of trust in our relationship with God. And that common thread will become the clue for how to deal with these issues.

Anger at God

People can be angry with God for any number of reasons, but nearly all of these issues can be summarized as resentments over either something good we think God should have done that He did not do, or something bad that happened to us that we think He should have prevented but did not.

These resentments can harden our heart. A person who is angry with God may deem Him to be untrustworthy or even worse, uncaring or vindictive. With that kind of internal stance toward God, the problem is not only difficulty hearing God, but even *wanting* to hear. As in any human relationship, when we hold another person responsible for our pain, we may also feel a lot of resistance to approaching them or explaining our point of view to them. Rather, we view the relationship in an adversarial light and regard the other person as our enemy.

Clearly, that is not the sort of context that makes it easy to receive mentoring or comfort or healing or anything else that God has to offer. In some instances, we can wrestle this out with God by expressing our point of view and asking Him to help us see things differently. Many Psalms demonstrate this approach to hammering out disappointments with God. At times, we may also need to seek help from others in order to see God's perspective and to rebuild our trust.

Again, the most common reasons people become angry with God are over things they believe He should have done or things they think He ought to have prevented from happening. Sometimes an illness, injury, or a painful childhood can lead people to view God as uncaring or highly conditional. Resentment builds toward God over what they think He would have done if He cared about them. Generally, no explanation of why bad things happen to good people will do much to reduce their anger, which seems very justifiable to them. And it is hard for them to be close to God when they are convinced He has betrayed them or failed them in some way.

This issue can be hard to deal with because it is hard to imagine that there is any other way to understand the pain we feel. We can find some clues to addressing the problem in a number of Psalms where the writer cries out to God and complains about the injustices he feels. Rather than stay away from God or pray only carefully sanitized prayers to Him, we need to let God know that we are angry and why we are angry. Taking the time to write out our rage and disappointment and listen for His response can be a very important step in our healing. We need to know that God can take our anger and still care about us. And God can say things to us in those moments that are very freeing and life changing.

Whenever we are motivated to keep God at arms' length, we must admit our attempts to defend ourselves and ask God to show us what we are missing in our perceptions and interpretations. If the problem proves to be intractable, then we need to seek help from others who know how to deal with these things gracefully. By whatever means, we must not allow our internal resistance to dictate the terms of our relationship to God.

Fear of God

By fear of God we do not mean the Biblical understanding of reverence and awe. Those are good things that actually contribute to a healthy respect of God's place in our life. What we are referring to here is a toxic form of fear that has many forms and many ways of motivating us to run from God.

As strange as it may be, many Christians are actually afraid of getting too close to God, even when they genuinely would like to have a better relationship with Him. Knowing intellectually about the goodness of God does little good, because the fear they feel comes from deep inside in places that do not respond to rational arguments.

Some people fear that if they get too close to God they will lose control of their life or God will "test" them in some painful manner. Some fear His disapproval and the shame they feel in His presence. Still others fear God because He often presents Himself as a father or as a powerful male, an image that has painful connotations for them. Despite the fact that God is their only real hope for the healing they need, they cannot approach Him because He is too scary. Walls of protection go up inside their heart and mind, and they are ready to bolt at any word He might say to them.

Many people are afraid of what God thinks of them. I know all the secret things about me that I try to keep private so people will not reject me. But God knows all those things too, so maybe He has as bad an opinion of me as I do. I hate it when I fail and when I have evil thoughts, and God knows all of those things, too. God hates sin. I know I sin. So maybe God hates me as much as He despises my behavior. The last thing I want is for Him to look down on me disapprovingly or to tell me how disappointed He is.

Or I might just be afraid of what He will ask me to do, what He will want from me that I'm not ready to give. What if He asks me to talk to that person at work I cannot stand, or do something at church, or even ask me to become a missionary? My concerns about what He might want from me may cause me to be too afraid to get close to Him at all.

Some fears of God even come from bad theology. Teachers who are steeped in legalism or shame-based backgrounds often view the Bible through the lens of crime and punishment, good people and bad people. Their teaching will reflect this distorted bias and can instill a deep fear of God watching us. I remember as a small child singing a song in Sunday School that went like this:

> Oh, be careful little hands what you do ...
> Oh, be careful little hands what you do ...
> For the Father up above is looking down in love,
> Oh, be careful little hands what you do. (origin unknown)

It made me wish God could not see me at all. If we are afraid of God for any reason, we will tend to try to hide from Him and to protect our heart from Him, which means we will not be very receptive to His leading.

What makes it so hard to address this toxic fear of God is the triple barrier that it presents. First, fear has a disabling affect on our physical brain, making it malfunction and far less able to relate to others or to consider the advice of friends or the voice of God. Second, the danger feels real. Everything in the person's body tells them that God is not safe, even when they know that isn't supposed to be the case. And third, their best resource for dealing with the barrier resides in the person of God, whom they do not want to approach.

So how do we resolve this dilemma? At least in part by a well-informed act of faith. Here is one very good reason why we need to learn how to walk by faith and not by sight. What looks and feels real to us may not be. Because the truth is, our emotions are not necessarily a measure of reality at all, but of our own internal belief system and inner process.

In Chapter 9 we will take an in-depth look at how we can resolve these faulty ideas in our inner world. But for now, just for the sake of argument, let us consider the possibility that my fear is coming from my own mistaken ideas of who God is, or whether He cares about me, or whether He holds me in His heart. What if, for reasons I do not yet fully understand, my ideas of who God is and how He wants to be involved in my life have been terribly malformed by my earlier experiences or by poorly thought-out theology? If that were the case, then my fear would be the cry of my woundedness, not the result of having a dangerous God.

If I am willing to take it as a matter of faith that my fear of God is actually due to my own malfunctioning soul and that God truly holds me in His heart, then I can ask God to help me with the healing I need to resolve the fear. I simply must come to the place of believing that the problem is not the trustworthiness of God, but my broken "truster," and that given enough quality time with God, this broken part of me will heal and become more trusting.

In the end, we need to take our fear to God, tell Him why we are afraid and why we are unable to change on our own. We must ask Him what we need to know and where we need to heal in order to be at peace with Him and participate with Him until our fear is removed by His love.

Fear of Emotional Pain

The other major form of fear that gets in the way of listening to God is the fear of emotional pain. Sometimes our healing requires that we revisit past experiences so that God can heal them, much like needing to cleanse a festering wound. If we have an intense fear of feeling that kind of pain, we may resist going to those memories and instead push them down as soon as they begin to intrude. If God begins to deal with us on a particular issue, whether current or past, and the intensity gets to be too much or it feels too painful, we may decide to back away from the pain rather than allow God to lead us through it. Sometimes people even think that the pain must be from the enemy, because they misunderstand the nature of old wounds. Whatever the cause, this type of fear motivates us to protect our heart and shut down our thoughts, which makes it very difficult for God to address the broken places in our heart or to talk to us about places where we need change.

Toxic Shame

One of the more complex emotions we deal with is shame. Sometimes shame can be very healthy and motivate us to become a better person. If I engage in a bit of "harmless" gossip, for example, and later find out that it got back to the person I was talking about, the shame I feel may cause me to change how I talk about others.

On the other hand, people can become burdened by a toxic version of shame that tears them down rather than encourages them toward change. When a child is humiliated every time they express themselves, they may come to believe their thoughts are stupid next to anyone else's. Even as an adult they may feel a flush of shame whenever they are asked for their opinion about something. This kind of shame can be so painful that a person will do almost anything to avoid feeling it.

We have all known people who seem to be completely unable to hear even the most legitimate or constructive criticism. They may respond with defensiveness and indignation, or with a complete meltdown and self-loathing. Any hint of disapproval or any possibility of being deficient in some way is extremely intolerable. Some people compensate with an air of superiority, some opt for blaming others, and still others simply feel overwhelmed with a sense of failure.

If we have a hard time dealing with shame, we will have great difficulty developing a vision for change and engaging in change, because that puts a spotlight on what is deficient in us. If we have learned to equate flaws, weakness, and sin with being "unacceptable" or "unlovable," we will be hard pressed to address areas in our life that need renewal. Getting stuck in shame and condemnation can lead to an unwillingness or an inability to see ourselves honestly. That presents a tremendous barrier to our renewal.

The great news of the gospel is that our brokenness no longer separates us from the presence of God, nor does our sin cause Him to walk away from us in disgust. He knows we are dust, and He knows it will take another hundred years to clean up our heart and mind from all of our malformed ways. But He delights in doing His work in us, to show that light is greater than darkness and that good is more powerful than evil.

As we will see in Chapter 10, toxic shame is based entirely on distorted perceptions of who we are and how God sees us. When we see the full truth of God's grace and His heart, we are set free from condemnation and any need to hide from God. Once we realize this liberating truth, we can run to God with every deficiency, every failure, and every sin we encounter and say, "Look, Papa! I found some more broken places for you to heal!"

When an emotion like shame overwhelms our emotional capacity, it can cause parts of our mental processes to shut down. In particular, it affects our ability to know how we are involved in a situation, resulting in an inability to learn or change. These are all ways that toxic shame can create major barriers to engaging with God.

Hopelessness

Hopelessness can set in for a variety of reasons. Many of us have issues in our life that keep coming back time and again. We try all kinds of ways to put and end to them, but they never seem to get resolved. Or we may hit a brick wall right after a really good retreat or a powerful encounter with God, and it takes the wind out of our sails. These experiences can discourage us to the point of disbelief. Following such letdowns, we find it harder and harder to believe that real change is possible, or that God cares about us, or that we will ever be able to do whatever it is we are supposed to be doing on our end of this relationship.

Some people experience a lot of difficulty when they try to hear God's voice. Repeated attempts end in disappointment, and their spiritual reflections seem to lack any fruit. In time this disappointment breeds disbelief and a feeling of hopelessness that they will ever be able to receive what they need from God.

Examples abound. This can be as simple as trying to forgive someone in your life that you know you should forgive, but you find that nothing seems to work. You end up feeling hurt and angry with every interaction, and the whole process has to start all over again. Or hopelessness can be as deep and complex as a recurring feeling of self-hate. No matter how many times you take it to God, every setback or disappointment with life just reminds you how much you hate your own life.

Whatever the issue, when we encounter any one thing for the tenth time we begin to wonder if change is even possible, at least for us in that area. Our faith in the process of renewal is challenged. Our expectations sink lower with each cycle, and we may even stop trying to hear God or receive anything from Him at all. In this way, hopelessness becomes an additional barrier in and of itself, because we simply give up.

To challenge this ever-widening gulf between our self and God, we may need encouragement and help from other people to breathe life into the process and to give us reasons to persist in engaging with God to restore our hope. We also need to take our hopelessness and disbelief to God and ask Him to restore our awareness of His presence and care for us. Many of the Psalms address this at length. In their despair and in their inability to see beyond their past and present situations, the psalmists cry out to God for some sign of hope and reason to believe. These psalms are great examples to us of how we need to re-engage when we seem to have lost our way.

The Problem of Trust

All of the above emotional barriers are heavily connected to the issue of trust. If I am afraid of what God might say, my fear is partly a lack of trust in His good will toward me. If I am too ashamed to talk to God or if I am concerned that He might really not like me very well, I probably have a lack of trust in His love for me. When I am angry at God over some way in which I think He failed me, I do not trust His way of caring for me or that He will protect me from harm. And when I feel hopeless, it is because I do not believe He will do anything to help me – again a lack of trust in His involvement in my life.

No matter what emotions are involved, trust issues always feel like we are dealing with someone who is not trustworthy, even if that someone happens to be God. Regardless of what our theology tells us, it *feels* like God is not trustworthy. When those feelings are strong enough, we may even doubt our theology about the goodness of God.

More importantly, it can be extremely difficult to accept the idea that the problem may not be about God at all, that the real problem in these instances is our broken truster. Whether due to prior experiences of broken trust or bad theology or a mistaken interpretation of God's character or His past actions, trust issues with God are always due to a broken truster. Feelings that tell us God is untrustworthy do not come from some proof that God cannot be trusted, but from our *interpretations* of God and our own *limited experience* of Him.

A poor relationship with our *earthly* father can also lead to developing trust issues with God. Lacking a good image of an available, safe, loving dad, we are already "wired" to suspect anyone with power, anyone we need to depend on, and anyone claiming to be a father. With just the slightest provocation or disappointment, our mind will reach back and pull up our prior experience and make the connection, and do so with very little awareness on our part that we are mixing the past with the present.

Whatever the reason, once we have raised the alarm bells and felt the anxiety that signals untrustworthiness, we will find it very hard to relax in the presence of God, open our heart to Him, or hear or see anything He wants to reveal to us. Nearly every emotional barrier to engaging with God contains some element of mistrust. We must to learn to notice these and believe that our real problem is our broken truster and that God is somehow truly trustworthy, despite our feelings.

Of course, making ourselves trust God fully by willpower alone is highly unlikely. As with everything, we must take our broken truster to God and ask Him to reveal what we need in order to trust Him more. So instead of trying to pretend that we trust Him when we really do not, what we *can* do, is accept the possibility that we are missing something or in need of healing in some area in order to make trust possible.

Believing the problem lies with our truster and that God can give us what we need is actually an act of trust in God. That minimal level of trust can then lead us to engaging with Him for the purpose of restoring our trust more fully.

COGNITIVE BARRIERS

Some of the barriers we encounter when trying to engage with God are actually due to how we think about the spiritual life. If we approach spiritual matters from a mistaken perspective, we end up missing a lot of what God wants to do in us and for us.

Assuming We Know

Interestingly, our very familiarity with Christian themes can become a barrier to our engagement with God. The more we learn about the Christian life, the more we run the risk of becoming less teachable and less open to new experiences of God. We begin to assume we know more than we really do, and inadvertently become less teachable.

A few years ago I attended an all-day guided retreat where the main passage to consider was the parable of the prodigal son. When I first heard the passage announced, my reaction was, "Oh, man. I've been through that about a hundred times. I really have a hard time believing I'm going to learn anything today." Fortunately, I recognized my inner voice as an assumption based on my prior experience, and asked God to help me surrender to the passage and let me see what I needed for that day. By the end of the retreat God had shown me several major ways in which the two sons are actually quite similar, especially in regard to how they both missed the Father's true heart for them. As a result, I felt a great desire in me to know the Father more.

Had I rested on my assumption of prior knowledge, I would have missed the insights I needed to see that day and perhaps missed the joy of desiring more of God. Too often we think of the material in front of us as "old hat" or having little to do with our everyday life. Assuming we already know most of what we need to know can keep us from listening to what God is trying to teach us.

But familiarity is not the only way we assume too much. Sometimes our theological training gets in the way of transformational learning because we substitute the "right" answers for the truth of what is going on within us. For example, when we read that we are to "Love the Lord your God with all your heart" it is easy to think, "Yes, that's right. I know this. I also know the second greatest command..." and so on, never asking ourselves, "What does it mean to love God with all my heart? What would that look like? How would I know? How can I love Him more?" We can be so preoccupied with what we already know that we never stop to see if our heart has caught up to where we think we are.

Or consider the way we often respond to such ideas as how God accepts us when we come to Him, no matter how messed up we are. It can be very easy to agree with that in principle, and at the same time feel very afraid of how God regards us personally. Without even thinking about it, we can confess that God accepts us and simultaneously try to hide from His gaze. Unless we are willing to question our assumptions, however, we are likely to miss our inner responses. Knowing a true thing intellectually can actually get in the way of knowing it experientially.

Another way that our assumptions get in the way of engaging with God is by substituting "knowledge" for experience. Psalm 139 begins by the singer declaring the truth that God knows him completely. If we have been taught anything about the all-knowing character of God, we could easily dismiss the thought with, "Of course, God knows all about me – after all, He knows everything" and go on. But to stop long enough to contemplate the wonder expressed here can be quite a revelation. The truth is that our deepest longing is to be fully known and fully loved at the same time. In fact, being known is foundational to our sense of identity and value. Here in this Psalm that dream is realized. What an amazing thing, this holy ground on which we stand! But so easily missed if we only look for what data there is to know.

Protective Assumptions

Cognitive barriers and emotional barriers are often heavily intertwined. For example, one of the most common reasons we make a lot of assumptions about the spiritual life is that we have an unspoken fear of not being as far along on the path as we would like to think we are.

For example, many Christians will answer correctly when asked if they know God is present in the room. But when asked, "How often do you feel abandoned by God?" or "Do you ever feel like your prayers are bouncing off the ceiling?" those same people will express concerns that sound as if they think God is far, far away.

Yet when they read in the Bible that "I will never leave you or forsake you" they nod in full agreement, because that is what they have learned is the right answer. In doing so, they assume that their understanding is sufficient, and consequently skip over the obvious questions that would arise if they were to stop and ponder their own lack of experience of God's presence. Their mental assumptions can blind them to their own insecurities about God and at the same time protect them from the discomfort of self-examination.

Our Prior Assumptions are Pervasive

There are so many ways our assumptions can show up, we would have to cover most of the New Testament in order to address this completely. When Jesus says, "Return good to those who mistreat you," it is easy to say to ourselves, "Yes, that would certainly be a good thing to do." But our agreement with the principle can totally bypass the fact that we may have no idea how to do that in the real world. We think that by agreeing with the principle we have indeed aligned with it, when in reality everything inside us may have already aligned with the belief that we should cut our enemies off at the knees (or perhaps run) whenever we see opposition.

Such assumptions can even show up after good teaching. For example, there are many good ministries that do a great job of addressing some particular area, such as dealing with marriage issues or healing the "Father wound." After attending one of these seminars it might be easy to say, "I have already dealt with that area," and never look at it again. However, for most of us, these areas need to be re-visited many times before they lose all their power to disrupt our life. Assuming we are "done" with an area of restoration or growth is a dangerous assumption, because we stop noticing where we still need help.

What these kinds of assumptions all have in common is the intent to protect our sense of self rather than the intent to learn and grow and heal. But any assumptions we make for the sake of bypassing self-examination will become barriers in our journey toward maturity.

Common Assumptions Worth Questioning

When we consider the fact that God's ways are higher than our ways, we are fooling ourselves if we think that we know most of what we need to know about the Christian life just because we have been in church for a few years and studied the Bible. There is always more for us to discover. One of the best ways to grow in our spiritual walk is to check with God about all those things we assume we know, to see if He has anything else He wants to reveal to us. Imagine the things God could show us if we were willing to question some of the following common assumptions:
- I already have a working relationship with God.
- I know God loves me.
- I know what I need to do, I just need to do it.

Remaining teachable is central to being reformed in the image of Christ.

Faulty Assumptions

Closely related to the problem of assuming we already know what we need to know is the problem of holding onto faulty assumptions as if they were true. Take the earlier example of how Psalm 139 can speak to our deepest longing to be known and loved at the same time by the same person. We can easily miss this treasure if we misread the passage. A great number of people even dislike this psalm because to them it sounds like God is looking at everything the psalmist does to see if it is good or bad. They feel judged and shamed by the very thought of God searching their heart.

But if we take the time to ask God to reveal the meaning of that Psalm to us, we may well encounter His true heart. Sitting for a while under His gaze and feeling His love at the same time can be a very healing experience: one that is easily missed if we have a mistaken view of what the psalm is about, or when we do not question our prior assumptions.

Another way that we dismiss possibilities for connecting with God is by thinking that a particular manner of engaging is too trivial to bother with. I once heard Dallas Willard suggest that we should turn our mind and heart toward God to contemplate His goodness every night as we are drifting off to sleep and for the first five to ten minutes after waking each morning. My first thought was that such an exercise would not do much. But knowing that Dallas was speaking from experience, I decided to give it a try anyway. After about three weeks I began noticing a change in the way I anticipated the goodness of God in my life. It was clear that I had been seriously wrong about the value of that exercise.

How easy it would have been to trivialize away an opportunity to be changed. I wonder sometimes if our tendency to minimize important things is one of the real reasons behind Jesus' insistence on obeying His words. The problem is not that what He asks is too hard. We just think what He asks is beneath us – like washing someone's feet. Making a space for God to be with us does not have to be dramatic or glamorous. We just need to show up, body and soul.

Mistaken Ideas About Discipleship

As Christians, some of the most common faulty assumptions we hold are in regard to spiritual development itself. As we have pointed out throughout this book, there are a lot of misunderstandings about what is God's part and what is our part in this process of growing up spiritually.

Historically, this imbalance has had a strong tendency to land on the side of trying to do too much of the job. We seem to think that given enough motivation and enough willpower, we should be able to do the right things and change our heart into something that is more Christ-like.

Every once in a while a group will figure out this is not true and swing the pendulum to the other extreme. They ask God to change their heart with a wave of His arm, thinking they do not have to do anything but wait for God to change them. But this is like asking a language instructor to make them fluent in Russian by the next day. They are bypassing their role as an apprentice and failing to participate in their formation.

One mindset expects to live the Christian life by determination, as if God were not even part of the equation. The other wants to be changed without any effort at all. Either way, the mistaken assumptions about how change happens get in the way of genuine development.

Variations on these themes are endless. When we introduce spiritual practices to people who are well trained in performance Christianity, their inclination is to add those practices to their list of things to do, and to try to do them better than anyone else. Their prior assumptions about how change happens colors their understanding of spiritual disciplines, which simply look like more things to work on.

At the other end of the spectrum, those who believe growth comes from exercising charismatic gifts over one another often have trouble with practices such as dialoguing with God. They tend to think of hearing God as primarily an avenue for ministering to someone else, and have difficulty submitting to God so He can mentor them in regard to their own life. Or they want God to "fall" on them and change them without ever having to learn how to work with God as a mentor who wants to speak into their life and train them in the ways of the kingdom.

Mistaken ideas about discipleship are the main reason people get out of balance and either try to do God's part or else neglect their part in spiritual development. Unless we are willing to question our assumptions, we run the risk of spinning our wheels rather than moving forward in life.

Difficulty Seeing Ourselves as God Sees Us

While this might be considered just another faulty assumption, it is so pervasive and insidious that it deserves its own space. In many ways this is related to the problem of having distorted images of God in our mind or misunderstanding His character, and thus missing His heart for us.

Whether or not they would profess this out loud, many Christians are quite convinced that God's regard of us is highly conditional, based on how well we perform spiritually. If we do well, then God is pleased and smiles on us. Perhaps He even blesses us. But if we mess up or omit things we ought to be doing, then God is displeased, and stands there looking at us sideways with His arms crossed and His jaw set, waiting for us to clean up our act.

Now it is very important here not to misunderstand this point. We are not saying that God dances with delight no matter what we do or how we respond to Him. God is far more concerned about the destructiveness of sin than we are. But the image of a judgmental God who disengages from us whenever we sin is simply not found in the New Testament.

What concerns God most about our sin is how it will destroy our life. That is why He came to rescue us in the first place, and why He wants to be involved in our life for good, to heal and restore us to an abundant life. Furthermore, He wants to grow us up into mature followers of Christ. So His primary approach toward us is that of a Healer and Mentor, who works with us in the same ways that He worked with His twelve disciples: teaching, training, enlightening, and admonishing them. Even when Peter denied Him, Jesus pursued him after the resurrection and worked with him to restore His faith and to help him understand that his desertion was not some kind of irredeemable sin.

If the Christian life were primarily a test of our resolve, then it might make sense for God to stand back and judge us at every turn. But the focus of our life is our relationship with Christ. So what makes the most sense is that God would actually step up His action in our life when we are at our worst. And since He is patient and loving, He starts with the most gentle of confrontations.

Usually, He begins by calling our attention to the matter, helping us notice where we have fallen, and inviting us to come to Him for help. If we hear and respond, He is then able to restore us, and in the process we strengthen our trust in Him and learn to turn back to Him more readily in future ruptures. If, on the other hand, we are reluctant to see our sin or deal with it, God will gradually find more pronounced ways of getting our attention. He may begin to speak through others, put a book in our hands, or intervene in some other way that is difficult for us to ignore. If all else fails, He may allow us the natural consequences of our action, or allow us to come to the end of ourselves so we will take our failures back to Him for help.

Either way, God's intentions are the same – to bring us through the experience cleansed and restored and stronger than we were before. He does not stand aloof, disgusted and resistant, until we figure it out on our own and patch things up in our own strength. Rather, He wants to help us in every way that we will let Him.

The challenge here is seeing ourselves as God sees us. We have a tendency to look at our inadequacies, flaws, sins, and brokenness and conclude that we are simply undesirable and unfit – that anyone who knew us well enough would most certainly reject us. If God knows us better than we do, He must certainly be disgusted as well.

At that point we may try to do something to get God to like us more or at least to demonstrate our intentions to try harder to be good. We might even confess and repent in an effort to get God to feel good toward us. Sometimes this issue is compounded by poor teaching or training in our families where we may have learned that mistakes are unforgivable or that mistakes prove how defective we are as human beings. If we project these feelings on God, we have trouble seeing our self as God sees us, and may opt for running from God instead of moving toward Him.

The Nature of Mind-Sight

One final problem to address is that of mind-sight – the ability to see an issue from a viewpoint other than one's own. Most people learn how to see things from other perspectives fairly early in life, and even improve on that ability as they get older. However, certain kinds of developmental issues can leave a person quite unable to do this on a regular basis. For example, this might be rooted in the fear that any other position on an issue is a threat to one's self worth. Or perhaps the only times a person has ever felt compelled to think of another person's perspective were when they needed to protect themselves. Also, simple indifference to what other people think or a lack of empathy and compassion could lead a person to disregard other points of view as irrelevant.

What is important about this issue is that when we have very little practice with looking for points of view other than the one we hold, we can have a great deal of difficulty grasping the significance of whatever God may want to reveal to us. Since His ways are higher than our ways, much of what He wants to show us runs counter to what we have known previously. If we are inexperienced in grasping new points of view and updating our perceptions, much of what God wants to reveal to us will be lost or misinterpreted.

Anyone who becomes aware that this is a problem area for them should seek professional help from someone who knows how to train a person for better mind-sight.

Removing Cognitive Barriers

The greatest difficulty with cognitive barriers is our inability to see them. These distorted ways of thinking function like blind spots in our vision, and it is very hard to name what we are unaware of. For example, if I have learned to keep people at a certain emotional distance as a way of protecting myself, it probably will not occur to me that I am also harming myself in the process. My mindset has already determined that my stance is "protective" in nature, not harmful. I assume I am doing what is best for myself. And since I am unable to observe any fruits of friendship, I also fail to see any loss of that fruit. So it does not appear to me that my isolation costs very much.

Consequently, cognitive barriers can be very self-reinforcing, and the "validity" of our faulty thinking can actually appear to us to be very self-evident. Continuing our example, the idea that *getting close to people is a bad thing* makes perfect sense to me and my prior experience of a painful breakup appears to support my conclusion. I have plenty of evidence to demonstrate how much it hurts to get close to people. But what has actually taken place is that I have misinterpreted my experience and drawn a faulty conclusion, at which point it looks like my experience proves my conclusion to be correct. Yet, all I have accomplished is to create a cognitive barrier to friendship and intimacy. Clearly, I need help to see my own blind spots.

Here is where humility and remaining teachable go a long way toward our restoration. As long as I am willing to question my assumptions about how life works for me, I have the possibility of seeing my own life from another perspective (God's) as well as noticing any corrective experience I might encounter.

Furthermore, by engaging in spiritual practices and conversations with God, I create teachable moments where insight into my own process will allow me to see what I could not see before. And finally, by engaging with other believers I can observe how relationships work in their lives and also experience their goodness toward me first-hand.

We are forever students of life, learning and re-learning what it means to be fully alive in the kingdom. Accepting the truth that we are all shot through with faulty assumptions about life will serve us well in our desire to be deconstructed and reconstructed in the image of God.

SUBJECTIVE BARRIERS

In addition to emotional and cognitive barriers to engaging with God, we also run into problems that come out of our personal experience as we try to learn how to live the Christian life. When we misinterpret our own subjective understanding of how all this works, we can actually create new barriers we did not have before. Once in place, these barriers can be very hard to see.

Bypassing Experiential Learning

For many decades, much of the Christian world has been caught up in an approach to the spiritual life that relies far more on educating the intellect than training the soul. A case could reasonably be made that our most common approaches to Christian growth are based on a model that comes out of a Western Enlightenment approach to education, which is primarily concerned with cognitive thought. When we couple that with a common belief among many Christians that professing the right doctrine is what makes a good Christian, we have before us a rather formidable barrier to true spiritual maturity.

At its core, the spiritual life is a relationship in which a person actually engages with God and experiences Him directly. One of the basic themes of the book of James is that when "faith" remains in your head and does not affect your real life, it is not a true faith at all. It may be a well thought out system; it may be pure fantasy. But it is not faith in the biblical sense. Faith in God is a life-changing experience, not an idea. And we do not grow in our Christian life without *experiencing* that growth.

Over-Confidence in Our Will

One way we miss the experiential learning process is to expect our will to do most of the work. If I think "loving my enemy" is simply a choice I need to make at the right moment, I have greatly over-estimated my own power and under-estimated the experience and practice it takes to learn how to love people who are hard to like. If I think forgiving someone is simply a choice and nothing more, then I do not really understand forgiveness, and I have placed a tremendous barrier in my path to learning; because forgiving is something that happens to me as well as something I offer to another.

Much of the mistaken approach to obedience today is deeply rooted in a belief that the Christian life is mostly about doing the right things, and that it is simply up to us to make the morally right choices. But as we have seen in earlier chapters, this amounts to nothing more than legalism dressed up in New Testament terminology.

Jesus made it very clear that there are things our will is incapable of doing: "Which of you by mental effort can add a foot to your height?" His point is well taken. We cannot grow by direct effort of our will.

Returning to our analogy of sailing, we cannot "will" ourselves to get to where we need to be. There is no direct way to make that happen. But we *can* choose to align the sails with a power that is capable of moving the boat in the right direction. That is a proper use of the will.

Trying to do what Jesus says by simply making the choice to do so, is like trying to grow a foot by sheer willpower. And believing that this is how we grow is a tremendous barrier to true spiritual growth.

Common Barriers to Engaging With God

Misinterpreting the Process

Whenever we try something new, it is easy to misinterpret our initial experiences whether they are positive or negative. For example, we may easily assume that our first few attempts at hearing God represent the sum total of what we can expect from conversational prayer, when in fact God has a wide variety of ways of communicating with us and an endless supply of issues to talk about. Or if we try fasting and do not see much fruit from that experience, we may give it up as if we had exhausted all there was to know about fasting, not realizing there is much to learn about connecting with God and depending on Him during that time.

If a person stumbles into an area where the learning curve is steeper than they had anticipated, there is always the danger they will back away from the issue before working through the reasons for their difficulty. Some people stop trying simply because it did not "work" the first time, and avoid the learning curve altogether. Others give up because the road is too hard, and they are unwilling or unable to do what it takes to walk it through. Sometimes people think they must have done something wrong or the whole thing would have gone better. Consequently, they back off when instead they should take the issue back to God for His help in pressing through the issue and continuing their learning process.

Encountering our own internal resistance is one of the most prevalent of these kinds of mistaken impressions. While seeking healing in some area of life, we may be surprised by the underlying pain and interpret it as an indicator that we are heading in the wrong direction. We might try to find another way that is less painful, or stop the process entirely.

Similarly, when we actually do make a breakthrough and experience genuine relief, if we encounter that same issue again at a later date we might second guess our earlier process and despair over our apparent lack of progress. The truth is that most of the wounds we carry have multiple layers, and we may need to revisit those issues more than once before they stop interfering with our life. Each time we deal with it, we may be addressing a different layer or a deeper cause for the pain. But if we fail to recognize that process and instead think we are simply going in circles, we might give up hope of moving forward.

For example, I was mentoring a man who was determined to heal from painful memories that came from the way his family had used shame and humiliation to control the children. In his initial conversations with God about this, he came to the realization that the contempt his parents poured on him in fact said nothing about who he was as a person – it arose instead from the unhealed wounds in his parents. That revelation immediately provided a great deal of relief from his feelings of worthlessness.

A few months later, however, his self-deprecating patterns began to reassert themselves. Taking this issue back to God, he discovered that the negative messages ringing in his head were no longer in his parent's voice, but his own. In asking God why he beat himself up so readily even when his parents were nowhere around, God helped him see how he had connected making mistakes with feeling condemnation. When God reassured him that mistakes did not get to define who he was, he again felt relief – and in the following days reported that he was no longer kicking himself around the room every time he did something less than perfect. After a few more years passed, he was back in my office uncovering an even deeper layer of his self-hate. And so the process goes. Each step along the way brings tremendous freedom and relief, and quite often makes it possible to dig even deeper to accomplish even more healing.

If my friend had become discouraged and stopped the process, he would not be so free of his debilitating self-hate today. But because he understood that restoration is a life-long process, he kept coming back to God with each new piece of the puzzle and so continued to grow and heal in many ways.

When Defeat Follows Victory

One final note regarding the process of restoration. Many people have noticed that right after a breakthrough in their spiritual life, it seems as if the joyful moment may be very short-lived before a new round of difficulties sets in. Such breakthroughs often happen on retreats, during times of wrestling with God, or at life-giving conferences. When adversity sets in shortly afterword, we can feel robbed of our progress.

What we most need to know about these backlashes is that they do *not* mean our victory was in some way insufficient or too shallow. Rather, there are two very common reasons why this happens. First, because the enemy of our souls cannot stand to see us moving closer to God or finding more life, we can expect him to step up his scorched earth policy in any way possible, to discourage us from seeking such things or expecting they will last.

Second, any time we move closer to the Light or allow that Light into deeper places in our soul, we can expect it to illuminate other things in the corners of our mind that we had not disturbed much before. Sometimes inner healing will open up access to areas of our heart that were too buried before to be dealt with.

A friend of mine in the Chicago area has been particularly blessed with the gift of helping people who have experienced the pain of physical or emotional abandonment. A number of years ago I spent several days with him, receiving his counsel and ministry, after which I felt more free than I had in decades. God met us there and gave me a lot of new ground to walk on that had been closed off most of my life.

About six weeks later, I fell of an emotional cliff. Rageful, violent self-hate came out of nowhere and flooded my mind. Even the slightest disappointment would send me into a tirade and ruin my day. I woke up angry and had to force myself to keep moving from moment to moment.

For the first few days, I thought this would blow over and go away of its own accord. But at some point I realized it was a backlash from the changes I had experienced six weeks earlier. So I got out my journal and started filling up pages – for the better part of three days – crying to God, yelling at myself, and working with Him to dig out the source of this horrible self-hatred. In the end, it became one of the greatest single moments of transformation I have ever experienced. God's light broke through the smoke and mirrors I had believed in all my life, and purged my heart and mind of the lies that kept me in bondage to self-hate. I have never been the same since that experience.

The point here is that the new layer of healing was only possible after the work God did in my heart previously. Had I misinterpreted my negative backlash as some kind of failure of that earlier work to "stick," I would have missed an incredible opportunity for deeper restoration. But by wading into the mess in the belief that God had even more work to do, it became another life changing-moment.

We must never forget that we are engaged in a spiritual war for our own restoration. Whatever the cause, whatever the timing, any intrusion by the enemy or anything triggered by the events of life in our world, or any mess that presents itself after important victories – it is all part of the messy war in which we are embroiled. But God has already broken the power of evil, and He is dedicated to the process of continuing to cleanse us from all the effects this broken world has had on our life.

Let us not misunderstand our victories, but celebrate them fully! And let us take the offensive whenever we see a followup that threatens to water down whatever gifts we have received.

Difficulty Quieting or Resting

People often find quieting down to be extremely difficult, even painful, for a variety of reasons. The problem is that this inability to quiet can make it very difficult to pay attention to the nuances of God's impressions on our spirit, impairing our ability to hear God.

No doubt there are many possibilities here. But one of the most common reasons a person might have difficulty quieting is some form of anxiety that drives them to distraction, often without any conscious realization of what is going on. Most of the time it does not even feel like anxiety. If the person is aware of anything at all, the emotion is usually given another name. For example, a child who develops an anxious attachment pattern may spend a lifetime feeling exceptionally lonely, and the loneliness may be so intense that they cope by training their mind to stop noticing any underlying pain. Or take the case of a person who gains their sense of value from being productive and who feels guilty whenever they slow down. While they may be aware of some sense of shame or guilt, they probably have little or no awareness of their anxiety about needing to feel productive.

There are many other sources of this kind of persistent low-level anxiety as well. Children who grow up in homes where parents demonstrate unpredictable patterns of abuse may develop a highly sensitized "radar," a kind of early warning system that tells them when to hide or run. An environment such as this creates a world for the child in which resting or relaxing is inherently dangerous. So much so, that any extended quiet actually generates anxiety in order to restore the hyper vigilance that is deemed necessary for survival. This fear-based lifestyle makes quieting nearly impossible.

When the inability to quiet is rooted in an underlying anxiety, it can be difficult to focus or to pay attention to impressions from the Spirit. In spite of this, people often find that they can engage with God directly about their anxiety and receive words or images that address their fears quite well. After receiving healing for their anxiety they can then calm better and have better conversations with God about other things.

Learning to Quiet

Generally speaking, quieting is a common skill that people learn as part of normal human development. An inability to quiet usually implies either an environment in which quieting was never learned, or some early injury to the soul, such as an anxious attachment pattern or other fear-based relationship style. For those who simply never learned to quiet their mind and body, the skill can usually be acquired through persistent practice. Others may need some outside help.

Intent to Protect

We all carry within us a map of life, a way of thinking about the world around us as well as who we are and how we fit into this world. As we go through our daily experiences, we all find areas in our map here and there that need to be revised or updated in order to better fit the reality in which we find ourselves.

Now much of the time, these changes are fairly minor. Our favorite restaurant has a new manager and the food is no longer good, so we revise our opinion of that establishment. Or during a really good marriage seminar we realize that we have been taking our spouse for granted lately, and resolve to be more deliberate about nurturing our relationship. These are relatively simple examples of updating how we engage with the world around us. But many of the changes we need to make can be quite significant.

Imagine that you are using a map to get around in a city, but your map is thirty years old. Or worse yet, your map has been altered by factors over which you had little control, and many of the streets are marked wrong or come to dead ends or do not even exist in the real world. Obviously, the more open you are to revising the map, the better things will be for you over time, while the more dedicated you are to the map, the more frustrated and angry you will become.

The same is true for our map of life. If we are willing to revise it as we encounter places where it fails us, we will be able to change and grow. If we insist that our map is right no matter what we encounter, we will make life miserable for us and everyone around us.

Please understand that we are not talking about changing our mind every time life is upsetting, or adopting whatever new thoughts come along. What we are referring to are the self-defeating patterns we all practice routinely, often with little awareness of what kind of map we are following until we bump up against reality. The mistaken ideas we have about self, life, God and others will repeatedly derail us unless we learn how to recognize them and get help with renewing our mind.

For example, a person growing up in a dysfunctional family can cause a person's idea of interpersonal conflict to be completely distorted into a need to destroy the opposition, rather than seek reconciliation. So when a conflict later arises in that person's workplace or church, their map takes them to a very destructive place even before they have time to think about what they are doing. These kinds of distortions in our map can play out in an almost endless number of ways.

Unfortunately, there are many people who are adamantly opposed to the idea that their map could have anything more than a few minor errors. When confronted with any sizable disconnect between their map and their experience, they will always accuse the circumstances and people around them of failure or malicious intent. They are convinced the problem *must exist outside* themselves. Their discomfort can never mean their map is incomplete, distorted, or out of date. For some reason they have come to believe that their map is who they are, and questioning their map feels like an attack upon their very sense of being. In many cases, challenging the map never even crosses their mind. They are determined to defend their map no matter how strong the evidence may be to the contrary, and no matter who gets hurt in the process. This is what we refer to as *the intent to protect*.

On the other hand, if we are willing to be uncomfortable within our own skin and to be open to revising our map whenever it makes sense to do so, we are then able to learn from our own mistakes and our own mistaken ideas about how life should work. Once we figure out that our map is much more flawed than we originally thought, and that revising the map leads to much more freedom and abundant joy, then life is no longer a fight to protect our status quo – it becomes an adventure in which we are continuously learning about who we are, who God is, and how life works in the kingdom. We have discovered the beauty and wonder of embracing the *intent to learn*.

Wherever we fall on this continuum — between intent to protect and intent to learn — makes all the difference in the world in terms of what kind of life we will have and whether or not we will be able to recover and grow. The more we are committed to protecting our map, the more we will remain stuck and continue to harm ourselves and others. The more committed we are to revising the map (or even tearing it up and starting over!) the more we will experience the abundant life Jesus talked about.

We are all subject to the intent to protect. It is in fact our default position. Whenever we react to life experiences without thinking, our most common basis for that reaction is an intent to protect our feelings, our self-worth, or our emotional investment. When we self-justify or shift blame or deflect negative comments, we are usually trying to protect ourselves in some manner and trying to minimize our feelings of loss or shame. For most of us, most of the time, this is really very automatic. We don't have to stop and think about what to do or say; we want to protect ourselves and these reactions just come out of us.

God is not afraid of how messed up our map might be. Nor is He disgusted with us, even when we have contributed to the distortions on the map ourselves. The only thing He cannot work with is any refusal on our part to deal with the map. But once we surrender our intention to protect our map and invite the Spirit of God to revise it to His heart's content, our life will never be the same and our joy will know no bounds! This is one of the most important keys to life we have open to us. We need to let go of our efforts to save our our own life (Mk.8:35) and embrace our Savior's invitation to become His apprentices and learn from Him (Mt.11:29).

Is Sin a Barrier to Engaging With God?

A common misconception many people hold is that when we sin God turns His back on us and stops wanting to have anything to do with us until we figure out what we did wrong, confess it, repent of it and ask for His forgiveness. Only then will God turn to face us and resume the relationship. This is a very distorted view of both God and sin, and greatly overestimates our ability to "get right with God." Above all, it assumes that sin is something I need to deal with before God will talk to me, and it reduces God's involvement to that of forgiving – as if we could accomplish the necessary change of heart in our own power. Frankly, this perception of sin and restoration is dangerously close to trying to earn God's attention.

My own experience is that the *opposite* is true. I may be engaging with God about some passage in Scripture, and as He begins to show me how it connects with my own life, it dawns on me that I have stuff that needs to be brought to God for His cleansing and renewal. Engaging comes first and reveals the sin, which God then offers to help me with. Or I may be dealing with some old wound that was left by earlier life experience, and in the middle of God healing it, I discover some resentment and unforgiveness I still hold in my heart as a result of the hurtful way I was treated. Again, my buried sin did not prevent me from engaging with God. Rather, by engaging with Him, the sin was revealed and dealt with.

Sin is not something that *we* can correct any case. It is something about which we work with *God* to put away. "If *by means of the Spirit*, you put to death the deeds of the flesh" (Rom.8). That requires engaging with God first, before the sin is dealt with, so that God can deal with the sin in ways that far surpass what we could "repent" of.

For those who really want to engage with God and are having difficulty doing so, it is important for them to understand that their sin is not getting in the way. Telling them "if you get right with God then He will connect with you" would be like asking a sick person to get well before they go see the doctor, because this particular doctor does not like to look at disease. No, the truth is that God wants to be deeply involved in our process of becoming whole.

So this may be a bit jarring, but it needs to be said. Generally speaking, sin is actually **not** a barrier to engaging with God! If it was, we wouldn't be able to engage with Him in order to repent. Jesus sat and ate with sinners all the time. He did not insist that they all repent and "get right" before He would have anything to do with them. "Blessed are the spiritually impoverished, because they are precisely the ones the kingdom is for!" (Mt.5:3). Jesus mentored His disciples for three years, and at the end they were still deeply flawed. That did not get in the way of their relationship. There is absolutely no evidence in the New Testament that our relationship with God is conditionally based on how cleaned up we are.

If God were to refuse to engage with us whenever we had some unconfessed sin, we would *never* be able to have a relationship with Him, because we are always missing the mark somewhere. The assumption that we can get righteous enough for God to connect with us is simply not biblical. The truth is, God *wants* us to come to Him with our sin and ask for His help in dealing with it so that we can actually be free of it, not just make some resolution about it. That requires us to work with Him as our Mentor and Healer, to dig out the roots of our malfunction and receive His love and truth experientially into those dark places.

There are actually only a few types of sin that can rupture our relationship with God or create a barrier to engaging with Him. And whenever the Bible talks about sin causing distance between God's people and God, the sin that is being addressed virtually always falls into one of these categories:

1. Wholesale idolatry, which makes sense, since in this sin the person is no longer even trying to connect with the true God. Idolatry disconnects us from God by definition.

2. Refusing to hear God, which again, makes sense. If the person has no desire for God to speak into their life, they have thrown up a major barrier.

3. Refusing to be impacted by what is heard (or by truth). If a person has decided not to respond to what God is revealing, they are effectively telling Him they are not interested in a transformative relationship.

4. Intentional self-indulgence. When a person is the center of their own universe and relegates God to the fringes of their life, there is very little that God can say to them that they would be willing to hear.

Notice in each of these conditions, we are the ones turning our back, not God. Even then He will pursue us for reconciliation and restoration. The idea that sin generally causes God to turn away is a misreading of Scripture and a misunderstanding of how this relationship works. God is simply not that conditional or that fickle. He is far more proactive in helping us with our failings than we can possibly know.

Summary

Barriers to engaging with God come in many forms with varying intensity and impact, and present us with a double edged problem: If I am encountering a barrier to God, how can I possibly engage with Him to get rid of the barrier?

Paradoxically, taking our barrier straight back to God in the belief that He knows what to do about it, actually makes the most sense. As a prime example of walking by faith instead of by our own understanding, holding our barriers up to God is not unlike coming to God as a lost sinner who is unable to fathom the wonders of grace. But come we must. That is our only way out.

Barriers between us and God are always God-sized problems. Our part is to bring them in faith and stay with Him as long as it takes for us to receive what God has for us in order to overcome whatever is in the way. Even more important is to recognize these issues, to notice when we are having trouble connecting with God, and to bring our concerns to Him. God wants our relationship with Him more than we can possibly imagine. Our task is to show up and begin to participate, even when we do not know how.

Resources for Further Study

John Townsend, *Hiding From Love: How to Change the Withdrawal Patterns That Isolate and Imprison You* (Zondervan) 1996

Interlude:
Practices for Christian Formation

> The things you have learned and received and heard and seen in me, practice these things, and the God of peace will be with you. (Phil.4:9 NASB)

Often referred to as *spiritual disciplines,* Christians throughout history have made use of various practices for connecting with God in ways that have proven to be beneficial for our soul. What we need to keep in mind, though, is that proper use of these practices is not at all self-evident. It would be best if we could all be mentored in how to engage in them, because it is the misuse and misunderstanding of spiritual practices that has led to their lack of use among Christians. For when these practices are misused, they become dead, often legalistic, exercises that have the opposite effect from what we would hope to gain from them. Learning how to practice spiritual disciplines in life-giving ways is very important to our spiritual health.

Our intent in reviewing some of the more classical practices as well as a few more recent adaptations of them is to demonstrate the manner in which they can be helpful for our Christian growth, how they can be life-giving instead of dry and lifeless, and what makes the difference between life-giving and life-draining practices.

Why Do We Need These Practices?

There are many reasons why people react to spiritual practices without much interest. Perhaps the actions required seem too disconnected from real life, too boring, or too trivial to make any difference. They may even recall trying to develop a devotional life that dried up after only a few weeks.

At first glance, it may be difficult to see how such simple practices could ever lead to any significant transformation. And without some vision of the value of spiritual practices, it is doubtful that anyone would take this approach to life seriously enough to engage in them. Hopefully the material in this book will help to alter those impressions, and I would encourage the reader to investigate the other resources listed as well. But before going any further, I would like to offer three very compelling reasons for making space in our life for spiritual practices.

First, we must understand that absolutely everything we do, everything we think or feel, every interaction we have with others, and everything that happens to us as well as how we react to what happens – all these things shape us spiritually and emotionally. This is how we are formed into the people we become. Once we grasp this truth, we can see the importance of doing whatever we can to involve ourselves in relationships and experiences that will contribute to the kind of formation we really want.

We see this principle played out all the time in marriages. When two people nurture their relationship and treat each other with kindness and respect and intentionally seek good for each other, then their love grows and their relationship becomes a source of joy to them. But when two people bicker and blame one another year in and year out, when they withhold kind words and actions, when they avoid each other for days at a time, their relationship suffers and they drift apart, finally ending in irreconcilable differences. In each case, the relationship is formed by every experience and non-experience they have with each other and eventually takes on a life of its own, for good or ill.

In the same way, our spiritual life is formed over time by the way we live. Given that all of our waking hours are spent interacting with a broken world and flawed human beings, we should expect that much of our experience is actually counter-productive and even harmful to our formation. For this reason alone it makes sense to deliberately carve out a space in our life to focus on those things that bring life, and to make a space for interacting with the Author of life, so that our malformation can be undone and our heart and mind can be renewed and re-formed in ways that strengthen us and shape us into the people God designed us to become.

That brings us to the second reason for spiritual practices, which is that they create a context for nurturing our relationship with God. More than anything else, our connection with God will shape our spirit in ways that we cannot even begin to imagine. This is what Jesus was talking about when He used the picture of a Vine and branches to illustrate the nature of the relationship He wants to have with us. Only by being connected to the Vine can we ever become a branch that bears fruit. Spiritual practices are designed to make a space for just that kind of connection. They also help us to grow that relationship into a way of life that is as real as any other relationship.

Third, this toxic world not only creates wounding and malformation in us that requires deliberate steps to reform who we are, it also *continues* to erode our soul and bring about loss throughout our lifetime. Only recurring encounters with God on a regular basis will offer us any hope of thriving rather than merely existing from day to day. Spiritual practices provide this resource to offset the corrosive effects of the world.

Far from being trivial or boring exercises, spiritual practices can open a doorway to an abundant life with God. This is why they have been used by all the great people of faith since the beginning of the Christian era. We would do well to learn how employ them in ways that bring life to us.

ENGAGING WITH GOD IN SOLITUDE

One of the oldest and most respected practices among Christians of all traditions is that of taking time to be alone with God. Getting away for an extended period of time to seek God, experience His presence, and listen to His voice can be incredibly refreshing. Just the quiet space by itself can be life-giving to your soul. When combined with moments of encounter with God, solitude can be a life saver.

Bear in mind that solitude does not have to last for forty days to be helpful. Genuine solitude can make a difference in our life no matter how long the time. What matters most is the extent to which we pull away from the distractions of everyday life and how closely we get connected with God. That said, spending more time away rather than less certainly allows us the possibility of experiencing much more depth.

Much of our identity gets tied up in daily life on the planet. Our work tells us we are a dentist, teacher, or bookkeeper. Relationships tell us how we matter to others around us. Even our home seems to say something about how clean or how creative we are. All of our successes and failures reflect our abilities, talents, and blind spots. With all of these messages coming at us from every direction, it can be very hard to remember at times who we really are and what really matters.

We can even get so caught up in maintaining day by day that we lose sight of what is really important. Demands at work can distract us from our family and friends. Shuttling between the children's soccer games and dance recitals can squeeze out quality time with each other. Even obligations at church can get in the way of experiencing God.

Solitude forces us to slow down, to set aside all these demands for a few hours and pay attention to our own soul, our spiritual condition, and our relationship to God. Without all the people, tasks, and other responsibilities telling us who we are, we are left with just our self and God to tell us who we are, whose we are, and how we matter. We have time to quiet our soul and listen more deeply than when we are rushing off to our next event.

As we make use of this space to engage with God for dialogue and reflection, we can go much farther into important issues than we can in any other context. We listen better, discern better, and have the time to pay attention to the quiet whispers of our heavenly Father. Areas in which we need His healing touch become more accessible, and God's words to us can penetrate far deeper. Truth we need for life has time to emerge. Everything good about appreciating the presence of God and directly interacting with Him becomes more enhanced in this sacred space.

There are many variations to the practice of solitude as well. We can set aside anything from an hour or two to an entire weekend, depending on what we need and what we want from our time. If we are on an extended retreat, it is usually helpful to alternate between times of connecting with God intensely and taking time to rest or go for a walk. Part of the time we may want to journal and dialogue with God, and part of the time we will want to just let Him hold us and rest in His presence.

Most of us do better with this when we get away somewhere that we cannot be easily reached. Retreat centers exist all over the world and are usually very reasonable in their daily rates. Some even offer spiritual guidance as an option while you are there. To be sure, we *can* make a space for solitude in our own home, as long as we are careful to turn off the phone and stay focused throughout our time and not get distracted by things that need to be done.

An alternative to taking a solitary retreat is to get away with your spouse or a close friend and share the experience. You can spend an hour or two apart and then come back together to share with each other the things that God is showing you or doing in your heart. Then you can enjoy a meal together before going back to more time alone with God. This rhythm of going back and forth can be very refreshing in itself. For those who are new to the practice of solitude, sharing the experience with another person can make a huge difference in dealing with any anxiety you might have about spending time in isolation.

There are good reasons why some of the most incredible stories we have of saints encountering God involve a time of extended prayer and solitude. Not that we should expect every retreat to be dramatic and life-changing. But we can expect solitude to be life-giving and renewing to our soul – if for no other reason than we need extended times with God in order to nurture our relationship with Him.

ENGAGING WITH GOD IN COMMUNITY

Because of our pervasive belief in individualism and our culturally biased distaste and distrust of community, we need to be reminded that we are designed for relationships We need each other far more than we know. While there is much we could say about the power of relationship and our deep need for one another, we will limit our comments here to just a few thoughts that are relevant to engaging with God as a group.

First, we must acknowledge that any gathering of Christians can have a wide range of possibilities from highly structured to formally polite to deeply personal. Getting together in a small group does not guarantee that we will connect relationally or emotionally. That depends on the intentions of the group and the relational openness of its members. If we focus on controlling the content of the discussion or teaching the correct answers to various Bible questions, we may find that the group has very little going for it relationally.

On the other hand, if we are openly honest with one another and supportive of each other's journey with God, whatever that may look like, then we may have the workings of a true community of believers. If we intend to build a communal space for engaging with God, such honesty is an absolute necessity. Corporate practices of engaging with God must be rooted in the belief that we can come to God as we are without putting on our best clothes or manners in order to be accepted. In this way we move toward a form of transparency that is refreshing and encouraging to everyone.

Second, we should always rejoice in another person's connection with God and with others. Joining others in their joy is an important aspect of building community. Some have referred to this as a three-way bond. Imagine a Mom, Dad, and Baby all enjoying the love bonds that exist between them. Dad looks on with joy as Mom and Baby connect; Mom enjoys watching Dad and Baby interact; and Baby is filled with joy in seeing Mom and Dad lovingly embrace. As Baby grows, interactions between the three of them grow, too, as roles and tasks are fluid and shared among them. These are all healthy three-way bonds.

In contrast, consider the possibility that because of her own insecurity, Mom becomes threatened by the bond that Baby has with Dad. Or what if Dad feels inadequate as a father and needs Mom to facilitate his connection with Baby? Or perhaps Baby is anxious about his or her connection with Mom and Dad, and becomes upset when the attention is focused between them instead of on Baby. Here the bonds are limited to dyads, and group bonds have become fearful.

Groups need to nurture these three-way bonds if they are to grow into life-giving communities. An environment like this becomes very affirming to relationships between group members, creates space for learning and growing, is far less susceptible to developing factions, and is capable of tremendous grace toward anyone wrestling with difficult issues.

Approaching spiritual practices together, a healthy community is thus able to proceed with anticipation and joy, knowing that people's experience will vary greatly from one another, yet without fear of that impacting any one's standing in the group or the relationships between the members. Any fruit that becomes evident is rejoiced over, and any frustrations are empathized with. Those who find a practice more life-giving will be graceful, helpful and encouraging toward those who are needing more time to learn. Those who are needing more help will receive hope and vision from the ones who are getting more from the practice. Together, they learn *how to learn* as a group.

We truly need each other more than we know. We need to learn what that means by our own experience.

Interlude: Practices for Christian Formation

Given the understanding that we can be formed spiritually by engaging in spiritual practices both in solitude and in community, we now turn our attention to the practices themselves and how we can make use of them in life-giving ways.

Making Space to Engage With God

	In Solitude	In Community
Appreciating God's Presence	Relational Quiet Private Worship Spiritual Reflection Abstaining or Extending Fasting Confession	Appreciation Stories Service to Others Recovery Support
Interacting Directly	Listen to the Word Dialog with God Repentance Healing Prayer	Encouragement Healing Prayer Forgiveness Intercession

PRACTICES OF APPRECIATING GOD'S PRESENCE

We begin with practices of appreciation, for several reasons. First, they are by nature far more accessible. None of the practices in this category require us to have much experience with conversational prayer or hearing God. Of course, there is nothing about these practices that precludes our hearing from God either. So for many, these can form a wonderful bridge to engaging with God more directly.

Second, these practices have stood the test of time because they help us to exercise our soul in life-giving ways. Just as a musician is helped by practicing scales and well-designed musical exercises, so also an apprentice of Jesus is aided by such things as spending five minutes every morning focusing on the goodness of God, or a few minutes at the end of the day reviewing all of the things they appreciate about their day. Many of the appreciation practices function much like aerobics for the soul. Since every experience of life impacts our spiritual formation, taking a few minutes to deliberately engage in a life-giving exercise can make a tremendous difference in our long-term spiritual health.

While the chart we are using lists several practices, in reality there are literally hundreds of ways we can exercise our heart and mind. Most books on spiritual disciplines, in fact, focus on these kinds of practices. I can heartily recommend any number of them, as long as you keep in mind the principles outlined in this book regarding the balance between God's part and our part.

Relational Quiet

This practice is about taking a few minutes to turn our thoughts toward God and how good He is to us, so as to quiet our heart and mind and experience the security of His presence. Perhaps beginning with a parallel in our human relationships is the easiest way to describe how to do this.

Nearly all of us know someone who is good for us. When we are with them we feel safe in their eyes. They know us fairly well, care about how we are doing, listen to our stories, and offer their encouragement and support. Spending time with them feels like food for our soul. In a word, we feel secure in their presence.

Furthermore, without trying very hard we can bring them to mind even when they are not around and feel those same feelings of security, goodness, and care. As we hold them in our heart and thoughts, our whole body seems to calm down and be more at peace. This is *relational quiet*: the ability to calm our nervous system by turning our inner focus toward someone we trust and with whom we feel secure.

If we hold that warm feeling for a moment, and then take notice that God is also with us in this way – safe and good for us – we can actually transfer our sense of relational quiet to Him and enjoy His presence with us without much difficulty. In this way, we can use a safe human relationship as a bridge to knowing how to be quiet in the presence of God. After we practice this for a while, we can begin to experience relational quiet with God very directly whenever we want, without first focusing on our friend.

Our soul needs rest just as surely as our body. Not all of our engaging with God needs to be in conversation. It is good just to "waste" time with God in quiet appreciation of His love and His presence. That is valuable in and of itself. From a health perspective, it is good for our soul and mind to move back and forth regularly between periods of activity and quiet. Being on the go all the time wears us down mentally and spiritually. And just like our body grows and repairs during sleep, we benefit greatly from dialing down for a few minutes several times a day.

In addition, once we learn how to quiet relationally whenever we want to, we can then make use of that ability in more stressful situations. We can then discern better and hear God better in times of stress. This ability also builds emotional capacity to tolerate greater amounts of stress without being overwhelmed, whether from fear, anger, shame, or whatever.

Resting with God can be practiced as a discipline all its own or as part of the time we spend with any of the other spiritual practices. For example, spending time in quiet after a conversation with God gives us a chance to absorb more deeply what we have seen and heard.

Those who find it extremely difficult to enter into relational quiet might want to consider seeking someone for help. Inability to quiet generally or to quiet relationally can wear on us in much the same way that sleep deprivation can, so this is important to address. Be aware that an inability to quiet may be rooted in anxiety that stems from distorted beliefs about safety or identity. In that case, asking God to help you see what keeps you from resting may reveal some important insights and lead to healing.

Spiritual Reflection

> Finally, brothers, whatever is true, whatever is noble, whatever is right, whatever is pure, whatever is lovely, whatever is admirable – if anything is excellent or praiseworthy – think about such things. (Ph.4:8 NIV)

Paul's famous passage on spiritual reflection calls us to ruminate on the things of God. The Old Testament encouraged God's people to meditate on their experiences of God's goodness. Often in the Psalms we see examples of dwelling on the things of God as a source of life.

There are several reasons why spiritual reflection is such an undervalued and under-practiced way of connecting with God among modern Christians. First, *we value productivity above listening.* We seem to think that listening to God is not very productive, and that unless we "do" something, we are wasting time or being lazy or self-indulgent in some way. But this is exactly why we get stuck in our Christian life and do not see much by way of transformation. We are still trying to master the Christian lifestyle and do enough in order to be good Christians. But as we have said repeatedly, no matter what we do in our own strength we cannot get to where we need to go. Rather, we need see and live life from God's perspective.

This is where spiritual reflection can begin to do its work. As we ruminate on God's ways and how different they are from our ways, we begin to see the futility of cranking out our spiritual development by our own effort. If God's mission in the world is overturning evil and reconciling people to Himself, then that work must begin with us – not by our physical contributions, but by our submission to the work God wants to do in us. I need to experience the defeat of evil in my own heart and mind before I have much to offer the world. I cannot export what I do not grow at home.

More than anything else, spiritual reflection is an acknowledgment that we need to deliberately counter the continuous assault of lies and distortions that come from the broken world around us. We need constant reminders of who we really are, and whose we are, and why we need God in order to live. Everything around us says otherwise. Meditating on the things of God helps us to retrain our mind to think in spiritual patterns and not in the patterns of the world. We need to be reminded of the unseen realities around us.

Furthermore, meditating on the truths of God helps us internalize them and make them part of our spiritual DNA. If we hold a word or phrase or picture during the day and ruminate on it, we can learn to see life more through the lenses of heaven and less from our earth-bound perspective.

For example, take the simple but profound picture of God being with us in all three persons. John (ch. 14-17) makes it clear that Jesus, God the Father, and the Holy Spirit are all with us, all the time. What if I begin to carry a picture of that in my mind with me? Suddenly, I am invited into the *community* of God, not just a dyad. Something in my heart rises to this and says, "Yes! I want that!" Such a life-giving image has amazing potential to reshape my feeling of aloneness or God's distance from me. Carrying that with me throughout my day can change how I see myself in the world and my place in the kingdom.

Consider the phrase, "You are not your own, for you were bought with a price" (1Cor.6:19-20). That brings to mind a whole host of ideas and images and questions. What does it mean for God to *own* my body? Where does that leave me? What is the difference between owning and being a steward of my own life? Am I relieved or disturbed by this prospect?

This is actually an extremely important issue, yet I would venture to say that relatively few Christians have thought much about it. What if we spent a few days or weeks contemplating this thought and having conversations with God about those areas we find difficult? What if we pondered at length the wonder of belonging to God?

Reflecting like this can go on indefinitely, because there is no end to the areas in which we might grow. Just meditating on the goodness of God over the span of several weeks can have a profound impact on our expectations and perceptions of God. Think of all the ways in which His goodness is expressed. Think of the character of God and what it means to have One that good and trustworthy dedicated to transforming your life. Imagine being cared about by someone who is more good than you can imagine!

Try wrapping your mind around the idea that God is in you and you are in God. What does it mean to be "in Christ?" What does Paul mean when he says, "I am crucified with Christ, nevertheless I live, yet not I but Christ lives in me?" How do I let Christ live in me? What would be different if I paid attention to Christ in me?

These are powerful thoughts and images to hold and reflect on. We need to marinate in them, let them soak deep into our mind and heart so we come to think this way naturally and do not have to constantly override whatever images we may hold from our past.

Truth takes time to emerge from our thoughts and time to sink into our heart. Spiritual reflection is a discipline that is terribly underrated, even trivialized. Yet it has the potential to reshape our thinking and aid us in renewing our mind. Furthermore, it forms a basis for dialoguing with God and a platform for listening to the Spirit.

Private Worship

One of the great things about music is that it engages parts of the mind that reading or reflecting may not touch. As we sing to God we literally worship Him with more of our mind, and internalize His love and care for us in the form of music memory and the images that music evokes in our mind.

Earlier we referred to the story in which Elisha asked for a minstrel to play for him so he could quiet his mind and focus on God better. "And then, while the musician was playing, the power of the Lord came on him" (2Kgs.3:15). It would appear that Elisha needed some help in focusing and quieting before God, and the music helped him to do just that. Music can be a great way for us to calm down and focus so that we can enter into dialogue with Him or listen to the Word better.

In our technological age we have a number of possibilities available to us. If you have the expertise, it can be very helpful to create a play list of songs that speak deeply to you and minister to you. You can even organize them into themes: perhaps one that focuses on the presence of God and how glad He is to be with you; another to remind you who you are in Christ; even one for times of repentance and reconciliation with God.

We can also make this a whole-body experience by moving with the music and learning to dance before the Lord as they did in Biblical times. (Finding time to be alone can be helpful here so that we do not feel self-conscious!) Allowing ourselves to feel the music in our body can be very freeing and helps to internalize it more deeply.

Music can be a powerful way to spend time with God in and of itself, as a way of receiving His love and experiencing His presence. We can be transformed by love just as surely as we can be transformed by truth spoken by God. So it is important to just be with God and enjoy Him.

Confession

Confession is another practice that can become very life-giving. As a discipline, confession has several forms, each with its own purpose. Traditionally, confession refers to the act of admitting the wrongs we have done and asking for forgiveness. While acknowledging that there is value in doing that, there is a lot more we can receive from this practice that can

Interlude: Practices for Christian Formation

foster healing and change beyond being forgiven. Perhaps it might be helpful to think of confession as *the practice of full self-disclosure before God*, in which we seek to be completely honest about where we are in our process. Such transparency is commonly seen in the Psalms.

Full disclosure is something we can incorporate into most of our other spiritual practices, especially when we are having conversations with God. Another way to describe this kind of confession is that *we are offering our best understanding of something in the hope of knowing God's heart in the matter.* With God's help, we dig deeply into our thoughts and feelings about something and participate with the Spirit to expose them to the light of day. In the process it is not uncommon to discover things we did not even know about our own heart.

For example, I mentioned elsewhere that on one particular day I had some difficulty with the verse, "To whom much is given, much is required." As I contemplated the feelings that it brought up, I felt led to confess to God the shame and dread I felt when I read those words. To my eyes, after all He has done for me, my actions were pitiful in comparison. I could never "catch up" as it were, to His generosity. I was not trying to repent of anything, but simply attempting to start what seemed like an important dialogue about my life and my purpose. This verse had touched something deep within me and I needed to talk to my Father about how I felt.

So when the thought came to me that I would *never* be able to live up to what was "required" of me, I suddenly sensed not shame but love, as if God was saying: "*Of course* you won't be able to keep up with me! I'm not that stingy!" The verse is not about repaying a debt as much as it is about honoring the gifts and the Giver. It may not even be about *doing* something as much as it is about changing and *becoming* someone different.

The point here is that by examining my heart as best I could, and by inviting God to examine my heart further, I was led to places I would not have otherwise seen, apart from my exposure to the light. I offered God what I saw and my interpretation of the data. He responded with love and an insight I needed. I ended that time with Him not by feeling ashamed and making some commitment to try harder, but by being drawn deeply by His love and grace to give my body and soul more fully to Him who gives so much to me.

When we confess to God our best understanding, it can include any of the following:

- Where we are in our journey.
- What deficiencies we can see.
- What we believe to be true, doctrinally.
- What feels true experientially.
- Our inclinations.
- Where we feel helpless or hopeless.

In response, God will offer us:

- His perspective on what we have observed.
- Details we have overlooked or minimized.
- How He interprets that information and our experiences.
- His heart in the matter.

In this way, confession becomes a way to open our heart and expose what is there, and to receive something of what we are missing.

Negative Confession

Now in some places there is a teaching that we should never say out loud the things in our heart that we fear or that are faulty. Referred to as a "negative confession," these kinds of statements supposedly give power to the enemy. Consequently, we should not say those things except in a prayer of renunciation or repentance.

The problem is that such teaching also assumes we can actually change what we believe by an act of the will. But except for a very select area of loosely held beliefs, this is simply not true. Most of the negative things that we assume about life have been learned from experience. And while some of these may be easily denied, they are not easily changed. This kind of teaching also ignores a great portion of the Psalms which are brutally honest about what is going on in the author's heart and mind.

Yes, we can espouse negative thoughts with an air of confidence that bolsters our belief in them, and that is not good for us. For example, if I speak with conviction and resignation that the reason a certain event occurred is because I live under Murphy's curse, my statement has a way of reinforcing that belief in my soul and my bondage to it. But that is not at all the same thing as exposing my dirt to the light in the presence of God so that He can show me what I am missing and renew my mind with His insight and teaching. With God, I need to be as honest as I can be about all the hate and anger and doubts and resistance in my heart and whatever else I harbor that is contrary to life in the kingdom. The deeper I dig the more I am able to see its extent and the more amazing will be His revelation to me.

When the prodigal came to his father, his intent was to confess not just his failings but his interpretation as well, along with his best idea for a remedy. He may even have been afraid of what his father would say. But his father responded with love and a redefinition of what had happened. "My son was dead and now is alive!" The older brother also confessed what he thought were the important facts along with his interpretation of the events and why he felt slighted. And it appears that he was not at all interested in his father's reasons for celebrating. But again the father reframed the experience and offered his perspective in the hope that his son would change his heart and reconcile with his brother. Confession was basically each son's part of the conversation.

We see confession at work in the life of Peter throughout the Gospels. Peter often gets bad reviews because he is always opening his mouth and letting something foolish come out. But such criticism is terribly unfair to Peter, because he is simply revealing what is in his heart and how he sees things. Chances are he was not the only one thinking that way at the time, but he was the only one willing to be exposed. He even argued with God when he was shown the vision of unclean animals and was told to have them for dinner. Peter was not one to roll over easily. But he learned how to be teachable. And that is why he was the perfect choice for the one to bring the gospel to Cornelius and to believe that Gentiles could be saved (Acts 10).

Positive Confession

At the other end of the spectrum is a practice that is referred to as *positive confession*. Again, we need to be careful. On the one hand, it is good for us to reaffirm what is good and true. For example, "I am truly grateful that I am a child of God and that He wants to be with me." We can all use reminders like this, and saying them out loud helps to train our perspective.

On the other hand, people are often encouraged to profess things they do not actually believe. For example, a person who is convinced they have done something unforgivable should not be asked to profess, "I believe God has forgiven me for everything" in an attempt to counter their difficulty with receiving God's grace. That is basically an effort to bury their feelings and talk themselves out of what they actually believe. Besides the fact that this is not how change happens, such a practice is a form of denial and an attempt to repress what is going on inside their heart and mind. A much healthier and more biblical approach is to confess what they *actually* feel and ask God for His help in healing their broken experience.

Confession is essentially a step in an ongoing conversation with God, a way of participating with the light God wants to shine on our heart and soul. When practiced in total transparency, it opens a space for God to do what only He can do. In that way it becomes a life-giving practice.

Fasting

Have you ever asked the question, "What does fasting have to do with my spiritual life?" After all, fasting is a physical act. How can that possibly improve my spirituality?

Well the reason why it is so hard to see a direct link between fasting and spiritual health is *because very little direct link exists!* Now that may be a bit jarring. But remember our premise, that spiritual disciplines do not change us by the act of doing them. We really must see this clearly. Fasting can be a purely physical act done for health reasons, with little or no impact on our soul. We may learn a little self-control in the process, and even experience a kind of calm that comes from fasting. But those benefits fall under the category of *human* development which is something anyone can learn and experience, Christian or not.

Fasting does however provide us with a unique context for encountering God, which is how it can be beneficial to us spiritually. First, I find out what happens when I say "No" to the desires of my body. I learn about the sway my urges have on my life, how much I *use* food, and the extent to which immediate gratification plays into my everyday choices. My dependence on God is tested in a way that I do not experience when I am always satisfied.

Second, it is really hard to forget that I am fasting! There is an almost constant awareness that I am denying my body what it wants. Ordinarily, it can be very easy to forget that God is with me, and I may have difficulty maintaining an awareness of the presence of God in my life. But I cannot forget I am fasting for any significant length of time. If I use that awareness to remember God and connect with Him, I will be almost constantly aware of Him, which can be an invaluable experience of His presence.

Third, on an extended fast, the body slows down after about three days, along with the entire nervous system. We experience an inner quiet and calm that is radically different from our usual state of hyper arousal. If we then enter into God's presence in this quiet space, we may be able to pay attention and listen to Him better than we are normally capable of.

There are other benefits as well, and I will leave them to other sources. Speaking of which, if you have never fasted it is important that you do some research before embarking on a food fast. Westerners are more accustomed to "fast food" than fasting. If a person goes on a fast without proper preparation, it is possible to harm their body. Especially with the significant increase in sugar-related illnesses in recent years, fasting requires some education and perhaps even a discussion with your doctor.

Had we grown up in a culture where fasting was common, we would have been trained in the proper ways to begin and end a fast so we do not get stomach cramps or have other physical problems that fasting can precipitate. But with good training and careful attention, fasting can be quite beneficial to our body, helping to purge out toxins and chemicals that accumulate over time in our modern diet. Again, this is my official disclaimer. Please do not attempt fasting without learning more about how to do it safely. There are many books available on the subject to help you.

We can also fast from specific types of food. Some people periodically cut out red meat. Some would do better to see what happens when they stop eating chocolate or ice cream. Especially when we are turning to certain foods for comfort, making a conscious decision to say "no" can help us get in touch with deeper issues that need God's healing touch.

Fasting has always been a useful form of spiritual practice, primarily because it involves our entire body and requires us to pay attention to our practice throughout the day. If we use each reminder as a moment to connect with God, we will be thinking about Him all day long.

Service to Others

God designed us with an intense need to give life to one another. In a life-giving community, people receive and give life to each other on a continual basis. Extending ourselves in this way is an important aspect of God's command to love one another. There are many ways we can do this. Most of the things we normally associate with "serving one another" are ways in which we can give life, such as:

- Providing food for the hungry.
- Offering respite for full-time care-givers.
- Stopping to offer assistance to someone in need.
- Giving our time to help someone move.
- Giving money to alleviate the suffering of another.
- Helping out in a soup kitchen.
- Joining the Big Brother program (or similar organization).
- Offering foster care (not for the faint of heart).
- Visiting the elderly.

Now at first glance, one might think these are all ways of "rowing" our way toward change – and they certainly have been that for many people. But as with the other spiritual practices, the spiritual value of serving depends on how we understand our part and God's part as we engage in these practices.

First, we want to avoid the pitfall of mentally dividing people into two groups – those who serve and those who are served. Although rarely done consciously or intentionally, Christians sometimes view the spiritual life as if it consists of three main steps: (1) conversion; (2) training for service; (3) and then service. Once you reach step three, you continue to serve until you die or until Jesus returns.

Closely related to this approach is the idea that service is simply a matter of obedience. Christians are supposed to perform good works to show God's love. If you are not involved in some form of service you are either lazy, disobedient or indifferent to God's commands.

When approached from either of these perspectives, service is clearly an attempt to "row." We try hard to do something good and keep doing it even when we do not feel like doing it, because this is what we are supposed to be doing. Consequently, we may even burn out from too much "service."

Of course, many people feel deeply called to some particular form of service, and do so with joy and satisfaction. Nothing said here ought to detract from that. Serving from the heart is in fact where we want to be. That is how God intends for us to serve. Doing so may even strengthen our relationship with God and deepen our spiritual life.

But for many others, even if they might be reluctant to admit it, service can be a real chore or viewed as an imposition on their limited time. It is here that we can benefit greatly by participating in service as a spiritual practice. Probably the most obvious place of healing in this regard has to do with any reluctance to get involved or any later regrets that develop after getting involved in some project. Suppose I decide to volunteer at a kitchen for homeless people. For a while, I get up on Saturday morning and go to the shelter to help scramble eggs, wash dishes, and serve those who come in for breakfast. Initially, it may even feel really good to be involved in something that makes a difference for so many destitute people.

Then comes the week where I would rather go to the lake with friends, or perhaps sleep in and have some down time. I go in to the kitchen anyway, and some drunken homeless person throws up on my clothes. I am so disgusted I am tempted to quit right then and there. A few months later I am beginning to resent all the time I am giving up, and it crosses my mind to stop coming altogether.

Each of these feelings might point to some level of inner resistance to the service I am trying to do. Or to put it another way, participating in this practice has tremendous potential to expose my limitations, my biases, my preferences for self, or areas of my heart that are yet unhealed. Once these parts of myself are brought to the surface, I can then bring these areas to God and ask for His help in restoring my heart and showing me what I need in order to continue to grow.

In this way, our service actually becomes training ground for our own spiritual development. Rather than viewing myself as "spiritual" for serving others, I see myself as a trainee in kingdom life, learning how to become more like Jesus and finding those places in my heart that need more of His mentoring and healing. I am learning by being involved.

God always wants to bring life to the minster as much as He wants to bring life to those we minister to. When we give a cup of water in Jesus' name, we discover something about our heart. If what we find is that we are rejoicing in being able to be part of what God is doing in the world, then we can move in closer to God in gratitude for what He has done in us. If what we find is that we have trouble giving joyfully, then we can move in closer to God for more healing and mentoring in some area of our soul. Service is as much for us as it is for those we serve. By engaging in a variety of types of service, we can place ourselves in numerous contexts, each with its own potential for triggering our "stuff." In this way, service becomes a spiritual discipline for our own growth.

A Life-Giving Task

From a developmental perspective, we all need to be needed. We all have an innate need to be of good to someone, to have a life-giving impact that makes a difference. Whether it has to do with helping our family survive, or easing the burden of someone, or simply being present with another person, we all need a life-giving task.

While it is good for us to practice a number of forms of service, most of us will find that certain particular kinds of service feel more like a calling or a mission that we can become intensely passionate about. And what seems like an absolutely essential endeavor to one person may feel like a bother to the next one. Each of us will be drawn to a different form of service because of who we are and how we have been formed.

Sometimes this compelling desire comes from what we might call "the main pain of our heart." For example, the woman who started Mothers Against Drunk Drivers did so because she lost a child to a drunk driver. Her greatest pain became her mission, and we have all benefited from her work. Our pain may be very different from hers, and our calling may be far less public. But having a heart that was forged in the fires of painful experiences or even our own brokenness can be a tremendous asset. Of course, we want God's healing in those areas as well. Serving from a place of pain is not what we have in mind here. But once we are well on our way to restoration, our experience can provide us with great motivation to make a difference in the lives of others.

On the flip side, instead of our main pain, we could be called to minister from what we might call "the main characteristic of our heart." For example, if I have a God-given passion for preschoolers and what they are discovering at that point in their lives, I probably need to find a way to give life to those children. Similarly, a person might have a heart for young single women who are facing an unwanted pregnancy, even though they themselves have never been in that place.

Finding a way to give life that comes from who you are can be one of the most rewarding experiences of your life. If you are unsure what is the main characteristic of your heart (or your main pain), be sure to seek God about this. Ask a trusted friend to tell you how they see you as well. It will be well worth your effort to join God in His mission to overturn evil with good.

God's Model for Serving

God never meant for us to burn out from serving one another or to dread being sucked dry from giving all the time. One of the best ways to envision service is to picture a multi-tiered fountain in your mind where the water cascades from one pot to another several times before reaching the lowest level of the fountain. God's model for serving is to be like one of the pots in the middle sections, so that you are being filled to overflowing and spilling into the life of another one downstream from your self.

"Freely you have received, freely give," Jesus said (Mt.10:8). We can only give away what we have been given. And giving is not draining when we give from an over-abundance of what God is pouring into us. This is how we can give joyfully instead of out of "obedience" from an empty well.

A Heart of Compassion

One final note on acts of service: our intent in all this is to find our heart formed in ways that allow us to serve others with joy, and to do so out of who we have become rather than just because we should. Our Father loves to give; that is His character. And as we develop a heart of love and compassion, in part by addressing any barriers we uncover in the acts of serving one another, we align ourselves with the heart of God and become more like Him.

What may surprise us in this process is how much joy there is in giving away life. God has not called us to burn out from giving. He has shown us how we were designed to live, and demonstrated by His own lavish gifts that our true nature is found in losing our life for the sake of goodness.

Abstaining or Extending

Rather than a single practice, this phrase actually encompasses two major types of spiritual practices. (In many texts, spiritual disciplines as a whole are divided into these two categories, which can be a useful way to look at them). There are three reasons why practices of abstaining and extending are often considered classical disciplines. First, they are within the ability of most people to do. Anyone can abstain from something they would otherwise normally do, or extend themselves to do something which they would normally not do. Second, when properly used, these practices can be far more beneficial than one might expect. Third, there are literally hundreds of ways we can abstain or extend for the purpose of fostering growth.

Before going any further, perhaps a few examples would be helpful. Fasting is in fact a practice of abstaining, and Service to Others is a main form of extending. We addressed those two separately in this book because they involve our whole body more completely than most other practices. But there are many other ways of abstaining and extending, each with its own context and purpose. For example, we can unplug the television for a couple of weeks and see what happens. We might discover a lot of underlying restlessness or boredom. Perhaps we will rediscover the wonder of books or of spending more time interacting with other members of the household. If video games dominate your time, that might be a better place to practice abstaining. For others it might be shopping or something else. Dropping anything that consumes us can be quite a wake-up for us and may reveal any number of things about our internal needs. Abstaining can also be as simple as refraining from saying anything bad about anyone for a couple of weeks.

As for extending, anything we normally think of as volunteer work falls into this category. We could put in time at a food shelf or a soup kitchen for the homeless. Short term mission trips, teaching Vacation Bible School, participating in a ministry at your local church, or virtually any other such activity can be a way of extending ourselves. Setting a goal of memorizing a chapter of Scripture or taking five minutes at the end of each day to list the things you appreciate could also come under this heading.

The obvious question then is how we are helped by these practices of abstaining and extending. Generally any such practice will create in us one of two main reactions. Either we will enjoy the change or else it will stir up things in us that need to be addressed with God. If our experience is more on the positive side, it will strengthen our soul and give us an opportunity to express gratitude to God.

For example, if I give up my daily latte for a few weeks and donate the money instead to my favorite charity, I might be surprised by how much joy I experience in deliberately making a difference in the lives of others. That is a great reason to rejoice and be grateful. I can then actively appreciate the work of God in my life for showing me how much I gain by giving away some of my resources. I may even ask God to help me find other ways I can contribute to the good of other people.

On the other hand, I might discover that I really resent not having my latte or resent how much I am giving away. In that case the practice has revealed an issue in me that I may not have been fully aware of before in regard to generosity. I can be grateful for the revelation and then begin to work with God to renew my heart and mind in that area.

On one particular Thanksgiving, my wife and daughter and I helped to serve a turkey dinner in an assisted living community. Frankly, it was hard work and we were exhausted by the end of the day. But what surprised us was how much joy we felt from all the interactions we had with the old folks and from the appreciation they expressed for our labors. We came away from that experience strengthened in our souls and glad for the opportunity. Thus, by extending ourselves we were formed and blessed.

Abstaining and extending practices can then benefit us in one of two ways. When our experiences prove to be positive, we are further formed in our spirit and strengthened in our spiritual journey. And when they stir up issues within us that need to be transformed, we can then engage with God for any healing or renewal we need. Either way, we benefit from deliberately practicing things that will create new contexts for growth.

Telling Our Stories

We have all been blessed by hearing powerful stories of redemption and restoration, such as the one portrayed in the movie *The Blind Side*, or by the personal testimonies of people like Joni Eareckson Tada, or even heart-warming stories that get passed around by email or that we might read in *Chicken Soup for the Soul*.

Stories like these impact us deeply for very good reasons, including the fact that our brains are designed to process stories of others. Research in recent years has validated what oral cultures knew centuries ago: that stories about life communicate meaning from one person to another in ways that are unmatched by direct teaching alone. We are designed to think narratively – about how one thing leads to another and how events and people are inter-related to one another. Many of life's lessons can be encapsulated in story form and passed on to others so that they can learn through vicarious experience.

Parables are one example of narrative teaching in Scripture. When you add to that the historical books of the Bible and the retelling of those stories in the prophets and apostolic letters, along with their interpretations and applications, much of the Bible consists of stories that were given to us to show us what it means to be connected to God. Hearing the parable of the prodigal son, for example, or the good Samaritan, we find ourselves *experiencing* the truths of those stories as much as we think about them. That is why they can have such tremendous impact.

When stories are personal, they reveal our heart and bring people together. We catch meaning from them that would be difficult to put into words or express as principles to be applied. Through stories we can try out the experiences of others to see if they "fit" for us; we download wisdom from both the wise and foolish choices of others; we can imagine our own potential solutions to problems to see if they match with who we want to be as a person; we can even see people and events from another person's point of view. Stories teach us about cause and effect in human relationships, express the value of things, and allow us to explore other ways of being and ways of engaging with one another.

Consequently, one of the most valuable means of engaging with God and helping others to engage with God is to share stories of our personal experiences with each other. What is God showing us? How does He do that? What happens inside us when we spend time alone with God? What is it like to forgive a family member of a long-standing problem? What does it mean to follow Jesus in our workplace? How has a short-term mission trip impacted our soul?

These are important messages to convey to one another. We need to hear how God is at work in others, as well as how other people wrestle with life issues. Story telling needs to become a formally recognized feature of our meetings together. More than just "checking in," our intention must be to share our hearts with one another, and to allow the Spirit of God to use those stories for encouragement, insight, and for binding us together.

Recovery Support

Unless a person has personally been involved in a healthy support group, it would be very hard for them to imagine how life-giving these small communities can be. For those who have needed such a group and found a good one, they can testify that support groups can be a life saver.

Many resources are available that describe what makes the difference between a good group and a mediocre one, so we will not go into much detail here. For our purposes, we will define a support group as a small gathering of people who share a similar life issue and who willingly offer one another their stories and their support.

When a support group has developed into a life-giving community, it offers its members a number of vital elements that foster their recovery process. To begin with, each member feels heard and understood by others. Whether people have come together for addiction recovery, grief support, or over some other life issue, everyone else in the group knows from their own experience something about what others are going through. They know the depth of what is being expressed in a given person's story and how it feels. That alone is worth a great deal.

Few things are as disconcerting and isolating as telling someone about your deepest pain and have them look at you like you are from another planet. But outside of support groups, such experiences are extremely common. A person going through a painful divorce might try to explain their distress to a married person, only to receive back a quizzical look conveying a complete lack of comprehension. Or someone might say a few words about being in counseling, and their listener pulls away from them ever so slightly, as if they might catch something. Such experiences can be incredibly painful or create tremendous distance between people.

On the other hand, when another person in your support group can effectively finish your sentence as you stumble for words, or when you see tears come to their eyes as they listen to your story, you feel cared about and less isolated and alone. Besides that empathy, when others exercise the kind of heart-sight that is truly encouraging, a support group can become one of the most important experiences of a person's life. God's desire is to restore people who are broken or sick or needy, and we can participate with Him in that process extremely well within the context of a working support system.

Because we feel heard in a good recovery group, we find a place to belong. Whatever the unifying issue, these become "our people." Members of such groups often report that they have found another family. This can be especially important for people who are dealing with family of origin issues or the loss of a beloved relative. God designed us to be part of something bigger than ourselves. And if our immediate family is not accessible to us or not supportive of us, these groups can become a highly functional substitute, even if only for a season.

Furthermore, since every person in the group is at a different stage of recovery, we benefit by watching others who are farther along than we are. For example, in a grief support group there will be people who have lost someone just a few days or weeks prior, as well as those who have been working through their grief for months or perhaps a year or more. To see someone else moving along in their recovery can provide a great sense of hope that perhaps I, too, can be there someday. Their encouragement has substance to it, because they have walked through that restoration process themselves.

The possibilities for support groups are almost endless. Groups exist for recovery from various forms of childhood abuse, addiction to substances or destructive behaviors, dysfunctional family dynamics, grief, uncontrolled anger, and almost any other type of trauma. The important thing to remember when looking for a group is that every one has its own flavor. Differences can range from variations in ground rules to the median age of the members to the length of time most people have been part of the group. For example, one alcoholics anonymous group might permit a lot of advice-giving between group members, while another might ban advice altogether. One group may be very empathic while another may simply push the program. It is even possible for a particular set of individuals to have been meeting together so long that the group has lost its original purpose or become ingrown. For these reasons it is important to keep in mind that not all groups are created equal, and it may take some perseverance to find one that fits well. But it is also worth the trouble.

The reason support groups are listed as a type of communal spiritual practice is because they provide a unique context for exposing what is buried inside us, as well as for encountering God. Telling our stories to those who can truly hear us is a spiritual exercise in and of itself (that is what many of the Psalms are made of). And since God can speak through others – especially others who have journeyed ahead of us – support groups are an ideal place for us to open our hearts and receive from one another the gifts that God is working among us.

Before moving on, it is important to note that in recovering from life trauma there are three different kinds of relationships that can be helpful, each in their own time. First, there may be a need for some intensely serious work requiring the skills of a trained counselor or prayer minister. Working one-on-one can provide tremendous initial relief, especially when the counselor knows how to involve God in the healing process.

Second, support groups provide a very homogeneous community where we can safely tell our stories and belong and be known. Unless there is a particular reason to continue long term (such as support for care-givers of disabled family members) most support groups work best as a transitional community. In order to finish the recovery process, we eventually need to move on to the third form of community.

At this third level, we need to become re-integrated with the larger diverse community. God designed us to be connected to a multi-generational group of people who come from all walks of life and who live daily with a wide variety of victories and problems. This is where we want to land, and not to remain indefinitely in support groups alone. Recovery implies that we seek to be restored to the larger community.[49]

Engaging with others to address significant life issues can provide us with the means to recover from what might otherwise be a much longer road to restoration. Walking alongside others and sharing our stories with those who have experienced similar hurts is far more powerful than one might expect. As with all spiritual practices, we are fed in ways that we could not achieve by any direct effort alone.

Practices of Engaging Directly With God

In addition to the many practices of appreciation, there are a number of spiritual practices that focus heavily on engaging directly with God. In general terms, these are all ways of creating a context for interacting with God, in which we are far more intentional about the quality of our connection with Him than we normally are, and we are more receptive to His Spirit, allowing Him to work in us and reveal His heart to us.

Dialogue with God

At the very core of spiritual development is our need to hear and see what the Father wants to do in us. That is, we must learn how to have two-way conversations with God so that He can mentor us. As this is part and parcel of having a tangible relationship with God, we sometimes refer to this step in our spiritual walk as developing a conversational relationship with God.

Much of this has already been discussed in Chapters 3 and 4 where the whole area of hearing God was presented. The point we want to make here is that since receiving from God is foundational to growth and change, this practice is a key component in our hope for renewal. As we stated earlier, spiritual disciplines are not in themselves able to change us. Each one simply makes a space for engaging with God within the context created by the discipline. While most of the other practices offer various settings and touch different areas of our life, being able to talk to God about what comes up

---

[49] This three-level model comes from Judith Herman, *Trauma and Recovery*.

during those practices allows us to go far deeper and to be further transformed by God.

For example, suppose I take time for a personal retreat with God. As I quiet down over the space of an hour or two, I begin to notice a kind of anxiety rising up inside, making it difficult to stay focused. So I ask God to help me see what is bothering me. I may then become aware that I am feeling particularly lonely. Then I might notice that my busyness for the last few weeks has really been about distracting myself so that I do not feel the loneliness. At this point I may have hit upon a major driving force in my life that I am not usually aware of. As I talk to God about my isolation and aloneness, I can ask Him how He can fill that space in my life, what I am missing in regard to my human relationships, and so on. As my Mentor, He can open my heart to old wounds that have led to my isolation, my disappointments with others, my lack of trust in Him, and any other factors regarding this area of my life.

Learning to have conversations with God is not only an essential practice in and of itself, it opens the door to a number of other ways of directly interacting with Him.

Listening to the Word

A special form of dialoguing with God is talking with Him about the words of Scripture. As we rely less on our own attempts to find applications and more on what the Spirit of God wants to say to us, He will often lead us to what we need at that moment in time. This can be far more transformative than trying to wring out some general principle to apply with our own wisdom and strength.

Again, this was covered in more detail in Chapter 3. It is being restated here because it is one of the more accessible and helpful disciplines. This is also relevant to the discussion in Chapter 6 about balancing God's part and our part. We do *not* want to do God's job of revealing Scripture to us. Trying hard to apply what we see in the Bible can actually be a sophisticated form of self-effort. It is trying to do God's part in renewal, and it will not produce very much change.

For those who are familiar with the Inductive Bible Study method, I do not want to discourage that. Properly used, it can yield some great principles. The problem is what to do with the principles we come up with. Simply trying to obey everything we learn will leave us really tired and discouraged over time. But if we take these principles to God and ask Him to show us why we have so much trouble following through on a particular thing, we will have a shot at real and lasting change.

Without the Holy Spirit teaching us, we are forced to "lean on our own understanding" (Prov.3:5). Just because we try to draw our thoughts from the teachings of the Bible does not mean we have escaped the problem of relying on our own understanding. Our best effort to apply scripture to our life is still dependent on our own wisdom and willpower, and is not really the kind of receiving from God that will set us free.

God's voice carries with it the power of life. When we read the text of the Bible, we may or may not hear the life in those words. But when engage with the Holy Spirit and ask Him to take those words and reveal them to us, we receive them deep into our heart and mind and are changed by them.

Repentance

Repentance is yet another way to participate with God for change that has become a dreaded practice for many Christians. In groups where life is viewed as a choice between obedience and disobedience, repentance is often taught as the primary means of changing our life by an act of the will. The underlying theory is that if a person is convicted deeply enough and is sorry enough for whatever it is that they are wrong about, they will repent and change their ways.

Thankfully, there are many places where repentance is seen in a much more graceful light, and people are not shamed into repenting. But even so, what we need to know is repentance alone cannot accomplish restoration.

Contrition and the desire to do better are good things. There are even some things about ourselves that we can change if we feel strongly enough about them. But many of the deeply ingrained thoughts and feelings that drive our life require far more than what we can achieve by making a resolution to try harder.

The truth is, repentance is far more powerful when approached as a *desire for change* rather than the change itself! Instead of asking for God to forgive me for gossiping about my co-worker and promising not to do it any more, what if I asked God to search my heart and mind for the things that caused me such contempt for my co-worker in the first place? The difference is that I am seeking a change of heart, not just a change of behavior. A change of heart is generally something I cannot do, even when I really want to be different than I am.

Repentance then becomes a process of engaging with God for greater change and not a single act of contrition. Feeling sorry for an action or inaction is a signal that something is wrong with my soul, and my spirit has noticed I need help. Repentance is acting on behalf of that urging to be more like my heavenly Father. But repentance does not presume to be the whole of it or even the direct means for change. Repentance is mainly the decision to go to my Mentor and show Him my brokenness and ask Him to do in me what I cannot do. God can then show me my own heart and reveal to me what He knows I need in order to become different in character, not just in behavior.

This is an act of aligning with our true self, the new identity that God has already given us. It may even take a while to work out all the underlying beliefs, wounds, and other issues that are involved in the matter at hand. But it is cause for rejoicing and hope. It is a move toward freedom from bondage, even an act of compassion for our own soul. Repentance is the choice to allow the work of the kingdom to rule in our own body and mind, however long it takes and whatever muck and goo it may uncover. And when the work of God is complete in us in regard to that issue, we can be sure that we have become more free than we were before we began.

One of the more profound and obvious forms of this kind of repentance can be seen when an addicted person finally admits they are out of control, and enters a support group for their problem, finds a good sponsor, and begins to work the program. No illusion of a one-time prayer enters the picture. Their recovery is seen as a life-long process that depends heavily on *help from outside* themselves. This is repentance as a *process*.

One time when I was reading Psalm 27, the phrase "Come, my heart says, seek the Lord" caused me some pain. I realized at that point in my life, my heart was not saying that very loudly. I had largely lost my passion for more of God. Realizing I really did want that longing, I *repented* by asking God to forgive me for my casual, cavalier attitudes and *show me how* to desire more of Him. He began a process that day to reveal more of Himself to me over time, and to grow my desire for Him in ways I could never have imagined that first day.

Repentance is far more effective when approached from the basis of *a desire for change* that needs God's help, rather than trying to make the change happen by an "act" of repentance. Such an approach opens a door for engaging with God that can truly change us from the inside out. As such, repentance is born more out of the hope of becoming stronger, rather than from the shame of where we are at the moment or a faulty dependance on our own ability to change.

Inner Healing Prayer

Although this will be covered more in depth in Chapter 9, inner healing is mentioned here as a way of highlighting how common it really can become. If we are paying attention well, both to our automatic reactions to events and during our times of engaging with God, the opportunities for healing will emerge quite often. Inner healing prayer is primarily an interaction with the Spirit of God in which we encounter love and truth at such a depth that they change us in some significant way. Some of the greatest barriers we face in our spiritual growth are the distorted beliefs we have about God, about ourselves, and about life. When these lies are destroyed and replaced by truth or through experiencing God's love more deeply, we can discover great freedom and the ability to live more as God intended for us to live.

Wounds we have received from bad experiences generally leave scars on our soul in the form of distorted interpretations of those experiences. In addition, many good things we needed in life that we did *not* receive can also cause us to lose our sense of value. These distortions lead us to fail in many areas of life. Those failures in turn breed still more lies.

For example, some children grow up in families where they are expected to fill the needs of their parents, while other children get ignored altogether. In either of these environments, these tender young ones do not experience being known for who they are, which is foundational to having a meaningful sense of self.[50] This can be very damaging to a developing mind and create a truly distorted self-image and even deep-seated self-hate. From that point forward, these children can become trapped in a never-ending effort to be heard or noticed or to have some sense of value. These efforts will then instill even more distorted beliefs about who they are and how they matter. At some point they will need to address these wounds and find healing before they can be free of the internal pain they carry and the coping tools they have adopted along the way.

When we engage with God, He will routinely show us ways in which our thoughts are not only deficient but quite often severely distorted, and He will show or tell us what we need in order to see things more that way He sees them. This is the very essence of what it means to renew our mind.

Encouragement

Larry Crabb tells a story in which he was talking with Brennan Manning one day, lamenting the many things about himself that he did not like and ways in which he fell short of God's Word.[51] As he was speaking, Brennan began to tear up a little. Larry stopped short and asked, "What's going on?"

Brennan replied, "Larry, you have no idea how much I feel drawn to Christ because of you." Larry was totally perplexed. "What? I'm sitting here complaining about all the things that are wrong with me, and you come up with something like that?" Brennan looked at him with all the love in his heart and said, "Yes, Larry, but the reason those things bother you so much is that you long to be more like your Heavenly Father!"

Larry says he left that meeting almost walking on air. He was encouraged by Brennan's remarks because he had been reminded about who he really was in Christ, and where his true heart was.

This is encouragement: pointing one another back to God and to the truth of who He has made us to be. We need to look beyond the surface and

---

[50] See Curt Thompson, *The Anatomy of the Soul* for an in-depth understanding of our need to be known.
[51] I believe this story comes from either *Connecting* or *The Safest Place On Earth* (both by Crabb).

ask God to reveal to us what He sees in them, similar to the way Brennan saw Larry, so we can truly encourage them.

Of course, we want our encouragement to come from a place of genuine interest for the other person and for their well-being. Trying to make something up that sounds nice would miss the point of learning to see others the way God sees them. The reason we have included this practice under the heading of "Engaging Directly With God" is because our part begins with asking God how he sees the other person and listening for God's perspective so we can share that with them. In this way, both of us are enriched because of what God has revealed. We come away with a greater respect and care for the other person, due to a better understanding of how God sees them and holds them in His heart.

We all need reminders of who we are and whose we are, as well as reminders of the unseen realities about the Kingdom Among Us. Our hope is that we would be more deliberate about encouraging one another in our spiritual journey toward God.

Forgiveness

Forgiving others for the wrongs we have suffered covers such a broad spectrum of experience that I wish we had more terms for this process. We have all experienced a range of injuries that run from slights that are so minor we would hardly consider forgiveness necessary, to violations so grievous we might think they are virtually unforgivable. Consequently, the kind of effort required and the nature of help we need varies greatly. Forgiveness is not a "one size fits all" answer.

First and foremost, we must understand that human relationships would be virtually impossible without forgiveness. We are all flawed, and we will all sooner or later hurt people we care about through both our interactions and our lack thereof. We will also offend many other people in our life with whom we have relatively little investment. Without forgiveness, we would eventually accumulate so much baggage in our relationships that being together would no longer be possible. Our resentments over past wounds always affects the present unless we find ways to cleanse our mind and heart of those injuries.

Again, many times our pain is so minor we hardly notice the process of letting go. An easily cleared misunderstanding can be forgotten in a matter of minutes, because we are able to make sense of the matter and to see the situation through the eyes of the other person. We might even laugh about how we missed each other in the process. Our forgiveness is so complete and immediate that we may not even think about it.

On the other hand when an injury is severe, when it happens over a long period of time, or when the act seems incomprehensible to us, our reactions come from another place entirely and any process related to forgiving is totally different. In some cases, the mere idea of forgiving can feel like an additional injustice over and above what we have already endured. In our mind this person needs to be held accountable for what they have done. Forgiving them is out of the question.

Of course, much of our life experience falls somewhere between these two extremes. A person dents our car or breaks an item we loaned to them. Our expectations of a friend are dashed. Or we find ourselves excluded from something where we thought we should have been included. These little ruptures are what we encounter every day. And perhaps it is here that we need to pay attention the most, in order to learn what it means to forgive.

Clarifying the Process of Forgiveness

Before going into what forgiveness looks like, it is important to say something about what forgiveness is *not*. To begin with, telling someone "I forgive you" because that is what good Christians are supposed to do, is not really forgiveness. That might be better called an *imitation* of forgiveness. We are all familiar with phrases like, "Oh, that's all right!" or "That's no big deal" but the premise is the same. If we say these things simply to do the "right" thing, we probably are not forgiving anyone.

Along these same lines, forgiveness is not something we do "out of obedience." Forcing ourselves to say certain words in order to act as if we are forgiving someone offers them nothing and changes nothing in us.

Forgiveness is a condition of the heart, not a phrase we say. It is not only for their sake we forgive, but for ours. Whether we refuse to forgive someone for what they have done (or not done), or whether we fool ourselves into thinking we have forgiven when we have not, either way our heart has not made the changes necessary to actually forgive. And any ability we have to repress our emotions or push the related events out of our conscious mind does not change this in any way.

I have often heard Christians talk about "the sin of unforgiveness" in ways that imply all we need to do is resolve to forgive that person and say the words in order to be through with it, as if it were some kind of task. But while forgiveness involves the will, it is not primarily an act of the will. It is a change of heart, and that is not something our will can do. For these reasons we need to redefine forgiveness, in order to clarify what we are actually trying to accomplish.

Forgiveness From a Changed Heart

Forgiveness is an act of surrendering any demand for restitution or desire for retribution, and if at all possible, responding to the offender with either goodness or an invitation to re-engage in the relationship. Such forgiveness is extended from a heart truly resolved regarding the issue at hand, through engaging with God to be restored to a place of love and release.

Now it is important to understand the implications of that description, so as to be able to embrace it in difficult circumstances. The point of the whole statement is to emphasize the kind of heart change we are seeking. In most cases where forgiveness is difficult, what keeps us stuck is our understanding about what happened. We may think that what the other person did was too awful to be forgiven, they need to pay for what they did, they owe us something, they need to be shaken up and brought to their senses, or perhaps even that we would really prefer revenge.

What we need is a change of heart. In most cases, the best thing we can do is check with God and ask Him how He sees that person. On occasion I have even had to ask, "How can You stand to be with them, God? What keeps you coming back?" Amazingly, He usually has an answer that changes how I feel about the person I am upset with.

The good news is that after we have engaged with God for a change of heart, forgiving is no longer hard – the hardest part of forgiveness is changing our heart! Forgiveness is then offered by expressing the matter from our heart. On the other hand, a good rule of thumb is that if we begrudge forgiving someone, or feel as if we are being ripped off by forgiving them, then it is a sure bet that our heart has not changed.

The Work of Forgiveness

So what does it mean to engage with God for a change of heart? What does that look like? How do we proceed? For starters, we need to allow God to search our heart and reveal to us whatever He finds there. We participate in that process by offering to God as honestly as we can all that we know and feel about our negative experience and our feelings toward the other person. Very often, it may be necessary to slow down the process and work through the various pieces one at a time, rather than trying to resolve everything at once.

Often we will find that our present issue has hooks into previous injuries that are not yet fully resolved. We may discover unspoken expectations we have about how we "should" be treated or what rights of ours we believe were violated. God may need to mentor us more in what it means to be in relationship with flawed human beings, or the difference between what is good and what we are entitled to, or even reveal to us something of the brokenness of that other person.

This is what makes forgiveness hard work. Only God could dream up something as bazaar as using an injury from another person to lead me to engage more with Him to restore *my* heart and mind! We tend to think it is the *other* person who should be doing all the work of repair. After all, they caused the problem. But this is what life in the Kingdom looks like.

Forgiveness can also require us to revisit the same issue multiple times in order to further the healing process. I have spent much of my adult life coming to terms with my early childhood experiences, despite the fact that in the broad scheme of things my parents were fairly good people. But the truth is I was miserable as a child and did not get what I needed from my family relationships. And every few years I run into yet another aspect of my life that stems from those wounds, very often resulting in another step in forgiving my parents.

None of this implies that I am holding out on them in some conscious way or that I am being "disobedient" in regard to forgiving them. As far as I know, I have done almost everything I can do to receive God's grace in this matter and to have forgiven them for the part I believe they played in my distress. But having revisited this issue many times over my life, it would not surprise me if I were to find yet another layer I had not dealt with before.

Whenever we discover that we still harbor resentments or ill will toward a person we thought we had forgiven, it is important that we embrace the process again and dig a little deeper with God to resolve more of the issues. No good can come from beating myself up for having an unforgiving heart. Nor is it good to hide behind the idea that "I already forgave them." Life is too complex to always get everything resolved at once. So when something like this resurfaces, we are probably looking at it from a renewed angle and God will help us through this again.

Stages of Forgiveness

One question that often comes to mind is, "How far does God expect me to go in forgiving another person? Do I have to act as if nothing happened?"

Dan Allender[52] offers us a fairly radical view of forgiveness which he defines as "the pursuit of the offender, by the offended, for the purpose of reconciliation." That certainly describes how God went about forgiving us. Although He was the injured party and we rejected Him, He proactively took the initiative to restore our relationship, even at great cost to Himself. Dan suggests that this is the kind of forgiveness we are called to as followers of Christ, and his book is one of the most comprehensive and provocative descriptions of forgiveness I believe has ever been written.

Regarding people who are important to us, this should in fact always be our ideal – to reach such a point of release and cleansing that we could not only receive the other person back into our life, but even take the initiative to make that possible. If we truly took this seriously and were willing to submit to God's work in our hearts, there is much that could be healed in our Christian families and organizations.

At the same time, we need to recognize that rebuilding trust is not always possible, or at least not easy. With God's help we can usually reach a point where we no longer hold the other person hostage for what happened. But what we cannot do is change the other person's heart. There are countless reasons why they might not *want* to have a working relationship with us or

---

[52] Dan Allender, *Bold Love* (NavPress) 1992

why they might not even be capable of a meaningful relationship with us. So along with releasing our hold on them, we may need to modify our expectations regarding what that relationship will look like in the future.

One perspective that can help us here is to view forgiveness as having two separate parts. First, is the essential step of releasing any debt we feel they owe us. That includes letting go of any desire or need for the other person to make restitution or to "earn" our forgiveness by apologizing or repenting of their actions. Any desire we have for revenge or to "make them pay for what they did" also needs to be cleansed from our heart. To use a recovery phrase, we stop holding them hostage.

Releasing that debt can be a very difficult process when the wound has been particularly harsh. For example, forgiving a drunken driver for killing your loved one might well require a supernatural act of God on your heart, because wanting the offender to suffer greatly would be a perfectly understandable reaction. And while that represents a fairly serious injury, it actually takes relatively little pain to put most people in the place of wanting some kind of retribution or restitution.

Letting go of what we believe they owe us may also include letting go of our desire to make the other person understand the extent of what they did. Often we feel compelled to make them realize how much they have hurt us. While helping them understand us may become part of the process of reconciliation, it does not have to be part of releasing the debt.

The second part of forgiveness has to do with reconciling. In many cases, of course, there was never any relationship to speak of prior to the injury, so there is virtually nothing to restore. But when a rupture has occurred in an existing relationship, we are faced with the process of restoring that relationship and perhaps having to discern what restoration will look like.

Now in many instances, the relationship is so well grounded in trust that we will be able to address the rupture with the intention of restoring our connection completely. There may be a need to talk about what happened and to reach an understanding of what that means to us, but there is little doubt about whether we can work through the difficulties and put the matter behind us. We care enough about the other person to make sure this does not create any long-term issues between us.

In other cases, however, the future of the relationship may need to be contingent upon the quality of the repair. This does not mean we will continue to hold something over their head. Rather, the nature of our relationship may need to change.

For example, suppose I have a ten-year-old daughter whom I let stay at a friend's house. Part way through her visit she calls and asks me to come and get her because someone in the home is acting inappropriately toward her. At that point, their family has ruptured our relationship. With God's help, we will seek to work through the first phase of forgiveness without getting stuck. But the nature of our relationship with that family will undoubtedly change, because I am not going to put my daughter in harm's way again. We might even make an offer to reconcile and work together toward finding conditions under which she could stay with her friend again, such as when the person in question is not home.

What we want to make very clear is that boundaries are not at all incompatible with forgiveness. Forgiving someone does not mean we have to be foolish about how we interact with them. At the same time, we need to be careful not to hide behind "boundaries" to avoid the work God may want to do in us.

Practicing Forgiveness

In addition to engaging with God at times when forgiving is difficult, we can also cultivate a forgiving heart though a very basic spiritual practice. One of the principles of spiritual disciplines is that there are things within our ability we can do in order to retrain our inner system, which will then enable us to do things we could not have done by direct effort. So as an alternative to taking on really big issues where we have trouble forgiving, we can begin by looking for really small things to forgive, and practice where we are able.

For example, when I am standing in a grocery checkout line, I can consciously forgive the person in front who seems to be high maintenance. When I am in a hurry and there are too many cars on the road, I can forgive the driver in front of me for being slow. When I am interrupted for the tenth time, I can forgive the person who is taking my attention away from my work. In short, every time I feel any slight setback or disappointment, I look for someone to bless instead of curse or resent.

Over time, this forms in me a desire for releasing people from any kind of obligation toward me, whether real or perceived. Now by itself this new strength may not make it any easier to forgive a bigger offense, but it will bring this process to mind much sooner and give me reason and courage to work with God in order to find a place of forgiveness. As I cultivate a lifestyle of forgiving, my heart is formed so I am more inclined to pursue this path than I would have been in the past.

Why Forgiving is So Important to God

Jesus once said something to the effect that if we do not forgive others, then God will not forgive us. This statement is a bit puzzling, because in many other places God's forgiveness seems unilateral and unconditional. But perhaps Jesus was thinking much deeper than merely making God's forgiveness dependent upon our behavior.

Suppose we want to be forgiven by God for our infractions and at the same time want to withhold forgiveness to another because we are not yet satisfied with their level of remorse or restitution. That is quite a double standard! If we really do believe that forgiveness must be earned (as indicated by the way we hold out on the other person) then the truth is we either have trouble believing that God forgives us unless we earn it, or else we do not believe His forgiveness means much, because He gives it away too easily.

On the other hand, if we really do believe forgiveness from God cannot be earned, then by holding out on another person we are effectively saying we have very little intention of learning how to forgive as He does. Either way, our double standard makes it impossible for us to live in forgiveness, because we are failing to allow it to penetrate our heart and to grasp its significance. Jesus is basically saying, "You can't have it both ways. Either you believe in offering and receiving real forgiveness or you don't."

Much of what we have said about forgiveness makes sense when we understand that there are multiple reasons for cultivating a forgiving heart. First, harboring contempt or ill will in our heart is toxic to our own soul. Second believing that another person must earn our good graces ignores the grace that God has extended toward us. Finally, God wants us to learn how to live in peace with others to whatever extent is possible.

Intercession

At its core, intercession is about considering the needs of others and interacting with God on their behalf. Regardless of whether we do this in their presence or not, it is best to think of this as a relational practice, because we are extending ourselves for the good of another person.

To begin with, we do not even have to know how to pray for them. One of the best ways to intercede for another person is to ask God how He sees them and how we can best pray. In doing so, we practice seeing others through the eyes of heaven and cultivating God's heart for them. The more we see others the way God sees them and the more we know of what God wants for them, the more we will know how to pray. Thus intercession becomes much more than just asking God to do something for someone. It is *joining with God for the good of another person, based on what God Himself wants for them.* How good is that!

In the process, we discover more of God's heart, our faith increases because we are more aware of God's earnest desire for their life, and we participate *with* God, not just ask for something *from* God. Not that there is anything wrong with asking God for what we want for others, but by first seeking God's heart for them we move our prayer from petition to intercession. When we join with others in praying for each other this way, we are actively pushing back the darkness, and making space for the life of God among us. Intercession becomes true kingdom work, done together for the good of all, both individually and corporately. We even learn how to think more communally and relationally as a result.

Intercession is also a great antidote for too much self-focus. It helps us turn our vision outward toward the needs of others and toward ways of giving life to one another. Developing a heart for others is a major part of our apprenticeship to Jesus, and intercession is one of the ways we can express compassion and consideration. What's more, our intercession may reveal to us ways that we can be actively involved in the other person's life.

Our hope is that we will begin to view intercession more as a way to be involved in the life of others, not simply a form of prayer we should engage in. Giving life to one another is one of the most important ways in which we can learn to be more like our Father.

SUMMARY

Hopefully, this interlude has helped to clarify how spiritual practices can become very life-giving ways of building up our relationship with God and growing our spiritual strength. Being deliberate about our formation is essential to long-term growth and restoration. Knowing how to employ these means for our good gives us many ways to be deliberate.

RESOURCES FOR FURTHER STUDY

Jan Johnson, *Spiritual Disciplines Companion: Biblical Studies and Practices to Transform Your Soul* (Downers Grove: InterVarsity Press) 2009

Chapter 9

Renewing Our Mind

> Do not conform any longer to the pattern of this world, but be transformed by the renewal of your mind. (Rom.12:2 NIV)

Having laid the groundwork for what it means to have a functional, conversational relationship with God, as well as how we can foster growth and change within that relationship, we now turn our focus to some of our deepest concerns as Christians who are trying to develop that new nature we have received from God. This chapter and the next two are going to investigate the process of transformation, including what exactly it is that needs to be transformed, why making those changes will have such a dramatic impact on our life, and how we can participate better with God so He can change our heart and mind.[53]

Transformation involves a broad range of changes that occur in the entire person including mind, will, body, and social context.[54] But transformation has only a handful of primary causes, namely truth, love, retraining, and corrective experiences, all in the context of joyful, healthy relationships. We experience *love* when we build authentic relationships with God and others. *Retraining* our soul is largely the work of maturity and spiritual practices. *Corrective experiences* come primarily from interacting with our community. Our focus in this chapter will be on how we can engage *truth* in ways that can literally change our heart.

Being transformed by truth is a very important process, which Paul refers to as *renewing our mind*. Learning how to engage with God in ways that change how we understand life is one of the most important aspects of Christian development, next to learning how to have conversations with God. Yet many Christians do not really understand either the importance of this process or the ways in which they can intentionally pursue it.

---

[53] This chapter is based on David Takle, *The Truth About Lies and Lies About Truth*
[54] Dallas Willard, *The Renovation of the Heart*

This chapter will explore the ways in which our deepest beliefs impact our life, how and why we all hold beliefs that conflict with our theology, and what it means to renew our mind to become more Christ-like. A thorough understanding and practice of this process can greatly enrich our life and our relationship with God.

Let's begin with a typical day in the life of John, who has been an active layman in his church for many years. He is married with two teen-age children and has a successful career as a computer software engineer. As the alarm goes off on Monday morning, John breathes a deep sigh and wishes the world would just stop for a few days and let him rest. If only he could find the time to finish his personal dream project, he could retire and do the things he feels called to do.

As he reaches the kitchen to get some breakfast, his teenage son is leaving out the front door without so much as a wave. A bit of anger rolls through John's body as he thinks about how hard it is to live with his own children. Pulling the milk from the refrigerator, he hits his elbow on an open cupboard door and drops the milk on the floor, and he clamps his jaw shut so that he does not yell something he will regret while he quickly picks up the carton and proceeds to clean up what spilled. He shakes his head as he mentally blames his son for leaving the cupboard door open. Part way through his breakfast, his daughter shows up with an attitude, demanding a ride to school because no one woke her up in time. John barks back something harsh, hoping to shut her up. But he takes one more mouthful and grabs his things, gives his wife a kiss on the way out the door, and drives his daughter to school in silence. On the way he takes a few deep breaths and asks God to help him through his day. He calms down as best as he can and tells himself he can do better.

Things start out well at work where John enjoys a good reputation for his skill and work ethic. He settles in to the tasks of the day and forgets about his earlier problems. But near the end of the morning he comes to the realization that the project he is working on cannot really be done in the time expected. He feels anxiety rising up in him as he plans how to tell his boss that his earlier estimates were too optimistic. And he chides himself for having quoted the job too low, thinking, "That's what I get for trying to give people what they want."

When lunch time rolls around everyone in the office seems committed to other things so John finds himself on his own and heads off to his favorite fast-food place hoping to cheer himself up a bit. That afternoon the talk with his boss is every bit as stressful as he expected, and he has to think fast and talk around the issue a lot in order to present himself in the best possible light. Later when he runs into a program bug that he has trouble tracking down, he cannot help but think of Murphy's law and how this additional disappointment was just par for his day.

Hoping for some down time as he arrives home that evening, his wife asks how soon he will be ready to go meet their friends for dinner. His voice says he's ready, but inside he is regretting ever having made these plans and secretly wishes something would go wrong so they could stay home. When John finally falls into bed that night he is fighting the thought that this day was a complete waste, and that life should not have to be like this. He thinks there must be a better way to deal with this stuff but he has no idea what that would be.

Now it's tempting to say that John just needs to lighten up or pray more or take a vacation. But the truth is that much of John's stress comes from his own understanding of life and his place in the universe, not from the events that confront him during his day. First, John is a man preoccupied with order and predictability. Since childhood he has fought against the chaos he finds in the world, believing that if everyone would just do what they were supposed to do, his life would be much better. So every unexpected turn that comes his way to upset his control of things taps into this reservoir of disappointment and frustration. Closely related to this way of seeing life is his perception that most people are more trouble than they are worth. Oh, he is cordial and kind most of the time, and is even willing to help others when he can. But relationships are far too messy and unpredictable, and while he wants to be known as a nice guy, he really prefers being on his own.

So in his view, his teenagers are rebellious and out of control, not the confused and immature young adults that they actually are. His boss taps into his long-forgotten experiences of an unforgiving father who believed that mistakes were inexcusable. And the reason he is gets so upset when he runs into a stubborn problem at work is because his self-worth is tied up with trying to create an error-free software environment.

John's greatest challenge to dealing with life is not the myriad of things in the external world that are out of his control, but the layers upon layers of his own deeply internalized beliefs *about* that world and what would make him happy. He knows a lot of good doctrine about relying on God and he prays for a better heart. But John cannot find what he is looking for because his mind and heart are in need of major transformation.

According to the Apostle Paul, John needs to be transformed by the renewing of his mind. But what does that actually mean? How can we go about changing the way we think about things? Why is it that when we first come to Christ we experience a lot of change in a short time, but then later on our growth seems to slow down to a crawl, even when we know we still have a long way to go? How can we rewire our mental processes so that we see life more the way God sees it and react differently?

The Truth About Lies

C. S. Lewis' well known classic, *The Screwtape Letters*, is an amazing little story of how the enemy attempts to distort nearly every aspect of our thinking. Lewis makes wonderful use of creative writing to give us an inside look at a well-seasoned demon named Screwtape who is mentoring his novice nephew demon in the art of deception. The nephew has been assigned to a young man for the purpose of messing with his life and leading him astray. Throughout the story, Screwtape takes into account almost every aspect of the human's daily existence – his interests, his relationships, even his opinions – and finds some way to distort them, redefine them, or distract the person with them (or from them).

For example, when the human begins to show interest in church, Screwtape chides his nephew for letting things get that far down the wrong path, but at the same time assures him that all is not lost. His advice? Try to get the person to think church is the ultimate goal; that by going to church he is better than anyone else; that going to church is what makes a good Christian. And so on with everything else in the person's life.

The value of Lewis' book comes from unmasking the endless ways in which the enemy's tactics of distortion and deception are applied over and over. Underlying this clever story is the undeniable fact that our enemy's greatest weapon is his ability to lie.

Jesus once told a crowd that lying was Satan's most basic character trait (Jn.8:44). If we are not careful, we might gloss over that statement or think it is simply a comment about the devil. But what Jesus has given us in this observation is a tremendous key to unlocking the mysteries of our own life.

For most of history, theologians have wrestled with the problem of sin in the lives of Christians. Sin destroys lives. Christians should not sin. When you become aware of sin in your life you need to confess it, renounce it, repent of it, and try not to do it anymore. We should resist by making the proper choices to not sin any more. As a result of this focus, we often think that willpower is our best weapon to eradicate evil from our life.

However, this is like a man who finds a hammer and then assumes everything in need of fixing must be a nail. The main problem with this approach is that the really serious issues in our heart do not respond to the will at all. Whether we are talking about persistent sins or areas of personal brokenness that continually drag us down, repenting and trying harder will not solve the issues.

More to the point, though, is the fact that sin comes at the end of long line of problems in the life of a Christian. Sin is the poison *fruit* of something else gone terribly wrong, it is not the initial cause. Furthermore, most of the things that repeatedly derail us are not sinful things *we* are doing, but the after affects of evil that has been done *to us*. I cannot repent of an emotional wound any more than I can rid my body of a disease by saying, "I'm sorry I got that." If self-defeating behaviors (such as addiction) are caused by trying to medicate an old wound and not from being morally deficient, then again, repenting will do no good.

To help shed some light on this, let's take a look at where sin began, in the Garden of Eden. What makes this story so relevant is the simple fact that neither Adam nor Eve had any "sinful nature." Most of us have been told that sin comes from something in our core that we were born with, something that will not be eradicated until we die. But aside from the fact that this does not fit very well with the New Testament's unanimous view of the victorious, abundant life, it also fails to explain why Adam and Eve sinned.

Saint Augustine and many other theologians have tried to find some fatal flaw in Adam that made him sin. It must have been his natural desire, an urge called *concupiscence* or some other base instinct. But this is reading into the text our own subjective experience and our own limited sense of what causes failure, not to mention how this sidesteps the truth that God created His creatures good in every sense of the word. Adam and Eve were not created with a defect that would cause them to sin. Their only weakness, if we can call it that, was their innocence, which is what the enemy made use of in his ploy.

We need to take a hard look at the facts of the story, to see what observations we can make about these two people and the event that changed our world forever. On that fateful day, what caused them to eat the fruit they had been warned about? Was it willful disobedience, a decision to disobey God? If so, on what basis? The truth is, they were too innocent to rebel. Nothing in their character would have given them such an idea in the first place. So what evidence do we have?

- Eating the fruit of that one tree was the first human sin.
- Prior to that sin, Adam and Eve were free of any distortion of character that would predispose them to sin.
- The option to make this choice had existed for them for some time, perhaps months before this event.
- The only difference here is that they were lied to about the fruit.
- It was because *they believed the lie* that they made a choice they had not made before.

What ought to be clear from this story is that they were *deceived*. The reason they acted differently was because they believed something different than what they had believed before that day. Up until this moment, they thought the reason they needed to stay away from the tree was because it was deadly. Suddenly there was this other idea – that God did not want them to have the power which the tree possessed. God was keeping something from them, and for no good reason.

If what the serpent said was true, then nothing more would be gained by asking God about the tree. They already knew what He wanted them to believe about it. In questioning their relationship to God and His intentions toward them, they were thrown back on their own resources for how to find the truth of the matter. The new theory about the fruit began to make sense, especially given how good it looked. Once they believed, they reached for what they would have otherwise ignored. What this story tells us is that *deception is sufficient in and of itself to cause us to sin.*

The reason this is true is because our beliefs and our limited knowledge about life are always involved in our internal process. We choose one course of action over another because of what we believe about the alternatives. We go to a doctor because we think it will help. We trust a friend to watch our dog because we believe they will do a good job. Our emotions and actions are driven by what we believe, whether consciously or not.

Even when we act contrary to our Christian beliefs, we are still buying into our beliefs about life. When a man seeks out an affair, knowing full well that it is wrong, he is also convinced that he is being deprived of something he needs, or that it is really harmless and no one will get hurt, or this is the only way he can stop the pain he feels inside. When a mother screams at her child and says terrible things, she knows on one level it is wrong, but deep inside she may have given up all options except to make the child stop their behavior, and this is all she knows to do. The truth is, we hold a great many such conflicting beliefs. We may or may not live out of our theological beliefs; but we will always find ourselves living from some belief we have in our heart.

How the Bible Views Deception and Blindness

The fall in the Garden of Eden is not just about how sin entered the world – it is the quintessential story about how we sin at all! Wherever we are blind, either because of deception or because of our limited insight, we are inevitably going to fail. This single truth is repeated over and over in Scripture, to the point of being almost too obvious.

At the doorstep of the Promised Land, the Israelites refused to go in because of their unbelief. Having seen the giants in the land and the fortified cities, they were convinced God had brought them there only to kill them. They were not being willfully disobedient, as is sometimes taught. They were fighting for their lives, as best they knew how. The problem was their faulty understanding of how God was at work among them (Heb.3:19). They acted out of their beliefs.

Even a cursory look at Scripture reveals how the authors repeatedly made the connection between spiritual darkness and failure in life.

> They have neither knowledge nor understanding; they walk around in darkness. (Ps.82:5)

> If you walk in the darkness, you do not know where you are going. (Jn.12:35)

Moving away from the metaphors, Scripture becomes very explicit about the cause-and-effect relationship between the lack of knowledge regarding spiritual matters and the resulting destruction in our lives. The most obvious is the entire book of Proverbs where the underlying premise is that wisdom leads to life and the lack of wisdom leads to death. But this theme runs through much of the Bible.

> Therefore my people go into exile for their lack of knowledge. (Isa.5:13 NASB)

> My people are destroyed for lack of knowledge … you have forgotten the law … a people without understanding comes to ruin. (Hos.4:6,14)

Even more pervasive are the twin themes of belief and unbelief. These two nouns and their related verbs (believe, have faith) are perhaps some of the most dominate concepts in all of Scripture. Without faith we cannot see God. With faith, all things are possible.

However, we must be careful about these terms. While there is an element of choice involved in faith – as in, I will trust You, God, even if I cannot see my way – the Bible also speaks of faith as the substance of what resides in our heart, not simply a profession that we make.[55] Christians often profess things they do not really believe. For example, many people know in theory that God accepts us unconditionally, but at the same time they harbor deep doubts about whether God accepts them personally. Or they may profess that they trust God, and at the same time wondering whether God is holding out on them.

---

[55] 1Sam.16:7; Mt.15:18; Eph.6:6; Phil.3:9.

The kind of faith that God talks about is that which comes from our heart, not from our lips. Sometimes that faith comes easy. Other times we need God's help to change our heart so that we are truly convinced of the matter. When God says He will supply our needs, we may want to believe what He says but find it hard to do so. The reality is that we worry about things all the time even though Jesus says not to worry. Our trust level is truly much lower than we would like to admit to ourselves, and probably lower than we might normally profess to be the case.

Our inner beliefs then consist of the assumptions we have about how life works, assumptions we have internalized over time either through life experience or from our training. Once we accept these beliefs, they then run our life. This explains why *what* we believe matters so much. If I truly believe I have done something that is unforgivable, I will live as if that were actually true, and carry around the guilt and shame of my error without any hope of ever being set free from that weight.

Unbelief matters. In fact unbelief is not really a lack of belief at all, but actually belief in something else – a faulty belief. We are told that when the Jews refused to enter the promised land, they were guilty of unbelief. In truth, they believed a great many things: that God hated them; that He brought them there to kill them; that they would have been better off in Egypt; and so on. Unbelief is not a vacuum, it is belief in a lie.

More to the point, believing lies leads to disaster. Nearly every major turning point in Bible history can be found to involve a battle between truth and lies in the hearts and minds of the people involved:

- Garden of Eden (the fruit will make us wise).
- Failure to enter the Promised Land (the giants are too big).
- Falling into idolatry (those gods will help our crops).
- Being "led astray" by false teachers (I think they are right).
- Pharisees missing their Messiah (He cannot possibly be the one).
- Galatians messing up the gospel (we need to keep the law).

Every one of these failures can be traced to the lies that people believed. Regardless of whether we are right or wrong about what we believe, we all act as if those things are true.

Consider what might have prompted the disciples to argue about who would be the greatest among them in the new kingdom. It was not simply because they fell into sin at that moment and allowed their 'flesh' to take over. The reason they started arguing was because they had preconceived notions about how a kingdom functions, and they carried their ideas about worldly power over into their vision of God's new kingdom.

So rather than chide them for arguing, Jesus went to the root of their problem and corrected their understanding of greatness. Jesus knew if they grasped the true nature of greatness – which was to live for the good of others – then there would no longer be anything to fight about. Once their internal beliefs were adjusted to reflect the truth of the kingdom, their relationships would change and their interactions would reflect these renewed inner beliefs.

Throughout His ministry, Jesus challenged prevailing beliefs about a great many things, turning His listeners' value systems right-side up. His famous Sermon on the Mount contains a treasury of insights into who God is, who we are, and how life works best in the kingdom. And because His ideas were so new and at times hard to grasp, He often admonished His listeners with words like, "Let those who have ears to hear, hear." He knew that if they were able to take in what He was saying, they would be enabled to live much differently from that point forward.

An Interactive Model

So how do we go about internalizing God's truth in ways that actually change us from the inside out? Why does that even work? In order to help make sense of what it means to renew our minds, we are going to use a model that demonstrates quite clearly how our internalized beliefs become such powerful influences in our life.

In practice, I am constantly interacting with the rest of the world in a never ending cycle. This cycle begins with an external event, person or circumstance that is significant to me or is impacting me in some way. I take in raw data from that event in the form of what I see or hear. My mind then begins to evaluate those perceptions and form some interpretations about what they mean. Finally, I respond in some way, emotionally, mentally, physically or verbally. My response may or may not impact the situation, which leads to another perception on my part, and the cycle continues. I can quite easily go around this cycle several times in a matter of seconds without even noticing how I am personally involved in the interactions.

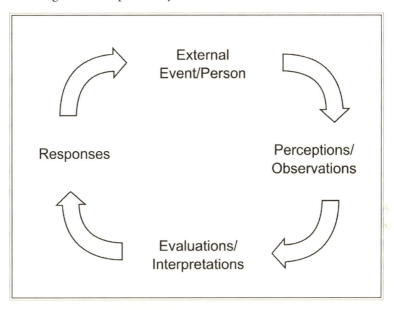

How We Process Experiences

We see this process at work all the time. For example, suppose I am trying to open a package I received in the mail. To my dismay it has a lot of heavy-duty packing tape on it. But my first reaction is to try to rip through it anyway. Taking notice of what I am doing, my wife asks if I would like a pair of scissors. My *perception* is that her tone is slightly off, and my *evaluation* of her comment is that she is mocking me for trying to tear through tape that is proving to be impervious to my efforts. My *response*, then, is to become a little irritated and I snap back at her with something to the effect that I am doing just fine.

Immediately my emotional antenna go up as well, as I expect to hear some sarcastic remark in reply to my response. Instead, I hear her voice soften and clarify that she just wanted to know if she could get the scissors for me (another *perception* on my part). Instantly I *re-evaluate* my previous interpretation and response in light of these most recent observations, and realize I had misunderstood her intentions. That also means that I had snapped at her for no good reason and should apologize. I *respond* to her with sincere regret and ask her to please get the scissors for me, and then I thank her for being helpful. Finally, I *observe* that she is smiling, which I *interpret* as being forgiving and understanding, and my internal *response* is to quiet down and feel closer to her.

While this is only a very simple interaction, the basic principles of the model are fairly obvious. At no point did my wife ever upset me. I was upset because of my own interpretation of what was going on. Most of our emotional life comes out of our own understanding of what we observe, and is only indirectly caused by the events outside us. Had I perceived and interpreted her initial comment more accurately, none of the negative events would have ever occurred. Even when our perceptions and interpretations are accurate, our responses are born out of our own internal processes.

But a very important element needs to be added to this model in order to make it truly useful, and that is the set of beliefs and assumptions about life we have gathered up over time from our own personal experiences. These beliefs might be very different from the theological propositions we hold, and they are even kept in a different part of our brain. Most importantly, they are very instrumental in how the rest of our internal process works. Inserting our belief system into the diagram, it looks like the one below.

Internalized Beliefs

To be clear, our internal belief system is something that grows over time, mostly without any conscious awareness on our part. These beliefs are tied very closely to what we have been calling *formation* and *malformation* in this book. All of my ideas about who God is and how He might interact with me, all that I have learned from relationships with others throughout my life, all of my anxieties, my hopes, what I think of myself, my secret beliefs about how life will turn out for me – literally everything I believe about my personal world is stored in this internal belief system. And once there, these beliefs effect everything else about how I interact with life.

In truth, I do not see things as they really are. My perceptions are actually filtered by my prior assumptions about reality. For example, if I believe I am more or less invincible (common among young people) I will fail to see the danger in many situations. On the other hand if I believe that danger is everywhere, I will see it in perfectly harmless circumstances.

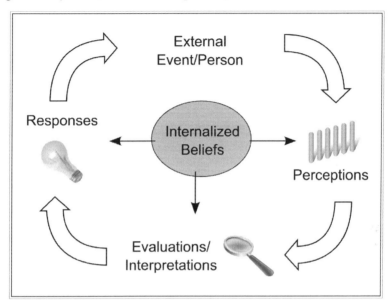

How We Interact With the World Around Us

Now let's turn our attention to how we go about interpreting our perceptions, because this is where the power of our internalized beliefs really comes into focus. What we need to realize is that our interpretations are almost entirely driven by deeply held beliefs about who we are, who God is, and how life works. This explains why two people can be in exactly the same place at the same time and have two completely different interpretations of what happened. And how we interpret a situation will greatly influence how we respond. What's more, our response will also be tempered by still other beliefs we hold in regard to what is appropriate, how much we care about how our behavior is viewed by others, and so on.

Let's take an example that is a bit more complicated. You and I are attending an important meeting in which a guy comes in late, and everyone is distracted for a moment. I might feel annoyed because my value system says that he was irresponsible and disrespectful. I might even claim that the guy's interruption made me mad, but the truth is I was angry because of how I interpreted his entrance. On the other hand, you may be relieved that he showed up, because you tend to assume something is wrong when people are late and you were worried about him. Our inner systems of values and priorities result in greatly differing responses to the same situation.

These differences often create conflicts between people, as well as govern what happens during a conflict. In fact, virtually everything we face in life is filtered, interpreted and impacted by our beliefs, and the thoughts and emotions that come out of this process are what drive our lives.

Now for much of life this is a very positive process, because this is how we make use of prior experience to make good decisions in the present. But what happens when we internalize faulty beliefs? What if that center circle is actually severely malformed and full of misunderstandings about life? Well, then we end up with things like dysfunctional family systems, self-defeating behaviors, discouragement, and struggles that we cannot seem to overcome – things we all deal with all the time.

As was evident from our survey of Scripture earlier, such misbeliefs are really quite pervasive and they wreak havoc with our lives. Only when we learn how to internalize truth in ways that alter these underlying assumptions about life can we hope to live differently.

While it may come as a surprise to some, none of us really knows all the things buried in our own heart. People who suffer from a deeply negative self-image may truly believe they are seeing themselves as they really are, defective and unable to measure up. But the truth is their internal belief system is badly distorted. On the other hand, those who feel pretty good about how they are doing may be as misinformed about their character as those who struggle with self-rejection.

Our greatest problem then is not willful disobedience or other evil inclinations. Rather our struggle as Christians is primarily due to the fact that our internal belief system has been terribly malformed by life in a broken world. However, even though our internal damage is greater than we can imagine, there is absolutely no condemnation or shame about standing completely exposed in the presence of God. He only asks that we come to Him and participate with Him in the process of restoration.

How We Come to Believe the Lies We Believe

Before we can address the means for changing our inner beliefs, we must ask two major questions: First, how do internalized beliefs become so distorted in the first place, and second, why are they so resistant to change?

The short answers are: (1) Our own life experience is the main source of the lies we internalize about who we are, how life works and how God is involved; (2) These lies are persistent because the truths we hear in church are no match for the lies we believe from our own experience.

When a child grows up in an abusive home environment, they learn how little they matter in the scheme of things, that no one cares for their soul, life is unpredictable, and they are powerless to impact their own world. Above all, they discover that they are alone; there is no one they can count on.

Beliefs such as these have a life of their own, a destructive power that wreaks havoc on every other aspect of a child's life, probably long into adulthood. All their judgments will be impaired because they lack any foundation for coherence and security. They may adopt a heavy facade to keep from being known, even though they desperately need to be known by someone who cares. Very likely they will develop a pervasive hatred of their own life. A large percentage of these children will end up "looking for love in all the wrong places" because of the desperation they feel, trying to make up for what they never got as a child. Trust in God may be almost impossible, especially if they believe God should have done something about their home life. On the other hand, they may adopt a fantasy view of God, hoping He will provide a safety bubble in which they can live where nothing can touch them ever again.

Most importantly, there is absolutely no way to talk such a person out of these beliefs. They were forged in the depths of trauma, and by means of these beliefs this person has managed to cope and survive. When you challenge their beliefs, in effect you threaten their survival.

And it is not just their defenses you are up against. The very gray matter of their mind has been woven into a pattern that revolves around the icons they have internalized over time in highly emotional states. Such paths do not dissolve because of a Sunday School lesson that says, "Jesus loves me," when the child has thousands of hours of life experience that cry out, "No one has *ever* loved me!"

Furthermore, lies from life experience do not end with childhood. Life provides a myriad of ways to add to our malformed set of beliefs. Any adult who has experienced a life-changing accident, divorce, or any other form of significant loss has to struggle to make sense of their life again. On the other end of the spectrum, people who have unmitigated success can get caught up in the power that seems to surround their life. And everyone anywhere in between these extremes must deal with dozens of experiences daily that impact how they view themselves and others, life, and God.

As if that were not enough to distort our inner world, we have all grown up in a world that exerts tremendous pressure on us in the form of materialism, individualism, mistaken goals, and distorted perceptions of how we matter. Witness the peer pressure a young person endures in middle school with regard to clothes, parties, cliques, sex, drugs, and countless other complex issues. In trying to fit in, that teen will internalize all sorts of new distortions about who they are and how they belong to the larger group. But in many cases, telling a young teen not to follow the crowd is almost pointless. Such admonitions may well be completely powerless against their beliefs about how they have value.

Yet our malformation does not stop there. Anyone exposed to our public education system is inundated with paradigms that are diametrically opposed to life. Universities today are notorious for their disregard of Christian beliefs and values, both openly and in many subtle ways that permeate the classroom material. Throughout their education, young people are trained in an environment that assumes God is non-existent, or at least irrelevant to the learning process, if not downright offensive.

Unfortunately, our distorted training is not confined to secular institutions. Throughout the preceding chapters we have noted a number of critical paradigm shifts that are needed by Western Christian organizations. Rarely do you hear of efforts to train people to engage with God in order to be mentored directly by the Holy Spirit. Most Christian training today focuses on behavior modification, which is deeply dependent on self-effort and willpower. These combined training deficits have a tremendous educational effect on the general Christian population, such that relatively few Christians have the necessary tools to foster spiritual growth. This in turn can only result in greatly distorted beliefs about what we can hope for and greatly lowered expectations regarding any life-long development or closeness with God.

On top of all that, we have an enemy who is so committed to distorting every thought in our mind that he has earned the title, Father of Lies. Taken together, this collection of mind-assaulting experiences is more than we can withstand. All of us, through the course of daily life, misinterpret countless life events that we internalize over time and thus become more and more malformed. Each distorted belief impacts our future efforts and interactions, compounding the lies we believe. Consequently, by the time we are old enough to reflect on this process, we have already adopted hundreds of lies that we may have never even verbalized or consciously considered.

These are the reasons why we need God in order to have any hope of renewing our mind.

Taking Stock of Our Malformed Condition

What can we say then about the condition of anyone who has come to Christ but is still human and therefore in need of life-long spiritual growth? It would not be too much of a stretch to say they are similar to a person rescued from a toxic waste dump who needs years of medical care and rehabilitation to restore their health. Paul says God has "rescued us from the power of darkness and transferred us into the kingdom of his beloved Son" (Col.1:13). Anyone would call that a new lease on life or the chance for someone to finally discover life.

But that is only the beginning. Paul goes on to tell us that this new life "is being renewed to a true knowledge according to the image of the One who created" us (Col.3:10 NASB). Bringing us into the kingdom offers us the opportunity to become whole. What we bring with us, however, are all the lies we have learned from the world, as well as our way of making sense of life which can lead to still more distortions. Only as we learn how to see life through the eyes of heaven and be mentored by God Himself will the lies stop accumulating and the truth begin to penetrate the deepest recesses of our mind.

Our world is a dangerous place for the human soul. Spiritual darkness is pervasive and it invades our very bodies like a solvent that gets through the protective layers of skin and contaminates our flesh. We know that being deceived about any aspect of life is sufficient in and of itself to cause us to fall, and that we are deceived in so many areas we cannot begin to comprehend the depth of darkness we have inside.

Everything that happens to us, everything we think about, every act we engage in, every success, every struggle – anything we encounter can be distorted in some way if seen through natural eyes or interpreted for us by the darkness we live in. Deception includes everything we see through distorted lenses, all of our thoughts that are faulty, and any blind spots we still possess. They all combine to create distorted views of God, of our own self, and about how life works for us. Only God is capable of working through that darkness and bringing us out. We can be as sure as the psalmist that "what is dark to me is not dark to You, God" (Ps.139:12) and cling to our hope as John has said, "In him there is no darkness at all!" (1Jn.1:5).

Now that we have made the case for the necessity of divine intervention to save our mind and heart, let us go on to discuss how this process actually takes place.

The Key to Transformational Truth

The basic premise here is that our internalized beliefs drive our perceptions, interpretations and responses to life. Distorted beliefs will impair those functions, while beliefs that are in line with truth will guide those same functions toward a better way of life. It then follows that if we can replace our faulty beliefs with truth, our life will change! The Bible confirms this idea in many ways.

> You will know the truth, and the truth will make you free. (Jn.8:32)

> Be transformed by the renewing of your mind. (Rom.12:2)

So how does this happen? Perhaps a few examples will show what we mean by replacing our faulty beliefs.

I still remember graduation week at Fuller Seminary. Having spent four long years working my way through a masters degree, I had to face the reality that our savings were gone and I had no job waiting for me. I could feel myself sinking into hopelessness, and a life-long dread of mine came bubbling to the surface: "I will never find my place. My life has no purpose, no meaning, and God has no use for me."

All these thoughts and feelings were running through my mind on Wednesday of that week as I walked into chapel on campus, and there on the screen in big letters was a paraphrase of Isaiah 41:9.
I have brought you here for a purpose, and I will not throw you away!
I nearly collapsed on the spot. It was God speaking directly into my heart, telling me my fears were all lies. Nothing outside me changed. I still had no prospects for employment. But my dread was gone. From that point on when people asked my what my plans were I just smiled and said, "I'm still waiting to see what God has in mind." This is how God changes our heart and mind in ways that we cannot.

Here is another example. After my wife and I went to see the movie *Evening*, I came home extremely upset and agitated. In the movie, the main character is near the end of her life, and she is filled with regrets about things she wished she had done differently. All I could think about were some of the painful regrets I had been carrying around for several decades. There were choices I had made and ways I had lived that I wished with all my heart I had done differently. So I spent a few hours talking to God, journaling, and trying to listen to His voice. As a result of the things He spoke to me that day, I came away with a new appreciation for God's incredible grace and forgiveness for my poor life choices. I felt cleansed and much more at peace with my own life.

Quite often this process of restoration washes over us in ways that are fairly subtle, but substantial nonetheless. Referring back to an earlier example, when I ran across the verse that says, "To whom much is given, much is required," I felt as if a spotlight had been turned on my life. I began to write, "God, You know how much You have given me. I cannot begin to list all the ways You have rescued me, taught me, brought mentors into my life...the list goes on. My response to that is pitiful! I have not even begun to give as much as I have been given to. What do I do with that?"

I immediately felt led to write God's heart for me at that moment: "I'm just not that stingy! You and I can talk about how to give more of what you have been given. But don't beat yourself up because you cannot keep up with Me. I am a generous God. And I will pour into your life far more than you can ever repay. But if you want to talk about how to get more involved with what I have for you, we can do that." Again, I could not help but smile at how God does what He does. My heart was not only lighter, but eager to do more of what He was calling me to do.

Over and over, we can be changed by God speaking His truth into our heart and soul. Every time He does, we see life a little better, with more clarity regarding the unseen things around us. Our heart is adjusted and attuned toward the kingdom more, and our soul is enriched with more light.

Misusing Truth and Missing Transformation

Now that we have come to the very core of what we need to know for transformation, we need to be very careful. We have explained how we can be changed whenever truth replaces any distortions, lies, or spiritual blindness we possess. But there is one huge caveat, and we all know it: *not all truth transforms.*

We have all read books, heard sermons, or attended conferences that were inspiring and encouraging in ways that we were sure would make a difference, only to discover a few months down the road that not much had changed at all. We might be a little more educated, even more articulate about some issue. But by and large, our life was pretty much the same as it was before our latest encounter with truth.

So the question we need to ask is, *How do we encounter truth in ways that actually transform us? What makes the difference between truth that changes us and truth that does not?* The answer to this not only opens the door to tremendous opportunity for a transformed life, it explains how so many of us have encountered volumes of truth with very little impact.

The next diagram shows graphically *the single most common reason we encounter truth without being changed.* That is, *we put almost all of our focus on how to respond* to people and situations.

Basically, we assume the function of truth is to tell us what we *should* do, how we *should* feel, and attitudes we *ought* to have. Then we try to force ourselves to respond in those ways by sheer willpower. All the time, our entire inner being is applying pressure to react according to our internalized beliefs. In a nutshell, this is an attempt to "row" our way to change.

In practice, putting all the focus on our responses looks like this: We read in I Corinthians 13 that "love is patient, kind, not jealous, not arrogant, does not seek its own, is not provoked, bears all things, endures all things." So what do we do? We try really hard to be more patient, less jealous and self-seeking, and so on. Of course, these are all *responses* we might have to people and events. In fact, we may never actually love the other person any better than we did before, but we are trying to do the things that a loving person should do around them.

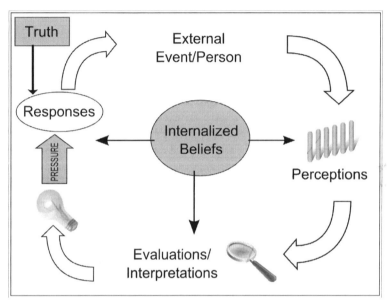

Focusing Truth on Our Responses

But Paul is *not* giving us a prescription on *how* to love. Rather, he is *describing* what real love looks like, so we will know it when we see it, and so we will know why he is bringing this matter into the larger conversation.[56] If we do not see these characteristics in our relationships (or some particular relationship) then chances are there is something *inside* us that still needs God's work. As we become more and more a loving person, this kind of love will flow out of us and be the basis for our interaction with others.

Much of what has been said previously regarding self-effort is clearly exemplified by this diagram. When we force ourselves to say the words, "I forgive you," we are trying to provide the correct response to the situation,

---

[56] The Bible tends to be more descriptive than prescriptive (Dallas Willard)

while overriding all of our internal processes that demand satisfaction. When we bake a cake for the neighbor we cannot stand in order to show our "love" for them, we are actually trying to offer a Christian *response* that looks to us like the right thing to do, but never truly changing our internal perceptions and beliefs about our neighbor.

This is actually what *legalism* looks like in graphic form. We know what we should be thinking and feeling and doing, so we attempt to get there by direct effort. If we could just control our thoughts and emotions long enough, perhaps we might be able to act the way we think we are supposed to. Some people train themselves to deny their inner thoughts and feelings so well that they become convinced they have changed when in fact they have only succeeded in losing touch with their inner life.

Viewing truth as primarily information we are supposed to "apply" in regard to right and wrong behavior, distorts the value of truth and puts us on a road that leads to self-righteousness instead of spiritual growth. Directing truth primarily at our responses to life tends to look for answers to the question, "What *should* I do in this situation?" Quite often this focus is reinforced through heavy use of terms like "obedience" and "accountability," as well as "making the right choices" and "being more committed." All of these phrases direct our attention to our external responses to the world around us, and are based on some highly questionable assumptions.

First, it assumes we can actually do the things God asks of us, as if the only thing standing between us and being able to forgive seventy times seven is our commitment to be obedient and the weakness of our will.

Second, this approach assumes that obedience is virtually the same thing as compliance. If I say the words, "I forgive you" then I am being obedient, regardless of where my heart is in the matter. If I bite my tongue and do not retaliate when you say something nasty to me, then I am being obedient, even if I hate you for it. Obedience gets equated with how well we adhere to the external standard of behavior. But that is not at all what Jesus meant by obedience.

Third, in some places it is even assumed that nothing can be done about our unruly, contrary emotions anyway. So obedience can *only* be a matter of external behavior. Our job is to fight those contrary feelings and do what is right regardless. They may even call that "getting the victory."

In truth, all this does is legitimize the power of the flesh and condemn us to internal battles we can never hope to win. The best we can hope for is to keep our inner life from leaking out or betraying us in a moment of weakness. We have given up on ever being able to "put to death the deeds of the flesh" (Rom.8:13).

But this whole effort to force the right outcome without changing our underlying process is exactly what Jesus called "cleaning the outside of the cup!" So although He actually commended the Pharisees for what they did, He also pointed out that their hearts were full of deceit (especially self-deception, because they thought doing the right thing was all that mattered).

Sometimes we hear that all we need in order to be obedient is to be more committed. But committed to what? If you have a distorted view of God (overly critical or judgmental) then the more committed you are, the worse it will be for you. And what good does it do if we are able to comply with the external appearances of goodness, while our heart is still full of regrets, disappointments, hurts, anger, and fear? We need more than commitment in order to grow up spiritually.

Do Responses Matter?

So do we just do whatever we feel like doing until our heart changes? Is our life to be ruled by our inner impulses, wherever they come from?

No, our responses *are* important. If we restrain our tongue when we would rather cut someone down to size, we have committed at least one less act of sin. But hopefully in the process we notice how much our soul still prefers to retaliate. Taking that awareness to God for His healing and restoration can truly set us free, so that the next time we encounter a similar situation we may want to bless that person instead of curse them.

If I get really mad at someone but stop myself from escalating the violence further, I have done a good thing. But rather than congratulate myself for doing the right thing in that moment, my best course of action is to take the whole thing to God and ask Him what I need from Him in order to heal my rage.

Focusing on our responses to life will not serve us well in terms of spiritual development. But that does not mean truth has nothing to say about morality or how God wants us to conduct our life. As with the Ten

Commandments, truth shows us God's character; it tells us the difference between right and wrong; it paints a picture of what holiness looks like so we can tell good from evil. But Paul also explained how the law brings us to the end of ourselves, so that we will realize how much we need God to do in us what we will never be able to do.

> For what the law could not do (because it depended on human effort) God did! By sending His Son and destroying the sin within us, He made it possible for us to internalize the law as we are led by the Spirit. (Rom.8:3-4, loosely paraphrased).

Knowing what is right and good is essential to life. It tells us which direction to go. Becoming a person who does what is right by nature is an entirely different matter. Not one of us is able to do that by our own direct effort. We need God to speak into our life and change our heart.

When we try to distill the principles of Scripture and then apply them by sheer resolve, we are effectively trying to live by external laws that are at odds with our internal circle of beliefs. As the diagram shows, when we are tempted to respond in a negative manner, it is due to the way our internal beliefs impact our perceptions and interpretations, which in turn apply pressure on our feelings and actions (responses). So any truth we try to apply directly to how to respond is at war with our automatic tendencies.

One of the biggest mistakes we make at this point is to think this internal war is normal for a Christian. We have even given it a name; we call it the conflict between the old nature and the new nature. Somehow our will is supposed to arbitrate between these two natures. But how is that possible? Does our will exist outside of our two natures? Do we have a third nature?

If we take Col.3:10 and other Pauline passages seriously, we have *one* nature which has been reborn a new creature – a *new* nature that is still contaminated from life in the world and needs renewing, healing, restoration, mentoring, and the impact of God's love before it begins to act more like its new self.

Our internal war is not due to having two different natures inside us.[57] A

---

[57] The only serious scriptural support for a two nature theory comes from a misunderstanding of the last part of Romans 7. See Douglas Moo's *Commentary on Romans* or N.T. Wright's *Commentary on Romans* for a better interpretation.

Renewing Our Mind

much better explanation for our experience is that we are still being renewed, and the internal beliefs we hold that have not yet been renewed are running on autopilot and wreaking havoc with our life. And as we will see, when we "take every thought captive" and bring them to God, we foster God's work in us so He can bring about the renewal we need so we can live better.

Above all, trying to force our responses to match the truth we see in Scripture assumes we actually have direct control over the fruit in our life (responses) without first changing the tree that is growing the fruit (our inner beliefs). Clearly, this is not how God wants us to apply His truth.

Proper Focus for Truth is Our Internal Belief System

Truth, when properly accessed and internalized, will not only illuminate our heart, but will transform our beliefs about who God is, who we are, and how life works. That is why we need to see truth as a way of bringing focus to our innermost thoughts. As we consider this next diagram, bear in mind that our internal belief system shapes our perceptions, guides our interpretations, and influences our responses.

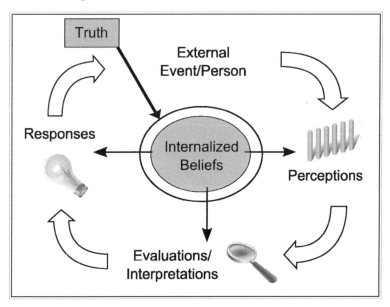

The Proper Focus for Truth

If faulty beliefs cause us to miss things or distort what we see, interpret them incorrectly, and respond poorly; and if correct beliefs help us to see clearly, interpret correctly and respond well; then the best way to change our life is to begin cleaning up this set of core beliefs. To whatever extent we can change these faulty beliefs, our inner war is greatly diminished and the whole system works better. We are then able to respond to life *as a result* of who we are, instead of in an effort to *override* who we are.

From this perspective, God's truth is not so much about what we need to *do* as it is about seeing what God sees, and about who we need to *become*. Only as we are changed on the inside can we ever hope to be able to respond to people and events the way Jesus did. This is what the Bible means by *renewing our mind*. And as we work with God to internalize truth, we are changed more and more into the character of Christ.

In terms of our primary metaphor, working with God to change our inner beliefs is like aligning our sail with the wind. As we 'catch' the truth that God reveals to us, we are changed in ways we could never manage on our own, and our spiritual life is propelled forward in ways we could never achieve by 'rowing' or trying to force the right outcome.

At this point it begins to make sense why we need to know what godly responses look like, even though we were never meant to produce them by direct effort on our part. In the earlier discussion of 1Corinthians 13, we talked about how truth can show us what love looks like. If we know we "should" forgive someone (the right response) and we know this is not going to be easy for us (something is messed up in the inner circle), then a light has been turned on and we now have a useful awareness about our soul.

A Story of Change

In Chapter 3, I related a story about Daniel who held deep resentments toward his parents and several of his siblings for nearly fifty years. Having done everything he thought a good Christian should do in order to let go of his anger and hate, he finally came to the end of himself and asked God what he needed in order to be free. God gave Daniel a picture of his family that revealed to him, "They're not being mean…they're desperate!" That revelation broke his heart, and he no longer felt bitterness and hate. Instead, he felt compassion for his family and longed for their healing.

Daniel's problem all those years was a distorted grasp of his family. All he could see were the ways they had treated him and each other, and he had long ago concluded they were mean-spirited people with very little redeeming value. Consequently, he could not make his heart care about them. But when God changed his internal beliefs about who they really were and why they behaved so terribly out of their desperation, his perceptions changed, his interpretations changed, and his responses to them changed.

Daniel had been trying to force the right response to his family all his life. But when God transformed his internal system, he immediately began to regard them with compassion. Notice carefully, that his compassion was a *natural* response based on the new condition of his heart. He no longer had to try to love his family – he just did.

Even though this example describes a major life-long issue, the principle is true even for minor distortions that cause us difficulty. As our internal conflicts are exposed by life experience, we can take them to God and ask for His insight into what is going on inside us that we have been unable to change. When He speaks into our heart, by word or picture or impression, He can transform our distortion with His truth and thereby free us to perceive, interpret and respond to life in ways that are more in line with who He created us to be.

Our Need for Transparency

When we approach God and His word for the purpose of being impacted for good, we need to walk into His presence expecting to encounter Light that brings Life. This was the joy of the psalmist when he prayed, "Search me, O God, and know my heart. Try me and know my anxious thoughts. And see if there be any hurtful way in me, and lead me in the everlasting way" (Ps.139:23-24 NASB).

Of course, this means we need to be able to stand in the Light without feeling overwhelmed by shame. That takes us back to Chapter 2 regarding God's character and His intentions for our good. When we fully grasp how His revelations to us can transform our internalized beliefs and how much He wants to restore us, we can come into His presence with all of our flaws exposed without any fear of shame or condemnation (Rom.8:1; Heb.12).

Refocusing Truth

Whereas focusing on our responses looks for answers to the question, "What should I do?" allowing truth to illuminate our internalized beliefs means we are looking for something else entirely. Focusing truth on our inner system asks, "What am I missing? How are my beliefs distorted in regard to God, self, or life?" This whole process sees truth primarily as God's worldview (if we can call it that) which is very different from our own worldview in many respects. He says, "My ways are higher than your ways" (Isa.55:9).

We see this process of redefining life throughout the earthly ministry of Jesus. In the Sermon on the Mount, He picked out several examples of ethical behavior and changed the focus from external action to internal character. Not killing someone is a good thing. But righteousness is more than refraining from violence. We need to purge hatred from our heart. Yes, we should keep ourselves from adultery, but the whole problem is better addressed by dealing with the internal issues that drive our lust.

When Jesus talked about the limits of Pharisaical righteousness, He specifically identified the problem of external compliance and the fact that on the inside they were still filled with the toxic ways of the world. When His disciples argued about power, He redefined for them the meaning of greatness. Rather than weigh in on the popular debate over paying taxes, Jesus reframed their understanding of who owns what, and the problem evaporated. In every instance we see Him revealing truth that clarified perceptions, provided better interpretations, and offered ways of responding that were rarely considered. Above all, He challenged their deeply held assumptions about who God is, who they were, and how life works.

How We Internalize Truth

An important question posed earlier was, "Why do we encounter truth so often without being changed very much? What makes the difference between truth that transforms and truth that does not?"

As we have shown, the most common reason we handle truth without much effect is because we put our focus in the wrong area – we focus on how we should respond to life instead of how we need to be changed by

God. But what does it mean to be changed by God in this way? How do we participate with Him to focus truth on our inner worldview?

I would point back to the stories of change that have been offered as examples. In each instance, someone had come to God with an issue that needed His help, and walked through the process of seeing where they had formed faulty views or lacked the necessary insight to move forward. As the person spent time listening to God, He revealed aspects of the problem they had not seen before, and through that insight they were able to receive healing and peace.

But all of this is predicated on whether or not we even notice these opportunities for healing and take the necessary steps.

Teachable Moments

From our personal experiences of transforming moments, as well as being present with many others in healing prayer, we have discovered that truth is best internalized when several elements are present.

- We are upset and have an emotional investment in the situation.
- We are able to perceive the presence and voice of God.
- We take the time to walk through the conversation with God.

These are what we call *teachable moments*. Our emotional investment is necessary because that is when we are most open to change. Internalized beliefs that are resistant to change are not simply ideas we have about life, but hard-won convictions we came to as a result of life experiences, usually emotionally charged experiences. Most of our faulty beliefs take shape in moments of emotional distress, including fear, shame, hopelessness, powerlessness, and sadness. When those painful emotions get re-triggered, it is because the underlying beliefs are making an active connection with our current situation. That is the moment when those beliefs become the most amenable to change.

By way of contrast, if we try to address an old wound in a dispassionate manner, as if we are discussing what we had for dinner the night before, any new thoughts we might have about the experience will get filed in the part of our mind that collects information. Consequently, we will not be changed much by the new idea. However, when we are involved in something in the present that has stirred up our emotions and triggered old reactions, or when God has taken us back to an old experience that has never been fully resolved and we are able to feel some of what we felt originally, then many of the circuits in our brain become active that were originally involved when we internalized and reinforced the old beliefs. Because of this, we are very open to new ways of making sense of that experience.

If we are connected well with God as we reflect on our distress, we can receive from Him what we need in order to change our beliefs. God may give us an image that captures the essence of what we need, such as an icon, or He may speak words of truth to us that we need to hear. Our insight might even begin as an impression of truth that forms into words only as we continue to dwell on it. In any case, the result is that God alters our way of making sense of the issue to be more like the way He views it.

What all of this points to is our need to learn how to identify these teachable moments when the conditions are right for transformation. These are not hard to find. Life itself brings us teachable moments all the time. Whenever we feel overwhelmed, anxious, hopeless or helpless, sad, or ashamed, we may have an opportunity for renewing our mind. If any of those emotions are accompanied by a sense of a split between our head and our heart, we can be almost certain we have a teachable moment and there are faulty beliefs providing the fuel for what we are feeling. For example, when we think:

- I really should forgive that person, even though I don't want to.
- I should volunteer for that ministry, but I feel so reluctant to do so.
- I really should be more generous and give more.
- I really should do something about the need that tugs at my heart.

If we will simply notice how ambivalent we are and how distressed we are about being ambivalent, we will identify many teachable moments. Our task is not to try to override our divided heart and "do the right thing" but to take our confusion to God and ask Him to show us what we need in order to heal our fractured heart.

Another teachable moment is possible whenever we find ourselves overreacting to something. It may only take a few words, a look, or a mistake to suddenly drive us up the wall, and we start acting in ways that are very disproportionate to the event we are involved in. These are all clues we are being triggered by an old internalized belief.

While attending seminary I once received a score of 75% on a book review and I was completely devastated. As I was ranting in my prayer journal about how horrible I was and how everyone else was smarter than me and why I should quit school, the light suddenly turned on. "Wow! That's a fairly big rant over one small paper! I think somebody needs a lot of affirmation in order to be OK!" My overreaction revealed a part of my heart that I did not know about until it was challenged. I was then able to dig in a bit deeper and engage with God for some healing about my own sense of worth and how for so many years I had depended on pastors and teachers to affirm my value as a person.

One reason we miss these moments is because they feel more like problems "out there" rather than opportunities to transform something "in here." A counselor friend of mine calls these moments, *Unwelcome Redemption*. They are unwelcome because we do not want to go through these experiences; but they offer us an opportunity for redemption because God can use these encounters to bring focus to those places in us that need more of God and more of His truth. Our main challenge in all this is to learn how to see these experiences as windows on our own internal process and as possibilities for change.

Sometimes these teachable moments come to us through very positive events rather than negative ones. They are "corrective experiences" in which we encounter something good that we have had little exposure to in the past. During a difficult period in my life in the 1980's, I joined a small support group in an effort to find some help. I distinctly remember sitting there one night listening to a number of heart-wrenching stories. As each person shared their pain, one or two others would respond with some of the kindest words I have ever heard, caring for the one who had spoken and offering comfort and compassion. It dawned on me that I had never witnessed such care before, having spent much of my life around people who were highly judgmental and fairly intolerant of emotional distress. In a matter of minutes, my whole idea of relationships was turned inside out, as I saw how these kinds of interactions were truly life giving. It was a corrective experience that led to a tremendous growth spurt in my relational life.

Finally, in addition to the teachable moments that are thrust into our world by life itself, we can *create* teachable moments for change very deliberately by making use of the spiritual practices that were discussed in the Interlude. Because when we intentionally put ourselves in a place where we can pay better attention to what is going on inside us, and at the same time set up a context that can stir up issues that need attention, we have all the makings of a teachable moment.

For example, when we engage in acts of service, all of our concerns about time and energy come to the surface. When we fast, we face the issue of what happens when we say 'no' to our cravings. Spending time in solitude, we discover how much we need to be needed or how hard it is for us to quiet our mind. Or while spending time in the presence of God, we may encounter His love more deeply than we have experienced before. All of these practices are have the potential to create teachable moments in which our heart and mind are open and receptive to the Spirit of God. Once we see this possibility, spiritual practices take on a whole new dimension of life for us as learners in the kingdom.

Transformation in a Nutshell

To pull this all together, renewing our mind is a life-long process we can engage in very intentionally, knowing that God is able to reframe our experiences and wounds, as well as reveal to us what we need in order to become the person we were created to be.

Most of our interactions with life around us are heavily driven by our internalized beliefs about God's character, our own sense of who we are, and our assumptions about how life works and how God is involved. Woven throughout those internal beliefs are far more distortions and gaps than we could possibly know. And those distortions disrupt our perceptions about the world around us, interfere with our interpretations about what we perceive, and limit or misdirect our responses. Consequently, to whatever extent our belief system is flawed, we will not be able to live out the vision we see in the New Testament of life in the Spirit.

The good news is that we have been given a Healer and Mentor who loves to reveal truth to us that is relevant to who we are and where we are in our journey; truth that is able to expose and transform our faulty beliefs about who we are, who God is, and how life works. Furthermore, we can learn how to participate with the Holy Spirit in this way to receive from Him what we need to change our heart and mind.

Then whenever we encounter teachable moments – whether through life itself or through spiritual practices – whether through negative emotions or corrective experiences – we can ask God to open our eyes to what we need to see and open our heart to His love and truth. Thus, one distorted belief after another, our mind and heart can be transformed to become more and more like the mind of Christ.

We must remember that we are forever the apprentice, a perpetual learner, a student of the kingdom, always in need of further renewal and in need of remaining moldable and teachable. Above all, we have a God whose ways are so far above our ways that we can only begin to see life from His perspective. And every revelation, every renewed thought, every transformed part of our soul brings so much relief and life that we will never be content to stop growing.

Implications for Christian Counseling

Before closing this chapter, I want to address one of the more serious implications regarding this issue of how God renews our mind. One of the greatest mistakes made by people who have trained as Christian counselors is the failure to grasp this process by which we are malformed. Counselors and other well-meaning Christians who operate from the premise that all behavior is volitional can do a tremendous amount of damage to those who have been wounded in childhood.

It is not uncommon for such ministers to insist that the person "repent" of their self-destructive behavior and change how they live (respond to life), when the adult child of abuse may in fact be unable to do so. They can no more rewire their mind by choice than they can command a lung to regenerate. Being unable to comply with the demands of the counselor, they are often left with an additional burden of shame and self-disgust. Often they are worse off than if they had not sought help at all.

The truth is we are so dependent on and familiar with our internalized beliefs that we often do not even know what they are. Just as we rarely think about gravity, but continuously operate under its assumption, so also we assume a great many things about how God regards us, about how we have value, and what we need to do in order to matter. Those thoughts may never be fully verbalized, but they drive our life as if they were the basic tenets of our faith.

When counselors are unaware of how these beliefs operate below the conscious level of the mind, and instead assume that all behavior is driven by deliberate choice (or the absence of necessary choices), they lay an impossible burden on those who come to them for help. Since no one can really live apart from their internalized beliefs, any external demands to do otherwise will create a painful internal conflict between their head and their heart. The usual results are either self-condemnation or denial, neither of which leads to integrity as a child of God.

Understanding the nature of spiritual renewal is essential to our own spiritual health. Learning how to internalize truth is a path that leads us to life. This become even more important when we take on the task of trying to lead others toward life.

A Model for Inner Healing

Through a lot of experience, Christian counselors and ministers who assist others with healing prayer have found a fairly effective way of helping people engage with God to permanently alter the underlying beliefs that cause so much pain and faulty living. The model for prayer outlined below is an adaptation of several of these approaches.[58] Please bear in mind that this is a very brief description of this kind of prayer. The reader is encouraged to check out additional sources on renewing our mind for a more in-depth discussion of inner healing prayer, especially any materials based on the "Immanuel Approach" to healing prayer pioneered by Karl Lehman.

1. Find a place of appreciation and ask Jesus to open your heart to His presence. It may be helpful to remember a time when you were keenly aware of His presence and ask God to stir up your memory of that time. When

---

[58] This model draws from several approaches to engaging with God for healing our internal beliefs about life. See the following authors: Koepcke, et.al.; Lehman; Wilder-Coursey; Takle.

Renewing Our Mind 289

you begin to have a sense of the presence of God, ask Him to come closer and reveal Himself to you even more. (If you have difficulty sensing His presence, ask Him to reveal whatever might be in the way. This then becomes the issue to take to step 3.)

2. Discern what needs to be addressed. If you have a specific issue that you want healing for, ask God if this is the time and place for that. Otherwise, ask God if He has some other way for you to spend your time together.

3. Once you have named the issue to be addressed, identify the emotions that are associated with it. Describe any reactions, beliefs and intentions that go with the experience and/or distress, and any means by which the issue may get triggered in your life.

4. Ask Jesus to help you bring the issue into focus, perhaps by using your memory of either an actual event or the people involved. Generally speaking, as long as you can stay connected with God, the more you are able to acknowledge the distressing emotions related to this issue, the more open you will be to change (it is not generally necessary to "re-experience" the trauma). If you identify a faulty belief that is involved, the more "true" it feels to you, the more deeply the real truth will be able to penetrate.

5. Check to make sure you are still connected to God as you talk to Him about this issue. If the emotions become overwhelming, be sure to back off and ask God for help in staying connected with Him.

6. Ask God what He wants you to know about this issue and be open to whatever He might say or do at that point. He may reveal truth in the form of words or images, or He may reveal His heart toward you, assure you that you are not alone, or whatever it is you need in that moment. If you are not receiving anything, make sure you can see Him or sense His presence, and ask Him questions about the issue that will help to expose any underlying fears and beliefs.

7. After you have received something that you believe is from God, check for peace and rest in the event. If you have experienced His joy or peace, then you may want go on to the next step, or you can ask God if there is anything else He wants to reveal to you. If the emotion has simply changed, say from

shame to sadness, then there may be more that needs to be addressed. Go back to step 3 and see what else needs God's touch.

8. Give thanks for the healing that has occurred. Tell someone else what God has done for you.

The most important factor in all of this is *staying connected with God*. If at any point it becomes difficult to sense the presence of God, then everything else becomes secondary to finding out what is preventing us from sensing His presence. Sometimes all that is needed is to notice that we have lost track of God and seek Him out again. Sometimes we will discover one or more obstacles in the way of perceiving His presence, such as fear of God, fear of pain, anger at God, vows we have made related to the issue or in regard to God, disbelief about healing or about God, and so on. These obstacles then become the issues that need to be addressed, taking them back to God just as the original issue was taken to God, asking Him how He wants to address these things.

For example, if you discover that you are angry with God because He did not prevent a certain thing from happening, then it is probably more important to deal with God about your anger than it is to seek healing in regard to that event. Or if you find that you are afraid of what God might say about the situation, tell Him what you feel and ask Him what you need in order to feel safe enough to move on. In any case, whenever anything gets in the way of your relationship and receptivity to God, your primary concern is to address those things rather than the original issue.

Looking back at the entire process, notice the level of participation that is required by both yourself and God. Seeking out the best evidence for a faulty belief can mean recalling a very painful event where the belief became anchored in your memory. You must be willing and able to hold significant levels of discomfort while remaining open to the voice of God.

It is often helpful to have another person present with you and interceding for you (even out loud, occasionally) while you engage with God for healing. But it is generally better for your intercessor to be patient as you wrestle with God, and not attempt to provide the truth that he or she thinks you need. (There is a time and place to receive wisdom from others. But in inner healing prayer, it is best to receive from God directly – His words have the power of life in them – Jn.6:63)

There are often multiple distortions embedded in single events, and there can be multiple events woven together to arrive at one or more faulty beliefs. Dealing with these complications and listening to God while in distress is a learned process for both the minister and the one being ministered to. That is why it is important to take into account all of the distress surrounding particular events, and why we should not abandon this process when we run into a few dead ends. Patience and persistence are valuable assets in any aspect of spiritual formation, and especially when addressing painful wounds.

Learning to engage with God and to let Him reinterpret our life experiences from His point of view is far more exciting and life-giving than anything we could ever hope to achieve through our own direct effort. We discover more of God's heart for us and find a freedom we never thought possible. May God richly bless your pursuit of His gifts.

Resources for Further Study

David Takle, *The Truth About Lies and Lies About Truth: A Fresh Look at the Cunning of Evil and the Means for Our Transformation* (Pasadena: Shepherd's House) 2008

Karl Lehman, *Outsmarting Yourself: Catching Your Past Invading the Present and What to Do About It* (IL: This Joy Books) 2001

Gary Smalley, *Change Your Heart Change Your Life: How Changing What You Believe Will Give You the Great Life You've Always Wanted* (Thomas Nelson) 2005.

Jim Wilder and Chris Coursey, *Sharing Immanuel* (Pasadena: Shepherd's House) 2010

Chapter 10

Healing Our Identity and Self-Rejection

We are what he has made us. (Eph.2:10)

One of the greatest challenges we face in our Christian development is that of coming to terms with our identity as children of God. What makes this challenging is that so many people suffer from some level of self-rejection or self-hate due to the distorted messages and wounds they have received from life in our broken world. More people than not can identify with the statement, "If you knew me better, you would not like me." And still more are convinced that God must not like them because He knows them better than anyone else.

During the 1980's there were several attempts by Christian authors to address this problem, with mixed results. Most of the discussions centered around the term *self-esteem*, with some teachers seeing a need for better identity models in the church and others insisting that self-esteem was another word for "pride" or that Christians ought not be concerned with their self worth.

In my opinion, the reason that nothing much came of those debates is that the proponents of self-esteem focused too much on symptoms and failed to offer a tangible means for healing a broken self-image. And frankly those opposing them seemed unable to grasp the discussion at all: they either confused self-worth with narcissism or tried to propose some form of anti-identity theology that left no room for an authentic relationship with God.

What we need to understand is that many Christians today find it hard to make sense of who they are in Christ or why that matters. And the single most common barrier to that end is self-hate in all its forms. So this is not a problem we can ignore. Our approach to addressing this issue can be broken down into three main areas: (1) Survey the many ways in which self-hate presents itself and affects our life; (2) Identify some of the root causes of self-hate; (3) Offer a means for healing from God Himself.

SELF-HATE SYMPTOMS AND EFFECTS

Many people who suffer from self-hate are not even aware that this is in fact what they are struggling with. Self hate is not confined to the obvious symptoms like suicidal thoughts or self-abuse. It can show up in some very direct ways and also some indirect ways.

Direct Forms of Self-Hate

Self-hate is often clearly visible in our self talk and in the ways we treat ourselves. Here are a few of the most obvious and direct ways in which we can express a negative sense of who we are.

Self-Derision and Self-Vindictive Criticism

We often here children say things out loud that demonstrate the extent of their disappointment in their own life. These statements can be startling, even horrifying when we hear them uttered by a five or ten year-old who has become exasperated with their limitations. Two phrases tend to top the list: "I can't do anything!" and "I hate myself!"

As we get older, we learn to keep such statements to ourselves and mostly say them in our head. The statements also get more specific:

- I hate it when I procrastinate or say the wrong thing or whatever.
- No matter what I do I don't matter.
- I wish I was dead; or I hate my life.
- Maybe if I got an incurable disease, I could get some consideration, and if not, I can just die.

These hateful expressions come out of us in moments of despair, when we are out of energy, or need things to go right, or when we experience the same setback for the umpteenth time. In our mind it is clear in that instant that we are somehow our own worst enemy, and we wish we could be a different person.

Shame and Self-Loathing

While less visible than the derisive things we might say to our self, the shame and self-loathing we feel can range anywhere from mild annoyance with our self, to deep seething rage and hatred. By the time we are aware of these feelings, we may no longer even know why we feel that way. These emotions can build over time from repeated rejection or failure, until we are so convinced we are failing at life that we can no longer stand who we are.

A closely related feeling is that of hating everything about my life without directly hating myself. I may hate the cards I was dealt, the circumstances surrounding my life, the family I grew up in, and so on. Rather than say, "I hate myself" the phrase that comes to mind is, "I hate my life!" On the surface this may seem quite different than self-hate. But these feelings of helplessness or victimization have a way of infecting our sense of value and meaning, eroding our self-worth in ways that we may not even realize. We may even spend a lot of time fantasizing about having a different life than the one we have. Or we might envy the life of someone we know and wish our life could be like theirs.

Dreading God's Opinion

For many people, the idea of being seen through the eyes of heaven is not a life-giving thought. When they imagine God looking at them, they feel shame or a crushing weight of judgment instead of love and hope. Whatever sin or shame they harbor feels like a giant blot on their soul, and they are certain that this is all God sees when He looks at them.

If I am afraid you would not like me if you knew all there was to know about me, then how am I to think God feels, given that He knows my darkness even better than I do? When I read scripture, all I see are God's judgments, His wrath, His demands, and so on. He may use the word "love" to describe His relationship to His people. But it sounds like the love of a strict authoritarian father who has no room in his life for nonsense, let alone failure.

Somehow all the good messages in scripture about how God sees us get lost in the terrible violent pictures of God's judgment. If I cannot stand myself then I must be one of those people whom God wants to punish. In any case, I can probably find plenty of evidence in my life that God is against me, not for me.

Minimizing Assets and Blessings

A rather minor form of overt self-hate is that of minimizing the good things in our life. When something great happens, we start waiting for the other shoe to drop. Murphy's law seems to be one of the more powerful forces we know: if anything can go wrong it will.

Unfortunately, because we live in a broken world, and because we are all quite limited by nature, this way of viewing life can feel quite accurate. But when we make this personal and view our circumstances as unusual or unfair, we may cross the line into wishing we could have someone else's life.

Those who struggle with self-hate generally have difficulty with compliments as well, which feel uncomfortable and are easily dismissed. "It was nothing," we say when someone tells us we did something good. It was a fluke. Or some unforeseen miracle made it all possible. But no way could it have been me. Anyway, if I try to feel good about it I'm being proud. And God punishes the proud, so I'm better off if I do not accept any credit.

Ironically, by going out of our way to dismiss complements, we may already be ascribing too much value to our performance. Our response is likely an attempt on our part to distance our self from our discomfort. Or we may simply be unable to believe what the other person has said. Either way, it somehow feels safer to retreat into a diminished view of self.

Indirect Forms of Self-Hate

Self-hate also takes a number of *indirect* forms, some of which are rarely associated with self-hate because they can look like the exact opposite.

Perfectionism

We do not normally think of perfectionism as a bad thing. In others it can be a bit annoying, but their dependability makes up for it. And in myself, perfectionism is just my way of excelling at everything I do.

But perfectionism can also come from an intense need to be perfect in order to be acceptable, either to myself or to others. Anything less than perfect makes me anxious and says something bad about me as a person. Making sure everything is just right is a way of keeping myself safe and making sure no one, including me, sees anything wrong in my performance.

Now there is such a thing as wanting to do well and doing our best in everything we put our hand to. That is not a problem. What perfectionism refers to is a drivenness to perform because of what someone might think about me. This is an attempt to over-compensate for internal messages of shame and self-doubt, an attempt to prove I am not as bad as I may have been told I am.

Illusions of Grandeur and Importance

Another way of compensating for feelings of inferiority or shame is to create an unrealistic view of ourselves as being significantly more important in some way than the average person. Images of who we might be can take a great many forms. One is to harbor a fantasy of being extremely adept at something that is difficult to measure, such as thinking I am more intuitive than most people. I might even believe that if you could see my real self you would wish you could be like me.

In its extreme form, this air of self-importance becomes narcissistic. Everything is about me. I am the center of the universe, or at least I think I should be. Anything that takes the focus away from me is a personal affront to my importance. But underneath this demand for attention there lies some tremendous insecurity about who I am and how I matter.

In children, illusions of grandeur are really a normal part of fantasy play. Imagining they are bigger and more important is very normal and may have nothing at all to do with a poor self-image. As we grow and mature, these illusions quite naturally give way to more realistic images of who we are. But when seriously unrealistic ideas of who we are or who we might become persist into adulthood, then very likely they are subconscious attempts to repress something far more negative and self-condemning.

Fear of Exposure

Even though shame is one of the main components of self-hate, a person may actually experience it more as fear. For example, people who fear exposure may not be aware of the underlying self-doubt, because the anxiety that keeps them hiding out is so overwhelming that it blocks any other self-awareness. In its simplest form, this is a fear that my worst ideas about me might be true. If you ever discover the real me, I might suffer terrible humiliation or rejection. You might see me as a fraud or totally undesirable.

Toxic Hopes

Another area that we do not normally associate with self-rejection has to do with chronic disappointment in our life that leads to toxic forms of hope.

God designed us with a yearning for more of who He designed us to be, and that is good. Longing to be more than what we are keeps us on the journey of discovery. But sometimes this ability to look beyond our current state gets distorted into something toxic, a rejection of the life we now have, as though we are on hold and unable to have a real life until this thing gets fulfilled. If only I had … the perfect job, the perfect family, or the perfect mate, then my life would be good. If only my boss would recognize me for the contribution I have made. If only my family would recover. If only.

The problem is not that we are desiring something better, but that these desires have become so overbearing and so important to our fulfillment that we are no longer living in the present. To whatever extent that we are unable to come to terms with where we are currently, we may be unable to accept that we have value and meaning in the present. And the more remote our hopes are, the more toxic their effect can be on our present life.

As Solomon so eloquently put it, "Hope deferred makes the heart sick" (Prov.13:12). Putting all our conditions for satisfaction in specific future developments can actually be a way of rejecting the life we now have.

How Self-Hate Affects Us

As we can see by the many forms of self-hate, this is not simply an emotion we carry around. It is a force that drives our perceptions, our interpretations of the world, and our day-to-day choices. Self-hate is deeply destructive in many ways that we may not even be aware of.

Distorted Images of God

Given that a negatively distorted self-image feels like a true reflection of who I am, it follows quite reasonably that God must also be disgusted with me, since He knows the real me. It is then a fairly short trip from there to the conclusion that God's love and perceptions of me are contingent upon my performance. If He loves me at all, it is because He has to, being God.

In short, self-hate is not only a lens that distorts how we see our self, it distorts how we think God sees us, and in turn, how we see God. Yet it never occurs to us that we are projecting our own disappointment over our broken identity onto God. Once in place, our distorted image of God will tend to drive us away from Him.

Lower Expectations of God, Self, Life

Convinced that we will only ever see the short end of the stick, our expectations will diminish in regard to God, self, and life in general. If I am as worthless as I think I am, then not even God will invest much in my life. He may judge me to be beyond help or not worth the bother, or too wounded or sinful to be of much use to Him.

If I cannot be fully known without being rejected, then I have to hide behind a facade and keep you at a distance. If you do happen to like me, you are actually befriending my facade and not the real me. So the value of your friendship is diminished and my expectation of what you can offer me is impacted as well.

Because of these relational barriers, nearly every meaningful aspect of life gets viewed as lose-lose. No matter what I choose, the best I can hope for is to exchange one set of problems for another. Better to lower my expectations than to be continually disappointed about how life turns out for me.

Weak Faith or Disbelief

Extending the impact of low expectations a bit further, self-hate will bring me to the place where I dismiss real change as merely visionary and without any basis in reality, at least for me. God is not going to heal my wounds, He is not going to give me purpose (why would He?), and He is not going to want to be with me. Thus I have little faith that He will speak to me, that He will meet my needs, or that I can hope for anything at all from Him. All that talk about the love of God and what He will do for us may apply to you, but not to me.

Difficulty Receiving

Viewing my life as a kind of black hole also means there is no reason for anyone to give me anything of value. Nothing will be enough to help me anyway, and I do not deserve it in the first place. What's more, I do not feel like I have anything to give in return, so receiving may even feel shaming.

Whatever gift you offer me I will discount as an anomaly, something that will not last and will not happen again. Since you cannot possibly know how bad I am (or you would not be so nice) I may feel as if I have deceived you into being generous, and your consideration may seem ill-gotten.

Finally, the idea of anything being freely given simply does not fit my world view. There must be some alternative motive, some string attached, or some expectation for me to reciprocate. Otherwise, if good things can be freely given and received, I have to make some sense out of the tremendous deprivation I have felt all these years. It feels safer to question the new gift and hold it at arms length.

Self-Exclusion

All of the above consequences of self-hate also function to keep me at a distance from those around me. When I am in a group, I tend to feel alone and isolated, out of place with those who have so much more to offer than I do. Assuming that no one really wants me around anyway, I limit my participation. Effectively, I exclude myself from the group, even though I may perceive it as the group excluding me. I may leave an event feeling as if everyone was closed and resistant, when all the while I was the one sending off signals that said, "Do not get close to me."

Still another way I might exclude myself is by trying too hard to compensate for my low self-image. In doing so I may become socially inappropriate in ways that distance people from me. Depending on my level of awareness, I may blame either myself or them for the disconnect. But the result is still the same.

Sometimes a severe crisis in a person's life can leave them with almost no ability to cope with reality at all, leading to extreme self-rejection. This is portrayed very dramatically in the movie "*The Martian Child.*" There a young boy who was abandoned by his parents retreats into a fantasy world in which he convinces himself that he is actually a martian child who was left behind accidentally when his parents were visiting earth. He is expecting them to return soon to get him, and in the mean time he is coping as best he can with the brighter sun and other inconveniences of the planet. The story is very compelling. But its basic story line is that deep unresolved pain can lead us to withdraw from everyone and everything around us.

Damage to Relationships

Having low expectations of how other people will respond to me can motivate me to severely limit my investment in any relationship. Believing that I will eventually be rejected means that I need to place safeguards on my heart and my hopes for any relationship in order to reduce my risk.

Also, to whatever extent I feel unlovable, I will notice that you do not love me well enough. I will eventually reject you for not being what I wanted or needed, or else I will get you to pull away from me, either because of my demands or my lack of investment.

This syndrome then creates a descending spiral. As my relationships become less reliable and less life-giving, my sense of isolation and self-hatred increases. And as my self-hate becomes more dominant in my life, my relationships suffer. Each gives momentum to the other and seems to add validity to my negative world view. Such a cycle can be very hard to break.

Difficulty with Developmental Tasks

As we will discuss in Chapter 12, normal human development requires a broad context of healthy relationships. The more self-hate a person internalizes, the less trusting their relationships become and the fewer resources they have available to them to continue their development. Here are just a few of the tasks that suffer from self-rejection:[59]

- Learning to receive with joy.
- Learning to regulate emotions.
- Learning how to return to quiet and joy from negative emotions.
- Learning to be consistently me over time.
- Learning to identify and ask for what I need.
- Learning to tame cravings.
- Developing a personal style that is uniquely me.

Again we are faced with a descending cycle of events. Watching others around me master tasks and develop skills that I cannot seem to learn, my self-image plummets further, making it even harder to grow into the person God intended me to be. The gap between my peers and myself continues to

---

[59] This list is drawn from Wilder, *The Complete Guide to Living With Men*.

widen and my self-worth falls even lower. Apart from some outside intervention, there is little chance that I will be able to break this cycle.

Certain Forms of Depression

Depression can be caused by a lot of things. One of those causes is self-hate. Over time, self-hate leads to a kind of dread of one's own life that can be very paralyzing. Combined with anger toward their failures, and maybe even themselves, this becomes a formula for depression that can further immobilize them as a person.

Of course, being depressed does not automatically mean that you suffer from self-hate, because there can be many other causes. But self-hate usually brings with it some level of anger directed at the self that leads to depression.

Chronic and Binge Addictions

Addictions can also have many causes. But for some people, an addiction can medicate the emotional pain that accompanies self-hate and at the same time deliver what feels like well-deserved self-punishment.

A major element of self-hate is the feeling that something is intrinsically wrong with the person. Even worse, this is usually accompanied by some sense that the defects are their own fault. Of course, feeling responsible for one's own demise is intolerable, so one way to cope is to engage in bouts of drinking, drugs, sex, or other mood-changing behaviors. Not only is the pain temporarily medicated, but the negative effects of the behavior make some kind of perverse sense. After all, a person deserves to be punished for sabotaging their own life.

If the behaviors are addictive, then once a person is hooked they have even more reasons to hate their life. Which of course leads to more binge behavior and an ever-deepening cycle.

Summary

Self-hate is not benign. It grows like a choking vine around all aspects of a person's sense of self and threatens whatever life remains. Unless a remedy is found, its crippling effects will be felt throughout a person's lifetime. In many cases, the layers of hiding and self-protection become stronger with time, and any hope of life being different becomes more and more remote.

THE ORIGINS OF SELF-HATE

How does self-hate get started in the first place? Where does it come from? In the segments to follow, we will look at some of the more common origins of this self-destructive process.

Wounding in Early Childhood

The single most common source of self-hate is childhood experience. Due to the fragile nature of a child's soul, care-givers can injure them quite easily without intending harm at all. Even in families that lack classic dysfunctional characteristics, parents are flawed and limited and may not be able to give their children those things that are necessary for a balanced self-image. When you add to that the number of days on which parents simply lack the energy to meet the needs of their children, there is ample opportunity to be wounded in ways that can have lasting effects.

Life events that cause injury to our soul can generally be divided into two types of wounds. A-type injuries are the *Absence* of good things that we need but do not get. B-type injuries are the *Bad* things that happen to us that in a perfect world would not happen. Sometimes these are referred to as the *intrusions* (B-type) and *deprivations* (A-type) of childhood.[60] Injuries can be further divided into various categories based on the general nature of the intrusion or deprivation. Here are some examples of the major areas of wounding:

- Emotional Injury
  - A-type: Lack of love or the loss of a primary caregiver.
  - B-type: Being terrified or unnecessarily shamed.
- Physical Injury
  - A-type: Malnutrition or lack of loving physical touch.
  - B-type: Getting beaten.
- Spiritual Injury
  - A-type: Lack of spiritual direction.
  - B-type: Being taught God is disgusted with you.

---

[60] From Friesen, et.al., *The Life Model*.

- Sexual Injury
  - A-type: Not being taught boundaries or basic sexual values.
  - B-type: Sexual assault of any kind (verbal, physical).
- Psychological Injury
  - A-type: Developmental needs not met; an absence of guidance.
  - B-type: Child required to meet emotional needs of parents.
- Developmental Injury
  - A-type: No help with attempts at problem solving.
  - B-type: Being shamed for asking for what is needed.

Notice that since B-type injuries are the result of *actual events*, they are much easier to remember and name. A-type injuries are *events that are missing* from the child's life, so there is nothing to remember, just a vacuum where something should have been. As a result, it is much harder to identify and name our A-type injuries and often harder to get healing for them as well.

A Diminished Sense of Self

Intrusions and deprivations can have numerous consequences in the life of a child. Generally speaking, children have very little capacity to withstand injury of any kind, let alone at the hands of their parents or primary caregivers. They internalize these injuries and interpret them as messages about who they are and how they matter.

Being slapped across the face, for example, tells a child that he or she is without dignity and can be violated at will by those around them. Even if they cannot find the words for it, they still internalize a sense of disdain, perhaps in the form of violent images of rejection.

When their needs and value are repeatedly scrapped due to rage or other parental limitations, children will come to see themselves as "less than" and expendable in some manner. Many B-type violations involve adults who behave shamelessly, which has a way of transferring the shame of the event onto the child. After living through hundreds of such events over a period of many years, a child will likely internalize the hateful behavior very deeply as self-hate. They may then act in hateful ways toward themselves and others, or else rebel against those feelings and become an overachiever or perfectionist in order to "prove" themselves to be better than the person they were told they were. Some children create a distorted reality where they can feel important in their own mind in ways that help them survive, but are counter-productive to their future relationships and continued development.

In addition, whether or not children experience such overt abuse, if they are poorly trained in their life tasks (A-type injuries), then as they grow up life will become increasingly frustrating for them due to a lack of necessary skills to meet the demands of adulthood. Inevitably, they will feel ill prepared to meet life and hate their own lack of ability to engage with others joyfully and competently.

Wounding From Later Life Experience

Besides the wounds we may receive in early childhood, there are many life events that challenge our sense of who we are and how we matter in this world. Experiences such as these can seriously damage our self-worth and cause us to hate our self.

Developmental Issues

To whatever extent a person fails to get the help they need to finish early developmental tasks, they will feel handicapped and deficient in their ability to handle the complexities of adult life. As these deficiencies become apparent and painful, the person will grow to hate their lack of basic skills and feel defective as a person.

Failed Relationships

Irreparable ruptures can be another important cause for a diminished sense of self. When we lose an important relationship for any reason, we may wonder why we were so easily mistreated or so expendable. Some of the greatest pains of divorce are the questions that come from the fact that the person who knew you best in the world rejected you. If they did not want you or could not live with you, what does that say about you?

Whatever the reason for the breakdown, failed relationships can seriously damage our confidence, our sense of value, and our hopes for sustained connections. And because God designed us for attachment and bonding with others, the pain of a lost relationship can have a very deep impact on how we see our self.

Failed Performance

When I fail at something important, like a business venture or school or staying financially solvent, I may come to believe that I myself am a failure. This problem says something about me that all the world can see and judge.

If I declare bankruptcy, it may seem like I am telling everyone that I have failed at a basic life task, or worse, that I have been irresponsible. If I get fired from a job, even if it is due to downsizing, it may be very difficult not to see it as an inability to compete in the marketplace. If I strike out at a critical time in the ballgame, I may feel as if I have let everyone else down. All of these failures can have a devastating impact on my view of myself.

Impossible Standards

Sometimes people continually compare themselves to standards they could not possibly live up to and then condemn themselves for being unable to do so. The shame from this seems inescapable to them, because the standards are clearly good and right, and their behavior is not. Every mistake is additional proof of their defective state, every faulty choice is evidence of their lack of judgment, and so on. They hate their inability to be the person they think they ought to be in order to be acceptable.

Poor Theology

There are certain strains of Christianity that believe the only remedy for pride is to beat our self-image into the ground. We may be saved, but we are still miserable sinners that God could hardly put up with were it not for Jesus interceding on our behalf. This is very poor theology and not at all in harmony with the love that Jesus demonstrated, especially in light of His declaration that "whoever has seen me has seen the Father" (Jn.14:9).

Every time this poor theology is taught, the teachers make at least one major error in logic, in addition to their misunderstanding of Scripture. Basically, they set up a false dichotomy: "There are two kinds of people in the world – those who are humble and know they are rotten to the core, and those who are proud and arrogant." The implication, of course, is that if you do not beat yourself into the ground you are an arrogant enemy of God.

What's more, this faulty comparison is based on a mistaken idea of humility. Scriptural humility is simply the recognition that I am a very small creature with a very big God. The universe truly owes me nothing, and everything I have is a gift. In my original design, I am totally dependent upon God for life, for value, and for meaning.

Now this has a lot of implications, especially when we start talking about how our relationship with God became ruptured and our lives filled with everything else except God. If there is going to be any restoration, God will have to initiate the entire process, provide the means, then call me, cleanse me, heal me, and mentor me in His ways. Understanding who we are and who God is and how we fit together is humility.

This also means, of course, that we have to acknowledge how we are involved in the process. That is why we need to confess and repent of our ways. Which does not mean that it is up to us to get our house in order. It means we acknowledge that our way of life apart from God is no life at all, and that we are going to need Him to restore us and to help us reconnect with Him and live for Him.

None of this requires us to beat ourselves up at every turn as a way of keeping our pride in check. Dependency is humility. But self-deprecation is actually a way of denying or refusing God's healing touch and His gift of true righteousness.

According to Paul's writings, God has transformed our very nature and made us into His child, with His image stamped on our heart and His Spirit residing within. We have His very goodness as part of our makeup.

Of course, that is only the beginning of our healing process. We still carry with us much of the damage we have internalized from life in a broken world. Some of the most destructive wounds we carry are those relating to our sense of self: how we matter, whether we will ever be loved or known, or for that matter, whether we are even lovable at all. These wounds strike at the core of our being. They cause untold misery, despair, depression, and loss of hope.

Self-hate is not a Christian virtue. It comes easily enough to everyone, Christian or not. Self-rejection (in its many forms) is a deeply destructive tool of the enemy, used to destroy our soul and ruin our life, and is not at all related to what Jesus called "self-denial." It is imperative that we learn to engage with God to be set free from this evil force in our life.

HEALING SELF-HATE

Who am I, really? This is our central question regarding self-worth. To answer that question we may need to go one step deeper and ask, Who is God, really? In many ways our self-worth depends on our answer to that second question even more than the first. But for the purposes of our discussion here, I am assuming that we have answered that question adequately in Chapter 2. Having settled in our heart who God is, we must then determine how it is that we have any sense of self in His presence.

For most people, the question of who they are brings to mind their total history – all the things they have done, not done, wished they could have done – including all their mistakes, poor choices, sins and regrets, as well as the good they have managed to do along the way. To be complete, they may even include things that have been done *to* them, not just what they themselves have done. Piling up all these elements into one big pot, they see their identity as the sum total of their choices and experiences, both good and bad. We refer to this perception of self as our *Identity of Past Experience*.

In contrast, the Bible speaks about a larger view of who we are. While in no way ignoring our past, God's perspective takes into account His presence in our life and His future for our life. We will call this our *Identity of Promise*.

The Problem with Inflated Self-Esteem

In recent years our culture has become increasingly concerned about the wide-spread problem of self-rejection and low self-worth, especially among school-age children. Unfortunately, the most commonly applied solutions are equally disastrous. To begin with, none of the precipitating causes for self-hate are being addressed. Instead, many efforts to deal with this issue try to confront the symptoms by direct effort.

For example, few things can be more mind-numbing than teaching a child to repeat self-affirmations like some kind of mantra. "I am good person ... Nothing anyone says to me matters ... I am perfect, just the way I am." What is being done here, is to teach children how to repress any negative thoughts about themselves, and to profess things they really do not believe. In terms of our model from Chapter 9, this is akin to changing our behavior (what we say about ourselves) without changing the underlying distorted perceptions (who we believe we are).

Even worse, many children make use of this type of self-affirmation as a tool for deflecting all negative feedback. They learn to tell themselves whatever they want to believe, without any regard to reality or corrective wisdom from those around them. That is how they can audition for a talent show without the least bit of talent whatsoever, and think the judges are idiots for rejecting them.

To be of value, our sense of self has to be rooted in reality. A grandiose or groundless view of self is as distorted and harmful as any self-rejection. Our goal here is to arrive at an understanding of self that takes into account all of the true facts about us, along with a solid and reliable interpretation of that reality; that is to say, how God sees us, in all of our totality.

Our Identity of Past Experience

When we view our value through the lens of past experience, we generally take into account all of our choices, both good and bad, all that we have done and all that has been done to us as well. This includes virtually every experience of our life:

- Bad things I have done, many of which I now regret.
- Things I regret not having done.
- Bad things I actually wanted to do but never did.
- Good things I have done and should have done but did not.
- Things I have said to people, some helpful, some hurtful.
- Things people said to me. Ways they treated me.
- Things people have believed about me, both true and false.
- Love and care I received from others.
- Love I needed but never got.
- What kind of impact I had or did not have on others.

We could probably go on and get more detailed. The point is that we look at this list not just as a litany of our experiences, but as the sum total of who we are. Our successes and failures define us. For people who might see the bad stuff in their life outweighing the good, this can leave them with a very painful image of who they are.

One reason why this kind of self-rejection is too hard to deal with is that the way we are measuring our life feels true. If I look at my life and my relationships and arrive at any of the following evaluations with any sense of self-honesty, I may well believe I am basically worthless.

- I do not matter.
- No one cares whether I am here or not.
- Nothing I do makes any difference.
- I will never get my needs met.

Whether or not these things are *actually* true is not the issue here. What matters is that we *believe* they are true. Because once we are convinced that we have no worth, we will inevitably feel despair or get depressed or find some way to medicate or escape our sense of failure. Self-rejection breeds a kind of hopelessness that is intensely and deeply felt. My life is terrible, and it is the only life I will ever have.

When this happens, we not only have a painful past and a painful sense of who we are, but we also see no future, and our present is only a continuation of the same old lines. Our past continually informs our present reality and tells us what we can never be or do. Again, this all feels true, because it is our own experience. And every new event seems to confirm for us our deficits and worthlessness.

Our Identity of Promise

So how does God see me, and how does that make any difference? If we go back to the last chapter, we see that our own perceptions and interpretations of our life are terribly flawed. For the most part, how we see ourselves is picked up from the feedback we get from others, who are also deeply flawed. How could we truly know who we are and how we matter unless we have that revealed to us by someone who is not filled with their own distortions? It only makes sense that God would be our most reliable source of truth regarding how we should see ourselves and our own life.

Healing Our Identity and Self-Rejection

First and foremost, God sees us *relationally*, not operationally. That is, He sees us primarily as His children (1Jn.3:1), not merely creatures who succeed or fail at what we do. Viewing the Christian life as a great test of obedience completely misses God's heart. The lens through which we look makes all the difference in what we can see. Once we understand that God loves us more than we can possibly know, that He wants our love and wants to help us grow up, then we have a workable foundation for making sense of who we really are.

Second, in order to know *who* we are, we also need to know *whose* we are. That is why the material in Chapter 2 of this book is so important, and why a true understanding of God's character is such a crucial step in developing our relationship with God. He is not an angry judge who demonstrates loves to us because He has to. Rather, He is a loving Father who is capable of anger. That's good news, because I need to know He can get angry enough to rescue His children and to do something about the things that will destroy their lives. Our future hope depends on it. But as a child eager to know Him and be close to Him, the last thing I need to fear is His disappointment or anger toward me.

Taken together, these first two elements tell us that God is a good Father who regards His children with love. That is the basis for God's perspective of who we are. Now let's take a closer look at how He regards the various elements of our life.

My Future Hope

When God looks at our life, He sees all of it: our beginning, our present journey, and our future – our distant eternal future as well as tomorrow morning. From the New Testament we know that His plans for our future are all about continuing our restoration and training, and deepening our relationship with Him. This is a future with hope, filled with the fruit of God's work in our life for our good and for His kingdom.

God desires our whole heart, mind, body, and soul – committed to Him and in relationship with Him. For that to be possible, we all need healing and to grow up in kingdom life. None of that is within our ability. God did not leave us on our own to flesh out the Christian life as best we could. Nor did He merely give us power to carry out His commands. Instead, He has made His home in us, so that His very presence and continuous mentoring would bring about the changes we need as we learn to participate with Him (John 14-17).

That is our future. When God looks at us, He sees all of the ways in which He wants to help us, all the ways He has in mind to draw us into closer relationship with Him, and the means by which He will cleanse us and make us into the people He created us to be. We are not merely the sum total of our history. *We are a work in progress* with a future that has depth and hope and meaning beyond our wildest imagination.

My Past

All that sounds so wonderful, but what about my past? What about all the stuff that is dishonoring to myself and God? The omissions and the transgressions alike?

Here again, our lens makes all the difference. We often have a way of viewing the past like a collection of events that are set in stone. But with God, our understanding of our own history is open to major revision, because He tells our story very differently than we would be able to tell it.

First, there are bad things that happened to us, leaving wounds and scars that fester from time to time and may still be painful to the touch. They might have come from an abusive parent or a cruel classmate. There may have been betrayal, acts of violence, or a long-standing pattern of character assassination. In addition to enduring specific acts of evil, we may have lived in a climate of continuous distress that scored and corroded our very soul.

From our perspective as a survivor, these are all violations, scars, or open sores left by those who overran our defenses and tore into our soul. These wounds stare back at us like derailments on our journey. But God does not stop there. To Him, these are all places where He can express His love through healing and restoring. Nothing is too big for Him to heal; nothing is too small for Him to pay attention to. All that has hurt us can be healed and resolved. When God looks at the bad things that have happened to us, His heart is stirred as a Father for His child who has been hurt by the world and needs His tender touch.

There were also those good things we needed that were not given to us when we needed them. Our mother may have been too wounded herself to

Healing Our Identity and Self-Rejection

offer much love; our father too preoccupied and distant or too violent. We may have felt alone or abandoned when we needed someone to be near. Our heart may still ache because of the emptiness we feel inside.

Again, God is on our side. He is the One who can fill our empty soul, and fill us with His love until we have enough to give away. His very presence and words to us will feed us until we are satisfied. When God looks at the holes in our life that need filling, He sees places where He can pour in His love and bring to us the resources we need.

Of course, there are those bad things we ourselves have thought or said or done that look like black marks on our record. Some we deeply regret. Some we felt compelled to do and could not have done otherwise at the time. A few we even did out of spite, for revenge. Some were plain stupid. We see all the mistakes we made, and they tell us we are unworthy of consideration, let alone of real love. If you knew us as well as we do, you would not like us.

But God was never hindered by our failures. He wanted us, period. "God demonstrates His own love toward us, in that while we were yet sinners, Christ died for us" (Rom.5:8 NASB). Even though we ruptured our relationship with God, our sin did not have the final say. When God looks at us, He sees a small creature in need of rescue. Our failures do not get to define us or stain us for the rest of our life. God in His grace not only forgives us, He cleanses us and gives us His righteousness. As we learn to work with Him to renew our mind, He even removes in us the causes for sin, so that we can become more whole. According to Paul, we died to sin, so that it could no longer have dominion over us or define us. We are by nature children of God, learning how to live in His kingdom. Because of that, our failures are no longer able to tell us who we are.

At this very moment, all that remains of our old identity are the ways in which we have been malformed by life without God – the distortions of life we have internalized that now impact our life in the form of destructive feelings and behaviors. That is why God has made transformation such a high priority under the New Covenant. Not only are we able to find healing for our past, God wants to change our heart so we can be sure of the future He envisions for us! Although we have a long way to go, we are not defined by the distance, but by our hope (1Jn.3:3) that God will complete the work He has begun (Phil.1:6).

Only God can tell us who we are; only the way He view us or tells our story has any credibility. So how does God view our past? He sees...

- Things done to me that He wants to heal.
- Things I have done that He has forgiven.
- A marred soul that He has cleansed and continues to cleanse.
- Ways I have been malformed that He will transform.

Our past is not a statement about who we are; it is a declaration of how much we need God and how great a work He wants to do in us!

My Present True Self

We are now prepared to understand how God can view us differently in the present. Instead of just being a person shot through with flaws, *we are a work in progress*! My true identity is the person God created me to be, a new creation, created to do good (Eph.2:10). We may need more healing and renewing and training in order to do those things well from a restored heart, but we are already His new creation. The greatest evidence we have that this is true, is our deep desire to be made clean and whole (Rom.8:23). God says I am:

- A new creation (2Cor.5:17).
- His child (Jn.1:12) (1Jn.3:1).
- A member of Christ's body (1Cor.12:27).
- Complete in Christ (Col.2:9-10).
- God's Temple (1Cor.3:16).
- A minister of reconciliation (2Cor.5:17-21).
- God's workmanship (Eph.2:10).
- A light in the world (Mt.5:14).
- A holy and royal priest (1Pet.2:5,9).

God is the only one who is qualified to tell me who I am. He has declared that I am His child by His choosing. And He has set me free so that I can pursue the renovation of my heart that He has in store for me.

Yes, I still have bad habits, negative attitudes, and do the wrong thing quite often. I even miss doing a lot of good things I really want to be able to do. But those issues are no longer representative of my basic nature. They are

Healing Our Identity and Self-Rejection

simply parts of me that have not yet been brought into alignment with my true self. They are malfunctions of who I am, not the essence of my identity.

When God looks at me, He sees my past experiences that He intends to heal and restore, He sees my future in terms of who He has called me to become, and He sees me in the present as a work in progress, on the way to the future He designed me for.

Anything that tells me I am irredeemable, unlovable, or unwanted; any message about not mattering to God or not having any purpose; any thought that I have no value – these are all lies! For the Christian, self-hate and self-rejection are always distortions of who we really are. Because whatever we have in us that is still bad, is simply reason to move toward God and to work with Him more closely for our renewal. We are not defined by our failures, but by our relationship with God.

Honest Self-Examination Without Self-Hate

Nothing said here negates our need for renewal, nor does it suggest that we should never feel regret or remorse for things we have thought, said, or done. In fact, as a child of God it only makes sense for us to be more concerned than ever about how we malfunction. We have been rescued from the kingdom of darkness and made into children of Light! Our lives have been spared by the grace of God. Those parts of our soul that have yet to be renewed are areas of legitimate concern.

If the revelation of our new identity in any way leads to a lack of concern over our sin or a tendency to ignore our flaws, then we have not really grasped the meaning of being a new creature. John's first epistle makes this abundantly clear. The more we truly comprehend who we are in Christ, the more we will want to be like Him (1Jn.3). So we will do whatever we are able to do in order to engage with the Spirit of God for transformation.

This, of course, requires us to take stock of where we are on our journey from time to time and make an honest evaluation of what needs to be addressed. But looking at where we fall short has its dangers, not the least of which is to beat ourselves up for all that we see wrong. In order to keep the necessary balance, we have to learn how to bring our stuff to God with all the seriousness of what we are dealing with, and at the same time hold tightly onto who we are in God's eyes.

Remember we are very small creatures who are loved by a very big God. We do not have to be finished, yet, because that is just not possible. And we do not have to do the heavy work of making ourselves clean. That is up to God. Our main job as His child is to stay connected with Him and invite Him to do His work in us.

God's Intentions Toward Us

Some of you may be thinking this is too good to be true or that this cannot possibly be my true identity. So let us approach this from another angle, through a better understanding of God's true intentions toward us.

As covered in Chapter 2, far too many of us believe that God's primary intention is to grade us on our performance and pay us our due. This view of God being so non-relational makes it almost impossible to recover from self-hate, because we can never measure up in the eyes of a Holy God.

That is why we need to have a clear vision of God's intention toward us as a loving Father who wants to be involved in His children's lives for their good. Fortunately, God did not leave us in the dark about this. The Bible is full of declarations regarding how much He loves us and how much He wants for us. Here are just a few of the references to God's intentions we can draw from Scripture:

- He does not condemn me (Rom.8:1).
- He planned to rescue me long ago (Eph.1:3-5).
- He lavishes His grace on me (Eph.1:7-8).
- He loves me even when I sin (Rom.5:8).
- He wants to live with me and in me (Jn.14:16-23).

These are not empty promises, nor do they only apply to super Christians. These are God's intentions toward each and every one of us who desire to be with Him.

Knowing God's true heart for us makes all the difference in the world. We are not loved by being good enough. Our worth does not depend on how well we measure up against the Apostle Paul as a standard of behavior. We are loved just because God loves. He loves to love – that is His character. He is good, and we can trust His heart for us.

Blessed are the Spiritually Impoverished

But again, "What about the stuff? Doesn't my sin turn His stomach? Isn't He disgusted with what I've done or not done, or with who I am in general?"

Perhaps one of the most illuminating passages in all of Scripture is that of the first Beatitude. In most versions of the Bible it reads something like this:

> Blessed are the poor in spirit, for theirs is the kingdom of heaven (Mt.5:6).

Now unfortunately, there is a strong tendency to turn this into a *how-to* verse. "If you realize you are poor in spiritual terms, then you will be able to get saved." But I think Dallas Willard has it right when he says that this verse is simply an announcement of the Good News. "The kingdom of God is now available to everyone, not just the super-spiritual!" Perhaps the following paraphrase captures the spirit of this statement better.

> Blessed are those who are spiritually impoverished, because they are exactly the ones the kingdom is for!

That is Good News. But for many of us, this sounds too easy. Something about the whole idea of spiritually impoverished people populating the kingdom of God does not seem right. Now God's kingdom is not a physical place as much as it is the realm of where His will is being carried out. It is where good overcomes evil, and truth and righteousness reign. Most of us would probably say that spiritually impoverished people are manifestly **not** in God's will, by definition. So how can they be in the kingdom?

Consider for a moment what it might be like to observe broken people entering the kingdom and moving about. They most likely would be very glad to be there, and would begin to get cleaned up and get some inner healing and start to grow, as would any child of the kingdom.

That is God's will! His will is restoration! That is how spiritually impoverished people can be in His will.

God invites all of us into the kingdom so He can heal and restore us and mentor us in His ways. As long as we are seeking to be with Him and seeking to be changed by Him, we are perfectly in God's will, *even if our life is still a complete mess*!

In light of this truth, it makes perfect sense that the psalmist can stand in the spotlight of God's all pervasive view and say, "Search me, O God, and know my heart" (Ps.139), because He knows God is good for it. He knows that being totally loved and known by God is completely safe, because that is what makes life in the kingdom possible.

We do not have to hide in shame because of something we have done that seems unforgivable to us. We do not have to beat ourselves up over our past or present behavior, or because we cannot seem to get past some sin. Our value does not depend on our performance. It depends on God's character and His love for us!

God Loves His Children

"See how great a love the Father has for us, that we should become His children! And someday we will be just like Him. And everyone who has this hope is already in the process of becoming more like Him" (1Jn.3:1 paraphrase). Recall for a minute the last time you looked at a little child who was all bright and cheerful, full of smiles and light. Think of how pure and innocent they can be in those moments, and how open they are to goodness and life and love. Oh, how much we want the best for them! We want to protect them and keep them safe! How much we want to keep them from any injury or sickness, or any mistake that would cause them to get hurt.

In a similar fashion, God has a tender heart toward any child of His that longs to be like Him. He desires the best for them and dearly wants to cleanse them of anything that would damage their soul. That is the kind of God we have, and that is why we can be sure He loves us even when we make mistakes.

Seeing Ourselves Through the Eyes of Heaven

Only God knows who we are, which means we can only know who we are when we see ourselves as God sees us. And that is only possible when we engage with Him in relationship. Nothing else will do. Any way that we view ourselves apart from how God sees us will distort our sense of who we are and move us away from our Identity of Promise. Any other means of evaluating our worth is like trying to use a ruler to determine the temperature of the air. It is the wrong tool, and it will only lead to a misunderstanding of who we are.

Healing Our Identity and Self-Rejection

It does not matter how bad we think we are. It does not matter how bad we have been. Any way in which we are not seen through the eyes of heaven will distort our identity.

The Importance of Grace

All of this takes us back to our understanding of grace described in Chapter 5. Because of God's grace, we get to have the relationship first. We get to be in relationship with God *before* we have any of our stuff cleaned up. It is not up to us to "get right with God" in order to be in relationship with Him. Our greatest hurdle is to believe how much He wants to be with us! How much He loves us! He wants to be with us now, before we have any chance to clean up, because He knows we need Him in order to cleanse anything at all. Whatever ugliness we have has no bearing on whether He will love us or not, or whether He will be with us or not. Grace means the relationship is cemented in who God is, not in what we do or don't do.

Furthermore, the whole process of changing me into the person God created me to be is a matter of *God's work* in me, not my effort to be good enough. Grace means it is alright to be small and unfinished (2Cor.4:7). Trying to earn God's approval is a faulty view of God, a faulty view of who we are and what we are capable of, and a faulty understanding of how God wants to be involved in our life. God wants to be with me in all my mess so He can do the work in me that I cannot do. Other than refusing to have anything to do with God (and even then He is very patient), nothing I can do will keep Him from wanting to be with me.

The more we see the beauty and wonder of God's grace, the clearer it will become that the bad stuff in my life has no right to tell me who I am. I am a child of God – wanted by Him, loved by Him, and in the process of being restored by Him. That is who I am.

Key Truth

Your true identity is the person God created you to be (Col.3:3). That means, self-hate is *always* rooted in a distorted perception of who you are.

Self-hate is always a lie. It is, in fact, a diabolical plan to get you to be your own worst enemy, fighting against God's intentions for you to grow up into an adult child of His love. Once Satan convinces you to hate your own self, then he can walk away and you will self-destruct. He does not have to bug you or harass you or tempt you with evil. You will be quite capable of doing all the necessary damage yourself.

The world usually tries to deal with self-hate through some form of self affirmation, which is basically an attempt to talk yourself out of what you really believe about yourself. Unless your denial system is really good, it will not take you long to see this does not work. The world's shallow effort at self-acceptance will fail.

As always, God takes a completely different approach. His perspective is more like, "*Of course you are small and flawed, but so what?* I love you and I want to walk this journey with you; the rest are just details we can resolve on the way as I bring healing into your life. And I really love doing that, *for* you and *with* you!" The truth is, self-hate is a house of cards, without substance. Once we see who we are in God's eyes, the whole edifice of lies comes crashing down around us. It has no foundation; there is nothing true about it. Self-hate is all smoke and mirrors, designed to keep you from seeing who you really are in Christ.

Toward Healing

In order to move toward healing we need only a few basic steps. First, we need to believe that what has been said here about self-hate is true; that it is indeed a pack of lies about who we are. Even if we still believe the lies, even if they feel true, we can – for the sake of argument, if nothing else – believe there has to be a way to see this all differently.

Self-hate can be a very stubborn thing. Everything said so far might make perfect sense, and yet our self-hate can rear its ugly head at any time. Seeing the truth on paper or hearing that self-hate is all lies may feel helpful and at the same time do very little to dislodge the feelings of self-rejection. But it helps to know that even if it does not yet feel true, there really is a way to resolve these feelings of hate and self-disgust that will free us up forever to live more like beloved children of God.

That brings us to the second part, which is to begin engaging with God for the truth we need to internalize experientially. In the last chapter, we presented a model of how we can engage with God to renew our mind and purge out the lies that drive us into darkness. What we have here in self-hate and self-rejection are a collection of lies that need to be removed and renewed by God. When He speaks into these areas of our life, He tailors His revelations so they will make it all the way into our heart and bear fruit (Isa.55:10-11).

But bear in mind that self-hate is generally not just one lie. When we develop self-hate early and carry it into adulthood, by then it becomes an entangled web of deeply held beliefs that reaches into almost every facet of our life. While tremendous relief is possible in a relatively short period of time, most people end up dealing with multiple areas of their life that have been impacted by self-hate. So do not despair or give up. Be persistent and ask God to draw you into this process. Among the separate areas that may need His words of truth are:

- Belief that I am terminally defective in ways that cannot be fixed.
- Belief that something I have done is unforgivable.
- Any driving need for perfectionism.
- Any driving need for approval from others.
- Any desire for a terminal disease or self-destruction (a way out).
- Any sense of feeling cheated by events or circumstances.
- Feelings of inferiority.
- Unresolved regrets.

As you can see, the list can become rather long. Our intention here is not to overwhelm you with what might be needed, but to help make sense of why self-hate is so stubborn, and to encourage you to not give up on this process of restoration.

Again, we have to return to our theme, that God is already in love with us as we are, and we have much to gain and nothing to fear in regard to going forward into our recovery. What we have said here is Good News! God is in the process of redeeming us in every way possible. He will leave no stone unturned, if we will take the time to talk with Him and let Him shine His light on our soul.

Bear in mind as well that we do not have to make this journey alone. We can ask God to bring others into our life to encourage us and walk alongside us as we wrestle with our self-hate and rediscover who we are in Christ. As we experience "God with skin on" from grace-filled men and women, we will begin to believe that God sees us through the eyes of grace as well.

Self-hate is not a life sentence. We do not have to carry it around with us until we die. God is more than able to free us from those lies, and He is eager to do His work in us to bring about our freedom. May we all trust Him enough to put our entire sense of who we are into His hands, and receive from Him a vision of our true self.

RESOURCES FOR FURTHER STUDY

David Benner, *The Gift of Being Yourself* (Downers Grove: IVP Books) 2004

Theodore Rubin, *Compassion and Self Hate: An Alternative to Despair* (Touchstone) 1998

Chapter 11

Disarming Our Fear and Anxiety

Casting all your anxiety on Him, because He cares for you. (1Pet.5:7)

God gave us the gift of fear to help keep us safe. One of the strongest motivators we have, fear moves us to protect ourselves from excessive harm and unnecessary risks. In the face of extreme danger, fear can fire up our adrenaline and help us react even before our conscious mind has had time to think about what is happening. In this sense, fear is a gift.

However, we often feel fear when we would rather be at peace. We can acquire fears from life experiences that persist long after the dangers no longer exist. We even project perceptions of danger into completely safe places, such as when one person's betrayal makes it hard to trust others who are actually trustworthy. And we develop still more fears from our general lack of trust in God's care for us. Collectively, we could refer to these as illegitimate fears or toxic fears because we are unnecessarily alarmed, overestimating the dangers or underestimating God's provisions.

Conquering illegitimate fear is an important part of our spiritual development, because fear interferes with our ability to hear God, as well as our ability to think clearly and discern well. This chapter will address the nature of toxic fears and provide some life-giving perspectives along with a few resources for disarming them.

Fear Has Many Faces

A fairly large vocabulary surrounds the issue of fear, allowing for the many ways that it presents itself. Each term has its own nuances. For example, *phobias* exist below the conscious level, can be entirely irrational, and generally cannot be calmed by logical arguments. *Foreboding* is fear of what might happen soon. *Suspicion* is the fear that something may not be what it seems to be. Some words such as *terror* refer to the intensity of our fear, while others like *distrust* describe fear within certain relationships.

A Sampling of Words We Use For Fear

- Phobia
- Distrust
- Apprehension
- Intimidation
- Threatened
- Scared

- Foreboding
- Trepidation
- Dread
- Misgiving
- Suspicion
- Stress

- Terror
- Panic
- Fright
- Unease
- Anxiety
- Worry

We Fear a Great Many Things

Even more surprising than the number of words we use for fear are the sheer number of things we are afraid of. Most people fear personal exposure of anything that could cause them shame. Consequently, they also fear any kind of visible failure that would expose their weaknesses or lack of ability. One very interesting fear is the fear of success. You would think that success would be what everyone wants. But a lot of people perceive some real down sides to success. For one thing, failure after having been successful can be even more painful than failing to succeed in the first place. It is one thing to not have your dream realized, and quite another to watch it fall apart. There are higher expectations that come with success, the possibility that you will be more visible, and so on.

Even before worrying about success, many people fear testing their dreams at all. While a dream that is never realized can cause some emotional pain, testing whether the dream will ever materialize can be far more scary. The fear of what might happen can be so great that no attempt is ever made.

A lot of fears revolve around relationships. Because of the fact that *belonging and being accepted* are so important to us, we fear rejection and anything that might make others pull away from us. After being rejected by a love interest, people often become afraid of intimacy, because the pain is so great that it seems better to be alone than to risk being cast aside by someone we care about.

Many of us fear negative emotions. Shame, hopelessness, and sadness are painful feelings we would rather not have. Attempts to avoid those feelings often take the form of denial, and when that is not possible, we may try "stuffing" our emotions, steeling our mind against any thoughts that might unleash this pain.

Anger, too, can create fear regardless of whether it is our anger or another person's. I may be afraid to get angry or afraid of how out of control I feel when I am angry. And when someone else is angry with me I may feel anything from mild nervousness to full-blown terror.

Things We Fear

- Exposure
- Public Shame
- Failure
- Success
- God

- Intimacy
- Rejection
- Needs Not Met
- Other People
- Testing a Dream

- Loss of Control
- Physical Pain
- Negative Emotions
- Change
- Legitimate Suffering

Some people even live in a state of perpetual fear. If they are at the office, they are afraid of what might happen because they are not home. At home they are afraid of what might happen at the office. No matter what they are doing, there is something else they are not attending to or something that is not under their control. When making a decision, they may find themselves paralyzed by fear because every option open to them is seen as a potential misstep, or at least a loss of other options. Such a pervasive sense of dread is not only a painful way to live, it can wear out a person's biological systems that were designed to manage fear.

Fear of Legitimate Suffering

The fear of legitimate suffering[61] is a very common form of toxic, self-defeating fear. Legitimate suffering comes about when there is some level of discomfort necessary in order to gain something worthwhile. The classic example is surgery. If we allow our fear of surgery to keep us from going to the hospital, we can end up far worse off. Rather, we need to accept the surgery as an experience of legitimate suffering, and be willing to endure

---

[61] This term and concept is taken from Scott Peck, *The Road Less Traveled*

significant physical pain and recovery time so that in a few months we will be far more healthy than we were before the surgery.

There are an endless number of ways in which this principle plays out in our life. Moms endure tremendous pain in order to give birth. Years later those same moms may experience emotional pain in letting their kids grow up and leave home. Repairing ruptures in our relationships is quite often a painful experience. It can be very uncomfortable to confront a friend and work through a problem, but winning back the trust and closeness of the friendship is worth the discomfort of addressing the issue. Going against peer pressure can be very hard, but again may be the best choice. Any time we make changes, risk asking for what we want or need, or try new things, we may need to face anxieties, or agonize over the best way to do something.

These are all forms of legitimate suffering, which if endured can bring about much good, and if avoided may cause much greater pain in the long run. Giving the fear of pain too much power in our life can be disastrous.

Discerning Our Fears

Legitimate suffering is only one example of the principle that *fear does not automatically mean we need protection*. There are many times when we need to feel the fear and do something anyway, because it is the best thing to do. In fact, there a number of things that can generate fear in us which, if allowed to control our choices will not help us at all, but instead create bondage and interfere with our spiritual development.

Remember that God gave us the ability to feel fear to help keep us from harm. Some fear is even wired in, such as the fear of falling. So fear is not a bad thing in and of itself. But many of our fears are learned from experience, some of which are helpful and some not. If we have bad experiences with those who are closest to us, we may learn to fear intimacy. If we experience a lot of pain from trying new things, we may avoid change or personal risk. If we have learned that our opinion is rarely welcome, we may be afraid to speak up even when it seems important to do so.

In other words, fear is not necessarily self-justifying, no matter how valid it may seem to us. This means we need to develop some tools for discerning our fears and disarming those that are not legitimate or helpful.

Fear Can Be a Signal

Rather than allowing all fear to motivate us toward self-protection, <u>being afraid may mean we need to grow or seek healing</u>. In that sense, our fear may actually be a signal that something is not working properly inside our soul. I once knew a man who was terrified of talking to strangers on the phone. He had no explanation for this irrational fear, and clearly, he was not in any real danger. Yet he would start to panic just thinking about making such a call. His fear was not about real danger, but a signal that something inside him was malfunctioning and needed help.

This principle actually applies to all of us in one way or another. If I am afraid of what God thinks of me, the answer is not to figure out how to protect myself from God. My fear is a signal telling me I am harboring some distorted view of who God is or how He sees me. I need to seek out God's help in uncovering my distorted perceptions, and allow Him to replace my broken view with a better perspective. The fear will then disappear.

If I am afraid that if you knew me better you would not like me, or that if I make a mistake you will think I am a fraud, the solution is not to keep you at a distance or take some other self-protective steps. The real answer lies in digging out the source of my distorted sense of who I am and what gives me value. I need God's healing of my identity, and then my fear about how you see me will diminish. My fear is really a signal of something malfunctioning inside me, not a message of real danger.

If I find myself avoiding certain kinds of tasks, it may be a signal that my capacity is too limited or that I need some help with my maturity.[62] Similarly, many anxieties about finances and relationships and other life issues are really places that need healing, or possibly evidence of holes in our development that need assistance. Giving in to these fears will stunt our growth and keep us in bondage to our distorted perceptions.

Many people find it very hard to repair ruptures with friends. They dread having the necessary "talk" in order to resolve the problem that exists between them. On the plus side, this fear may be a reflection of how much that relationship means to them. If anything went wrong and the rupture became worse, the grief might be more than they want to risk. But on the other side of the question, there may be fears about any shame they might

---

[62] The issue of human maturity will be addressed in Chapter 12

feel for their part in the problem, or fear of what the other person might say that they do not want to hear, or even fear of how angry the other person might be. These fears might be signaling their internal weaknesses, a need for healing in regard to shame, or any number of other issues.

In Chapter 9 we discussed how internalized beliefs drive many of our emotional responses. That being the case, fear can arise out of our internal map of what might cause us pain or discomfort, as well as from our thoughts about what resources we have for dealing with a problem after things go wrong. That means the fear we feel may be rooted in distorted beliefs about who we are or how life works, and have relatively little to do with the external reality we are facing.

Feeling fear then, does not necessarily signal a need for self-protection. We may instead need to stop and ask God if there is something inside us that is in need of help.

Fear Bonds vs. Love Bonds[63]

Where toxic fear has its most damaging effects is when it keeps us from forming close bonds with other people. God designed us with the need and desire to attach and bond to others. Bonding is so critical that infants can literally die from lack of love and attention. As children get older they develop survival strategies to deal with minimal nurture, but even then bonding is so important that any insecure attachment can severely distort their sense of reality. What we need to know about bonding though, is that we not only have the ability to bond through love but also the ability to create bonds that are rooted in fear.

Love Bonds

Love Bonds are created with others who are glad to be with us and regard us well in their heart. This is a primary source of joy, which is the single most important emotion for building emotional strength. When I have a love bond with someone, I am motivated to be close, to receive and give life, and to intensify our joy through shared experiences. When we are together, I feel known and loved. When we are apart, I remember your goodness and long for our reunion.

---

[63] Friesen, et. al., *The Life Model*

Fear Bonds

Fear bonds are created with people who are important to us, but at the same time are a major source of distress. For example, a child will bond with their parents regardless of what kind of people their parents are. If an adult is dangerous to the child or emotionally abusive, that bond will be rooted in fear instead of love.

When I am fear bonded to someone, my main reason for getting close to them is not for joy, but in order to better manage their feelings. Yet I have to keep some emotional distance in order to manage my own feelings. Much of the time I will have the sensation of "walking on eggshells" and living with pervasive anxiety. The relationship as a whole revolves around painful interactions and pain avoidance behaviors.

Fear bonds are common in parent/child relationships where the parent is unpredictable, abusive, or a practicing addict. But fear bonds can also develop within the context of a marriage or any other close relationship.

While difficult, it is possible to change a fear bond into a love bond.[64] However, this generally requires intentional commitment by both people involved, and usually means seeking outside help in the form of good counsel and support. But even prior to getting such resolution, a person can benefit greatly from the other approaches to disarming fear discussed here.

Fear Bonds With God

Our main reason for raising the issue of fear bonds here is because fear bonding with God is an extremely common problem. Although rarely talked about, the truth is that a great many Christians have more of a fear bond with God than a love bond. This can present itself in many ways, including:

- Afraid of getting too close to God – He may overwhelm me.
- Afraid of getting too far away from God – I will not be able to find Him when I need Him.
- Afraid of God taking over my life in ways I am not prepared for.
- Afraid of what God thinks of me.
- Afraid of what God might do to me or expect from me.
- Afraid of not knowing God's will for my life – that I will be judged.
- Afraid of finding out God's will for me – that it will be too hard.

---

[64] See Friesen, et.al., *The Life Model* for more on changing fear bonds.

Such fears can create a tremendous barrier in our relationship with God, because they tend to crush our trust level with Him. If we do not trust God, then we will put barriers and boundaries in between Him and us to keep God at a certain emotional distance. It is as if we are afraid to get too close to Him or for Him to indwell us too much.

While working through a course[65] based on Dallas Willard's book *The Renovation of the Heart*, there was an exercise in which I was supposed to lay down in a comfortable place, and beginning with my feet and working up towards my head, dedicate every part of my body to God. About the time I got to my knees, I started feeling an anxiety rising inside me. As I talked with God about my fear, it dawned on me that I was afraid of giving up my whole being to His ownership. I was alright with Him "renting" space in me, occupying a few rooms in my heart. But I was not really ready for Him to take ownership. It was a truly frightening perspective. So I stopped the exercise and began working through my fear with God, asking Him for help in uncovering the deeper reasons why I was afraid of Him taking ownership of my life. As He healed those places in my heart where I was afraid of losing myself, I actually began to experience great joy in knowing that He owned my life and my body, and that I belonged to Him.

As discussed in Chapter 2, if we have any hope of developing a relationship with God that is vibrant enough to change us from the inside out, we have to come to a place of complete and utter trust in His goodness and His intentions toward us. Working through our fears about how He wants to be involved in our life is crucial to this process.

For many people, understanding *where their fear of God began* can be very helpful to the process of resolving their anxieties. For the most part, causes for an unhealthy fear of God tend to fall into one of three main categories.

Life Trauma: Whenever we experience traumatic events, there is always the possibility we will end up blaming God for what happened to us. "Why God?" is a cry we have probably all uttered at one time or another. Wondering why God did not prevent some tragedy can generate all sorts of emotional reactions, not the least of which is fear of what He might do or not do in the future. Such fear can leave us feeling very insecure about how God works in our life.

---

[65] Gary Moon, *Renovation of the Heart* (GA: LifeSprings Resources) 2003

Some of these traumas are experienced as children, when we are most vulnerable to forming distorted ideas about how power gets used. Given that adults are very nearly omnipotent in the eyes of young children, any harmful behaviors by their parents can be totally devastating to their worldview. From that point on they may see any power greater than themselves as inherently dangerous. Starting from that perspective, it would only make sense to be afraid of a God who can do anything.

Of course, trauma is not restricted to youth. As adults we may experience rejection, life-threatening illness, serious accidents, the loss of loved ones, or any number of painful events that can lead us to question the goodness of God or His willingness to protect us. These issues can then quite easily lead to a fear-laden relationship with God.[66]

Spiritual Abuse: Another form of life trauma that is particularly devastating can occur when an abuser directly links some distortion of God's character to the abuse itself. For example, continuously threatening a small child that "God can see you and He will get you if you do something wrong" can lead a child to develop a fear of God's presence and intentions. Any unwarranted use of the Bible to create self-condemnation in Christians or to shame them for not being able to live up to God's standards is also spiritual abuse. Such wounds can inject fear deep into a person's soul and leave them with a fear bond with God that dominates their spiritual life.[67]

Poor Theology: Since the days of Paul the church has had to deal with distorted views of how God is involved in the lives of Christians. As covered in Chapter 2, one of the most prominent ways we see this today is in portraying God primarily as a judgmental deity who is always looking for ways to punish people for their evil ways. It would be very hard not to be afraid of such a God.

We see a closely related problem arise when people try so hard to "take sin seriously" they actually obscure the grace of God and turn the Christian

---

[66] It would be impossible to address this complex set of questions in depth without opening up the whole issue of why there is suffering in the world, which is a topic beyond the scope of this present work. Our focus here will remain on how we can disarm our fears.

[67] See Dave Johnson and Jeff VanVonderan, *The Subtle Power of Spiritual Abuse* for more on this issue.

life into an anxiety-ridden venture in which God acts more like a divine correctional officer than a mentor or ally. Among other things, they fail to realize that fostering toxic fear of God is as much a sin as anything, and carrying a toxic fear of God is falling short of God's best, as much as any sin of omission or commission we might be guilty of.

Perfect love casts out toxic fear. And God's love is perfect. Whatever else one may want to teach about sin in the life of a believer, it must take into account God's mission to destroy the power of sin itself, so as to keep us from sin in the first place. He is not just waiting to judge sin after it happens. Joining with God to defeat the power of sin in our life is one of the great privileges of being His children and a reason for great joy. Viewing sin as a barrier to a Christian's relationship with God distorts the nature of sin, disregards God's desire to work with us, and denies our primary means of restoration, which is actually our relationship with God.

Toxic fear of God is one of the single most damaging forces we will ever deal with. Since the Garden of Eden it has motivated us to run from God, to hide our sin, and to depend on our own strength and resolve to live well. That is why we need to know how to disable this kind of fear.

Disarming Our Fears

Thankfully, there are a number of strategies available to us for dealing with fear. Internalizing and practicing these approaches will open the door to healing, more freedom, less anxiety, and better discernment.

Redefining Safety

When dealing with matters of actual danger, fear drives us to seek safety, which is a good thing. Fear motivates us to get away, to make something stop, or to oppose with force whatever threatens us. These are all ways of ending the danger and feeling safe again.

Unfortunately, our built-in responses to fear do not always distinguish well between real danger and perceived danger. Furthermore, as we grow up we tend to develop limited patterns for dealing with fear that keep us from seeking alternative ways of addressing issues that cause us so much anxiety.

Disarming Our Fear and Anxiety

For one thing, the word *safe* is itself a tricky word. We tend to think of safety as the absence of danger or an absence of anything that would disrupt our peaceful existence. But that view of safety promotes strategies for managing fear that can take us down a very disappointing path. Unless we broaden our understanding of what it means to be safe, we will be hard pressed to find long-term answers to our fears.

Efforts to Control

No one really likes to get hurt or disappointed. So we generally think about being safe in terms of preventing things from going wrong. When something happens beyond our control, our first response is usually to try to make it stop so we can regain our control. Sometimes people can become very controlling in their attempts to maintain peace and safety in their life.

In its extreme form, this attempt to control the world around us can lead to a preoccupation with pain avoidance. Perhaps you have heard the term "Control Freak" to describe people who try too hard to keep everything just right. But this is almost self-defeating in itself. A person can become permanently stressed out in their attempt to prevent any distress!

The truth is we really have relatively little control over the things that can go wrong. People get sick or die, often from things that no amount of effort can stop or avoid. Things go wrong. Mistakes happen. Oversights abound. Realistically, we probably have control over no more than a small percent of what happens in our life. So any hope to stay "safe" by preventing problems from happening is a toxic hope destined for disappointment.

There are two other kinds of safe that are far more realistic and far more helpful in our unpredictable and broken world.

Restorative Safety

Whatever goes wrong, God is able to restore us to a place of peace. God is the God of restoration. His entire venture in the world today is a mission to overturn evil and all of its impact.

He is the God of resurrection. He was able to bring us to life when we were dead. How much more will He be able to give life to us now that we are alive! (Rom.5:10). If He can resurrect us after we have died, surely He is able to restore our heart and mind when we suffer in this life.

This is the kind of safety that made creation possible. God could have created a world in which nothing ever went wrong, where everything was controlled and limited by God so that no sin and no pain would ever occur. But God knows of a stronger kind of safety, where no matter what goes wrong, redemption is possible. That is why He could create human beings who were capable of poor choices, and still call His creation good.

As we experience God's healing hand in our heart and mind and discover how much He wants to restore us, we begin to see how nothing is beyond His reach. Our hope is not to live in some sort of spiritual bubble wrap where nothing can harm us or touch us. Rather our hope is in a God who can bring good things out of ruins and life out of death (Rom.8:28).

We live in a broken world and things will go wrong, of that we can be sure. Knowing that nothing can destroy us beyond restoration is far more reassuring than any short-term peace or calm we might achieve through our limited efforts to control.

Relational Safety

Not only can we count on God to restore our heart no matter what goes wrong in life, we can also count on His actual presence with us as we go through difficult times.

Imagine a small child who lives in a house with an old dark basement. On their own, the child may be very afraid to see what is down there. Whatever unknown things might be in the dark are too scary to risk. But if Daddy holds their hand, they can feel safe enough to venture down the stairs with him. So it is when we have God with us. Life on our own is justifiably scary. Anyone who is not afraid of life on their own is either not paying attention, has been lulled to sleep by our affluent society, or has already become cynical and given up any hope of goodness in this life. But as we learn to live in the presence of God, we find hope and peace in all circumstances simply because He is with us.

This was the secret Paul knew, leading him to declare that he could be content whether he had an abundance or lived with scarcity (Phil.4:12). His security and his peace did not depend on the events of his day, but on the person of Jesus. *God with him* was enough, even in death. That is also why the Psalmist could declare, "Even though I walk through the darkest valley, I

Disarming Our Fear and Anxiety

fear no evil; for you are with me" (Ps.23:4). God was with him, and that is what mattered most.

Basically then, fear is an issue of trust, because fear is the opposite of trusting. Perfect love engenders our trust, and that is why perfect love will disarm our fear.[68] So the more time we spend with God and the more we let His love into our soul, the more we will trust Him and the less fear we will experience. Or to put it another way, whenever I am afraid, some of the questions I want to ask myself are, "Who do I want to be with right now?" and "Where are you God?"

We really are small creatures, far too small to manage the complexities of life by ourselves. But we have a God who knows what to do in every situation, what matters, what our heart needs to know, how to speak, how to respond, and so on. He is our reason to feel secure, no matter what. Security is not the absence of fear; security is being with someone who is good enough and strong enough to handle any situation, who will hold us as we go through hard times, and who can restore us when we need to be restored.

Redefining Our Goals

Understanding restorative and relational safety leads us to redefine what we do with fear. While there is nothing wrong with preventing unnecessary suffering, we need better strategies for dealing with fear than simply rearranging our circumstances. Besides the myriad of things we cannot control, there is the issue of anxiety itself and its negative impact on our life. In the big picture, the main question is not how to minimize our pain, but:

- Who do I want to be with when I am afraid? (Relational safety)
- Is my fear a signal that I need healing? (Restorative safety)

Again, we need to check in with God to see if this fear is rooted in our own distorted perceptions of life. Many of our fears and much of the intensity of our fears are due to our inability to interpret life correctly, not due to the actual nature of some danger. Our energy might be better spent seeking out the cause of our fear and building our trust, rather than trying to avoid the

---

[68] "There is no fear in love, but perfect love casts out fear … whoever fears has not reached maturity in love (1Jn.4:18)

pain or control our circumstances. Having conversations with God about our reasons for being afraid is one of the most important things we can do for our healing and our mental health.

Refocusing Our Need for Self-Preservation

Just to make this abundantly clear, let us take one more look at what our fear is trying to do. At its core, and by God's design, fear is intended to keep us safe, to insure our self-preservation. But here is an important question. If my fear is causing me to lose my sense of self, my stability, and my ability to think clearly, what am I actually preserving? Has not the fear itself then caused the very thing I was afraid of – being diminished as a human being?

If I am afraid to speak up because I may be misunderstood or seen as foolish, my fear has already trumped any possible negative response from other people and cost me something of my self. At the very least, it has cost me my own voice. If I hold back on trying something new solely because I am afraid of failing, my fear has already kept me from any chance to learn something new by experience. This kind of safety is an illusion, because I have already lost something by letting fear have its way.

If I do not repair a rupture with my friend because I am afraid of the confrontation, have I not already lost my friend? My fear is allowing the rupture to go unhealed, and that alone is enough to leave the distance intact. Again, giving into my fear is actually contributing to the very problem I am afraid of.

We even see this in areas of life that are distinctly spiritual. If I avoid engaging in conversational prayer because I am afraid I will not hear anything and be disappointed, my fear has already insured I will hear nothing at all. What's more, I have rationalized my way out of trying to learn. How is that self-preservation? Such fear has much more in common with defeat than with safety!

These are examples of toxic fear that are almost certain to hurt us as much, if not more, than whatever it is that we are afraid of. Once we see how counterproductive toxic fear can be, how self-destructive it can be, we can begin to see why Jesus thought it was important to call us to an anxiety-free life! "Do not worry" (Mt.6:25) is not some command we are supposed to follow. It is a life-giving prescription intended for our own good.

Learning to Suffer Well[69]

This may be a strange sounding phrase, but *learning to suffer well* is far more valuable than developing strategies for avoiding pain. That means learning how to stay emotionally present and relationally connected while suffering, rather than trying to avoid suffering or deny it or blame someone for it.

Unpacking that description a bit further, staying present means that you keep all of your relational faculties when you are afraid rather than go to fight, flight or freeze. We can then take our fear to God and ask Him what we need to see in order to disarm its toxic effects in our life.

As we mature and develop greater capacity for fear as well as receive healing from our distorted fears, we become more and more able to stay focused whenever we are afraid, and better able to discern what to do, who to seek to be with, and when to ask God for more insight.

REBUILDING OUR TRUST

Fear is the opposite of trust, which is why the psalmist says, "When I am afraid, I put my trust in you" (Ps.56:3). He knows from his own experience that he can counter his fear through trusting in God. This is like the small child who can face her fears when her daddy is holding her hand. In another passage we read, "The Lord is the stronghold of my life; of whom shall I be afraid?" (Ps.27:1). Again, we see that once the psalmist knows who God truly is, he can lay down his fear because he trusts God to take care of him.

From our limited perspective, there is a strong tendency to believe that the reason we have so much anxiety is because there are so many things to legitimately worry about. We truly believe that our anxiety is justifiable. We *should* worry about those things, otherwise we might not pay enough attention to them. When Jesus says not to worry about what to eat or what to wear, we find it real hard to take Him seriously. Surely He does not mean for us to ignore basic responsibilities for living, does He? How can we not worry about food, clothing, and shelter, not to mention layoffs, downsizing, and other hazards of modern living?

---

[69] This concept is taken from the Life Model training.

Aside from the fact that we tend to see these things through the lens of false dichotomies, we need to come to terms with a fundamental truth. Toxic fear is not an unavoidable emotion because of circumstances around us over which we have no control. It is not really caused by external forces at all. Rather, toxic fear is an internal response to life, born out of our insecurities and the beliefs we hold on to because of our lack of trust.

Remember that emotions arise from processes that go on inside us, not directly from the external world. The fact that some fears are legitimate does not negate this truth. The main difference between healthy fear and toxic fear is whether or not our internal reactions and interpretations are correct. If we are accurate in our perceptions and interpretations, then the fear is good and intended to keep us safe. If on the other hand our perceptions and interpretations are distorted due to our limited trust, then our fear is toxic and self-defeating.

Our basic problem then is not that life around us is dangerous and unpredictable. Jesus knew that. Our problem is that our truster is broken and we do not know how to trust God, whom we cannot see, in the face of life events that we do see. The problem of toxic fear lies within us, not outside us.

Trust that Overcomes Fear

What does it mean to trust God enough to stop worrying about our basic needs? How do we build that kind of trust? How do we actually become secure enough to quiet our anxious heart? The answer is found in going back to the kinds of safety that God has provided.

First, we need to find His healing touch and discover for ourselves what it means for Him to heal the wounds we carry around that foster our fears. When a person finds healing for an old relational wound, they will then discover that they are much less afraid of intimacy than before. When a person's sense of value is healed from the humiliations of their childhood playground experiences, they will be far less fearful of what people think of them in the present.

These are simple examples of God's ability to restore. The more we experience His healing, the more we will come to count on His restorative safety. Once we get this, life becomes much less dangerous to us, because we

Disarming Our Fear and Anxiety

always know where we can go when we get hurt. When we have little or no experience of God's healing hand in these areas, we are naturally more self-protective in regard to our circumstances, because we have no recourse other than prevention. If we think all wounds are permanent, we will also believe we have good reasons to be afraid of anything that might hurt us. Only when we experience first-hand God's redemptive, life-giving restoration will our fears begin to dissipate.

As discussed in previous chapters, we can take our trust-breaking life events back to God and ask Him what we need from Him in order to get free from our pain and fear. For when God speaks into those events in such a way that He reinterprets them for us, we actually experience them differently. They become part of our story of redemption, instead of remaining a story of loss and pain.

I assure you this is more than just a theory about healing; it is a reality that many Christians have experienced first hand. The more we know by our own account how God can redeem our past, the more we trust Him with our life and the less we worry about things we have no power over. The more we experience God's ability to restore, the more we will be able to trust His restorative safety.

The second thing we can do to disarm our fears is to proactively build trust with God through deepening our relationship with Him. Just as our experience of His healing will give us a sense of restorative safety, our on-going experience of His presence and goodness will increase our sense of His relational safety. We all need to know that no matter what happens *to* us, God is *with* us. In fact, He has come to live *in* us, so that absolutely nothing can separate us from His love.

For most Christians, it takes time to build trust with God that goes deep enough for us to have a sense of genuine security. Whenever we spend time with God, whether in conversation or simply appreciating His love and life within us, we grow our awareness of Him in all His essence inside the very cells of our body. Gradually, this awareness becomes for us an ever increasing sense of His goodness and a deeper sense of peace and security than we ever thought possible. In some ways, this relational security is even more powerful than restorative safety, because God is with us all the time, even before we begin to see the fruits of restoration.

All of this is possible because of the tremendous love that God has for His children. "See how great a love the Father has bestowed upon us, that we should be called 'Children of God' – and we are!" (1Jn.3). As we live more and more in His love and actually experience this relationship we have been called into, our trust level grows like a tree that is planted and watered in rich soil (Ps.1). Our trust in turn pushes anxiety and fear right out of our mind and body. That is why John could say that when we experience God's perfect love, it decimates our fears (1Jn.4:18).

Conclusion

Fear can be a good servant, but it makes a terrible master.[70] In Christ we have a remedy for fear, because He walks alongside us and loves us well enough to restore us, and because His light of truth can penetrate our insecurities to heal our mistaken beliefs that lead to fear.

Security is not the absence of danger. It is the presence of God no matter what the danger. Being connected to God and trusting Him in a fearful moment will go a long way to calming our fear. And if we can find another person who is not afraid of what we are afraid of, God can use that person to help us see what we cannot and respond in ways that we have not yet learned.

Growing our trust will disarm our fears.

Resources for Further Study

Brennan Manning, *Ruthless Trust: The Ragamuffin's Path to God* (San Francisco: Harper Colins) 2009

---

[70] From Dallas Willard (multiple sources).

Chapter 12

Two Kinds of Maturity

> As a result, we are no longer to be children, tossed here and there...but speaking the truth in love, we are to grow up *in all aspects* into Him. (Eph.4:14-15 NASB).

Most of the material in the preceding chapters focused on learning how to engage with God so that He can do in us what we are unable to do for ourselves. This is the basic function of grace in the Christian life. At each step it has been emphasized that spiritual healing and development cannot be achieved by direct effort, but instead is received through interacting with God. That emphasis is necessary in order to correct the mistaken approaches many Christians have tried that are rooted in self-effort to reach an ideal standard of behavior.

However, it would be misleading to leave the reader with the impression that *all* growth is received by interacting with God. There are, in fact, two very different aspects of maturity, each based on very different principles and requiring different approaches regarding our participation. Unfortunately, many people are mistaken about *both* forms of development, which is why they find it so hard to keep growing throughout their lifetime.

On one hand, people commonly assume that *spiritual maturity* comes from trying hard to be a good Christian. At the same time, they mistakenly think *human maturity* happens more or less automatically as we get older. But as we have seen in the first eleven chapters, spiritual maturity can only be received through direct interaction with God. And the piece we want to add here is the fact that *human* maturity *is* actually achieved through hard work and the practice of certain life skills within the context of healthy relationships.

Human maturity includes all of those life skills that any person can learn, whether they are a Christian or not. Consider for example, our ability to make friends, delay gratification, resolve conflicts in ways that are satisfying to all involved, how to regulate our emotions so that we can stay connected to other people (even when angry or afraid), and so on. *These are all things that people can learn how to do whether or not they are Christians.* God designed human beings to grow up and mature in certain ways, whether or not they acknowledge their Maker.

What this means is that while spiritual development is largely *received*, human development is largely *earned* through hard work. Both types of growth are necessary for balance, for developing our identity, and for building strong sustainable relationships.

Predictably, *the Bible talks about both aspects of maturity*, because God wants us to "grow up in all things." That is why so many admonishments in Scripture are about things we can actually do, such as "do not gossip" (1Tim.3:11) as well as things that seem impossible, like, "forgive seventy times seven" (Mt.18:22). The one we can learn through careful awareness of what we are saying, how we are saying it, and how it affects others. In fact, anyone can learn it, not just Christians. For the second, however, nearly everyone requires the work of God in their heart and mind in order to truly forgive that willingly and that regularly.

When these things get mixed up, we can easily form the impression that the Christian life is something we can learn to do if we just try hard enough. This is why so much of this book has focused on how much we need God and how He works in us to give us what we cannot do by our own effort.

But those of us who have grown up within the context of Western culture have another problem. Collectively, we have lost the map of how God designed human beings to grow up and mature. Evidence of this abounds as we watch adults all around us, even in positions of power and leadership, who demonstrate very obvious symptoms of immaturity in their behavior, their emotions, and their relationships.

Even the secular world has noticed this phenomenon in the last few decades and identified certain elements of these changes in our culture, referring to such things as the "me generation" and the dramatic rise in narcissism. Failure to mature today has become the norm, and relatively few people seem to know what it is that we have lost or how to recover it. So if we are going to grow up as Christians in every aspect of our life, we need to know what it is that we are not finding in our surrounding culture, and how we can acquire the relational skills we need in order to mature.

THE LIFE MODEL

Most Christian models of human development have come about by surveying various forms of secular psychology, gleaning from them whatever elements seemed to be consistent with Christian principles, modifying them when necessary, and supplementing them with wisdom from Scripture. Unfortunately, most secular models of maturity assume that proper development can be deduced from observing high functioning adults in the surrounding culture. That is assuming a lot, to say the least.

Over fifteen years ago, the professional staff at Shepherd's House[71] developed something called *The Life Model* to describe the ways in which God designed people to grow and develop. What they decided to do differently was develop an *idealized model* of how God intended for people to grow and mature. In essence, they began with questions like, "What would it look like if people grew and matured the way God intended? How would the resulting community function? What would relationships look like? How would they train children to internalize the necessary skills and values for maturity? For that matter, how does God define maturity?"

Admittedly, attempting to create the ideal model is quite an undertaking. But as an organization they not only had God's Word from which to draw a vision of an abundant life, they also had thousands of hours of clinical experience to draw from to see what kinds of deficits had brought people into counseling, what sort of help was most helpful to them, and what sort of "help" was not so helpful. Beginning with a blank sheet of paper, they proceeded to create a map of how they believed God designed human beings to grow up into thriving adults. This became the basis of the Life Model.[72]

When they took this model back into the counseling sessions, it produced significant results in the lives of people, thus providing more validation that they were on the right track. Today the Life Model is used and taught all over the world. The initial publication has been edited several times and translated into multiple languages. Life Model study groups abound, and have proven to be life-changing for thousands of people.

---

[71] See www.lifemodel.org for more information on this organization.
[72] Friesen, et.al., *The Life Model*.

What is the Life Model?

The short answer is that the Life Model is a comprehensive blueprint for building:

- Strong individual identities.
- Strong community identities.
- Strong relationships between people.

In order to live well, we need to have a good sense of who we are as an individual, as well as who our people are, who we belong to. Our community as a whole needs to have a strong sense of who they are as a people. Strong relationships are rooted in love bonds with others with whom we can build joy together, endure hardships together, and recover well when there are hurts or ruptures in our relationships. When we have a strong identity, we are able to live out of who we are and connect to others with competence, confidence and joy. A strong identity also includes the following characteristics:

- Our primary motivators are joy and love and concern for the good of one another, not fear or shame or rules.
- An increased capacity to experience strong emotions (both positive and negative) while staying connected to others.
- Resiliency: the ability to return to calm and joy after strong negative emotions and experiences.
- An accurate picture of how God sees me, as the person He designed me to be (not based on my accumulated malfunctions).
- A strong sense of who I belong to, who my people are, what characterizes our group, and how we receive and give life together, as well as how God sees us corporately.
- Integrity between what I say and what I do, between my stated values and my behavior.

All of this is based on the premise that *relationship is the organizing principle of life*. People often organize their lives around things other than relationship. For example, people often organize their lives around fear, consumption, pleasure, pain avoidance, career advancement, personal recognition, or even their addictions. But God designed human beings in such a way that we function best when we organize our lives around our relationships with God and other people. That is why the two greatest commandments are, "Love God" and "Love one another."

Consequently, building strong relationships is the cornerstone of the Life Model. A strong group identity combined with strong personal identities is necessary for building strong relationships; and strong relationships are necessary for building strong identities. These two elements are completely interdependent and mutually beneficial.

A great analogy to this interdependence is that of words in a sentence. Each word in the language has a range of possible meanings, and the only way we can be sure of what a word means is to see it in a sentence. But the sentence in turn is made up only of words. If we see the word "cook" by itself, it is impossible to know whether it is a verb (he is going to cook dinner) or a noun (he is a cook by profession) or even a metaphor (they are going to cook something up for the program). The meaning of the word depends on the sentence, and the meaning of the sentence depends on the words it contains. There is no sentence without words, and yet apart from a sentence, the words are indeterminate. *Context determines meaning.*

The same is true of the interdependence between individuals and groups (families, communities, churches, and so on). A group character comes out of the people who participate in the group, and people are shaped by the kind of group they are part of. When the group is made up of people at all levels of maturity from infant to elder, all working well together, all growing and maturing as God intended, then the group will be strong and resilient. People who are part of such a group will be blessed with mature examples to follow and life-giving mentoring to help them grow. People readily share, engage with one another, and build up one another. When conflicts do arise, they are handled in ways that lead to still stronger relationships and deeper personal growth of those involved.

Communities like this do not happen by accident. They are the result of careful interaction between generations, involving all levels of maturity from infant to child, to adult, parent and elder, all working together in ways that reflect the training they have had in how to receive and give life.

Why Christian Organizations Need a Life Model

Western culture has for the most part lost its relational foundations. Whatever sense of community that existed prior to the urbanization of the modern world has all but disappeared. Hardly anyone even knows any longer what has been lost, what its value was, or how to recover it. Individualism and autonomy are so ingrained in our way of life that the very idea of living as an interdependent community is now a frightening thought to many people.

Predictably, along with the loss of community we are witnessing a growing immaturity in the population at large, both individually and collectively. One of the many losses we have experienced is the truth that human maturity is heavily dependent upon a functional community that has a strong sense of who they are. Since community is almost non-existent, we no longer have in our possession the primary means necessary to grow up and mature as human beings.

Now this may sound a bit strange to people who appear to be functioning quite well as adults. But maturity is not the ability to stand on our own two feet in an individualistic culture. *That is a set of coping skills, not maturity.* True human maturity is the ability handle increasingly complex relationships with competence and joy.

All we have to do is look around to see that this is in short supply in our culture. Marriages are ending at an alarming rate, and many of those who are still together are miserable at best. Young people are dismissing the older generations earlier and more completely with each passing decade. And being self-centered is now treated like a virtue.

We Need More than Good Theology to Live Well

Despite what many Christians have been taught, proper growth and development requires a lot more than good doctrine. First, spiritual maturity and human maturity are very different processes and require very different resources. Hopefully, that will become more clear as we proceed. While the Bible has a lot to say about both types of maturity, unless we understand the differences we will be at risk of trying to apply human solutions to spiritual problems and spiritual solutions to human problems.

Second, the Bible gives us a lot of directives that are left to the readers to understand and apply. For example, "Love one another" may sound simple enough. But do we really know what this means? Or is this partly a learned way of interacting with others for which we need some training? Why do you suppose there are so many "marriage enrichment" seminars and sought-after speakers like Gary Smalley who can help us flesh out what it means to be in a committed relationship? Because while the Bible correctly points out the importance of marriage, it does not give us very many step-by-step details on how to develop a really good one in a community-starved culture.

We all know that good Christians should try to raise children who will be mature and resilient in our broken world. But how do we do that? Every parent wishes their children had come with instructions! What do infants need from us? How do those needs differ from the needs of toddlers and adolescents? These are not easy questions. There is, in fact, a lot of terrible advice available on these issues, some of which comes to us in the name of Bible-based instruction, often written by people who know virtually nothing about child development. The Bible underscores the importance of raising children well, but it does not provide a lot of detail on how to do that.

Or take the problem of those among us who have suffered terrible abuse. What is the best way to help them recover? Do we simply quote edicts about what they ought to do and then expect them to "get over it"? Or are there more loving approaches that require something of us who are stronger? How do we bear another's burden without being either an enabler or co-dependent? Again, we need some wisdom here that is not easily discerned.

Jesus told us to seek reconciliation wherever possible and do our utmost to transform adversarial encounters into relational moments of grace. But how many of us find ourselves embroiled in conflicts that seem like a matter of principle to us? Why is that? How do we discern when to take a stand and when to lay aside our "rights"? What are the means of resolving conflict?

Paul writes that we should build up one another into a corporate body that works together well, a community that fosters life and practices love between its members. But how? What are the tools necessary for this job? How do we build relationships in an individualistic environment?

We could go on. These are all very important questions, which require much more than simplistic answers and proof texts. What we need to acknowledge is that the Bible is fairly silent about many of these issues; and the reason it is silent is because God expects us to learn many of these life lessons from our elders. But that raises a very serious problem for those of us in the modern world.

The Task of the Church

If our culture is rapidly losing the means for transmitting relational skills and developing human maturity, and the Bible is often silent or ambiguous about how to handle many of these issues, sooner or later it comes down to a very basic question: Who is going to teach us what our culture cannot, in regard to how to grow strong people and strong relationships?

It bears repeating. Human maturity and spiritual maturity are vastly different processes. Human maturity is possible for both Christians and non-Christians. And it is so important and makes so much difference, that a *mature non-Christian* will often look and act a lot more loving than an emotionally and relationally *immature Christian*. A Christian can have a heart full of compassion for another person, and at the same time be completely lacking in either the capacity to handle upsets in a relationship or the relational skills necessary to be of any real help. We need both kinds of development.

The key issue is this: our culture cannot significantly help us with either one. Just as it is up to the church to preserve and pass on the message of the kingdom, so also *it is up to the church to learn how to build and preserve and pass on a well-functioning community* in which relationships are powerful enough to bring about growth and life change in one another. This is the focus of the Life Model.

"FIVE TO THRIVE"

Earlier we said that the Life Model was about building strong identities and strong relationships. While that points us in a direction, it still begs the question, "How do we do that?" Over a period of several years, the Life Model authors identified five major areas of human development that are absolutely foundational in order to thrive as God intended. They are affectionately referred to as the "Five to Thrive." They are:

Two Kinds of Maturity

- Healthy Attachment and Belonging.
- Receiving and Giving Life.
- Knowing How to Recover When Things Go Wrong.
- Developing Maturity.
- Living From the Heart Jesus Gave Us.

Each of these areas has been written about and taught extensively[73]. Only a small introduction is possible here. Most of our emphasis in this chapter will be on the fourth element, *Developing Maturity,* because that is the area that most significantly complements spiritual formation as described in the first eleven chapters. Highlighting that contrast will provide some extremely helpful insights regarding what it means to "grow up in all things."

Healthy Attachment and Belonging

Our most fundamental needs as human beings are a place to belong and people who know us and love us. Attachment and bonding are vital to our well-being. God designed us for relationship, and we function best when we have strong bonds to depend on.

Our brains are literally wired for bonding. Deep inside the right hemisphere of the brain is an area that functions below the conscious level which is responsible for our bonding and attachment. Infants bond quickly and deeply to their parents and feel deep emotional pain when separated from them. Around the age of puberty our mind undergoes some changes that prepare us for building bonds with others and forming a group identity. (In our culture this happens primarily with peers, even though God's intention was for much broader bonding with our entire adult community).

We can also see the importance of human connections by looking at what happens when the opportunity for bonding is not present. Infants who are left alone except for basic physical care can become very ill (called "failure to thrive" syndrome) and actually die from lack of attention and love. Even in prisons where one would expect to find men who are so hard that they do not need anyone, solitary confinement is considered to be one of the most debilitating forms of punishment. And finally, the most painful emotion we can feel is *attachment pain,* that pain we feel when someone we

---
[73] See annotated bibliography.

need has died or left us for an indefinite period. We are designed to attach deeply and for life. When we lose those to whom we are bonded, we suffer greatly. Some of the saddest love songs are songs about attachment pain.

Clearly, God designed us for relationship. Few things are as necessary to life as healthy attachment. God designed us this way because He wants to be connected to us and have us as His people. Throughout the Scriptures God relates to both Israel and later the church as a Father to His children.

> See what love the Father has given us, that we should be called children of God (1Jn.3:1).
>
> I will be their God, and they shall be my people (2Cor.6:16).

The very heart of the gospel is about God's love for the world (Jn.3:16). When God says that He wants us to become one with Him, He is not talking about doctrinal unity. He wants us to be joined to Him in love.

Relationship is also the basis for joy, which is primarily relational in nature, not situational. We see this in Scripture as well:

> In your presence there is fullness of joy (Ps.16:11).
>
> I hope to come to you and talk with you face to face, so that our joy may be complete (2Jn.12).

Even more exciting is the realization that joy is our intended state.

> Jesus: "I have said these things to you so that my joy may be in you, and that your joy may be complete" (Jn.15:11).

Meaningful, long-term connections are essential to life and well-being. These are the relationships where we learn to receive and give life, where we mature, and where we discover our God-given identity.

Receiving and Giving Life

This segment of the Life Model is roughly the equivalent of "Love one another" fleshed out in ways that are beneficial and life-giving to everyone involved. We need meaningful interactions and joyful sharing of time, energy, and resources within our bonded relationships. To that end, we need to know what is life-giving and what is not, how to develop healthy connections with one another, and how to send and receive both implicit and explicit messages of love, life, and good to one another.

For Christians who have always tried to live up to Biblical standards and may be thinking how important it is to be the one giving, it may come as a surprise that the first task in giving and receiving life is to learn how to *receive with joy*. That is, an infant should not have to wonder when and if their needs are going to be met. They should not have to perform well before being given what they need. Their primary task is to learn what it feels like to be on the receiving end of love. If the adults around them give with joy, without any resentment or contempt for the baby, the infant will come to believe that giving is good and that it makes people joyful.

But receiving with joy is not always the norm. As infants and young children, if our needs were met only sporadically, or if we learned not to ask for what we needed because it invited shame or upset the people around us, then we learned early on that receiving was not a life-giving experience. Instead, we were told that our requests were unreasonable or inconvenient, we felt fear or shame for having needs that inconvenienced others, and very likely we came to believe that giving was an imposition, not a joy.

The wounds that come from these kinds of interactions go deep into our soul where joy and peace should have taken root. We learn that our needs mean very little to others, that meeting our needs must not cost anyone anything, that gifts usually come with expectations, and that whatever the "good stuff" is, it is in short supply. Love is scarce, not abundant.

In many homes the roles are even reversed, and children are expected to fill deep needs in the adults. Couples sometimes have babies in the hope that the little ones will bring enough love and purpose into the home to save the marriage. Women who have had little or no unconditional love in their life may long for an innocent infant to love them without any conditions or historical baggage. These children are born with a job that they should never have been given. Assigned with the task of meeting adult needs, and no defenses to guard against those expectations, they readily capitulate to the emotional demands because that is how they find acceptance in the eyes of their parents. The damage done to their tiny souls can be crippling.

Then there are homes where the caregivers are also a major source of fear for the child. One or both parents may be actively addicted to some mood altering substance, or so wounded from their own history that they are unable to regulate their emotions and thus melt down at unpredictable times and overwhelm the defenseless child. In any case, children in these environments live in fear of upsetting the adults in the home, and generally blame themselves when things go wrong. "If I had only behaved differently, then Daddy would not have gotten so angry." Again, they are doing relational maintenance work they should not be required to do, instead of receiving the care and nurture they need.

All of these problems make it extremely difficult for a child to build an experiential understanding of how receiving and giving can be life-giving and a source of joy. Infants and children need to experience not only the joy of receiving love with no strings attached, but they need to see joy in the faces and lives of the people who are giving to them. Receiving with joy allows the child to know what a free gift feels like, what constitutes a good life-giving gift of love, and why a person would delight in giving away their time and resources for the purpose of blessing and connecting with another person. Then when a child begins to experiment with giving to others, that child already has both a model to show them how to give and a motivation to do so. *They want to be the cause for others to feel what they felt when <u>they</u> received with joy.* Receiving with joy is how we learn to give with joy.

When instead we try to shame people into giving time and resources, we destroy both the motivation and a major part of why people give in the first place. The point of giving is not to comply with some moral law or to keep from feeling guilty about hording. The best reason to give is because we have learned the joy of receiving and giving, and have a deep sense of the goodness we can offer one another. When we try to get people to give before they have learned to receive, we can perpetuate their beliefs in scarcity and create a faulty understanding of what it means to be a servant to others.

In many ways, our need for learning how to receive before learning to give is very similar to the fact that we must have a "no" before we can have a "yes." That is, unless we are empowered to say "no" to routine requests, our "yes" has very little meaning. If every time we are asked to do something or give up something we immediately say "yes" without thought or hesitation, it may well be because we do not believe we have any voice in the matter. Our "yes" does not really mean "yes" if we have lost much of our ability to say "no." Only when we can turn down a request without fear will we be able to say "yes" with integrity. Only then will our "yes" be the result of a choice rather than from a belief that we have to do whatever we are asked. Similarly, until we have learned how to receive, our giving will most likely come from some place other than joy. But when we know how to receive, our giving can come from a heart that is free to do so.

Knowing How to Recover When Things Go Wrong

Because we live in a broken world, things will inevitably go wrong in our life. Other people or circumstances may create difficulties for us, our own judgment errors will cause damage to ourselves, and immaturity, foolishness and other limitations will also impact our life in negative ways. If we lack sufficient strategies and resources for the work of repair, then mistakes and mishaps can be devastating. So the third element we need in our "Five to Thrive" is the ability to recover when things go wrong.

In the chapter on self-hate we described two major kinds of injury that we can experience, A-type and B-type injuries. B-type injuries are the Bad things that happen to us, and A-type injuries are the Absence of good things that should have happened. Both types of injury can cause spiritual damage in the form of internalized beliefs that are not in tune with the way God sees our experience. That kind of damage often requires the Spirit of God in order to heal and correct our understanding of our own life experiences.

But A-type injuries also require something more. Healing the wound is important, but that still does not give us the good that was originally absent from our life. For example, instead of being taught the relational skill of asking for what I need, suppose I was always discouraged from asking for what I needed and learned instead that I was somehow bad for being needy. As an adult, I require two separate resources for full recovery. I need some healing from my distorted sense of what it means to be needy, and I need training and encouragement to practice finding my voice in regard to advocating for what I need and to do so in a balanced and respectful manner. The healing is *received* from God and the new skills are *achieved* through training and practice with the help of other people.

Spiritual and Human Resources for Recovery

A great many spiritual resources necessary for recovery have been identified throughout this book.

- We have a God who wants our healing more than we do.
- God offers forgiveness for mistaken choices.
- God gives us truth for understanding our own story.
- God heals our wounds and ministers to our brokenness.
- God will help us identify the missing pieces of our development and help us find the people we need to learn from.

But restoration from type-A injuries would be incomplete without other people to help. They can be an invaluable resource in two ways. First, God may use them as part of His way of speaking into our life or as an aid in seeking God's direct healing. Second, as we will see in the maturity section below, much of our recovery work involves relearning developmental skills that we missed earlier, and these can only be learned with the help of other people. We also need:

- Someone who is glad to be with us, even in our weakness.
- Someone who can see us through the eyes of heaven.
- Someone who is not afraid of what we are afraid of.
- Someone who can show us what to do in our situation.

When we combine both human and spiritual resources, our healing is far more complete and life changing.

Living From the Heart Jesus Gave Us

This phrase was coined during the development of The Life Model as a way of expressing what it means to live out of our God-given identity.

In order to better understand what it means to live from our heart, let us begin by listing a few of the basic principles people often use as a compass for life. A few of the more common include:

- **Peer influence:** I do what my peers think is cool (or good).
- **Emotions:** My feelings tell me what to do.
- **Rules:** I figure out what is right and wrong for every situation.

As pervasive as these approaches are for navigating through life, they are all woefully inadequate, and sometimes even dangerous. We need a better way. God designed us to live from a pure heart, not from internal urges or external pressure – not even external rules. The more we become the person God created us to be, the better our boundaries, the stronger our relationships, and the more life-giving our interactions will all be.

Part of this process involves distinguishing between our true heart and our identity of past experience, as discussed in Chapter 10. Extremely important is knowing the true characteristics of our heart as seen through the eyes of heaven, not as seen through the lenses of the world or our woundedness. Then also the unique style and giftedness that each of us brings to the community of believers must be taken into account. We need Peter's willingness to risk, Andrew's desire to include others, and John's sensitivity. All are important.

When we properly grasp who we are, our true character gives us direction and discernment in our daily walk. I will know what to do when I make a mistake, when I find someone else's cell phone or wallet, and when my co-worker sets me up. Jesus was the ultimate model of this way of life, and He knew how to respond to events and to those around Him because of who He was. And in those moments where we find ourselves unsure of the next step, we know how to listen to the Spirit of God and other Christians for the vision and heart we need to decide what to do.

All of this results in very intentional and purposeful living, aware of where we are in relation to the unseen realities around us, the presence of God, and our ultimate purpose for being. We are able to remain relatively consistent through various circumstances and when encountering different people, rather than letting those things squeeze us into whatever shape provides the least resistance.

For Christians this also means living from our renewed heart instead of from a set of laws. Our whole emphasis on sailing instead of rowing explores this issue in detail, so we will not belabor it here.

Human beings are designed to live out of who they have become, whatever their level of maturity. As we continue our process of life-long growth, integrating both human and spiritual maturity, and developing a strong identity, we will live more fully as God intended.

UNDERSTANDING HUMAN MATURITY

Acquiring the skills necessary to mature is something that God designed into human beings. People do not have to be Christians in order to grow and mature in this manner. That is why tribal cultures who have never heard of Jesus still understand there is a difference between children and adults, who have elders among them that exhibit great wisdom and place the welfare of the group above their own interests, and so on. Once we see the scope of human maturity and what people are capable of, we begin to see how it is that a mature non-Christian may very well show more character than an immature Christian, and why all of this makes human maturity important for Christians to pursue.

In short, *spiritual maturity* is largely *received* through interacting with God, while *human maturity* is largely *earned* through interacting with people and developing relational skills. This distinction is crucial to understanding both our means for growing up and our resources for recovery when things go wrong. Most of the first eleven chapters were devoted to reshaping our vision for spiritual maturity through interaction with God. This next section will explain what we mean by human maturity so that we can then revisit this idea of two different aspects of maturity and how they intersect.

A Developmental Model of Human Maturity

To understand this model of maturity, it is important to view human development as a series of steps. Beginning with infancy, moving on to childhood, adulthood, parenthood, and finally elder, these stages of maturity represent qualitative differences in the ability of people to engage in relationships with joy and competence.

To put this another way, we naturally expect more of children than infants in their interactions with others, just as we expect more from adults than children, and so on. But age is not the only determining factor. We all know someone who is walking around in an adult body, but emotionally and relationally is still very much an infant. They have little insight into the thoughts and feelings of others, they have difficulty controlling their impulses, and they view many of their interactions from the perspective of a transaction in which they win or lose something (and we could go on and list many more such characteristics).

While conditions like this are unfortunate, they are really quite common. And the reasons for this kind of immaturity are best understood within the framework of a model that explains how maturity happens in the first place – or not.

Part 1: Skills

To begin with, there are five discernible stages of maturity, each one represented by a specific set of relational and emotional abilities. For example, one of the skills that separates a child from an infant is their ability to calm their cravings and wait for things that are not immediately available to them. An infant simply gets overwhelmed by any unmet desire and cries. At the child level of maturity they can quiet that desire in most cases without much ado, and ask for what they need.

Moving on from child maturity to adult maturity, one of the key relational abilities that must be learned is how to meet the needs of two people at the same time. A child's job is to learn how to take care of their own emotional and relational needs and to ask for help when necessary. But adult level relationships require more mutuality, and a person must learn how to take care of two (or more) people at the same time, without viewing such needs as competitive or win-lose propositions. It should be fairly easy to see this skill is fundamental to the success of any marriage. Because when two people get married who have not yet reached adult level maturity, they view every conflict of needs as a problem caused by the other person and as a win-lose proposition. They are unable to approach the situation as a problem "we" have and need to work through together.

Thus each stage of maturity can be described in terms of certain emotional and relational skills that people must learn in order to continue growing and developing as human beings.

Part 2: Needs

But we do not learn relational skills in a vacuum. We must have some basic needs met in addition to a great deal of careful mentoring. If none of the adults or peers around us have these skills, we will probably not learn them. Which in turn implies that we will remain immature in those areas.

For example, in order for an infant to learn child-level skills, they need an encouraging family around them and a lot of help with their attempts at child-level tasks. If instead they are criticized or humiliated for their efforts, they will not only fail to learn the needed skills, they will likely learn a way of working around the lack of relational skills in ways that are detrimental. Without the proper support from family and community, they simply cannot acquire the relational tools to handle more complicated situations.

The charts on the following pages provide a snapshot of some of the more prominent needs and tasks that are required to achieve each level of maturity, along with a few of the symptoms that might be present many years later if those tasks are not completed. Please be aware that these charts are by no means exhaustive, and a far more complete list of maturity needs and tasks is available in the works cited.

As to the age references on each stage, these represent the earliest possible age at which a person might accomplish these tasks. Most people do not grow at that rate. It would not be unusual to find a thirty-year-old who is still mostly at child-level maturity. Also note that the stages may not be rigid. A person can be at child-level in regard to most tasks, while having done well at one or two adult level tasks.

Maturity as a Coherent Picture

In each of the five stages of development, we have a particular set of needs that must be met by significant people in our life, and a set of relational skills we need to learn. As we master each stage of maturity, we are able to handle relational situations that are more complicated than we were capable of dealing with previously. Not only that, but we are able to do so with joy and a sense of competence and satisfaction.

For example, a major parent-level task is learning to give sacrificially to their children without any expectation that the children give something back to the adult. But having children does not by itself move us into parent-level maturity. It is not enough to merely spend time, money, and energy on the children. Our entire way of relating to them must be one based on the joy of doing for them what they cannot yet do for themselves, and on being able to do most of the work of the relationship itself, and do so joyfully.

Stages of Human Development / Maturity*

Infant Level Maturity (birth to 3 years)

Needs to be Met by Others	Tasks to be Accomplished by Person	Possible Symptoms of Unfinished Tasks
Strong, loving bonds with parents Important needs met w/o asking Others synchronize to infant Help regulating emotions Be seen through eyes of heaven	Receive with joy Develop trust Organize self into person through imitation Regulate and quiet every emotion Return to joy from distressing emotions Learn to rest	Weak identity Difficulty bonding Withdrawn, disengaged, unresponsive Inability to regulate emotions Gets stuck in emotions Addictions

*E James Wilder, *The Complete Guide to Living With Men*; and Freisen, et.al., *The Life Model*
Please note that the chart shown is incomplete, and that the phrases used can be fairly technical.
For a more complete description of the stages of maturity, please refer to Jim Wilder's book.

Child Level Maturity (4-12)

Needs to be Met by Others	Tasks to be Accomplished by Person	Possible Symptoms of Unfinished Tasks
Help doing what the child doesn't want to do Help sorting feelings, imagination, and reality Feedback on guesses, attempts, and failures Love that is not earned To be taught the big picture of life	Take care of self, emotionally/relationally Learn to ask for needs Learn self-expression Develop persistence for doing hard things Develop personal resources and talents Tame cravings Learn what satisfies See self through eyes of heaven	Frustration over unmet needs Consumed with fantasy life Life filled with unproductive activity Fails to develop personal style Addictions

Adult Level Maturity (13 to birth of first child)

Opportunity to form bonds with peers Inclusion by the adult community Observe adults using power fairly Opportunity for important involvement Opportunities for mutual relationships	Discover main characteristics of heart Develop personal style reflecting heart Move from "me and you" to "us" Remain stable in distress Learn to protect others from self Mutual satisfaction	Self-centered Leaves others unsatisfied with interactions Conforms to peer pressure Tendency to isolate Controlling, blaming

Two Kinds of Maturity

Parent Level Maturity (until youngest child becomes an adult)

Needs to be Met by Others	Tasks to be Accomplished by Person	Possible Symptoms of Unfinished Tasks
Encouragement and guidance from elders Peer review with other parents Secure and orderly community	Giving without receiving in return Protecting family unit Serve and enjoy family Meet needs of children Help children with their tasks	Other family members at risk of being deprived Children taking care of parents' needs Children do not mature

Elder Level Maturity (after youngest child becomes an adult)

Needs to be Met by Others	Tasks to be Accomplished by Person	Possible Symptoms of Unfinished Tasks
A community in which to belong Recognition by the community A proper place in community structure Opportunities to be involved in lives of community members	Hospitality Give life to those without family Nurture community identity and purpose Able to guide group through difficulty and return group back to joy	Disintegration of social structures Fragile people do not heal or survive Increased crime, disregard of others

At this point, we are ready to present a coherent definition of maturity that takes all of these factors into account. *Human maturity is the ability to handle increasingly complex relationships, and to do so with competence and joy.* This maturity is *earned* by learning the necessary relational skills to function appropriately at a given stage of development. And these skills are learned through interaction with others who already possess them and who will meet that person's needs and mentor their growth process relationally.

In broad strokes, the progression from infant to elder looks like this:

Infant: Main task is to learn how to receive. Main need is for others to give to them unconditionally and with joy.

Child: Main task is to learn how to care for self in relation to others. Main need is for others to help them with their attempts at self direction.

Adult: Main task is to learn how to care for two people in relationship. Main need is for models to follow and mentors to help them.

Parent: Main task is to learn how to care for another who is dependent upon them (in a non-mutual relationship). Main need is encouragement and guidance from others who have learned how to do this.

Elder: Main task is to learn how to care for a community and to mentor them in their various relationships. Main need is for the community to respect their role and make a space for the elder to speak into their lives.

As you can see, each stage adds something new to a person's ability to manage relationships, which are increasingly more complex and require more from the person.

Traceable Threads of Maturity

Some of the characteristics of maturity can be observed developing throughout the various stages, like threads that weave through a person's overall experience, becoming more complex and layered with each stage.

For example, one relational skill we need is the ability to see ourselves and others gracefully "through the eyes of heaven." As we learn to do this well, we become far less judgmental and for more life-giving in the ways in which we interact. But it is really helpful to see how this skill changes and grows as we mature.

The following list summarizes the progression.

Infant: Be seen by others through the eyes of heaven.
Child: Learn to see self through the eyes of heaven.
Adult: See self and peers with the eyes of heaven.
Parent: Help children see themselves through the eyes of heaven.
Elder: Help everyone in the community see one another and the group with the eyes of heaven. Train parents how to see and train their children.

Another fairly visible thread can be seen in the skill of knowing what truly satisfies. Many people never know what satisfies their soul, and as a result try to use food, thrills, alcohol and other things to satisfy them. Taken through the stages, it looks like this:

Infant: Receive from others what truly satisfies.
Child: Learn what satisfies self.
Adult: Learn what satisfies self and others at the same time.
Parent: Help children discover and learn what satisfies.
Elder: Help everyone in the community learn what satisfies both individually and as a group.

Summary

God intended for human beings to grow up and mature in the context of a thriving community, one which is capable of passing on the relational skills everyone needs in order to receive and give life to one another. This is a highly interactive process requiring a multi-generational context. In order to mature, we must have our needs met by those around us, especially by those with whom we are most bonded, and learn a number of relational skills that allow us to function more joyfully and competently within our community.

Emotional Capacity

One particular element of human maturity deserves special attention, partly because it is often misunderstood and partly because it has implications for spiritual growth as well.

Capacity in this context refers to the ability to feel intense emotions without being overwhelmed by them. A good synonym for capacity might be "emotional strength." We all possess some capacity to maintain our normal way of relating to others when experiencing minor levels of distress.

We sometimes refer to this as "acting like ourselves." But our capacity is limited. At some point, when the distress becomes great enough our capacity is overwhelmed, and our ability to stay relational and rational is diminished. In the early stages of overwhelm, we may experience being "at a loss for words" or "unable to think straight." In more severe cases of overwhelm we might freeze or lash out at those around us in ways we later regret.

Capacity is something that can grow over time. The greater our capacity, the more intensely we can feel emotions like fear, anger, and shame without becoming overwhelmed by them. We must of course recognize that as human beings we all have limited capacity. So becoming overwhelmed is not in any way a moral failure.

It may even be helpful to understand some of the physiology behind this phenomenon. Our brains are designed with a hierarchically arranged control center in the right hemisphere that processes everything we pick up from our surrounding environment before passing it over to the left hemisphere where we finish making sense of things and put words to our experience. Under stress, that control structure can alter how it processes. It may even short-circuit our rational mind and cause us to react before we have had time to think through the situation. This system is very helpful in cases where we really do not have time to evaluate what is happening. For example, if a dangerous animal were to suddenly show up, the lowest levels of our control center can make a "fight, flight, freeze" decision and pump adrenaline into our body to move, even before we have had time to consider our options.

This control center will begin to take over whenever the intensity of our emotions exceeds our emotional strength; that is, whenever our capacity is overwhelmed. But getting overwhelmed is not usually an all-or-nothing process. In less stressful situations, only some of our processing will get by-passed. We experience this all the time when we snap back at a person without thinking, or when we cry without knowing exactly why.

Interestingly, the most reliable way to grow greater capacity is to spend a lot of time building joy. When the psalmist says, "The joy of the Lord is my strength," he is describing his own empirical observations of this truth. As we develop strong relationships and engage in joy-building interactions, we actually strengthen the emotional circuits in our brain that provide more resilience and capacity!

Two Kinds of Maturity

Many of the relational skills we need in order to mature depend on our capacity. For example, learning how to remain consistent over time over a broad range of circumstances requires that we have the capacity to work through uncomfortable situations and interactions. So emotional capacity plays a large role in human maturity.

Infants and Capacity

An important note in this discussion is the fact that we are all born with *virtually no capacity* for stress or discomfort of any kind. That is why a baby will cry when it is hungry, when it is wet, when it needs attention, and for almost any other reason that comes along. They may even get angry and fuss and act "demanding" in their attempts to express how distressed they feel. Almost anything can overwhelm their emotional and relational circuits and create more distress than they are capable of handling. So they cry a lot, which is basically an involuntary response to being overwhelmed and the body's way of discharging some of the stress. We also see symptoms of overwhelm at the toddler stage in the form of tantrums.

Here is where authoritarian styles of parenting make the terrible mistake of assuming the infant or toddler is being "bad" and needs to be punished or ignored. At a time when the parents should be helping the young child to grow their capacity for emotional stress, they instead react in ways that *increase* the child's distress, often to the point of a complete shutdown. The parent may then misinterpret this as good compliant behavior which they have properly induced in the child by their disciplined approach. Over time, this parenting style will train the child's control center to shut down whenever he or she is overwhelmed so that strong emotions are often not processed at all. Unfortunately, this gives the appearance of a well-behaved, compliant child who rarely disagrees or complains, when in fact the child is losing touch with their own inner world in an effort to accommodate their parents' demands.

To add no small irony to this mistaken approach, it basically stems from the parents' own lack of capacity and the ease with which they are overwhelmed by their child's behavior. Unfortunately, their ability to coerce the desired behavior leads them to believe they are using a good parenting style. Children quite naturally react to being overwhelmed by expressing anger, sadness, hopelessness, and other negative emotions. When parents mistake these symptoms for willful defiance, they may react in ways that are very harmful to the emotional health and development of their child.

Parenting is far more complicated than making children behave well. Our goal is to train them in relational and emotional skills so they can deal with the increasing complexities of life they encounter as they grow. If parents discover they are ill equipped to train their children in this way, our hope is that they will first give attention to the holes in their own maturity, and then seek help in how to raise their children to be joyful and secure.

Implications for Spiritual Development

Emotional capacity is something any normally healthy human being can develop with the right help. If our capacity is so limited that we malfunction quite often, it is likely that we have had fairly weak relational connections for much of our life, especially when we were young. We need to find the necessary resources to grow our capacity so that we can become more stable.

However, a very common mistake is to interpret low capacity as some kind of spiritual problem and try to pray for that person for healing or expect them to overcome their difficulties by repentance. Such an approach is like adding a ton of bricks to an already overloaded bridge. We need to understand capacity in order to properly interpret what is going on for a person and to offer help that is actually helpful.

Another factor to keep in mind is that capacity must be taken into account when engaging in inner healing prayer. In Chapters 9 to 11, we presented a model for inner healing in which a person learns how to engage with God in ways that allow Him to be present with them in their traumatic events, and to speak into their wounded areas and reinterpret their experiences from His point of view. This is a wonderfully life-giving answer to our brokenness and weaknesses. But our capacity can put limits on how far we can go with this process.

Imagine for a moment a person who has fairly limited capacity for shame, who is trying to engage with God for healing in regard to their self-hate. Suppose they remember a particular incident in their childhood that captures very well the kind of verbal and emotional abuse they suffered which helped to create their self-rejection. But when they try to go back to that experience and ask God to speak into that moment, they lose sight of God and cannot hear anything He says. One possible cause is that they get overwhelmed by the pain of that event whenever they reflect on it, and their relational circuits begin to shut down. As a result, they are unable to perceive the presence of God.

When this happens, it becomes more important to deal with the fact that they are losing their connection to God than to deal with the self-hate. In many cases, they can reconnect with God by backing off the healing process and spending time in appreciation. Once they have a strong connection, they may be able to address the painful experience again without losing sight of God. However, some people may need to put certain past experiences on hold for a time while they continue to build up their relationship with God, which will increase their capacity for these negative emotions. After that they can try addressing these areas again.

Building Capacity

Capacity is built throughout our lifetime. But before describing how we do that, it is necessary to make one more clarification. Capacity is not the ability to hold emotions at bay or the ability to override strong emotions with willpower. Those are actually attempts to manage stress by shutting down important functions in the right hemisphere of the brain.

Capacity is the ability to feel strong emotions and stay relational at the same time. When Jesus cried out, "Oh, Jerusalem, how I have longed to gather you together ... but you would not allow it," He was expressing deep grief in regard to His desire for His people, while at the same time remaining fully relational. When He healed the man with a withered hand on the Sabbath, He was able to feel intense anger toward the teachers of the law and intense love for the man at the same time. That requires emotional capacity. And if ever there was a time to be overwhelmed, it would be on the cross. Yet Jesus forgave His executioners, made arrangements for His mother, and connected with the thief on the other cross. These are the kinds of relational things He might have done if He were *not* suffering. His ability to maintain His normal self under duress is an example of incredible capacity.

Capacity is not about feeling less, but the ability to feel more intensely and stay relational at the same time. To build this capacity, we must train our emotional circuits how to return to joy from distress, as well as how to hold both joy and distress at the same time, at various levels of intensity.

What this means is that when we feel anger or shame or sadness, for example, we know how to be with God and others in ways that allow us to quiet down (which may take a few moments) and how to return our inner focus to a place of appreciation. During this process we may need to be comforted and to allow ourselves to receive that comfort. This in turn implies that we can sense we are not alone and are able to reach out to others or allow them to reach out to us in our distress.

That brings us to a very important and liberating truth, that joy can coexist quite well with any one of a broad spectrum of distressing emotions. Human beings are fully capable of experiencing both joy and grief at the same time, or joy and disappointment, and so on. If we think about this, it only makes sense, because reality is very complex. We can be in the throes of a significant loss and at the same time be in the presence of God or a trusted friend. It follows then, that we can experience the grief of one and the joy of the other at the same time. By training ourselves to notice both, and building the capacity to hold both at once, we are able to experience what the New Testament writers were describing when they talked about rejoicing no matter what else was going on.

If we get the help we need in this process and learn how to experience joy in our distress, we effectively train our mind how to trust God and others when under duress. Every time we are successful in returning to joy from a painful emotion, we reinforce the emotional circuits that keep track of this process. So the next time we feel a similar pain, our mind knows better how to move toward rest and quiet without as much effort. We become more secure and less concerned about managing the intensity of our emotions. As a result, we can experience much stronger emotions without losing touch with our relational faculties, and we are able to stay relational with others in the face of greater distress. This is what it means to build capacity.

INTEGRATING HUMAN MATURITY AND SPIRITUAL MATURITY

It is now time to return to our major premise, that there are two quite different aspects to maturity, human and spiritual. As should be more clear by now, human maturity is largely *earned* through hard work and interaction with family and community. On the other hand, spiritual maturity is largely *received* through interaction with God. In this section we will demonstrate how these two different aspects interact and why we need them both.

We Need Both Kinds of Maturity in Order to Heal

Suppose I grew up in a dysfunctional family where shame and humiliation were used as tools to control the children and as weapons to win arguments between siblings. Once a person had been properly shamed, they were automatically "one down" and lost their voice in any dispute. Not only that, but the humiliated person was then left on their own to deal with the rejection, while other people in the family simply forgot about the incident and went about their lives.

That being the case, there would be every reason to suspect I would reach adulthood with very little ability to quiet down and reconnect with others whenever I felt shame. More likely, any time I thought my flaws were exposed I would wish for the ground to swallow me up or try to disappear. I might even become super sensitive to constructive criticism, or low grades on a test, or getting passed over for recognition. Whenever I felt shame I could expect to get stuck in that feeling for many hours or even days before feeling like myself again.

So what do I need in order to break free from this trap and to be able to handle making mistakes without getting overwhelmed and losing my sense of belonging or beating myself up for being imperfect?

First, there is no way that I would have made it into adulthood with this problem without also internalizing a ton of lies. I probably believe mistakes are totally unacceptable, that being flawed is inherently shameful, and that I am defective in some terrible way. I have internalized a distorted view of myself and of what it means to make mistakes. Most likely these lies are so deeply embedded that they cannot be dislodged through any rational argument or carefully worded admonition. I need healing that only God can give, or in other words, I need to *receive* something, not just overcome the problem by my own effort.

But once I get some of those wounds and lies healed, I still need to learn how to get back to peace and joy from the feeling of shame. Healing may resolve the illegitimate triggers that sent me spiraling into shame, but I still need to learn how to deal with the healthy form of shame that we all feel in those moments when we mess up and no one wants to be around us. I still need to work on and accomplish the task of learning how to return to peace and joy from shame. Someone needs to show me how to recover from instances of public exposure and other kinds of mistakes, so I can learn what to do and how to do it.

Getting to a place where shame is no longer debilitating takes both spiritual resources and human resources. There are things I need to receive from God and there are tasks I need to learn with the help of other people. Generally speaking, almost any such gap in our maturity must be dealt with from both angles. There is something I need from God, and some training I need from my community.

But there is more. The ways in which we experience inner healing prayer can grow and change as we continue our human development. At infant level maturity (assuming the person is actually much older, physically) a person who seeks to receive healing is best guided by an adult who knows how to identify a need for healing and minister faithfully and sacrificially for the benefit of the infant-level person. When a person reaches child-level maturity they can often see for themselves when they need to seek healing and either ask someone to help or, in some cases, initiate a conversation with God for healing. But not until they reach an adult level of maturity are they ready to minister to adults.

Therefore, since most adults have not reached elder maturity, it is helpful to keep in mind how their participation in inner healing prayer might change as they continue to grow.

Infant-level adult: Able to receive healing when guided by an adult who knows how to minister.
Child-level adult: Able to identify need for healing and participate well with an able minister. Able to initiate time with God for healing.
Adult: Able to minister to others who need healing.

Parent: Able to help children learn how to identify a need for healing, and to mentor them in how to initiate prayer with God for healing.
Elder: Able to train parent-level adults in how to train others, and able to help troubleshoot problems that arise.

While it is possible for children to minister to one another under the supervision of someone at parent-level maturity, at a child-level they are not going to be prepared to deal with the kinds of issues that can arise from the complexities of adult problems.

It is often helpful to notice where we get stuck in this process, because that shows us where we need to grow. For example, when a person ministers to others and finds that they themselves are getting pulled into the other person's issues, taking on their pain and unable to recover from the prayer sessions, it is time to reassess what they are doing. These are signs that they have not yet developed sufficient maturity or capacity to deal with the nature of the problems being encountered. Like everyone else, they need someone who is "upstream" from them to help continue their restoration and growth.

We Need Both Aspects of Maturity in Order to Grow

Much of the discussion so far has been presented as if these two sides of maturity might function quite independently. While it is possible (within certain limits) for a person to develop human maturity without any sense of God at all, God's design for us is that we would incorporate both aspects of maturity into our lives. In fact, the closer we look at these two developmental branches, the more they appear to be intertwined.

To begin with, spiritual formation looks differently for people of differing levels of human maturity. Intuitively, this makes sense. For example, we do not want to encourage five-year-olds to "die to self," since they are still trying to figure out who their "self" is, and the concept is too advanced for them to wrap their minds around anyway. That is really a message meant for adult-level listeners.

Going back to the earlier discussion of maturity threads, it is fairly easy to see how spiritual practices could grow and become more complex as we mature in human terms. Our example of how we learn to see ourselves through the eyes of heaven illustrates this quite well, because it requires some connection with God in order to learn, yet it changes as we develop the ability to deal with greater complexities in our relationships. Another such thread can be seen, for example, as it relates to the practice of solitude:

Infant: Listen to stories of others who practice solitude. Learn to rest.
Child: Try short periods of solitude with direction from parent or elder, both in preparation and followup afterword.
Adult: Practice solitude on your own initiative. Practice joint retreats where you alternate between solitude and sharing your experience with others.
Parent: Mentor your child (or very close friend) in the practice of solitude, preparing them ahead of time and following up with them afterward.
Elder: Lead retreats for community members and train them how to train others in the practice of solitude.

As you can see, developing better relational skills and greater capacity for the complexities of community allows our participation in the kingdom to change and grow with us.

Conversely, when a person attempts to function in a spiritual practice in ways that are beyond their maturity level, it can become quite dangerous for everyone involved. For example, when a person of child-level maturity attempts to lead a retreat, they will be unable to deal with problems that arise between group members or help anyone who becomes overwhelmed by the process. They may even lack the mind-sight or discernment necessary to validate someone's experience that is very different from their own.

Christian formation can look very different at each stage of human development. The ways we engage with God, the ways that God can work within us, and the interpersonal dynamics of group spiritual practices are all approached differently, depending on how mature we are relationally. The more we mature and the more capacity for discomfort we develop, the deeper God can take us in the process of restoration, and the more available we will become to those around us who need help.

As people mature, their range of activity in the kingdom becomes more complex, and they are able to deal with greater demands to manage complex human relationships with joy and competence.

Human Maturity and Spiritual Growth Are Interdependent

In truth, these two forms of maturity aid each other incrementally, and are in fact, inseparable. As human growth is *achieved*, it opens ways to *receive* more spiritual life. And as spiritual growth is *received* from interacting with God, human development becomes more *achievable*.

Suppose in my particular ministry there is someone named Gary that absolutely drives me up the wall, and I have a terrible feeling of dread every time I see him. He completely wears me out with his "stuff." I take a few deep breaths when I see him coming and try to remind myself he suffers from a lot of relational handicaps and needs someone to talk to. But the only real coping system that ever works for me is simply checking out emotionally while he is talking. I am not really listening or empathizing, and in fact I really do not want to hear what he has to say. I only pretend to be his friend.

What is needed here? Partly, Gary overwhelms my nervous system, so I could use more capacity for his kind of intensity. That is an issue of human maturity, which may take some time to develop. But the problem is deeper. My heart may not really be in a place where I want to have more ability to engage with him anyway. If I am honest with myself, I would prefer that Gary found someone else to talk to.

Of course it is possible that God would rather I find someone else who can shoulder the burden of coming alongside Gary. But suppose God is truly calling me to be Gary's friend. In that case, I need help from God. Once God has opened my eyes to see Gary the way He sees him, and altered my heart so that I truly care about him, then I can begin to do the hard work of taking Gary in small doses. I can also talk to Bob, who genuinely seems to enjoy Gary, and have him encourage me and mentor me in what it means to be with someone like Gary. Over time, I am able to develop more relational maturity though interaction with both Gary and Bob.

Let's take another example. Suppose I decide to learn how to hear from God, but give up when my first attempts end in disappointment. If someone encourages me to try again I resist, and express my certainty that trying again will not do any good. One possibility is that I never learned the persistence to do things that felt hard to do. And the reason I never learned it was because someone either did the hard things for me or ridiculed my efforts. I just learned to give up and take the path of least resistance.

What might be helpful at this point is for someone to come alongside me and help me find something that is rewarding but not easy, and encourage me until I begin to get the hang of it. Then they may be able to help me transfer that willingness to persist over to the problem of hearing from God. As they encourage my reflections and mentor me in the process, I begin to discover the joy of engaging long enough to find life. Once I gain the skill of persisting in conversations with God, a whole new world of spiritual development opens up to me.

The number of ways this interdependence takes place is almost limitless. Peter says to "support your faith with goodness, and goodness with knowledge, and knowledge with self-control, and self-control with endurance, and endurance with godliness, and godliness with mutual affection, and mutual affection with love" (2Pet.1:5-7). A careful evaluation of these terms would reveal a very interdependent and complex collection of human and spiritual qualities that work together to form character. In fact, the biblical authors mixed these two areas of maturity quite often.

One-Sided Maturity

From time to time we hear of a minister or leader with a solid footing in the Word and theology who has a major meltdown or moral failure that destroys his career and family. Although we often look for a spiritual cause for these kinds of messes, more than likely they are the result of the leader having been at infant or child-level maturity. They ran into an issue for which they have never received adequate help maturing, and consequently behaved in ways that were much more in line with their true level of development.

Many years ago I was a member of a church that called a new pastor who had just retired as a major in the armed services. Unfortunately, the man had not matured very well in that heavily disciplined context, and was far more accustomed to receiving and giving orders than building relationships. So when a conflict arose between the pastor and the elder board, he got up one morning, packed up his family, and moved to another state without so much as a goodbye to the congregation. Of course, in his mind he had a host of "scriptural" reasons why this was necessary. But the truth is that he was stuck somewhere between infant and child-level maturity.

When we fail to grow in one of these areas of maturity, we develop an imbalance that affects both our theological outlook and our life. For example, if we never learn how to receive what we need from God, our efforts to grow spiritually will focus on the skills we can acquire through hard work. This is precisely what takes place in much of the Christian world today, and why discipleship often looks more like a behavior modification program than a relationship with God.

On the other hand, if we never had the training to develop the basic skills of adult human maturity, we may be unable to handle the complexities of adult life or stay relational with people when problems develop, despite whatever ability we might have to hear from God. We see this most often when a person is gifted in some area but lacks the maturity to work well with others or to lead in a way that brings life. We can perhaps think of a pastor who approaches all conflict as a win-lose proposition and sees the parties to the conflict as good-guy and bad-guy. This is not a spiritual deficiency but a lack of maturity. Putting immature people in positions of leadership can be very dangerous to the group, no matter what "spiritual" qualifications may be evident. We need both human and spiritual maturity in order to live well.

Recovering Missing Steps In Human Maturity

So what do we do when we discover holes in our human maturity? First, we need to remove any sense of self-condemnation from this problem. If I grew up in a shame-based family system where shame was used as a way to control and overpower others, would it be any surprise that at forty years of age I could still have a near heart-attack any time I make a public mistake? Would anyone think it strange if I still responded to any form of public embarrassment with anger and rage? If none of the adults in my extended family knew how to restore a sense of peace and joy after feeling shame, or how to stay relational while feeling shame, then my siblings and I probably would not learn how to do it either.

The truth is, we all have holes in our maturity, because none of us had parents who flawlessly covered every need we had for our development. That means the first step to filling the holes in our maturity is to let go of any shame of being stuck in child-level or infant-level tasks for which we were never trained. We have plenty of company, because quite honestly there are very few places in our culture where adult maturity is the norm.

When we discover holes in our maturity, we need to find someone who knows how to do whatever we are having trouble with and ask them to tell us what it is like for them to encounter these situations. For example, a friend of mine once told me a story about her experience with a very unpleasant person. She had gone to the Post Office with a package to mail. When she got to the window and put the package on the counter, the Postal worker took one look at it and said in a nasty tone, "You can't mail that! It's wrapped all wrong!" She pushed the package back at my friend, waving her away. Without skipping a beat, my friend replied, "You know, you are absolutely right! I really have no idea what I'm doing here. Could you help me and show me what I need to do differently?" The Postal worker suddenly calmed down and became extremely helpful.

When my friend told me this story, my immediate reaction was, "How did you do that? If someone talked to me like that I would have been humiliated and either frozen up or said something really rude."

My friend then took some time to slow the story down and explain her process and why she did what she did, and how it had worked well in the past, and so on. Noticing that she was able to do something that I could not do and asking her to explain her way of responding, was a very helpful step in my recovery of a missed developmental skill.

My early training would have left me speechless in that circumstance, or triggered me to escalate the issue into a power struggle. But ever since I listened to my friend's experience, I have made it a practice to view the people in customer service as potential allies rather than problems. Whenever I need to return a product, for example, the first words out of my mouth are, "I wonder if you could help me with something" instead of some comment like, "This product you sold me is a piece of junk!"

Holes in our maturity are *not* due to bad DNA or some other inherent defect in us that makes us less acceptable than others. We simply cannot learn these relational abilities on our own. God designed us to learn these skills from others. When our developmental needs are not met or the training is deficient, we predictably fail to develop essential skills for dealing with life. This is not about blaming our parents, either. If they lacked certain skills, it is for the same reason that we lack them. This stuff can go back for many generations.

There are two main strategies, then, for overcoming the gaps in our training. One is to stay alert and notice the things our friends can do easily but that we find difficult, as when I heard my friend's story about the postal worker. The other approach is to identify an area that we need help with and start to ask questions until we find someone who can help us with our task. Either way, we need to observe someone while they exercise this skill, or hear full-bodied stories about what it is like for that person to do what we have trouble with. In both cases, it helps to share our struggles with this person and ask them for help in developing that ability in us.

One final point that needs to be made here is the fact that we cannot achieve human maturity simply by praying for it. We can ask God to bring people into our life who can share these tools with us, but there is no way to short-circuit the necessary practice involved. Relational skills are not bestowed on us. They are acquired though an active training process in which we must participate and practice until the skill becomes a natural part of who we are.

Conclusion

Hopefully, this approach to understanding both sides of maturity has helped the reader to grasp the importance of engaging with both God and people in order grow and mature over a lifetime. At the same time, it is important to see how our relationship with God is so radically different from our relationships with people, both in terms of how we are impacted and in terms of how we grow. Let us end now with a great vision of what Church can be, as described for us by the apostle Paul.

> "Speaking the truth in love, we will in all things grow up into him...From him the whole body...grows and builds itself up in love, as each part does its work." (Eph.4:15-16 NIV)

This vision can only become a reality when we meet several conditions:

- We must fully understand what it means to grow up spiritually through engaging with God, and we must each develop a strong, personal relationship with Him.
- We must understand what it means to grow as a human being, the way God intended.
- We must find (or help create) a healthy Christian community, because that is the only place capable of providing the resources necessary for our development.

Even though we dedicated only one chapter to this issue, it is every bit as important to living a full life as learning to connect with God. For further help in the areas of human maturity, please check out the bibliography at the end of the book.

Resources for Further Study

Jim Wilder, *The Complete Guide to Living With Men* (Pasadena: Shepherd's House) 2006

Friesen, et. al. *The Life Model: Living From the Heart Jesus Gave You* (Pasadena: Shepherd's House) 2000

Peter Scazzero, *Emotionally Healthy Spirituality* (Nashville: Thomas Nelson) 2011

Curt Thompson, *The Anatomy of the Soul* (Tyndale Momentum) 2010

FORMING: A WORK OF GRACE

Throughout all of salvation history, there is a single message that rings out loud and clear. ***God deeply desires to restore people to life and to gather them together as His children.***

To that end, He has sent us His Son, inaugurated a new kingdom, overcome the power of the enemy, and made it possible to come and live within us and among us.

Our part in that reconciliation, among other things, is to receive Him personally into our life as our Savior, Father, Lord, and Mentor. Within the context of that relationship, we are then able to participate with Him so He can form us more and more into the image of His Son, Jesus.

Knowing what is God's part and what is our part makes all the difference in how we are formed by God. Our prayer is that this book will help to point the way to this path that leads to an abundant life.

Lord, I pray for all who read this book, that they will be blessed with new hope and life as they practice the things we have spoken of here. For those who are new to this way of life, I ask for both peace and anticipation in the good things You have prepared for them as they begin this journey. For those who are more familiar with the things we have covered, I pray that You would encourage them and renew their desire to make space in their life to connect with You. Continue to lead us and work in us and draw us ever deeper into relationship with you, as we look forward to a life of never-ending growth and discovery.

Amen.

Appendix

THE TROUBLE WITH OBEDIENCE

In a world bent on having its own way, it is tempting to believe that everything would be a lot better if people would just do the right things. We often have a tendency in Christian organizations to talk about obedience as if it were the basis for the Christian life. We can even find a ton of verses to back that up. What's more, we can name a number of areas in our own life where we have done the right thing simply because it was the right thing to do, and have been better off for it. Unfortunately, that kind of obedience will not take us very far in the Christian life.

It would be one thing if everything Jesus asked of us were things we could actually do, like feed the dog or take out the garbage. But He asks us to love our enemy, return good for evil, forgive seventy times seven, never lust or harbor contempt — and the list goes on. He has in fact asked us to do things we really cannot do!

Of course, one approach to this problem is to, "Go ahead and do the right thing even if you don't feel like it!" Well, there is something to be said for making good choices when I am able to do so. But if the only reason I do something or don't do something is because of what I am supposed to do, what does that say about the condition of my heart? If I have to override my whole internal process in order to say the words, "I forgive you," then I clearly do not have a forgiving heart, and it is quite doubtful that I have forgiven the person at all.

It seems to me, that kind of obedience is what Jesus called, "Cleaning the outside of the cup." I'm thinking God had more in mind than strong willpower and compliance when He talked about obedience. And if we look a little closer, the problem gets even more interesting.

First, Paul says that no one was ever able to keep the *old* law. Then along comes Jesus with His Sermon on the Mount and other sayings, and basically raises the bar higher than the law ever was! Not only can you not commit murder, you are not even supposed to wish you could. Not only should you not commit adultery, you should not wonder what it would be like to do so. Well if we could not keep the old law, there is surely no way we can measure up to the new standard set by Jesus. So what does it mean to be obedient if the commands are impossible? And why do we keep preaching "obedience" as if it were a simple matter, when no one can actually do what we have been commanded to do? We need to back up and take another look at what Jesus must have meant by way of "keep my commandments."

Under the Old Covenant, obedience to the written law was paramount to their way of life. But no matter how hard they tried to keep it, the law could not produce character transformation. That was why God established a New Covenant founded on different principles (Heb.8). "For if a law had been given which was able to impart life, then righteousness would indeed have been based on law"(Gal.3:21 NASB). But that was not possible, so God gave us something else entirely.

Tragically, the Christian world has by and large failed to grasp the enormity of this paradigm shift, and has instead opted to substitute New Testament Principles for the Old Testament law, all the while continuing in the belief that trying to do the right things will make you a good person. But Jesus did not just give us better principles to replace the law. He did away with the whole process of achieving righteousness through human effort. And claiming that God gave us the Holy Spirit to provide the power to keep the new principles, only obscures the seriousness of this error on multiple levels.

1. That is not the main role of the Holy Spirit.

2. Whatever power the Holy Spirit does give to us, it clearly does not change us just because we tried hard. If it did, we would be a lot farther along than we are. So something else must be involved.

3. If change comes from our hard work aided by the Holy Spirit, we would have to conclude that how much effort we supply is what makes the difference (or worse yet, that God only helps those who try really hard) which runs contrary to Scripture.

4. If the Holy Spirit's job is to give us the power to keep His commandments, how do you explain burnout? How do you explain why people remain in bondage in spite of all their effort to be free? Wouldn't all that effort elicit the help of the Spirit and make it all possible? The evidence would suggest that is simply not the Holy Spirit's job.

5. God never intended to empower us to keep an external set of principles. He chose instead to write his laws on our heart. That means he wants to change our heart to act naturally in accordance with his laws so that we do not have to keep trying to do what our heart resists doing.

Writing His laws on our heart is a primary characteristic of the New Covenant, but it does not happen all at once. The reason we try to finish the task by committing ourselves to an obedience-driven process of growth, is because we do not know how to receive what we need from God. So we make the same mistake that the Jewish nation made. "Not knowing about God's righteousness and seeking to establish their own, they did not subject themselves to the righteousness of God" (Rom.10:3 NASB).

If we intend to become Christ-like, we must acknowledge from the start that we cannot get there by direct effort. Our goal is to learn how to engage with God in ways that change our heart. As our heart becomes molded by God, we will then be able to live in the way God designed us to live, the way we are called to live. If that seems hard to grasp, it is only because we have not been taught how to live this way.

In order to begin finding our way out of this mess, we need to see clearly the fallacy of trying to grow up by following principles, and return to the original message of following a person, developing a functional relationship with Him that gives life, and getting to know our Mentor who can actually help us with our struggles, not just cite laws from a distance. Because rather than try to coerce obedience from us, the Holy Spirit reveals to us the underlying causes for our malfunctions, heals the wounds that keep us bound in fear and anger, and shows us what we need to see in order to move forward. Our part in the process is to run to Him when we are in trouble, open ourselves to His teaching and training, and receive from Him what we need in order to grow and change.

Obedience to a beloved Mentor is very different from obedience to a set of rules. Take for example, Psalm 51, our quintessential psalm of repentance. Interestingly, no where in that psalm does David promise to not ever do those terrible things again. He makes no resolution to be different. He simply comes to God and acknowledges that his heart is a lot worse than he had imagined, and that he wants God to create a new heart for him that would never conceive of such things. In short, he is asking God to do for him what he cannot do for himself. That, my friend, is obedience! Submitting to the work God wants to do in our life.

Before we try to keep all the commandments that have to do with how we act in the world, we must first learn how to obey the invitations to be transformed: "Come to me" (Mt.11:28); "Abide in me" (Jn.15:4); "Believe" (Jn.6:29); "Listen" (Isa.55:1-3); "Drink" (Jn.4:14); "Be filled" (Eph.5:18); "Be transformed" (Rom.12:2). These are not euphemisms for going to heaven. They are the very basis for our life in God. And once we learn "the obedience of faith," coming to His table and eating what He has set before us, listening to His voice as He mentors us in our own life – then and only then will the other things become possible for us. Because once we give Him a chance to write His laws on our heart, we will become "obedient" by our very nature, not by trying hard to do what is right.

What About Sin?

From time to time a question is raised, "When teaching about spiritual formation, why don't you talk more about sin? After all, the real problem people have is sin, and they need to confess, repent, and ask for forgiveness in order to be free of sin."

Now obviously behind this question there is a goal in mind, which is that Christians should be enabled to live lives of purity and continue to become more and more free of sin as they grow in their walk with God. With that goal, I can entirely agree. We need to pursue holiness, and encourage and train others how to pursue it as well. But also behind that question there are a few other assumptions that I find to be truly problematic.

More to the point, however, is that when we teach spiritual formation, we are actually addressing the sin problem *constantly*, because we are training people how to deal with the *causes* of sin and showing them the means of *overcoming* sin. This can be quite a new process for Christians who have been taught to focus on the sin they have already committed as a way of inducing change. They have been told they need to feel enough remorse to confess their sin and ask for forgiveness, and to promise to try hard to change. Unfortunately, this is like waiting for the dandelions to go to seed, and then cutting off the tops and trying our best to get to them next time before they go to seed.

Christian spiritual formation, on the other hand, digs out the roots and kills the weeds so we no longer have to deal with them over and over. This, by necessity, requires us to use a different vocabulary and different means. For those who have been trained to focus on dandelion seeds, that can sound like we are neglecting something very important.

And yes, we do need to go to God whenever we become aware of sin in our life, and ask Him for help in our restoration. We are not suggesting we should ignore such things. But once we learn how to engage with God for healing, growth, and inner transformation, we can proactively defeat the power of sin before it bears fruit. Why focus entirely on how to deal with seeds when we can kill the roots? Why not do both?

Now before proceeding much farther, it is necessary to correct a very common misunderstanding in regard to "repentance" itself. Most teaching on repentance assumes that our part is to confess, ask for forgiveness, and change our behavior or attitude to be more in line with what is good. The problem here, is the assumption that we are capable of making the necessary changes simply by choosing to do so. Granted, there are many areas of life that we can decide to do differently. Non-Christians can choose to do many things differently as well. If they truly believe it is their best interest, most people can restrain themselves from lying, cheating, or killing, without supernatural intervention.

But what we cannot do is *change our soul* by direct effort, any more than we can talk ourselves out of a phobia. We might be able to repress some of the symptoms of the problem, but we cannot simply choose to not have it anymore. Many people who struggle to give up an addiction, for example, end up replacing it with another. They give up alcohol and take up smoking; they give up smoking and start over-eating. What they are unable to do is stop the underlying cravings that are driving the addictions. In many cases, they may not even be aware of those cravings or know what causes them.

The same is true for many problems we deal with, such as feeling hatred toward a person who harmed us, desiring revenge, feeling anxious about our life, being unable to forgive someone for the tenth time, harboring unresolved regrets – the list could go on. Many of the spiritual issues that we struggle with are driven by areas of our mind and soul that are not governed strictly by the will and do not change by an act of the will.

Creating the conditions necessary for the changes we need in our soul is what spiritual formation is all about, including how to change the internal parts of our mind and heart that we do not have direct access to. Once we learn how to care for our soul in this way, we have the means to move forward. And often this process requires engaging with God very directly so He can change our heart and mind.

Repentance then, is best envisioned as "engaging with God for a change of heart that is far deeper than we could accomplish on our own." We actually see this in Psalm 51, one of the most famous psalms of repentance in all the Bible. Nowhere in the psalm does David ever promise to not commit adultery again or not set up anyone to be killed so he can have their wife. Instead, he engages with God and asks Him to "create in me a clean heart."

The reason this is so important is that sin is not a self-initiating cause. *Sin is caused by something else.* If our only approach to dealing with sin is to repent every time we sin, there are a lot of sins that we will never be free of, because we are failing to deal with what is causing the sin. For a more comprehensive explanation of this whole issue of what causes us to fail and how we can deal decisively with sin (as well as our wounding) I would recommend the book, *The Truth About Lies and Lies About Truth*.

The problems that most often get in the way of our relationship with God are: distorted images of God; being afraid of Him or angry with Him for what He did or did not do; hiding from God because of the shame we feel; or feeling hopeless about connecting with Him. Paying attention to these emotional barriers is important because they are often overlooked or viewed as something we need to "overcome" by willpower.

Worse yet, anger, shame, fear, and hopelessness are sometimes viewed as sin or caused by sin – something that should be "repented" of and repressed. In truth, these emotions are most often caused by wounding or by our lack of spiritual eyesight, not by sin we have committed. When we categorically denounce these as symptoms of sin, we usually end up blaming the victim, and condemning people for having been hurt by those around them. If instead, we see these emotions as symptoms of a broken soul, we have the freedom to approach God with open heart and hands, asking Him to reveal the causes of these issues and what He wants to do with them. If He shows us that the emotion is caused by sin, then so be it. Either way, He will also show us what we need in order to renew our mind and heart.

God wants to rid us of sin, far more than any oncologist would want to rid a patient of cancer. But we must never limit His involvement to that of addressing the aftermath of sin, hearing our confession and offering forgiveness. God wants to remove in us the causes of sin and the power of sin! That way we can escape the continuous cycle of repent – restore – fall again – repent, and so on. But He does not expect us to heal ourselves. We need to learn how to work with Him so that He can do in us what we cannot do for ourselves, which is to write His laws on our heart and to change us from the inside out.

Christian formation focuses on practices and ways of engaging with God that change our heart and mind, because this is by far the most effective way of purging our lives of sin and filling our lives with God's love and grace.

Please also see "Is Sin a Barrier to Engaging With God" in Chapter 8.

Reference

SCRIPTURE RESOURCES (NIV)

God's Vision for His People

To prepare God's people for works of service, so that the body of Christ may be built up until we all reach unity in the faith and in the knowledge of the Son of God and become mature, attaining to the whole measure of the fullness of Christ. Then we will no longer be infants, tossed back and forth by the waves, and blown here and there ... Instead, speaking the truth in love, we will in all things grow up into Him. (Eph.4:12-14)

That your love may abound more and more in knowledge and depth of insight, so that you may be able to discern what is best and may be pure and blameless until the day of Christ, filled with the fruit of righteousness that comes through Jesus Christ. (Phil.1:9-11)

So that you may become blameless and pure, children of God without fault in a crooked and depraved generation, in which you shine like stars in the universe. (Phil.2:15)

Asking God to fill you with the knowledge of His will through all spiritual wisdom and understanding. And we pray this in order that you may live a life worthy of the Lord and may please Him in every way: bearing fruit in every good work, growing in the knowledge of God, being strengthened with all power according to His glorious might so that you may have great endurance and patience. (Col.1:9-11)

God's Provision for His People for Healing and Change

Come to me, all you who are weary and burdened, and I will give you rest. Take my yoke upon you and learn from me, for I am gentle and humble in heart, and you will find rest for your souls. For my yoke is easy and my burden is light. (Mt. 11:28-30)

The Spirit of the Lord is upon me, because he has anointed me to preach good news to the poor. He has sent me to proclaim freedom for the prisoners and recovery of sight for the blind, to release the oppressed. (Lk.4:18)

If anyone is thirsty, let him come to me and drink. Whoever believes in me, as the Scripture has said, streams of living water will flow from within him. (Jn.7:37-38)

If the Son sets you free, you will be free indeed. (Jn.8:36)

The Counselor, the Holy Spirit, whom the Father will send in my name, will teach you all things and will remind you of everything I have said to you. (Jn.14:26)

The Spirit of truth ... will guide you into all truth. (Jn.16:13)

The reason the Son of God appeared was to destroy the devil's works. (1Jn.3:8)

We were therefore buried with Him through baptism into death in order that, just as Christ was raised from the dead ... we too may live a new life ... For we know that our old self was crucified with Him so that the body of sin might be done away with, that we should no longer be slaves to sin – because anyone who has died has been freed from sin ... You have been set free from sin and have become slaves to righteousness. (Rom.6:4-7,18)

Now that you have been set free from sin and have become slaves to God, the benefit you reap leads to holiness, and the result is eternal life. (Rom.6:22)

I pray also that the eyes of your heart may be enlightened in order that you may know the hope to which He has called you, the riches of His glorious inheritance in the saints, and His incomparably great power for us who believe. (Eph.1:18-19)

To Him who is able to do immeasurably more than all we ask or imagine, according to His power that is at work within us. (Eph.3:20)

For He has rescued us from the dominion of darkness and brought us into the kingdom of the Son He loves. (Col.1:13)

His divine power has given us everything we need for life and godliness through our knowledge of Him who called us by His own glory and goodness. Through these He has given us His very great and precious promises, so that through them you may participate in the divine nature and escape the corruption in the world caused by evil desires. (2Pet.1:3)

Our Participation (Grace is opposed to earning, but not effort)

Everyone who hears these words of mine and puts them into practice is like a wise man ... everyone who hears these worlds of mine and does not put them into practice is like a foolish man. (Mat.7:24-26)

Whoever follows me will never walk in darkness, but will have the light of life. (Jn.8:12)

If you hold to my teaching, you are really my disciples. Then you will know the truth, and the truth will set you free. (Jn.8:31-32)

If a man remains in me and I in him, he will bear much fruit. (Jn.15:5)

If by the Spirit you put to death the misdeeds of the body, you will live. (Rom.8:13)

Do not conform any longer to the pattern of this world, but be transformed by the renewing of your mind. (Rom.12:2)

Continue to work out your salvation with fear and trembling, for it is God who works in you to will and to act according to His good purpose. (Ph.2:12-13)

For this very reason, make every effort to add to your faith goodness; and to goodness, knowledge; and to knowledge, self-control; and to self-control, perseverance; and to perseverance, godliness; and to godliness, brotherly kindness; and to brotherly kindness, love. For if you possess these qualities in increasing measure, they will keep you from being ineffective and unproductive in your knowledge of our Lord Jesus Christ. (2Pet.1:5-8)

What Does Not Work

After beginning with the Spirit, are you now trying to attain your goal by human effort? (Gal.3:3)

Such regulations indeed have an appearance of wisdom, with their self-imposed worship, their false humility and their harsh treatment of the body, but they lack any value in restraining sensual indulgence. (Col.2:23)

Receiving Life and Giving Life Away

Sermon on the Mount. (Mt.5-7)

Love the Lord your God with all your heart and with all your soul and with all your strength and with all your mind, and Love you neighbor as yourself. (Lk.10:27)

Freely you have received, freely give. (Mt.10:8)

ANNOTATED BIBLIOGRAPHY FOR FURTHER STUDY

These are the resources referred to throughout this book, along a few other of the best works on Christian development I have found. They are listed alphabetically by the last name of the author.

David Benner, *Desiring God's Will: Aligning Our Hearts with the Heart of God*
   The best book on aligning with God's will I have ever seen. It goes far beyond the traditional concept of seeking guidance from God about decisions, and addresses the bigger issues of how to seek out and desire the heart of God. (IVP Books) 2005.

David Benner, *The Gift of Being Yourself: The Sacred Call to Self-Discovery*
   A wonderful job of describing how God sees His children. An excellent resource for understanding our Christian identity. (IVP Books) 2004.

David Benner, *Surrender to Love: Discovering the Heart of Christian Spirituality*
   One of Benner's best works, in which he helps us discover why we both want to and need to be closer to God. (IVP Books) 2003.

V. Raymond Edman, *They Found the Secret: 20 Transformed Lives That Reveal a Touch of Eternity*
   Edman does a wonderful job of giving us the stories of some of the most famous Christians of the last two hundred years: Hudson Taylor; John Bunyan; Amy Carmichael; Oswald Chambers; Finney; Moody. Most importantly, we get a glimpse of how they underwent the transformation from overburdened Christians to joyful, fulfilled people of God. (Zondervan) 1984.

John Eldredge, *The Journey of Desire: Searching for the Life We Always Dreamed of*
   With a passion that is rare in prose, John stirs his readers' longing for more of God in ways that few authors can do. (Thomas Nelson) 2001.

James Friesen, E. James Wilder, Anne Bierling, Rick Koepcke, and Maribeth Poole, *The Life Model: Living From the Heart Jesus Gave You*
> This is the book that launched the Life Model, a Christian view of human development. Contains great descriptions of what it means to have a strong identity, the difference between fear bonds and love bonds, and much more. (Shepherd's House) 2000.

Dave Johnson, Jeff VanVonderan, *The Subtle Power of Spiritual Abuse*
> A tremendous resource for anyone dealing with the after-effects of life in a highly legalistic community. (Bethany House Publishers) 2005 reprint

Jan Johnson, *When the Soul Listens*
> Personally, I consider this to be one of Jan's best. She paints a picture for us, an invitation to spending with God that so good, we cannot help but respond. (NavPress) 1999.

Karl Lehman, *Outsmarting Yourself: Catching Your Past Invading the Present and What to Do About It*
> A wonderful combination of current neurological insights brilliant observations from Karl's private practice. A must-read for anyone involved in Christian counseling or pastoral care. (This Joy Books) 2001.

Brennan Manning, *Ruthless Trust: The Ragamuffin's Path to God*
> A very passionate presentation of how God's love will build our trust. (HarperCollins) 2010.

Steve McVey, *Grace Walk*
> A great description of how grace changes everything about life, and how it differs from the kind of legalism most of us have learned. McVey knows what he is talking about, because he used to be a legalistic preacher himself. (Harvest House Publishers) 2005.

John Ortberg, *The Life You've Always Wanted: Spiritual Disciplines for Ordinary People*
> A layman's guide to spiritual disciplines. Inspired by his own spiritual growth after learning from Dallas Willard, this book is recommended for those who find Dallas a bit too difficult to digest. (Zondervan) 2004.

Theodore Rubin, *Compassion and Self Hate: An Alternative to Despair*
Probably the best description of self-hate ever written. Rubin delves into the causes and effects of this toxic evil in a way that is very readable and yet precise. Although a non-Christian author, Rubin employs sound psychological methods that can be very helpful. (Touchstone) 1998.

Peter Scazzero, *Emotionally Healthy Spirituality*
Great book regarding the need for integrating emotional health with our spiritual life. Very readable. (Thomas Nelson) 2011.

Gary Smalley, *Change Your Heart Change Your Life: How Changing What You Believe Will Give You the Great Life You've Always Wanted*
Gary discovered that we can only live out of our heart. Whereas we have emphasized the use of conversational prayer for inner healing, Gary has found ways to apply a great many other disciplines to this process of restoration. (Thomas Nelson) 2005.

James Bryan Smith, *The Good and Beautiful God: Falling in Love with the God Jesus Knew*
One of the best books available on learning to trust the goodness of God. (InterVarsity Press) 2009.

David Takle, *Whispers of My Abba: From His Heart to Mine*
For those who need more help with conversational prayer, this book was written with the intention of mentoring the reader as much as possible on the written page. Many have found this to be a life-changing book. (Kingdom Formation Ministries) 2013.

David Takle, *The Truth About Lies and Lies About Truth*
An in-depth look at the nature of deception, how it corrupts our mind, and how we can renew our mind by engaging with God. (Shepherd's House) 2008.

Curt Thompson, *The Anatomy of the Soul*
The best book on Christian neuro-theology that I know of. (Tyndale Momentum) 2010.

Jim Wilder, *The Complete Guide to Living With Men*
This may be the most complete explanation in print of the relational and emotional skills we need in order to mature. (Shepherd's House) 2005.

Jim Wilder and Chris Coursey, *Share Immanuel*
This fairly short booklet does a great job of walking the reader through the steps of Immanuel Healing. (Shepherd's House) 2010.

Dallas Willard: *The Divine Conspiracy: Rediscovering Our Hidden Life in God*
One of the best descriptions ever written of the Christian worldview. Often considered a difficult read not because of the vocabulary, but because the concepts can be quite challenging. (Zondervan) 2010.

Dallas Willard, *Hearing God: Developing a Conversational Prayer Life with God*
Lays out a theological basis for listening to God in the present day, describes what it is like to hear God's voice, and discusses various issues surrounding this topic. (IVP Books) 2012.

Dallas Willard, *The Renovation of the Heart: Putting on the Character of Christ*
The more we know about how God transforms us, the more we will know how to anticipate the work He wants to do in us. One of the best works available on various aspects of transformation. (NavPress) 2012.

Dallas Willard, *The Spirit of the Disciplines: Understanding How God Changes Lives*
A wonderful explanation of why spiritual disciplines are helpful, and how to approach them so as not to misuse them. An excellent guide for anyone attempting to teach spiritual disciplines. (HarperOne) 1999.

Other Works Cited

Dan Allender, *Bold Love* (NavPress) 1992

Larry Crabb, *Connecting* (Thomas Nelson) 2005

Larry Crabb, *The Safest Place on Earth* (Thomas Nelson) 1999

Melvin Deiter, Anthony Hoekema, Stanley Horton, J. Robertson McQuilkin, John Walvoord, *Five Views on Sanctification* (Zondervan) 1995

Judith Herman, *Trauma and Recovery* (Basic Books) 1992

Douglas Moo, *The Epistle to the Romans* (Erdmans) 1996

Scott Peck, *The Road Less Traveled* (Touchstone) 1978

J. B. Philips, *Your God is Too Small* (Touchstone) 2004

John Townsend, *Hiding From Love: How to Change the Withdrawal Patterns That Isolate and Imprison You* (Zondervan) 1996

N. T. Wright, J. Paul Sampley, Robert Wall, *The New Interpreter's Bible: Acts to First Corinthians (Commentary on Romans)* (Abingdon Press) 2002

Forming: Change by Grace

A course in Christian Formation
by David Takle

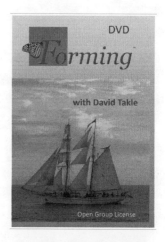

Forming is a fresh, life-giving approach to spiritual growth and restoration that may be very different from what you have tried before. What makes *Forming* unique is that instead of relying on your willpower and self-effort to bring about change in your life, we help you build a relationship with God that is vibrant enough to change you from the inside out.

Forming: Change by Grace is a twelve-session course based on the book *Forming: A Work of Grace*. The course follows the same twelve chapters, and is designed to involve your whole body and mind in the practice of building an authentic relationship with God for growth and transformation. It includes a **workbook** as well as a set of **DVD's** in which David provides complementary material on each of the topics. The workbook contains exercises tailored to help you internalize the material and actually experience more of God. A **facilitator version of the workbook** is also available for facilitating *Forming* in a group setting. Both seasoned believers as well as those new to the faith who have taken this course report that it has been one of the most important experiences of their entire Christian journey. (Note: while *Forming: A Work of Grace* is not necessary for the course, it is a great resource for anyone facilitating a group).

Please visit www.KingdomFormation.org for more information.

The Truth About Lies and Lies About Truth

by David Takle

"I've been waiting for someone to approach spiritual formation, recovery and inner healing in an integrated way. This is it! In doing so, David Takle has described how interactive life with God grows and results in transformation into Christ-likeness."
– **Jan Johnson**, retreat speaker and author of *Invitation to the Jesus Life*

Chapter 9 of *Forming* introduced the process of renewing the mind, including what actually happens in the process of renewing our mind, how this differs from conventional study, and why trying hard to live the Christian life fails to transform our character. In *The Truth About Lies*, David fleshes this out in much greater detail and provides in-depth support from Scripture and stories of healing to demonstrate how God can restore our distorted perceptions of life.

If you are eager to learn how to engage with God in ways that bring about lasting renewal from the inner lies that keep you stuck, this is the book you are looking for!

Please visit us at www.KingdomFormation.org under "Resources" for more information.

Whispers of my Abba: From His Heart to Mine

by David Takle

In *Whispers of my Abba*, David greatly expands the material from Chapters 3 and 4 in *Forming*, and discusses conversational prayer with far more depth and breadth to help the reader discover the joy of listening to God.

Whispers includes actual journal entries that demonstrate what it can be like to engage in conversations with God, and also contains a troubleshooting chapter on what to do when hearing God is difficult.

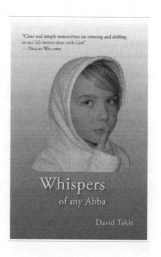

If you want to know more about how to have conversations with God, or if you want to give a gift to others that will change their life forever, this is the book that will make the difference.

Please visit us at www.KingdomFormation.org under "Resources" for more information.

Made in the USA
San Bernardino, CA
11 September 2014